G000078451

# Critics Review

*"Before sitting down and reading this book, pour yourself a double Jack Daniels and Coke and contemplate the most atypical lawyer and military officer you've ever known, then exaggerate what you know about him and you'll have the author, Mike Sciales, the original "Regular Guy." I served with Mike in England and Panama and have known him for thirty years. His stories were legendary and now finally part of military lore. Two thumbs up!!!"*

Bob Blevins, Colonel, USAF (Ret)

*"Its a fun read!"*

Robert Burns, National Security Writer at The AP

*"Through a collection of entertaining and well-woven vignettes Major Mike Sciales shows how things get done in the insular world of the United States Military. He is a delightful story teller with admirable attention to detail. If you enjoyed J.D Vance's memoir, Hillbilly Elegy," you'll like COMBAT JAG" even more."*

Ron Wilper, University of Idaho
Class of 1987

*Immensely entertaining and contemporary look into the life and times of a JAG Officer. I laughed, I cried, I held my sides. A good read. Think a bit Tom Robbins, a bit Patrick McManus, a bit Hawkeye Pierce. Highly recommended.*

*Wade Porter*

*I served from 85 on to 2005 so a lot of the experiences Mike talks about, I could relate to. I know a guy who was stationed with Major Mike in Kuwait so that was a good reference point as well. Either way, this JAG is a smart and funny man whose ability to write about his experiences in the military is only exceeded by his amazing vocabulary. Smart, witty, endless entertaining. Told from the side of a lawyer, an enlisted man, a diplomat, a bartender, and many other things. Imagine the stories a JAG has from Europe, the Middle East, Idaho, Japan, and all points in between.*

*John K. Lennon*
*Major, USAF (ret)*

# FOREWORD

People see the military through a hazy macro-lens. We see all the hundreds of thousands of men and women, military and civilian, who serve in the defense of our nation as a huge machine that goes where we ask it to go and does what we ask it to do.

Beyond that, we don't think very much about the military except during movies, or the Super Bowl, Memorial Day, the Fourth of July, and maybe Veterans Day. What we don't get is that the military has evolved into a professional warrior class. We don't understand much about the people who choose the profession of arms because we don't really know them and never see them through a micro-lens.

Fewer than 7% of Americans have ever worn a uniform and still fewer serve on the front lines as vanguards of freedom around the world. While working on being professionals, we are all still humans, bearing all the faults of the human condition.

These are some of those stories.

# Acknowledgments

First and foremost, I want to thank my long suffering editor and wife of over thirty years. Laurie brought her decades of experience teaching English to her really smart high school seniors, most of whom actually liked writing and cared about the rules of English. She brought that professional acumen and work ethic to this task. Never one to be shy with her professional opinion, she not only introduced me to her admiration of the Oxford comma, but produced a mini-lesson on the sad amount of "action" verbs I was using, (I can hear her right now, saying, "You don't use "amount" there; it's "number" if it's countable!") and I'm pretty certain a bunch of colorful nouns, but absolutely no improper capitalizations, whatever they actually are.

Honey, I wouldn't have finished without you; thank you, you **are** the best.

Wade, thank you for taking the time to go through each line catching those missing letters, words, and spaces. It made a difference in readability; and I appreciated all your comments and observations. YITB #113 NE

I'd also offer my profound thanks to my technical directors, old drinking buddies, and occasional wingmen:

Catfish, for reeling me back into the blue and knowing all about helicopters.

The "Other Regular Guy" for your professionalism, and taking me under your wing. You showed me a good time while having more integrity than anybody I've ever met. I'll bet Don Rice still brags about meeting you. I know those Norwegians won't ever forget you.

Mongo, for your comments on those fast-burner questions I had. Thanks for leaning against the rail those many nights at Osan and flying me into Kunsan so takeoffs equaled landings. It meant more to me than you'll ever know.

Skipper, knew everything there was to know about submarines, baking bread, and building a bar. You kept ever steady and the party rocking, and you never let them see you sweat.

Rocco, fun times at the Khan Khalili, in a place as strange as Cairo.

Finally, the legendary Tony Bennett: singing mailman,  part-time beer baron, board member and assistant master planner of the Oasis Lounge. I enjoyed our time reading all those dirty magazines and bondage catalogs you brought in for destruction.  I'm sorry I put the hot hibachi under your chair while we were playing poker that cold evening, Pepino made me do it.

+++

They all did their part; any factual errors or omissions are mine alone. Nothing libelous to be found, I did change some names just to protect any delicate sensibilities.  The events and remarks made were real.

## Benediction

For everybody in blue who signed up for clean sheets, hot coffee, and air conditioning, and got way more than they bargained for, and for all those warriors, like Cliff and Salty, who never came home. I list the dead and ask you take a moment and say those names aloud; don't forget to thank them for their service and sacrifice.

## Dedication

I wrote this for my brother-in-law, Ted, the son of Greek immigrants from the South side of Chicago, a genuine Vietnam-era fighter pilot. Not interested in waiting for the Army to draft him off to Vietnam, he came into the blue in 1970. He was a weapons school grad and proudly wore his mustache out of regulation. He taught me how to drink Johnny Walker blended whiskey by setting out a bowl of ice, two glasses and crushing the cap saying, "Nobody leaves until the bottle is empty."

We were telling war stories while sitting in Moran's bar in Syosset, New York, on Christmas Eve in 1979 when he told me I ought to write a book. I did, it just took me a couple of decades to live it and put it to paper. He took off for Korea in 1982 and said he'd be back in the spring, but March never came.

He was the best guy I ever knew.

Captain Theodore T. Harduvel, Jr.
80th Fighter Squadron "Juvat"
8th Fighter Wing,
Kunsan Air Base ROK
Call sign: Gamble
15 Nov 1982

# Table of Contents

**Epilogue**

Footnotes

# Prologue

I was minding my own business and keeping my nose in a law book. I was a clerk to the Chief Judge of the Idaho Court of Appeals and I was miserable. For all of my adult life I'd had jobs that involved being outdoors at all hours and never had an eight to five office job. I enlisted in the Air Force in 1971, right out of high school and was made me a cop. I'd gotten discharged from Mtn Home AFB, Idaho, institutionally known as "The Airbase Time Forgot," so I enrolled at Boise State University just up the road and went for a year on the GI bill. As money got tight, I took a job for three years as a cop in a small logging town in Oregon. After three years I'd had enough of the never-ending rains and finished my undergraduate degree work at the University of South Florida to get some sunshine.

After graduation it was "what to do?" I knew didn't want to be a cop forever and while walking down the University hallway I passed a bulletin board and saw a notice for learning how to be a long-haul truck driver. Next to it was something from an art school looking for talented students that invited me to draw the Pirate or the Turtle and send it in for an evaluation. Neither one of these inspired me, but then I saw it: The Arthur Kaplan LSAT review course. The Law School Admission Test was something I hadn't considered but it sounded good, so I took the coupon, signed up for the course, took the examination, scored very highly and was accepted as a student at the greatest law school in the state of Idaho, and conveniently, the only law school in the state of Idaho, located in Moscow, just a few hundred miles from the Canadian border.

For some students of the law, the quest for meaningful employment after graduation starts in the summer of the first year. The top students are head-hunted by big name law firms who wine them and dine them, seducing them with dreams of a partnership. All of this was a ploy to sucker them into signing up and beginning a miserable five-year death race with all the other new associates while enjoying ten hour work days (plus eight hours on the weekend) all for a shot at the dream, because not everybody gets a partnership offer.

My third and final year was underway and I still hadn't given any real thought to my future because I believed in a more serendipitous approach; karma would sort it all out. I was then working twenty hours a week on a limited license as a prosecutor under the supervision of a licensed attorney, in the small city of Clarkston, Washington, population 6,903, about thirty miles from Moscow. Situated where the Snake River pours into the Columbia, the area was originally named Jawbone Flats. Clarkston was chosen to honor William Clark, of the Lewis and Clark Expedition fame. Lewiston, across the Idaho State line from Clarkston, is named for Meriwether Lewis, and is the older and larger of the two cities, leading to a sense of undeserved superiority since neither Clark nor Lewis ever visited the Clarkston side of the river.

I'd spent the past two summers painting houses and also snagged work staining the deck of Sheldon, our dean, so I was surprised when he made a first time ever appearance in the basement of the law school library to personally invite me to a hosted reception at his house. The basement was a haven for those students who smoked, drank, and played cards between classes, while the more serious students preferred the upper floors. His appearance was unusual because he preferred to be able to say he had no idea what was going on downstairs. While looked upon with disdain by the "smart kids," our basement group produced one Idaho Supreme Court justice, a District court judge and several magistrates while the upstairs folks produced one guy who got disbarred for stealing an old widow's life savings.

Confused as to his motives, I asked Sheldon why I'd made the social "A" list and he told me, "The Court of Appeals is finishing sitting here today after hearing cases and I need somebody to lighten things up tonight at the reception because all the smart students are rather dull." Ignoring the left-handed compliment, I was hesitant because, while I agreed those students were dull, it was knowing most of them would be on best behavior and shamelessly sucking up to the three appeals court judges that painted the bleakest picture of what I might consider fun.

The sycophants would be gathered round all their future employers and shining as best they could. They'd be attending with great interest if any guest should choose to hold forth on any subject in law and engage in deep philosophical discussions to intellectually spar with classmates to demonstrate and distinguish their brilliance from the others. The prize was getting a judicial clerkship, touted as a "masters degree" in legal writing, and another area I never aspired to work in. Sheldon sensed this adding, "There will be plenty of food and free drinks!" I was sold, thinking if nothing else at least I'd have a good time.

I drove several miles out of town on an unpaved road until I came to his château perched along the side of Moscow Mountain and made my way inside. Although I was spot-on time, the party was in full swing, all the smart students having arrived thirty minutes earlier to demonstrate how keen they were for those jobs and arrive before anybody else. I saw students talking animatedly with a couple of guys I'd never seen before so I knew they were judges. I did a bit of eavesdropping and quickly realized there would be nothing I could offer to any of those conversations, so when an indentured servant/student waiter came by with a tray of hors d'oeuvres containing some of those "pigs in a blanket," I grabbed one, asked where the bar was and was pointed outside.

I went out on to the deck and saw the student bartender, his white jacket glowing in the light of a full moon, so I made a bee-line for him and got a drink. It was about that time I noticed an older guy with a head full of white hair leaning against one of the deck rails smoking a pipe. After getting my drink, I ambled over and asked, "Is this the smoking porch?" He nodded and I introduced myself and he told me his name, Jesse. Looking to make conversation I said, "I know you aren't on the faculty so I'm going out on a limb and guessing you're on the court, right?" He nodded and I offered, "So what exactly do you do there?", hoping to get him to discuss the process, which meant he could do all the talking, but was rewarded with, "I'm the Chief Judge." I nodded and said, "I guess I probably should have known that, but I was wondering more about how you guys figure out who gets what case."

He was happy to oblige and I paid close attention. It wasn't that I had any burning interest in this, but, as long as he was talking, there wouldn't be any awkward pauses in the conversation. The bartender discreetly kept refreshing our drinks and on that late September evening the air was still and the temperature comfortable.

Over the judge's shoulder I could see the moon rising above Moscow Mountain and illuminating the endless sea of wheat rolling west. The Palouse is an integral part of America's bread basket and I idly wondered if the Ukraine, the bread basket of the Soviet Union, also looked like this. We spent the next two hours uninterrupted because the other judges didn't drink, so by default, neither did the suckups.

Out of the blue the judge said, "How would you like to clerk for me?" I almost spat out my drink. He looked at me, startled by my reaction. I took a moment and said, "Listen Jesse, I know we've had a fun time out here and maybe we both had too much to drink, because I'm pretty comfortable that if you call Sheldon on Monday morning and tell him about your offer to me, after he stops laughing you can reconsider and find somebody way better than me."

He nodded and said, "So I've made the offer, do you have any questions?" I thought about it and asked where the court was located and if I got free parking downtown, then asked about the hours and if it was OK to leave ten minutes early on Friday to get to a happy hour and was promptly out of questions. He said, "Don't you want to know about the pay?" I nodded towards the lights and polite laughter going on inside and told him I was certain it was generous given all the activity in Sheldon's living room. He told me to consider the job mine and a contract would be coming in the next week. He remarked that it was supposed to be left open for applicants until the beginning of November, but just to not say anything to any of the students. Still mystified about why he thought I'd be a good clerk, I finally asked him point blank, "Why are you offering me this job?"

He took his time tamping his pipe and relighting it before saying, "You were the first person to ever ask how it all works."

We left it at that.

# CHAPTER ONE

## 𝔈ngland

# Back into the blue

I graduated and spent the next two weeks with my Army Reserve unit as a firefighter. We were assigned to Gowen Field, an Air Force base operated by the Idaho National Guard, but attached to the airport in Boise. We burned a lot of jet fuel and got a lot of great training and experience with aircraft rescue and fires although nothing crashed or burned while we were there. I liked Boise, it was a pleasant city but the thought of starting my job as a legal clerk, a scribe, filled me with dread. The mental image of spending my days at a desk reading boring legal briefs and then researching the laws cited by the opposing counsel to make sure they weren't misinterpreting the ruling they cited made my head hurt.

All too quickly my summer drill was over and I loaded the car with my few possessions and drove to the City of Trees, found an apartment, took a law school friend, Jimmy the Loon, as a room mate, and began the next phase of life.

The job was straightforward enough. I'd sit with my judge and we'd talk about the case he assigned me and how he thought the matter should go. My job was to chart that course and write a legal opinion consistent with his views while recognizing that two other judges of differing judicial temperament would review the proposed opinion. Those who could not agree in whole or in part would offer that different position in a dissenting opinion. Jimmy the Loon had likewise been selected to be a clerk for another judge on the court, one who fancied himself a scholar and master of jurisprudence.

Each night Jimmy and I would walk back to our apartment and talk about the day. A legal opinion never gets approved with the first attempt because the judge always has comments and changes which are incorporated into the second draft, then a third, and even a fourth. Jimmy was complaining because he'd had an especially bad week. He asked me how many cuts it took before my drafts were approved and I told him usually three, sometimes four. "Judge sets out the legal position and then all I do is pick the first seven points of contention and dismiss the rest, they either have it or they don't." He looked sad and said, "I just don't get it; he takes everything I write, crosses it all out and tells me to start again." I asked, "Don't you talk about it with him and get guidance?" Jimmy, who'd just spent the week working on his twelfth draft, looked at me as if I'd just dropped in from Mars. "We talk about it, but he's just wrong." All I could think to say was, "Well, if you tried giving him what he wants, maybe he'd sign off on it." I added, "After all, it is his name going on the opinion, not yours."

Judges hire clerks based on grade point average, class standing, legal writing style and a sit down interview. Jimmy's judge, who had been off on the lecture circuit and teaching at the judicial college, simply hadn't had the opportunity to get together for an in-person interview and somehow, although Jimmy was one of the top ten students, he had not received an invite to the cocktail party.

I began to wonder about how this happened and got to talking to his judge's other clerk, the senior one, a Jewish guy from Philadelphia who graduated with honors from Stanford Law and spoke two languages. We were both taking the bar review course at night and became friends over coffee. I learned he'd taken the job and moved to Boise on a whim because he thought a judicial clerkship would look great on his resume when he moved back to Philadelphia, and he wanted to experience living in some wide open spaces. We discovered this judge had a bias towards Jewish students, believing them better academics. This was evidenced by his three prior clerks all being Jewish. We figured he'd offered Jimmy the job based on a review of his legal resume and class standing and by his name, believing him to be Jewish. It must have been quite a shock to discover he'd hired a not so erudite Episcopalian.

Each day brought new cases and an assurance that there would never be any end to it. There were six of us in a large room, each having a cubicle made up of shelves of legal opinions bound in court reporter volumes, with every Idaho and ninth Federal circuit decisions, all updated monthly by our state law librarian in our full reference library in the back. The mornings were quiet and that was the best time for reading and writing because by ten I was exhausted and needing a break from the analytical work. I'd walk to check the court's post office box to collect any mail and, if it was Wednesday, continue my walk a few blocks to a cigar store. I'd buy the latest copy of the Weekly World News, that faux-newspaper given to outrageous stories of celebrities, aliens, and mystics. Although Jimmy's judge exuded a patina of brilliance and enjoyed a reputation as a notable scholar of law, he also managed to walk by my desk Wednesday afternoons knowing I had picked up a copy of the WWN that morning when it came out. He delighted at picking up the paper and holding it aloft while mocking the headlines as he read them aloud, headlines that often screamed:

"UFO seen near Mt. St Helens moments before eruption!"

"Joan Collins abducted by Aliens!"

"Hippo eats dwarf!"

He'd often chuckle and remark how silly those headlines were as he slowly folded up the paper and, putting it under his arm, would wander back to his office where he'd close the door. It'd reappear on my desk the next day as if by magic. I think he just didn't want to be seen buying it.

In the short amount of time I'd been there, I knew I needed to be doing something else. I needed something completely different. The cosmic wheel of fortune heard me and delivered.

I was recruited back into the Air Force when Rick, an old basement buddy from law school, popped round one day. He was a former Army Cobra gunship helicopter pilot and trailer park neighbor. He told me there was a bow wave of Vietnam guys who were retiring and they were looking for attorneys in the Judge Advocate General Department (JAG), and I could have my pick of any number of assignments world-wide. He'd joined a few months earlier and had been assigned to Mountain Home just down the road. Laurie, my new English teacher wife, was up for the adventure and she selected the F-111 base at RAF Upper Heyford, solely on the strength of "its near Stratford upon Avon, the home of William Shakespeare!"

I took a commission and, after some initial training in Alabama, we found ourselves in the Cotswolds, one of the most beautiful parts of England, resplendent with rural farm land and dramatic scenery. I was an Assistant Staff Judge Advocate assigned to the 20th Fighter Wing.

That was something completely different.

## Dickhead jobs

Not many folks want to be a dickhead. There could be an occasion when circumstances demanded being one, but it's not enjoyable, besides, there are plenty of dickheads in every walk of life and profession to fill that square. We all know or have met some, like the traffic cop who really likes writing tickets and collecting "another rock in the box" for the monthly stats. Some dickheads come by it naturally and enjoy it. Most folks hate them, but they're OK with that.

But sometimes a dickhead gets a job even they don't want to do, because while being a dickhead requires a lack of empathy, there were also times when hard jobs come that need some finesse. It was no surprise that dickheads routinely lacked both finesse and personal courage, resulting in that day when I got stuck being a reluctant dickhead.

Major Jack Tipton was the Services Squadron commander. A former enlisted man, he'd gone to University on the GI Bill and later received an officer's commission. This was at a time when race relations were given significant attention and being a black man was a huge plus. He believed the USAF had given him everything good in his life and was fully committed on his end. He was a hard working, capable officer dedicated to leading the best Services Squadron in the USAF, no small thing since airmen were the fussiest eaters in the DoD. Of course at that time the USAF believed that its "Cold War" warriors might as well be comfortable, and well nourished, as they lived and waited for the "balloon to go up" and all of Europe, including our RAF base, to be reduced to obsidian, that glass left behind after a thermonuclear explosion raises the ambient air temperature in excess of 6,000 degrees.

Driven to be the best, his squadron ran award-winning dining facilities, temporary quarters and hotels, clubs and the library. It was a big job because if the slush puppy machine at the NCO club was out of service he'd hear about it, regardless of the hour, given how much kids liked slush puppies and parents hate screaming kids. The same was true if a dignitary came to visit and stayed on base and the mini-bar hadn't been stocked with their particular drink. This was no joke and were some of the things learned as a "project officer" for a visit from a VIP or other dignitary.

The "project officer" title meant you were personally "on the hook" for anything that didn't go perfectly. The duties involved inspecting the guest quarters and included mundane tasks like: Making sure the alarm clock was set to a soft music station with volume low and alarm set for six, flushing the toilet, checking for two spare rolls of soft toilet paper, not the government issue stuff, count the towels, scan the complimentary toiletries, verifying the desk pen worked and there was ample embossed base stationary for thank-you notes, then checking the room temp was set at seventy and flicking on every light on to see if working.

The highest priority was to make sure the minibar was stocked with a good variety of liquors and any particular visitor favorites. I would call the services desk and always instruct the clerk to bring up additional bourbon so at least I'd be covered when invited to have a drink, a precaution that served me well on several assignments. Finally, a function check of both phones, commercial and the secured STU-3 for classified discussions to make sure they were working. The well-trained staff always made certain everything was perfect and I never did note any deficiencies. Even the billeting clerk eventually caught on to always add the bourbon if I was listed as the project officer.

From somewhere in the deep south, Jack was not only an efficient and effective leader, he was a genuine "people pleaser" and that made him well-liked in the base community. He was married to a lovely woman, also well educated, and as a direct result of the "Spouses Preference Hiring Act" had gotten a great job in the base Education office where she was likewise very well regarded for her own considerable people skills. I knew her because they were neighbors and we all went to the club every Friday afternoon for Happy Hour from half past four until seven for cheap drinks, long pours & heavy hors d'oeuvres as befitting servants of the nation on the front lines of the Cold War. We also regularly saw each other at lunch because Upper Heyford was a small American community in a foreign country, so we stuck together and knowing "faces in spaces" got work expedited. She and Jack lived just a few identically cramped duplex houses away, just around the corner from us. Ours was a British Royal Air Force installation with a history back to WWII and her majesty believed a nine hundred square foot three bedroom house with one bath was perfectly satisfactory for a family of four. Our house was utilitarian, frugal, and adequate. It also looked as if designed by George Orwell and approved by the British General Post Office.

One of the many challenges a new JAG faces is "drinking from the legal firehose" and in very short order learns, and becomes familiar with, all the applicable Uniform Code of Military Justice (UCMJ) offenses, various Federal, State and foreign civil and criminal laws as well as understanding the rights of US Forces overseas under the Status Of Forces Agreement (SOFA). There were always any number of small fires needing attention and this included providing counsel to commanders on all matters legal and relating to their operational world. This included environmental considerations and recommending dropping incendiary munitions on an enemy's phosgene poison gas manufacturing facility to ensure destruction of the gas and not just the facility.

To that end, a JAG has to work to not only understand the exact nature of the job — the installation mission — but also understand the military culture and work to provide relevant guidance to the war fighter. At least that's what they said in our evaluations. No small part of this education consisted of varying degrees of mentoring by your boss and others and how well you responded to fluid and constantly changing mission requirements. If you're told to do something, it's very important, even if seemingly unimportant, because nothing you are directed to do by a superior is ever unimportant.

So it was an unhappy occasion when Jack Tipton learned that not everybody enters their profession bent on being the best every day and you really do "get what you pay for" in law just like any other services.

I was in my office having just attended to the needs of some walk-in legal assistance folks when my boss, the Staff Judge Advocate, or **SJA**, summoned me to his office. Lieutenant Colonel Dan Haas was a man who bore more than a passing resemblance to Mikhail Gorbachov, the last Soviet Premier. He was calling for me to either chew my ass for something, or to discuss a criminal justice matter. I was Chief of military justice and therefore responsible for any and all preparations and analysis for the administration of justice on the installation. The reason for the summons was really OK either way, because I needed a break and his office was much larger and had a great leather couch and comfortable leather chairs. Walking inside I saw another lieutenant colonel, the commander for the Mission Support Squadron (MSS), our admin paper-pushers, a man who was poorly regarded as a rule-bound bureaucrat and general dickhead. I took my seat.

From behind his desk, Dan said, "We have an interesting problem, a case of first impression, and we need your advice on how to proceed." The MSS commander pulled out a message he'd received from the big personnel office somewhere in Colorado and handed it to me.

The subject of the message was none other than Major Jack Tipton and the content of the message was that he was a bigamist.

It took a moment for that to settle in. Bigamy is a crime, defined by military law as being married to more than one woman at the same time. It was no small matter either, the penalty potentially being a dismissal from service, a "dishonorable discharge" for an officer, forfeiture of all pay and allowances, and confinement for two years. Although at first blush this punishment is harsh, the government already spends large sums of money on legitimate dependent benefits, and was loathe to pay the often huge medical bills for more than one wife at a time.

The report told the story:

Before coming to England, Jack had been a Services guy down in San Antonio, Texas. It was during this unhappy period in his life that he was married to the first Mrs. Tipton, an odious woman given to running up large clothing bills while screaming about all of Jack's personal and professional shortcomings. As so often happens in military marriages, Jack had occasion to stop at a lawyer's office in a strip mall near the entrance to the base. He was intrigued by an electric sign saying, "All Military clients get a 10% discount!" with a lit arrow pointing in towards the office. He retained the lawyer to attend to the matter, paid a hefty fee, sat back and watched as the legal machine churned out the paperwork to deliver him from his personal hell. He went home that night and shared that he was done with her being so mean and cruel; he'd filed for divorce.

As so often happens, she promptly maxed out all the credit cards, cleaned out the joint bank account and split, leaving him with some hefty bills. It took Jack a lot of work and time to pay off all those debts she'd amassed, but the divorce was finalized and he was finally free and legally clear.

Armed with that sure and certain legal decree from Texas, he married the current Mrs. Tipton and brought her on a three-year, fully subsidized honeymoon in jolly old England. And that's the way it was until that afternoon in late November 1988.

It seemed Jack's Texas attorney had filed all the paperwork and, since Jack didn't know where she was, he filed a notice in the local newspaper of record, which is all the law required, and then waited the prescribed time and took a default judgment when she failed to respond. From that failure to respond, the Judge signed the final decree of divorce and the deed was done, so the participants in that union touted as "until death us do part" got a reprieve from a life sentence.

What nobody in Jack's piece of the former union ever expected were a couple of things:

- That the flamboyant first Mrs. Tipton would ever reappear on the scene with a lawyer saying, "She never got the personal invite to the divorce." She had only moved a few miles away and even though Jack didn't know, or care, where she was, the lawyer was

supposed to make some effort to see if she was still in the area. The most rudimentary search would have found her listed in the phone book.
- That the attorney of record would not notify his client about any of this in time for him to respond. Jack had left his forwarding address with the lawyer.

We were quickly able to dispose of any notion of criminality as simply ridiculous because Jack had every legitimate reason to believe he'd been properly divorced. Criminal matters being my area of expertise and since there was no attempt by him to keep two wives in the government health care system, my work was done. I started to rise from my chair when Dan motioned me back down.

"Well, it seems there is a bit of a problem" he intoned, his voice heavy with concern, and he nodded to the Commander who said briskly, "Under the personnel regs the Air Force position is only one Mrs. Tipton can be in the system at any time. The former Mrs Tipton is now in fact legally the only Mrs. Tipton. This doesn't mean the new former Mrs. Tipton has to leave the country, but it does mean she cannot remain in her job at the Education office because she was hired under the Spousal Preference Act and she no longer being a spouse, means she can no longer be...ummm, preferred."

He really said that, she could no longer be "preferred." I'd never heard that before so I looked at him, astonished, because the personnel machine in Colorado couldn't possibly care if she remained employed, but that was his call, not mine. Being insensitive, he took my astonishment for interest and continued.

"The really difficult part is how to tell this to her because she's really quite a character." He was trying to say he was scared of her and he had reason to be. She was from Chicago, a five-foot ten-inch black woman with Jamaican roots and big hair who was prone to wearing heels to look even taller. The commander was five foot five on a good day with lifts. It was at that point I noticed both of them looking at me and I could tell where this was going. Dan broke the ice, "Say, you know Jack and his wife don't you? Aren't you neighbors?" Of course he knew we were neighbors and the commander knew it also, who piped up saying, "Well, since you know her, and this is a rather delicate matter that might be upsetting, we were wondering if you wouldn't mind breaking this news to her?"

That wasn't really a request and really didn't surprise me. This was a crummy job, like giving a death notification. Nobody is ever going to say, "Thanks for coming by!" and this would be no different.

I stood up and asked for the message so I could answer any questions they might have. As I made my way to the office door, the commander asked for one more small "favor." He said, "Would you mind collecting her DD Form 2AF, the dependent ID card? It's an accountable item."

It was full dark by the time I left the office, as winter is long in the northern latitudes. It had snowed a few days earlier and there were still some crusty skiffs of snow on the walkways as I made my way home. I stopped in, dropped my gear and told Laurie I'd be gone for a little bit, and was back out the door. I walked around the corner, came up the short front walkway and rang the doorbell.

The soon-to-be-other woman opened the door and gave me a big hello as she ushered me in and asked if I'd like a drink. I told her I would and while she got that, Jack came into he room. Drink in hand, I sat them both down and said I had some bad news it was my unpleasant duty to tell them, and so I told them.

I'd seen a fair amount of people in varying degrees of distress during my years as a cop and was pretty good at reading emotions. All I saw was shock and disbelief.

She spoke first. "So I'm not his wife anymore?"

"Yes, that's correct because legally you aren't. It doesn't mean you're a bad person, just that now Jack will have to go through the process again. The really bad news is that the divorce was several years ago and since then Jack's gotten a promotion and several pay raises…"

"And *she* gets that?" the now unknown civilian woman asked. She turned her head slightly towards Jack, tucked her chin down and set her eyes upon him and I knew it would be a long hard night at Casa Tipton.

"Yes, the entire divorce proceedings have been nullified and, under the rules, her claim for a percentage of his retirement check goes from the day married until the day the divorce decree is entered." I then explained how the calculation for her new piece of retirement pay would be determined because a simple formula is used.

"A spouse gets two and a half percent per year for every year of marriage up to a maximum of fifty percent." This new period of marriage would boost the usurper's haul to forty-two percent of Jack's final pay when he retired. I looked at Jack who was staring morosely at me because any settlement would be a lot of money for nothing, while making another person miserable.

The best Jack could hope for was to die on active duty so his newly former wife could at least collect on his serviceman's group life insurance policy. He mused about one NCO who hated his wife so much that to deny her any of his retirement pay he went absent without leave several times until he was finally tossed out at nineteen years of service. That cost him his retirement because you must complete twenty years to receive it. Because his retirement never "vested," the ex-wife received nothing.

The room was silent except for the hum of the florescent light in the kitchen and the pronounced ticking of the Hermle-Anstead grandfather clock near the door. They'd just gotten that clock a few weeks ago, imagining how great it would look when they moved into their new, larger quarters he'd qualified for when he got promoted six months earlier. I looked at my now empty glass wishing it'd been a bigger drink.

Say what you will, but for a now governmentally declared "camp follower," she was remarkably poised and gracious as she stood to show me out. She took my hand warmly, looked me in the eyes and said, "I know this wasn't what you wanted to do, but thank you for being strong enough to come and tell me" and kissed me softly on the cheek.

Remembering my other mission I looked at her and said, "There's no way to put this right and I'm sorry as hell to tell you, but I was also asked to collect your ID card so they can log you out of the system."

She drew back, her eyes narrowed and she reached for her purse, asking "Will you destroy the card?"

"No, I have to bring it to the Mission Support Squadron Commander he's the one who asked for it."

She nodded to nobody in particular, rummaged through her purse and handed me the card. I thanked her, opened the door and went back into the cold night.

The next day when I came into work, Dan saw me in the hallway and asked about the night before. He said, "How'd it go?" I just shook my head and said, "She was calm, but boy was she pissed." Later that morning I walked over to the MSS offices and gave the ID card to the Support Commander. He was sitting back in his leather chair as I put the ID card on his desk. He leaned forward, picked up and examined the brown card, turning it over in his hands.

With a concerned look he asked, "How'd she take it?"

"About as well as anybody could be expected to, I suppose."

He looked back at the card in his hands. "Was she angry?"

"I imagine so, but she seemed fine."

He looked up nervously and said, "Good."

I left the office and wandered down the long central corridor to the service desk to check on the status of some administrative packages due us. I passed a junction which led to the outside. A sign on the wall directed visitors to the different functional areas at one end and the command section at the other end.

I didn't hear the door open, but I turned to a loud sound I recognized was the former Mrs. Tipton speaking in a deep, full-throated, and now Caribbean accented, voice that could have easily announced the end of the world as she screamed "WHERE IS THAT LITTLE WORM?"

The little worm in question had gone across the hallway to talk with his deputy and was caught in the open like a deer in the headlights. Between him and any exit was one very angry black woman whose Jamaican roots were showing as she pivoted ninety degrees right to stalk the now visibly shaken lieutenant colonel who had no immediate way to escape her.

I was reminded of LBJ who said about Vietnam, "Its like a West Texas hail storm, you can't run or hide from it. You just have to take it."

I continued strolling towards the exit and the last thing I heard as I left the building was **"You are such a fucking coward…"**

+++

# Rules Of The Mess

Part of the day's activities included the "legal assistance" hour. Starting each morning at eight and lasting until nine, any military member or their spouse could come to the legal office and be seen by an attorney to discuss whatever civil legal concerns they had on their minds. Most of these involved debt owed to sleazy businesses that operate outside of every one of America's military installations. They offer a place where young airmen, many recently married, would take on a load of debt to furnish their homes or buy a new car. Being young, most were not interested in the fine print, so they often found themselves making minimum payments with interest in excess of twenty percent, a formula guaranteed to make paying off the loan impossible. Other cases involved domestic discord and requests for information on obtaining a divorce in the UK, or any one of the fifty United States, were routine and my expertise on the subject matter grew.

In the course of assisting people whose lives were disintegrating around them, I found myself sitting across from a pilot who'd once again driven the eighty miles to RAF UH. He'd come from the Empire Test Pilot "*Learn to Test, Test to Learn*" School located at the Ministry of Defense (MoD) installation Boscombe Down in Salisbury, Wiltshire, on the Salisbury Plain and convenient to the ancient Druid monument at Stonehenge.

He'd visited several times and today came all that way just to conclude the last chapter in his sad story about a wife who declined the opportunity to move to the UK to accompany him while he attended this highly competitive and career enhancing course. During her time away from him, she also decided she no longer wanted to see herself as a romantic and tragic figure in a nomadic and lonely lifestyle. She had no desire to become a young, and at some time guaranteed to be pregnant, woman left to make her way in a foreign country for weeks or months at a time by a husband whose career demanded so much. She preferred to remain behind with her family and had written a note to her husband saying she'd retained a lawyer and he'd be getting papers. Those divorce papers had finally arrived and I translated the legal "mumbo jumbo" for him and went over each document while explaining what it all meant in dollars and cents. When he felt he understood everything he whipped out a pen and signed off while I notarized his signature. The only comfort I could offer was to assure him that, unlike Jack, his wife had brought this case so it could never be contested at a later date.

With that sad and onerous portion of our visit completed, I asked him if there was anything else I could do for him because there was nothing left to be done. He thought about it for a moment and said, "Well, I've been here for almost a year and in that time you're the only American I've met who isn't in school with me. I'm graduating next week and there's a formal dinner in the officer's mess on Friday night and I'm allowed to bring somebody. I'm wondering if you'd like to come as my guest?" After receiving his assurances I wouldn't have to put out for him when the night ended, I agreed.

The Brits have a lot of traditions, which is what happens when you have a lengthy history of people fighting someone or another. This one came about when the Roman Magnus Maximus withdrew all his legionnaires from northern and western Britain in 383 CE, and left local warlords to take on the marauding Vikings and Franks. Twenty-seven years later, those put-upon locals kicked out all the remaining Roman administrators because of those troop reductions, leaving them to fight without Roman assistance. The exiled administrators appealed to Emperor Honorius for help and he told them "Sorry, I got problems of my own  fighting the Visigoths in Italy and I'm under siege, but thanks for asking."

By the mid-6th century, Britannia was entirely lost to the Romans and the Brits spent the next 1,500 years building an empire and celebrating generations of warriors with lavish feasts and song became the standard. The RAF was the latest bunch to save the Old Blighty during the "Battle of Britain," that protracted series of dogfights in the skies over the island that lasted from July 10 through Oct 31, 1940. Germany's Luftwaffe failed to gain air superiority over the RAF despite months of targeting Britain's air bases, military posts and ultimately, its civilian population. This battle ended Hitler's dream of invading England. So great was this victory, Prime Minister Sir Winston Churchill remarked, "Never in the field of human conflict was so much owed by so many to so few."

Fifty years on, those drunken bacchanals had morphed into an orderly and regimented formal dinner which meant setting the highest standards for all the other services. The RAF was particularly keen to show those older and more storied services that they were equals. Nowhere was this more evident than in the Officers' Mess at the Empire Test Pilot School. A formal affair,  the mess is overseen by a president and vice president and violators of the formal etiquette of the dining-in are "punished."

The following are examples of what could be considered "Violations of the Mess":

1. Untimely arrival at proceedings
2. Smoking at the table before the lighting of the smoking lamp
3. Haggling over date of rank
4. Improper wear of uniform
5. Inverted cummerbund
6. Wearing a clip-on bow tie at an obvious list
7. Gaffes
8. Loud and obtrusive remarks in a foreign language
9. Foul language
10. Discussion on a controversial topic (politics, religion, and women are commonly forbidden topics)
11. Improper toasting procedure
12. Toasting with an uncharged (empty) glass
13. Rising to applaud particularly witty, succinct, sarcastic, or relevant toasts, unless following the example of the President
14. Leaving the dining room without permission from the President of the Mess
15. Carrying cocktails into the dining area before the conclusion of dinner
16. Haggling, whinging or quibbling over penalties or fines imposed
17. Drawing a sword for other than an authorized ceremony

After dinner there was always a loyalty toast, a salute given to the head of state of the country in which a formal gathering is being given, or by expatriates of that country, whether or not the particular head of state is present. The toast is usually initiated and recited by the host before being repeated by the assembled guests in unison. There is sometimes a tradition of smashing a glass used for a loyal toast, so that no lesser toast can be made with it. This toast always involves "passing the port." Both port and madeira decanters are placed at pre-determined spots in front of the President and Vice President who remove the stoppers simultaneously and pass the decanters to the left. The glasses of the President and Vice President will be filled last, after which they are to re-stop the decanters. The President calls upon the Vice President to propose the Loyal Toast. The Army and RAF stand for the toast, while the Royal Navy remain seated (they having ships with low bulkheads). While passing the port, the RN would ensure the decanter does not leave the table, a tradition arising from spillage on high seas, while in the RAF it's passed from hand to hand without touching the table as if flying from glass to glass and I assume the pouring represented aerial refueling.

On the appointed day, I arrived at the club's guest quarters and enjoyed a single bed with a well-used and quite worn mattress, ancient wardrobe, small sink, and washstand. I shaved again, put on my formal mess dress and was out the door and down to the casual bar, where I met my host and downed the first of several whiskeys. I mingled with an array of officers, enjoying a bit of a chat before snagging another drink. Wishing to avoid any controversial topic with an Australian Colonel, we confined our chat to the contributions of the Little River Band[1] on American pop culture, both agreeing their music was crap.

At precisely ten minutes to seven, a steward in livery came through hitting some notes on a hand-held chime announcing ten minutes remained until the doors were closed and not again opened until the mess was closed by order of the President. This was the time to make a last visit to the loo and people took advantage of that.

At seven the door opened, everybody was seated, the doors closed and the dinner called to order. A string quartet played while stewards served a lovely dinner in several courses, as the wine flowed and flowed.

The large dining room was laid out with a long dais for the twenty-five dignitaries and long trestle tables ran vertically up to the dais with seats for twenty-four, twelve on each side. The staff was efficient and discreet, and it was after the main course but before the cheese plates, that one young RAF test pilot discovered he was testing the upper limits of his bladder capacity, as he was now in some considerable discomfort and had to leave the mess. He could have stood up and begged permission from the President but would that have been a Rule 14 violation since he'd certainly had notice and time to attend to his personal needs, but failed to do so through neglect. He also knew he would incur a penalty that might involve singing the squadron song or otherwise entertaining the mess, and would absolutely involve a trip to the grog bowl for a drink of some very potent potable.

---

[1] Formed in Feb 1975, in Melbourne, Australia, the LRB originally called themselves *Mississippi*. Tired of people not knowing what Mississippi was, the name change was made while traveling down the Geelong Road from Melbourne. They passed the turn-off for Little River, and from the back of the truck Glenn Shorrock shouted, 'What about the Little River Band?' and the name stuck.

Thinking discretion the better part of valor, he scanned the room and saw the senior leadership and VIPs on the dais engaged in animated discussion, while the stewards moved about. That commotion provided a perfect opportunity to leave and not be noticed. He also knew this window of opportunity was closing and he had to move before the plate removal finished and the next course started. He slumped slowly down in his seat until he was able to duck under the table and crawl on hands and knees past his comrades, none of whom would disclose his secret, as he made his way to the wall and slithered across a few feet of open carpet. Once safely behind some floor-length crushed red velvet curtains with gold embroidery, a remembrance of a more elegant time, he slowly made his way towards the black kitchen door where he could make his escape from the room.

What the pilot didn't know was that while none of his comrades would comment, the people sitting on the dais, while older, still possessed keen eyesight. In the candlelight, the movement of the curtains first attracted their attention, and the urge to laugh had to be stifled while they elbowed each other. In short order the kitchen door slowly opened and closed as if by an unseen spirit. After a few beats the President rapped a gavel and said, "I believe there has been a gross violation of ettiequte and will not stand for it." He then directed the stewards to remove the empty chair from the table and the diners on either side of the AWOL dinner guest to move closer to close the gap.

Conversations were resumed with everybody keeping one eye on the swinging door, the porthole window giving a glimpse into the life of the scurrying kitchen staff. After several minutes the door slowly opened and closed and again the velvet curtains began to sway. Like he was taught in evasion school, the pilot had counted his steps while crawling out and that effort now eased his return. He reached his table and low crawled back under the trestle as the mess grew quiet. For several long moments the progress of the pilot could be determined by the smiles on the faces of his table-mates marking his passage as he crawled back and forth looking for a chair without a body and finding none. Realizing the jig was up, he went back to the end and stood up, coming to attention while announcing his presence and requesting the return of his chair saying, "Sir! I believe my chair has gone absent." The President directed him to the small table that had been set up near the exit. His food had been brought there as well as the chair. He ate his dinner alone but was allowed to rejoin the Mess after a short song and dance at the grog bowl.

+++

# Road Trip

It was late October 1989 and I'd been on station in England for a year when a training course on updates to Military Law sent me to a conference in West Berlin. Occupied by four nations: France, the UK, USSR and USA since WWII ended, it was considered the epicenter of the Cold War. All the war scenarios practiced by our general officers told us the war would start in Berlin if anywhere and Germany was certain to become a nuclear battlefield which explained why their modern architecture was so utilitarian, it making zero sense to build something beautiful only to have it get blown up again.

I began the journey by driving east towards RAF Mildenhall, the military transportation hub northeast of London, in Suffolk, East Anglia, a region famous for its beautiful countryside, quiet market towns and Cambridge University. It was still two hours to dawn as I made my way down the A-421, passing through the bypass for Milton Keynes New Town, a city born out of the carnage that was WWII.

Nearby Coventry and Birmingham had been destroyed during the Blitz, sacrificed to keep secret "Ultra," the designation adopted by British intelligence in June of 1941, for wartime messages decoded by breaking the cypher on the Nazi *Enigma* device. That destruction resulted in the need for tens of thousands of new houses, and thanks to that domestic migration, Milton Keynes New Town opened in 1967 and was all the rage as a vision for cities of the future. Broad streets and never-ending roundabouts made the journey uninterrupted, but removed all the fun, like I found a few miles on when I came into a small village. The narrow, two-lane main road made a slight turn around a building and I narrowly avoided colliding with a milk float, those ubiquitous three-wheeled battery-powered electric dairy delivery carts the Brits are so very fond of.

This particular cart was carrying seventy-five imperial gallons of milk when it pulled out from a side street. Armed with confidence that comes from a rapidly flashing rotating yellow beacon on the roof announcing it as a slow moving vehicle, the dairyman turned onto the roadway and was working towards his max speed of 10 mph, in a 40 mph zone, at night, in a light drizzle. I slid across to the on-coming lane and drove the wrong way for a bit before recovering and continuing on, unlike my heartbeat which stayed elevated, thanks to the adrenalin rush. I arrived on time and met my traveling companions, several prosecutors from the other airbases on the island and, as the dawn broke we boarded a C-130 Hercules propeller driven transport for the flight to Rhein-Main Air Base in Frankfurt. We enjoyed a two and a half hour plane ride that would have taken a little over an hour in a commercial jet. We sat tightly belted as our machine labored like its namesake and lumbered through the cloud-laden skies that provided more than a bit of turbulence.

We landed shaken, not stirred, and told to experience Germany, then report back that next evening, not later than half past seven, to the Frankfurt Hauptbahnhof, the central train station. There we would board the Berlin Duty train, a 115-mile ride through the "Iron Curtain." This train averaged twelve miles per hour and typically took nine to eleven hours, depending on the time needed for the Soviets to check passports and orders at the checkpoints. These trains were composed of a first class car and anywhere from sixteen to nineteen second-class carriages and baggage cars containing a company of soldiers rotating in to begin duty as part of the Berlin Brigade. They'd be joining the other 2,500 US soldiers specifically assigned to duty in Berlin, part of a unit formed in 1961 as a response to Soviet aggression.

The Soviets couldn't stop the train, but they made it inconvenient. The train could only travel at night, departing at half past eight and arriving in Berlin just before seven the next morning. The trip took so long because of mandatory stops at Hemstedt to switch the engine to an East German one, and then back again to a West German locomotive at Potsdam. Traveling at night also worked to defeat any US photographic espionage efforts since the countryside was black due to a lack of electrification. We were also cautioned that drinking was not permitted aboard the US Army Troop train.

The next afternoon found me sitting in the Armed Force Hotel bar having a drink when the senior lawyer in US Air Forces Europe (USAFE), "Uncle Tom," came strolling into the lounge with his fourth or fifth wife. A USAF Academy (USAFA) grad and former instructor there, he remained immaculate in dress and appearance while enjoying a remarkably full head of thick silver hair. He cut an impressive figure made more so when you saw the silver eagles identifying him as a Colonel to all the world. He looked my way and nodded. I raised my glass in a toast and since I didn't gamble said, "You might want to try the third slot from the left. I've watched a guy dump a load of dough into it and it should be hot."

With nothing further to discuss or offer, I watched as they strolled over to the slot, one of thirty that lined the walls of the club. He signaled the waitress for drinks and they settled in to play. The waitress was just delivering the drinks when that slot hit a payment of three hundred dollars, which was pretty good for an investment of five bucks. The manager paid them out, they tossed back their drinks and left the lounge without so much as a "fare-thee-well," or a free drink for me.

Uncle Tom was just one of a number of cheap bastards in the USAF, and being stingy always made me think less of him and guys like that. I got my revenge later by refusing to kick in on a going away gift from our office when he retired. He was so disliked that all Dan could raise from our entire office and staff, numbering twenty people, was five dollars and that sum being Dan's own contribution.

As time passed, in drips and drabs, the group of lawyers traveling by train was growing. The contingent from the United Kingdom was joined by colleagues from across Germany, Holland, Belgium, Italy, Greece, and Turkey. It was the Cold War, so smoking, drinking, gambling, squadron bars and carousing were still permitted, but the vanguard of "humorless Puritanical weasels," the ones who were never a part of the Vietnam Era Air Force were growing, and voices against such vices were starting to be heard. Some of the fast-burner weasels were moving into senior leadership and began calling into question those long treasured uniquely American military traditions. These new airmen repudiated a cultural legacy forged in the crucible that was WW II, by hard men of the Greatest Generation, the ones who fought to save the world. Over 69,000 airmen fell from the skies from December 7, 1941, until the Japanese surrender on September 2, 1945, and now the term, "Politically Incorrect," a term first coined by the Soviet dictator Joseph Stalin, was being touted and things would change, but not that evening.

That evening we boarded our charter busses for the trip to the Hauptbahnhof and it was not surprising, nor remarked upon, when we all heard the clinking of bottles as suitcases where thrown into the bottom luggage bay for the trip. More than a few riders, already unsteady on their feet, were holding bloated shoulder bags or briefcases.

We arrived, per US Army instruction, one hour prior to the boarding. Each train was assigned a train commander, a Russian-English interpreter, two Military Police, a radio operator, and a conductor. The Train Commander was almost always a Transportation Corps lieutenant responsible for the safety and security of the train during its journey. The radio operator maintained constant contact with Brigade Headquarters while traveling through the Soviet zone. The Transportation Non-Commissioned Officer acted as the conductor. The crew rode in a special escort car adapted from a German caboose.

While the Army folks were busy assembling, having their papers checked and being yelled at, several of us drifted off to a nearby "Imbuss" bratwurst stand and passed the time in idle conversation. Those who had been a bit more feint of heart when originally cautioned about train-drinking took advantage of the wait and stocked up on liquor for the trip. Two of the more celebrated JAG team were Rita and CarraLee, both very attractive women and enthusiastic equal opportunity drinkers. Rita was perpetually single and CarraLee, tall, beautiful and leggy, was not. She had been featured in Playboy's "Girls of" series while in undergrad and was certain to let you know. I'd seen that issue but wished Laurie hadn't thrown them all out as I couldn't recall her in particular. CarraLee was married to another lawyer at her home station but neither was happy, so they were married in name only. Both women had been early shoppers at the liquor store and now took the opportunity to scope out the Army troops milling about to see if there were any cute ones since most of the soldiers were between 18 and 22 years old and in prime physical condition.

Officers were assigned to the first class car, each compartment having four bunk beds. We had a very senior Colonel from the States, Papa Joe, who was on a three-year assignment in a highly coveted, "Retired on active duty" slot. He now spent his days traveling the globe, sitting in on conferences and keeping abreast of how the troops were doing, as well as scouting talent to body snatch and drag off to the Pentagon.

Some JAGs loved being a JAG, they just hated being in the military, so they focused their efforts towards safe career progression which meant finding a hiding spot in an anonymous office somewhere on the E-Wing at the Pentagon, where they would labor for twenty years like a monk in a monastery. These scriveners would work in small offices, packed three or four tight and transferring electronically to another nondescript job, keeping the same desk and never having to leave the comfort, safety, security and anonymity of the magic military bubble that was Washington DC. They avoided onerous duties, like temporary foreign deployments for exercises or assignments to combat zones. Many had fine careers, because those judicial technocrats, in their tiny offices, were spectacular when you needed somebody to spend a year or two drafting and revising some regulation or interpreting what a new policy meant, but were likewise uniformly awful when thrust into real world situations where commanders needed intelligent answers instantly. Papa Joe was always looking for real-world operators.

An earnest young Army second lieutenant, wearing a brassard that said, "Troop Commander," came up to announce that we were free to begin boarding and reminded us that drinking was not permitted aboard the Berlin Brigade troop train by order of Army Regulations. Since we were not in the Army and really just guests there on a visit, and not for the occupation, after no deliberation of any kind we simply nodded and thanked him. As people saw us grabbing our suitcases they also began to load on up knowing berthing assignments were first come, first serve.

The entire time I'd been back in the Air Force, my work had been routine, but on occasions, and as a part of the certification process, met and became great friends with Bob, the Circuit trial counsel. He went to different European bases from Iceland to Greece to work difficult or complex criminal matters as a full time job. Bob was an Air Force brat from Biloxi, Mississippi, although he'd been raised in Germany. I was surprised to see his wife, a figure mentioned a great deal in passing, standing on the platform. I'd only seen her briefly once when she came to pick him up after a trial at Heyford but we'd never been formally introduced. She pulled into the Commander's parking slot and started tapping the horn, and when I passed by she yelled "can you tell him to get his ass out here right now?" Bob was fond of bragging that she had been Miss Nicaragua when he found her, married her, and brought her to America. In reality, she had Nicaraguan parents but had grown up in southern California. Short in stature, but capable of pulling off skin tight jeans and a clingy sweater, she was tapping the toe of her calf-high dark leather Italian boots with stiletto heels, on the concrete platform as I walked up to introduce myself.

She asked me, "Do you know where my husband is?" I confessed I didn't but told her I felt confident he wouldn't miss the train. She looked at me coldly and said, "I'm not going on *that* train." Miss N was laboring under the delusion that Bob was having an assignation with Rita, and had taken an incredible dislike to her, so when she saw the perceived "other woman" on the platform she simply went ballistic. Bob was already busy making hasty arrangements with another JAG and his wife to share a car and drive into Berlin. Feeling the ambient air temperature dropping and sensing I was no longer needed, I wandered aboard and made my way down the car until I came to a compartment near the middle, which was fortuitous, since Papa Joe had assigned himself the center compartment. Given his seniority, and at his immediate direction, this would also be where the bar was set up.

With everybody aboard, the Army conductor gave a signal and the train lurched as it began to roll out of the station. We were all making ourselves comfortable in our respective cars and out of consideration to the two non-smokers, smoking was only allowed in the passageway.

Curiously enough, this was also the spot where most of the drinking was taking place. As the lights of Frankfurt and "the West" fell behind, the train moved into the looming darkness that was then East Germany. An hour was spent at the border as the authorities checked the accuracy of all the travel documents with the Commander and Conductor while the engines were being switched. We spent the time enjoying cocktails and sharing war stories of trials. One lawyer from a base in Holland saw a Soviet soldier on patrol outside our carriage. He spoke a little Russian, so he opened the window and asked the kid how much he wanted for his Soviet Army watch, then bought it for two packs of Marlboros. Another lawyer bought the same soldier's hat with red star emblem for a bottle of Jim Beam Kentucky bourbon whiskey.

About an hour inside the "Evil Empire," as it was referred to by former President Reagan, the party was in full swing and that was about that time the Troop Commander walked into our car escorting a mildly inebriated Rita and CaraLee. He came to Papa Joe, now thoroughly in his cups, and reported he'd found the two attorneys in the enlisted men's carriage where the women flirted outrageously with the troops and created a disturbance. He was now asking if we could we please keep them in our carriage for the good of all concerned. Papa Joe, who was showing all the effects of both jet lag and consumption of a half liter of vodka, smiled benignly at the clearly unnerved young officer and said, "You bet! Now get the fuck out of here." The troop commander fled, not to be seen for the duration of the trip. The party ratcheted up a notch and finally ended around 0400 and the few hours remaining passed in short enough order.

+++

---

## How Merv Griffin Ended The Cold War

We got off the train before seven, as promised, but our rooms at the Templehof airport hotel were not ready, so we spent Sunday morning visiting the Egyptian Museum of West Berlin. While I enjoyed seeing the Nefertiti Bust and pondering the intervening 3,500 years, I was hot to visit East Berlin. American officers could walk unimpeded from Checkpoint Charlie through the "no man's land" kill zone, past barking dogs, bright lights, and East German Vopos, the folk or people's police. They had no authority to speak to us and we were ordered to never acknowledge them in any way. Giving us the stink eye was the infamous STASI, the Ministry for State Security, a much-feared secret police agency. One in sixty-three East Germans provided information on neighbors and friends, and those agents behind mirrored glass regularly photographed people transiting through to add to their collection of known US Military. I didn't care about any of that; I was more interested in seeing the city and enjoying the fact that while the West German mark was worth $1.89 US, the East German "Ost" mark was worth six cents.

We came through the "wall" and I was walking with another lawyer, Steve, ready to see what was on offer in East Berlin. We'd stopped at the Checkpoint, picked up our identification placard and proceeded uneventfully into this most restricted-access city. We wandered down the Unter der Linden, a broad avenue famous for its Linden trees; it was denuded during the war, and we spent our time simply observing the cityscape.

We passed department stores and I noticed, that while display cases in the West would showcase high-end luxury goods, these windows enticed entry with items of more pedestrian and proletarian interest like shaving cream, green-colored shampoo, toothpaste and hair brushes. As we walked, I had the curious sensation that we were being followed. Using a shop's window-pane reflection, I could see two twenty-something guys taking more than a passing interest in Steve and me. At the next block we made a right turn, then again at the next corner. We were now off the main thoroughfare where the buildings were largely unchanged since the end of WW II. These exteriors were still sooty, with scorch marks from fire and pockmarks from bullets fired forty-four years earlier. For all the Russian talk of the modern Soviet Man and Society, the Russians were still punishing the Germans for the carnage of WWII by leaving much of the city in ruin as a reminder; besides, they knew where the nuclear battleground would be.

We stopped in front of the shell of a building and I tied my shoelace. The two guys then had to walk ahead of us and went around the corner. We ambled up that way, then made the next right to get back on to the main thoroughfare. It was only about a block later that I spotted the tail back in place. They'd subbed out one guy for a woman of about the right age and the couple were walking hand in hand. The guy changed his jacket, but he hadn't changed his patterned socks which matched his shirt in the European fashion.

We smiled and waved at them, receiving only a scowl in return. We headed to the InterContinental Hotel, at the time the finest hotel on that side of the wall. When the waiter saw us come in, he pulled the "reserved" sign off a table and invited us to enjoy the best view in the house. We tried Berliner beer and the 600 year old cheese he touted. Paying the bill in east marks but leaving the tip in west marks, the waiter enthusiastically asked us to come back and visit again. Having checked out the process of going into East Berlin, we promised, despite the 600 year old cheese, to come back and bring a group the next night.

Walking back toward the checkpoint, we passed a small market and I went inside. Certain staples reflect a society: I purchased a container of milk, a loaf of bread, some wurst, and a packet of cigarettes. Once outside Steve and I sampled each one of the products. The milk was watery, the bread dry and tasteless, the wurst was fatty and the cigarettes tasted like they'd been put together using the sweepings from the factory floor. This society was in a bad way.

What we didn't know was that six weeks earlier, on September 4, 1989, after a weekly prayer for peace at the church in Leipzig, people began holding rallies and protests against the government of the German Democratic Republic (GDR). With the confidence that came with knowing the Lutheran Church supported their resistance, and would do its best to protect them, these demonstrations began to accompany the weekly prayers, swelling in size as groups emerged to better organize the growing resistance.

Groups around the country rapidly duplicated the actions of the protesters in Leipzig, and the weekly rallies became known as the "Monday Night Demonstrations." A month after the initial rally, a few hundred protesters had become 70,000. A week later, on October 16, there were 120,000. The next week, there were 320,000 people demonstrating in Leipzig alone, and groups of citizens held protests at churches across the country. It was during this period that resistance groups experienced enough popular support to go public with their ideas and materials.

So it was the next night, Monday, that a group of six of us presented ourselves at Checkpoint Charlie where the MP (Military Police) warned us to avoid any public demonstrations that might occur, and keeping that stern admonition in mind we made our way across the killing zone and into the East. We were held up briefly while some papers were checked. A small booth with mirrored glass was where the Stasi would be recording our information and checking it against their data banks. A second visit in two days would be noted.

We began walking up Friederikstrasse and after a few blocks turned right on to the Unter den Linden. We'd been told by some old Berlin hands to have dinner at the exclusive Golden Goose restaurant. It offered an outstanding view of Alexanderplatz, the social center of East Berlin, with many restaurants and shops offering goods for sale to anyone with any cash other than the almost worthless Ost marks. It was late autumn, just before Halloween, and the low German sun had dropped behind the horizon shortly after five.

We turned on to Karl Liebknecht Strasse, a broad avenue lit only by an occasional lamp post. As we drew up to the Soviet Monument against Fascism, we could see lights blazing from the imposing GDR headquarters across the street. Its impressive size and brightly lit exterior was enhanced and made sinister by the more than one hundred AK-47 toting Vopo ringing the exterior, ready to repel any threat from insurrectionists.

As we drew alongside the monument, I saw a lone German in civilian clothing standing in front of us, looking across the street at the armed guards ringing the building. Recalling my best German from ninth grade language class and every World War II movie since, I began my conversation by asking him what was going on.

"Guten Abend. Was ist los?"

The man had seen us walking up and recognized us as Americans, aided by our uniforms, no doubt. Once I'd given the greeting, he cast a furtive look up and down the broad avenue and across the street before turning slightly and presenting his back to that evil building. Smiling broadly and speaking in lightly accented English, he exclaimed happily, "Tonight we are making a demonstration for democracy!" The group of us murmured appreciatively, not wanting to be so loud as to attract the attention of the Vopos our way. While we were immune from arrest or detention, this fellow was not.

At that point, we wished him well and began to move away. But before we left I leaned in towards him and said, "You know, our own experience in revolutions is that you really need a few more people to show up." He drew himself upright and looked me evenly in the eyes and with absolute conviction said, "More will come. You will see."

We ambled on, approaching Alexanderplatz, when suddenly, from an intersecting street we were startled to see a hundred or more East German protestors, walking with banners and carrying candles in cups, calling for freedom and democracy. Just as the German gentleman back at the monument had predicted.

As the senior officer and designated group leader, and heeding the advice of the MP at the checkpoint, I looked about to see if I could find a way to get out of the area because I knew none of us wanted to end our foray into the heart of the Evil Empire this early. It was then that I eyed the rathskeller, a basement bar, just a door away. The demonstrators were drawing abreast and the time to leave was upon us. I led the way downstairs, pushed open the heavy wooden door and we entered the dim interior of a place that was a European version of Moran's, a small bar back in my home town on Long Island. We saw eight representatives of the modern Communist man quietly drinking the evening away.

I was instantly reminded of those old Westerns where the strangers walk into the saloon and the piano playing stops. In this case, it was manifested by the simultaneous movement of all eyes upon us and conversations coming to an instant halt. This is also where the stranger has to decide how to reveal his intentions in the clearest possible way to avoid misunderstandings or bad outcomes.

My very rusty German provided the solution and I said loudly, "Guten Abend, meine Freunde, die Getränke sind auf mich!" Buying a round of drinks is a universally understood offer of friendship, and that caused the crowd to come alive with offers of many thanks and a few shouts of "Machen sie meine ein doppeltes!" (Make mine a double!) Those fine working men shouted their orders to the now animated barman who began rapidly pulling bottles off the top shelves to satisfy the desires of our new friends.

We settled in with our drinks and I paid the two dollar tab. We knew we had a few minutes' wait to be certain the demonstrators had left the area, so we relaxed and started chatting. The TV volume picked up again and in a few minutes I would come to understand how it was Merv Griffin who had ended the Cold War.

For whatever reasons, television signals from West Berlin were not being blocked by the GDR, whether that was a recent development or routine I could not know, but what I did hear was the unmistakable sound of the opening music to "*Wheel of Fortune*," and I glanced to see the syndicated West German version of Pat and Vanna spinning that wheel and the happy West German contestants winning speed boats and ceramic Dalmatians.

I watched those men watching that television, those workers of the proletariat, and I saw something in their eyes, some yearning that would be explained a few years later in the movie "*The Silence of the Lambs*" when Dr. Lector told FBI agent Clarice Starling, "People covet what they see."

Finishing our second two-dollar round and having earned the good will of that entire drinking establishment, we made our way out the door, up the stairs and off into the evening.

Just half past seven found us in front of the restaurant. As we were walking inside, we ran into two other JAGs from the conference. They were both assigned to bases in West Germany and one, Mary, spoke fluent German. They joined us, and the tuxedoed maitre d' escorted us up thickly carpeted stairs. We entered a huge open dining room and were seated at a large table set inside a bay window with an unobstructed view of the Platz. The few local diners were mostly elderly couples. We were either early by European standards, or not a lot of folks could afford to eat there. The men wore jackets and ties and the women stylish dresses. They all looked our way and many nodded pleasantly. The diners were being serenaded by a gray-haired gentleman playing a dirge-like tune on his electric piano, but this ended as we were being seated when he broke into some snappy American show tunes from "Oklahoma" and "South Pacific."

Our waitresses were young and pretty, both spoke limited English, but their enthusiasm for the movement towards democracy was unmistakeable. One of them greeted us by sharing her name and saying proudly in practiced English: "I cannot wait for democracy! As soon as I can leave here, I am going west and then if I am lucky, I will go to America and to live with my sister in Chicago."

Now satisfied that she wouldn't be spitting in our soup, we began to work on our selections for dinner. The first order of business was ordering drinks. Since most of us were having white wine we demurred to her suggestions after reminding her that, "Geld ist kein problem" (money is no problem) and how about a nice selection of appetizers?

She came to Jimmy-Jam, a wild man from a base in the UK, who fired off "I want you to bring me the best thing on the menu, what you only bring out for the big shots." He leaned back conspiratorially, "You know, without telling all of us good folks about it."

Some might say Jimmy had problems with voice projection as his volume was always set way too high. He got his nickname because of getting jammed up when the US government shifted from handing over Temporary Duty (TDY) pay in cash and instead issued government credit cards for recording and reimbursing all the credit card expenses. This required the card to only be used for government business which Jimmy came to understand did not include Valentine's Day chocolate, fancy lace underwear, and a spa day for his wife.

Confused, the waitress leaned in and said, "I'm sorry, your English is too fast for me, please." Jimmy began to pantomime shoveling an imaginary fork towards his mouth and turning up his volume just a notch in case she couldn't hear him and which was now attracting the attention of other diners while saying, "Something good!" and he gave her a thumb's up gesture and big smile. Unable to remain quiet and allow the loud American stereotype to be further denigrated, Mary, the German-speaking attorney blurted out "Bringen sie ihm ein schweineschnitzel mit spätzle und salat!" (Bring him breaded pork with noodles and salad) Jimmy, stunned by the rapidity of the order, sat back, cocked his head and looked at her appraisingly. "Yeah, that sounds good," he told the waitress while closing the menu he couldn't read, and turning to Mary saying, "That's good, right?" She nodded and told him it was a very good choice, so the entree was settled.

The liberty-loving waitress probably should have left it at that, but she further inquired as to Jimmy's drink choice, in English. He decided he wanted some red wine, which was fine except there really was no red wine in East Germany in 1989, maybe some Bulgarian red for cooking, but for drinking, only white wine. He looked up at her and said, "I don't know, maybe have some red wine." Again, she leaned forward and said,"Please? I'm sorry?" Jimmy looked at her and said very slowly and much too loudly for the room, "I said REEED WIIIINE!" dragging the vowels. The waitress was confused and looked to the same attorney who said, "Bringen sie ihn einfach ein glas, er wird trinken, was wir trinken!" (Bring him a glass, he'll drink what we're drinking) Grateful to be done with this big-voiced American, she nodded, finished up the order and left for the kitchen, and no doubt telling any other future immigrants what the Americans were like.

As the evening progressed and courses began to roll out, we made another judicious use of "Drinks are on the Americans!" and the place became even livelier. A later crowd arrived and people were being serenaded by a now lively piano player who was stoked by the appearance of American dollar bills in his tip jar and had amped it up to selections from *Cabaret*.

While we were chatting amiably, somebody glanced out the bay window and said, "Would you look at this!" We stopped talking and looked out and on to the Platz. The shops had closed a half hour earlier and the square was no longer brightly illuminated, but still, there was no mistaking as thousands of ordinary Germans began walking into that square from all directions. There were hundreds more banners and every single person had a candle which blended into a peaceful, but determined, mass of humanity petitioning their government and the world for freedom. As they converged and coalesced, a phalanx of helmeted Vopos surrounded the plaza on several sides. They were backed up at a distance by other officers in riot control vehicles. The protestors chanted and waited for the carnage that never came. We finished our dinner, said our goodbyes, and made our way back to the West. Ten days later that hated wall starting coming down.

I wonder if our waitress made it to Chicago.

+++

## Black History Month

The base at RAF Upper Heyford, was just a little slice of America transplanted and set in the bucolic and rolling farm lands of rural Oxfordshire. Despite the pleasant and docile exterior of the base, inside it was ready to unleash nuclear armageddon against the Soviets and had been that way since 1955. Clubs for officers, and a combined NCO and Enlisted mess, offered a place for camaraderie and relaxation.

I'd completed all my required trials to be certified as competent and, when the position came open, I was re-assigned from the Wing at RAF UH and to become the Area Defense Counsel. A "tenant unit," located on the installation, I would now be reporting to a colonel in Germany. This was necessary to free me from any undue influence by any base personnel or the commander, because my job was simple: to represent any airman who had been accused of an offense, and airmen accused of crimes are never very popular.

Each club on a military base had its own culture and atmosphere that likely had developed over the preceding decades. Since figuratively if not literally, nothing every changes in Britain, an entire nation that profits nicely from being frozen in time and looking charming, the clubs were no different. The Officers' Club had a pub in the front plus a casual back bar, and even a drawing room with overstuffed chairs and a "no women allowed" rule. The front bar looked like any proper British pub with a resident barman, Bobeslaw Jandy. A Pole displaced during WW II, he'd helped the Allies hunt down fugitive Nazis. For this service, he was brought to the UK and given citizenship. He was hired on as the barman, and would remain there until he died or the base was closed. Although friendly to all, he would never serve any German pilots who visited the base, so an American officer would, by necessity, do the drink-ordering for them.

The louder, and more athletic, "Bunker Bar" was in the back of the building, just past the Royal Dalton gift shop. The junior officers would hang out, engage in youthful shenanigans, and commit certain indiscretions which is what kept me so gainfully employed. The bar had sandbags around the support columns, less for ambiance, and more to protect the drunken aviators they served. Many were the clients who came to me on a Monday due to some transgression occurring the weekend prior.

The NCO club across the way had a similar lay out. A dining room with twenty tables and a section of booths along the wall looked out into an open courtyard surrounded by the three-story drab, but functional, red-brick single-person dormitories. The senior NCOs had a small ancillary pub and a private section of the dining room because the younger NCOs filled those booths each weekend, taking their spouses out for dinner and drinks. Two large interior rooms served as meeting rooms, but jazzed up as dance halls over the weekends. One side piped Country Western and Rock, while the other side spun Soul, Disco and Rap. During any particular ethnic/gender celebration month, the clubs offered promotions and giveaways to tap various interests to encourage club membership and camaraderie.

February was always Black History month and, although the banners and placards around the base reminded us of that fact, it really didn't mean much in the day-to-day life at Heyford. Sixteen years after race riots at west coast air bases resulted in the 1972 creation of the social actions and equal opportunity programs, such issues had been virtually insignificant on the base. Because the USAF was a firm believer in racial equality, equal opportunity and treatment, these months were really just a reason to encourage club patronage and more fun.

In addition to the top shelf liquor brands at bottom shelf prices, Upper Heyford was the beneficiary of the added attraction of what was now the third generation of "Tesco girls." Saddled with a nickname that referenced the Tesco Grocery Store bags they used for their next day change of clothes, these young ladies stepped lively on to the base every Friday afternoon. They were looking for their "Golden Ticket," ideally to include marriage and that life-changing DD Form 2AF dependent ID card. When failing that, the dawn would find the young ladies in the slow walk of shame to the bus stop, perhaps a broken high heel sticking out of the plastic Tesco bag. In one well-told case, some young lads were discovered "in flagrant delicto" in the dorms with the eighteen-year old daughter, the thirty-six year old Mum, and fifty-five year old Granny, all of whom had shared a cab for the short ride from Oxford, and then again for the long ride back.

Kenya T. Weber was a life support specialist at one of the flying squadrons. From a rough part of Chicago, Ken had grown up in Englewood, west of 63rd Street near where I-94 becomes I-90. He'd been working as a hotel night clerk when the robbery and murder of the night clerk at a hotel in nearby Sherwood park helped him decide to broaden his horizons. He'd dropped by the Air Force recruiter for information and was bound for Lackland Air Force Base in Texas just a few days later.

He liked working in the squadron. He'd learned a lot in technical school and was glad to be a part of the fight against Communism; but, mainly he was glad for getting out of Chicago, a city with 744 murders so far that year. He was grateful for landing in a place with women who reminded him of home, full-figured women who liked a strong man, and Ken was that strong man, an operator who liked to burn that candle at both ends.

Ken liked a particular style and body shape. He liked big women, bigger-than-him women. Ken was slight, maybe 140 pounds on a good day if he was wet. He favored women who came in above 180 pounds (or 13 stone), and expressing that preference made him quite successful in matters of love during his fifteen months in the UK. He loved this assignment because he had met many healthy women in Oxfordshire and Buckinghamshire. Ken had watched a lot of British movies growing up and he liked England because, unlike Chicago, things were quiet. He remained a happy guy until he ran into that wrong Tesco girl.

Ken came to his grief on a Friday night during Black History month, which was pretty much the same as any other Friday night not during Black History month. The music was loud, the lights were low, a disco ball perpetually threw out sparkles, and the drinks were full and unmeasured. In fact the only difference was that Ken had gotten in between a power struggle involving two Tesco girls.

Ken was nothing if not consistent, for in addition to enjoying the comforts and charms of zoftig local lasses, he was also fortunate in making the acquaintance of two women with the same name, Agnes. For clarity, the two will be referred to as the former Agnes and the current Agnes.

This entire sequence of most unfortunate events was set in motion when, a month earlier, Ken dumped the former Agnes rather unceremoniously one evening. Making matters worse, he did it in a public place, the NCO club ballroom on Soul Night, because Ken was afraid of her and wanted their relationship ended in public. He later confessed that upon reflection saying, "Step off, bitch!" might not have been the best choice of words. Sadly, Ken had no inkling of the depths of emotion in Agnes the former, but that depth became clear when Ken showed up at the next disco night parading the current Agnes, late of nearby Bucknell, who made her living killing chickens at the factory.

As might have been expected, the former Agnes showed up that night as well. When she saw her Ken making time with the current Agnes, it didn't take too long, just two rum and cokes, for her to stride across the darkened dance floor, indelicately weaving and hip checking strangers as she pressed through the gyrating flesh until she stood before Ken and his "harlot."

Former Agnes didn't say a word; she simply grabbed the current Agnes by her long and silky black hair, wrapped that hair around her hand at the palm, gave a quick yank down and out, splaying the now screaming Current on the carpeted floor. That's when Former began kicking Current until the bouncers could race over, separate them and toss her out. As one prescient senior NCO working as a night manager said later, "This shit won't be over until he goes to jail."

Another week passed and it was the middle of February, at the height of the Black History Month Celebration. The cover of the base weekly magazine, "The Guardian," drew awareness to this. The cover was a photo of a volunteer dressed like an African slave, a chain around his neck, then superimposed was the same guy dressed in his Virginia Military Institute graduation dress to show how far the struggle had come.

It was Saturday night and the crowd was well oiled and getting into the evening. Ken had just purchased a new mocha heather blended cotton cashmere mixed stitch crewneck sweater and liked the way he looked in it. So did his Current, and as they danced to slow songs, all was well and good. That is, until Former, not constrained in any fashion at all, stepped into the lounge to see the two dancing and she started to boil. The song ended. Ken had just escorted Current to her seat, when he saw Former boiling over as she raced to her nemesis. Ken yelled for help as she knocked Current out of her seat, fell upon her, pummeling with both fists. It took longer than it should have for his frantic screaming and waving to catch the attention of any of the night managers, given the blasting music and just-short-of-pornographic gyrating in his purview. Finally the senior manager noticed Ken waving wildly and tapped his assistant, signaling him to hurry along. Cutting a line through the tables, they were able to grab the two brawlers. Ken continued to yell in absolute frustration.

The senior manager, a cop during the duty day, realized Ken was the only military link to this problem, so he decided to toss him from the club and the two brawling women along with him. Things went poorly. Hearing this news, Ken screamed in disbelief at the irritated night manager. Now the manager from the country side bar rushed in to help with the crisis, taking an Agnes outside while the other two managers handled a near hysterical Ken.

Then, as he was pulled through the double doors to the hallway, his new sweater brushed a wall thermostat which snagged it, creating a hole, instantly trashing the garment. This proved to be too much for Ken and like Popeye the Sailor man, he'd had '*all he could stands and he couldn't stands no more.*' The rage manifested as he punched the senior manager in the mouth, stunning him, and causing the assistant manager to throw Ken into a wall. Finally the cops arrived from the station house just one hundred yards away. Three of them ran down the long hallway past the cashier's cage and continued toward Ken's screams.

The first of the three, a six and a half tall buck sergeant named Kozink, saw Ken struggling with the assistant manager and moved in. Kozink grabbed Ken by the sweater and pulled him up while the other two cops, Germane and Zippen, moved to either side to get the cuffs on. The security police academy used the theory of "one cop, one arrest." Ideally, when taking a person into custody, one cop handles the arrest and cuffing while the others watch unless needed, as too many hands can cause confusion. Unfortunately, in this case confusion already reigned, and the cops ignored that admonition.

Ken was still struggling, so Kozink used a prohibited choke hold to restrain him. This dangerous maneuver involved applying pressure against the opponent's carotid artery by putting his neck into the "**v**" where the forearm meets the bicep. Squeezing the bicep restricts the artery and the arrestee is rendered unconscious. Improperly applied, you choke the life out of the guy. This technique was no longer taught after 1975 and was not permitted under regulations in 1990.

The part of that practice Kozink didn't understanding is that pressing solidly completes the arterial constriction. Kozink was trying to apply a choke hold while wearing a thick sleeved jacket and was only able to cut off the air supply, which produced a wildly violent autonomic response to suffocation from Ken, who could no longer breathe. This was interpreted as resistance by both officers and each had a different reaction, as both cops shouted directions and commands to Ken, resulting in more confusion and a greater application of force on Ken.

Ken's violent thrashing about made Kozink lose his grip and Ken slumped downwards. He'd begun gulping air and began to stand back up when the other two cops slammed him to the ground. Zippen pulled out his handcuffs, forgetting that he'd double-locked them to prevent any movement of the ratchet into the pawl. When he tried to snap them over Ken's wrist, the ratchet stayed in place. Frustration made him draw the steel cuff back and mash the ratchet hard against Ken's slender wrist, making Ken howl and writhe in agony. Germane grabbed a set of unlocked cuffs and together the three policeman succeeded in handcuffing Ken. They pulled him up and moved him down the hallway toward the door where they were assisted by a manager.

Concurrently, the other managers had decided "too much bad behavior." They shut off the music, turned on the lights, and informed their customers that the club was now closed. Since this was a night when nothing went right, chaos would continue. As the police procession turned left to go back down the main hallway towards the front entrance and the waiting police car, the double doors for both ball rooms opened up and the drunken crowd flowed into the center of the hallway, jostling toward the exit. Just then one of the cops tripped over Ken's legs as he was dragged along, causing a collective balance disaster and ensuing fall onto a sofa along the hallway wall.

Handcuffed, Ken couldn't catch himself falling and went down screaming. His head smacked into the thigh of the assistant night manager near Germane. The manager screamed that Ken was biting him which led Kozink to lift Ken off the manager. He applied the choke hold correctly this time and he caused Ken to pass out, slide down, and fall face first onto the floor. These three cops took the opportunity to reposition themselves on each side and behind him, but were so intensely focused on this crazy man-biter, they failed to notice the crowd was no longer moving towards the exit but stopping to revel in the excitement.

Germane knelt down, yelling at Ken to "Wake up!" believing Ken was playing at being unconscious. He decided to apply a pain compliance technique. He jumped up, grabbed his night stick, and struck Ken's left thigh a mighty blow. When that got no response, he tried it two more times in quick succession while using a batter's grip, but had to finally realize that Ken was, in fact, unconscious.

The crowd watching the action kept growing larger, and, at seeing Germane wailing on prone and unconscious Ken, some started raising objections. As Ken began to stir, the cops stood him up, moving him forward and continued towards the now sympathetic crowd. After just a few feet and abreast of the cashier's cage, Ken regained his senses, saw the crowd and quickly appealed to them for help, yelling, "Help me, brothers help me! Abraham Lincoln freed the slaves! Don't let the white man take me away in chains!"

The crowd in its entirety became agitated, and one wanna-be pitching star hurled a whiskey glass towards the group of cops. Thankfully, owing to a lack of physical coordination, and perhaps some inebriation, the glass struck and shattered one of the mirrors on the wall. Ken's incitement led to more shouting and crankiness among the displaced revelers. Calls brought more police to restore order before things got much worse. Now perceiving Ken as a potential black-history-month-agent-provocateur, the cops were finally taking no chances. They bound his feet using yellow nylon ropes with eyelets at both ends. Called "Hobbles," they allowed a flailing prisoner to be bound up like a piece of American Tourister luggage. They ran another line from his bound feet to his bound wrists; and, treating Ken exactly like a piece of odious baggage, they tossed him into the waiting police car for transportation right across the street to the police station.

Ken was ultimately charged with creating a riot, assault on the punched manager, assault on the bitten manager, and resisting arrest. At trial the judge was astonished when an eager Germane demonstrated his ability with the pain compliance technique using his nightstick which he'd named "Mr. Licorice Stick of Love." Holding Mr. Licorice, Germane came off the witness stand and stood in the center of the courtroom. Germane then struck the carpeted floor with enough ferocity to make the trial judge wince and raise his eyebrows in disbelief.

Ken was ultimately convicted of "breach of the peace" for creating the disturbance when team Agnes were brawling around on the floor and for hitting the night manager. Taking into account the abuse and beatings he suffered at the hands of the cops, the judge gave Ken no jail time and only a reprimand.[2]

+++

# Can I Ask You A Question?

I heard phrase a lot, usually uttered by someone nervous and not familiar with the judicial system. I never bothered to inquire if it was for a friend, I always assumed the question was a hypothetical asked out of curiosity.

Leaving the club after lunch one day, I was in no hurry to get back to my office in a building that formerly housed the base veterinarian during the sixties and which still smelled of antiseptic. I was walking down the carpeted hallway to the exit when Richie, a Weapons Systems Officer (**WSO**) with another squadron, came limping in. He'd recently jumped out of an F-111 departing Incirlik Air Base in Turkey. The crew was just five miles east of the base when they sensed smoke in the cockpit. In efforts to fix the smoke issue, they switched off the yaw / pitch dampers and central air data computer system, causing a stall and complete loss of control, which necessitated their immediate departure from the now doomed and out of control aircraft.

The pilot pulled the yellow and black handle that fired the escape crew capsule that jettisoned from their crippled bird. The two-man crew remained encapsulated and protected until "such time as the external environment is suitable for direct exposure or the capsule reaches the ground." So while the aircraft plummeted to its destruction, they floated like angels down to earth where an air bag automatically deployed to cushion the impact. I noticed his limp and asked what it was like ejecting and how he was getting on. With a wan smile he said, "OK I guess, we landed pretty hard. It felt like falling off the roof of your house while sitting in a rocking chair."

---

[2] Later over drinks in the bar, he told the prosecutor and me that he wished he could have thrown those two cops in jail. Curiously enough Kozink would come to me for criminal defense services when he was accused of having sex with a subordinate on duty. I got him acquitted at a jury trial.

I was impressed with his nonchalance and was going to commend him as riding the original "Mr. Toad's Wild Ride" which was not without considerable risk, when he said, "Can I ask you a question?" His words tumbled out that, while in no way related to any malfunction that might have doomed the ten million dollar government asset, there was a matter of some twenty-four handmade and terribly expensive Turkish carpets that had been loaded in the bomb bay by the maintenance squadron commander. Since all were purchased and paid for in advance by the local customers who were even now expecting a delivery and would be asking questions in fairly short order, what was the chance of a happy fix?

It was no secret in the USAF that aircrews often hauled private cargo as "baggage" when space allowed it. This usually amounted to a few cases of wine, beer, Bavarian cuckoo clocks, and the like. There were the occasional excesses, like the C-141 pilot in the late sixties who flew his new Mercedes from Germany to his home station in Alabama, a non-title state, to avoid customs duty, but in most instances it was small items of negligible weight.

Here the question revolved around a commercial rug selling enterprise operating out of a flying squadron. That meant the Uniformed Commercial Code Section 2 would control the answer. I'd gotten a B in that class and the answer came right to me. I told him the rugs were shipped "F.O.B. RAF Upper Heyford." Richie looked confused so I explained F.O.B. stood for "free on board," a delivery term under which the seller **must,** *at his own expense and risk,* transport the goods to that place and tender delivery of them to the buyer. In addition, the seller, at *his own expense and risk,* must load the goods on board.

All the risk was on the seller, which meant fiscal liability was on the broad shoulders of full-time pilot and part-time rug merchant, one Capt "Ali bin McGinty" who'd already made several carpets runs. He'd talked Richie and his pilot into taking a load for him and this had been their first run. Given these were the truly greatest fighter pilots on earth, nobody ever expected them to do some Turkish carpet bombing on that fine and sunny day.

I put a gentle hand on Richie's shoulder as I explained the potential legalities to him. I saw his face grow pale which suggested he might have been a silent financial partner and the thought of being on the hook for $25,000 or more was not a pleasant one. Dejected, he thanked me and started to hobble off when I called after him, "Of course there is the whole matter of what the aircraft accident review board's thoughts will be on the issue, if the matter even comes up." Richie stopped and looked back at me wide-eyed as he realized what that meant. I continued, "There is also the matter that aside from the expectations of your clientele regarding losses and possible remedies, you might expect some questioning of just how many folks knew about the delivery process, if that ever even comes up in any subsequent OSI investigation, so I'll just leave it there."

+++

## Deviants

Not everybody who went to jail was a bad person.

Chuck was a rising star at RAF Upper Heyford. He'd graduated with distinction from the Virginia Military Institute, taken an Air Force commission and took a position with the Security Police. A handsome man, very much the poster boy image of a VMI grad and USAF officer. He was personable and well regarded by everybody who knew him. Sadly for him, he was a homosexual at a time when homosexuality was as feared and hated as Communism. He'd been accused of attempting to sodomize a young enlisted man one night after they'd both spent the evening drinking and flirting, when Chuck had asked for a blowjob. The "victim" then threatened to out Chuck and did so after Chuck told him to fuck off. Although the complainant was clearly a mean and spiteful little queen, the evidence was sufficient to prove the attempt and Chuck was promptly convicted of Conduct Unbecoming an Officer. He was given a small term of confinement and ordered to be dismissed from service. Chuck took his punishment with grace and even though he wasn't my client, I liked him and made a point of visiting him when I came to see my clients housed in the regional USAF jail at RAF Lakenheath. I had enough clients serving time there that they could field their own basketball team. So, when I went over it was an all day affair. As their defense counsel I made it my duty to visit them during their incarceration and I'd bring some comfort items: homemade cookies, paperback novels, and cigarettes. I liked that Chuck even took part in the base Christmas tree sales; because, officers, even former ones, cannot be made to perform manual labor.

On the other side of the "sexual-criminal" coin was a "chicken-hawk" captain, a predatory homosexual who sought out naive young airmen. This one worked in the Services Squadron at a "geographically separated unit," the bomb dump storage facility at nearby RAF Fairford as a "morale and recreation" officer. His approach was making a habit of finding vulnerable airmen, plying them with strong drink and seducing them. On one occasion, he'd found a choice young airman and invited him to visit his off-base residence for dinner. The airman was flattered to be receiving such personal attention and seeming friendship from one of the more senior officers on the tiny installation. Besides dinner, this captain gave the young man a combination of wines and liquors, then put on a slide show that started with a guy in a flight suit standing by a fighter plane. In the next slide the guy has his flight suit center zipper down, then the suit is dropped to the waist. He asked the drunken airman if he ever wanted to wear a flight suit, which of course the young man did, and of course the hawk had one in the closet, but of course, the young man needed to take all his clothes off "because the flight suit was tight" and besides, he assured the tender young man, "real fighter pilots go commando."

Come dawn's early light, the hungover airman woke up beside the sleeping captain, instantly recognizing the enormity of his prior evening's bacchanal and he, reasonably, panicked. As soon as he could get there, he reported the incident to his First Sergeant who called the cops. Charges were brought forth and at his trial that legendary prosecutor, now Major Bob, was examining the complaining witness. The charge was sodomy, a serious business under the Uniform Code of Military Justice. Bob was an experienced and savvy advocate, with a straightforward, yet folksy, manner used when he had to elicit certain explicit testimony from the witness in order to prove the crime occurred. In this case, Bob had to prove the accused had visited, "… unnatural carnal copulation with another person of the same or opposite sex, or with an animal." An essential element was "penetration, however slight" which was a nod to U.S v. Sanchez, an Army private assigned to Germany who was interrupted while having a tryst with a chicken.

To that end, Bob had to find the exact phrasing to get the statement he needed. In a trial a few weeks earlier Bob had asked a female rape complainant to describe what happened to her and she testified, "He put his penis in my uterus…" and all a startled Bob could say was,"Some reach!" For this, Bob received a stern, non-verbal warning, from our regular judge, Mike, who knitted his caterpillar eyebrows together while leaning forward on the bench. Bob plunged on with his examination:

"Airman, did the captain attempt to put his penis into your anus?"

"Sir, yes sir!"

"And was he successful?"

"Sir, NO sir!"

"How can you be certain?"

"Sir! I squeezed my butt so tight you couldn't have gotten a Mercury dime up my ass!"

The defendant was properly acquitted of the sodomy charge, but was found guilty of the attempt and Conduct Unbecoming an Officer. He was ordered jailed for four years and dismissed — *cashiered*, the officer equivalent of a dishonorable discharge. While the other prisoners worked outdoors, this fellow was lazy and still felt superior so he preferred to stay indoors. The rules forbade sitting on his bunk before five PM so he'd sit on a metal folding chair. He was a creep and I never gave him any cookies.

+++

# The Jandy 6

"There are old aviators and bold aviators, but there aren't any old bold aviators."

Old Air Force adage

In those halcyon days before Desert Storm, while the Free World was still enjoying the "peace dividends" that came from the collapse of the Soviet Union, I was minding my business on a lovely Sunday morning. My perusal of the *Stars & Stripes* comics section was rudely interrupted by a persistent knocking at my door. I opened it to see Sully, my pilot neighbor from across the street. He was holding a Bloody Mary saying, "Hey Shyster, we'd like you to come on over and visit."

I'd taught every flier the Laws of Armed Conflict, the Code of Conduct and ethics. When I briefed the 79th Tactical Fighter Squadron, a NATO "Tiger" squadron, those guys said I made them laugh and invited me to be initiated as a Tiger, which meant I could use their bar. I would also be addressed by my call sign and could address any other Tiger using theirs, regardless of rank, but always mindful of surroundings. The naming ceremony involved eating a whole raw egg still in a shell. You put it in your mouth and then had to eat it all without using your hands. Breaking the egg upset the air pressure inside your mouth and shot the yolk towards the back of your mouth and that would cause some initiates to gag or vomit. You couldn't be a member until you ate that egg, which was then washed down with a tumbler of Jeremiah Weed, possibly the most awful tasting liquor available for sale anywhere on the planet. Thank God, I succeeded on the first time and was given the radio call sign and *nom d'guerre*, "Shyster," which, while unoriginal, was a natural. When I later became the Area Defense Counsel (ADC), a full-time defense lawyer, they designated me their squadron, "*Legal Mouthpiece,*" the first squadron to ever have, or, as I would soon learn, need one.

I looked at my watch and, while half past eleven on a Sunday wasn't too early for the offer of a drink, I knew it wasn't being offered because I was fun to drink with. I walked across the street and wasn't

surprised to find six other Tigers in Sully's kitchen, and all of them pacing and looking very nervous. I started the ball rolling by asking, "OK, what's supposed to have happened, who was allegedly involved, and were there any witnesses or pictures?" I asked this to see if they followed my standard legal advice, which consisted of "Admit nothing, deny everything, and issue counter-allegations."

The story emerged that, on the Wednesday just past, they'd been drinking a few beers in Jandy's with a couple of the wives when a most unfortunate and absolutely understandable misunderstanding occurred.

Jandy's Pub was located just to the left of the main entrance, in the front of the club. Double doors led into the bar proper and eighteen stools stood around the long wooden **J**. There was no service hatch because Jandy didn't ever have to come out from behind the bar and there was no waitress service. If you wanted a drink you needed to order from him, and timing and tips were everything.

Friday afternoon was "Commander's Call" which every officer was expected to attend for a briefing from the Wing Commander. Next we would all listen to the "Hails and Farewells," welcoming new arrivals, and witnessed the people who had earned medals have them pinned to their chests. A smart guy would show up at four and order two Guinness stout beers, one to enjoy immediately and the other to take into the briefing while asking Jandy to please have one ready upon his return. There were often a hundred or more officers in attendance, and while not all drank, plenty did.

During the week, the pub was open from four until eight or nine, depending on the crowd. On this particular Wednesday night there were fourteen people in the pub. While Jandy was pouring the beers, six Tigers and two wives sat or stood along the hook in the **J**. Opposite them were the base commander, his deputy, and Oscar, the new Tiger squadron commander.

Sitting out of sight, in a booth behind a stained glass privacy barrier, was Phil, the airfield manager, and his wife Susie. In the ordinary course of events this would have been a perfectly uneventful evening but for the names of two of the wives. At the bar, drinking shots with her husband and five of his squadron mates, was effervescent Suzy

Morton. Meanwhile, in the booth with her long-suffering husband, Phil, was the equally inebriated, but terribly sour and dour, Susie Wharton. The main difference between the two women was that Susie Wharton was a nasty drunk.

A lively discussion was ongoing at the bar and Suzy was giving as good as she was getting. In fact she was so passionate that the best reply one of the tipsy aviators could give was "Fuck you, Suzy Morton!" said out of exasperation, and not malice, by Mr. Will, whose wife was not present or she would have smacked him.

Meanwhile, back in the booth, Susie Wharton was just finishing her third double whiskey and about to rip into Phil for no other reason than it was Wednesday, when she misheard Mr. Will saying, "Morton," and thinking he said Wharton, immediately took great offense, not realizing nobody even knew she was there. She didn't share this outrage immediately, preferring to wait and have Phil bring the matter up to the Wing Commander in the morning at Wing standup. Phil didn't relish carrying this water on her behalf, so he slow-rolled it until the following morning and finally broached the matter shortly after the daily "stand up" briefing which, strangely, was conducted while all were seated. This was a time when subordinate commanders and various support officers gathered first thing in the morning to discuss upcoming requirements and any other issues with the wing commander.

Larry, a former Thunderbird pilot originally from rural Montana, would give them guidance and direction as needed. While the "Wing King" was filling his coffee cup, Phil begged a few moments when, hemming and hawing, he related that sorrowful tale of unseemly and ungentlemanly behavior that Susie had been made to endure. When Phil finished that tale of woe, Larry leaned back in his brown leather swivel chair, lit a Marlboro and said, "So what do you want me to do about it?" Phil told him his wife was pretty mad but had to admit she was always pretty mad and left it there. After Phil left, Larry called his lawyer, Dan, the Staff Judge Advocate. As Wing Commander, Dan served as his Larry's lawyer, with no other client on the base. Asked for a legal reading, Dan opined that nonjudicial punishment would be the answer for ungentlemanly behavior and Larry told him he'd ponder it.

Larry then put in a call to Oscar to bring him up to speed on the allegation. Of course Oscar had no knowledge of any of this; he recollected having been engaged in his own conversation with the base commander about a skate board park for the kids. He acknowledged that foul language was not unknown in the club at any given time, but he would certainly look into it.

Oscar had only recently arrived in the squadron; his report date had been moved up, a necessary response after the squadron hosted a "NATO Tiger Meet." That exercise involved Tiger squadrons from NATO countries coming to Heyford for a week to discuss and work on joint tactics. They flew together to improve readiness against the now nonexistent Warsaw Pact. The farewell "Combat Dining In" (flight suits and party shirts, no wives) was a debauch which that year included sending two Portuguese Tigers to the hospital when a firecracker landed on a china plate and sent shards flying. A Canadian from Lahr Air Base Germany won the best skit award when the cross dressing F-16 pilot came out in an orange bikini after tucking his junk up and out of sight, and lip-synced to Madonna's "Like a Virgin."

The total damage sustained by the club exceeded five thousand dollars and all involved took up a collection to pay the tab. Even the Portuguese Tigers said they had a swell time and couldn't wait for the next one. Still, Larry thought it'd be better if the commander left earlier than anticipated so he could enjoy a few months leave with the family before he went on to his next assignment at Somewhere-not-here Air Force Base. When Oscar reported in, Larry shared his opinion that a more seasoned and steady-handed commander was what the squadron needed, and he hoped Oscar was that guy.

The moment he hung up the phone, Oscar broke into a sweat. Each squadron had its own personality and the Tiger war cry was "Tiger, Tiger Roar!" They also had an impressive and storied history dating back to the first world war and that made them some very bold NATO Tigers. A few months earlier Larry had soft-fired another squadron commander, removing him from command and leaving him turning in the breeze until a replacement was announced some time later, as an example to others. Oscar knew Larry wouldn't hesitate to find a replacement who could better manage his warriors if the need arose.

Leaving those nervous and pacing Tigers and heading home, I thought back just a month earlier to the last time some overly bold NATO Tigers had used a lot of legal time.

---

## Canadian Rodeo

Vinnie was a Tiger who hailed from just outside of Worcester, Massachusetts. Average height with a stocky build, thick jet black hair, low sloping forehead and caterpillar like eyebrows, he enjoyed a perpetual five o'clock shadow and a loud, gregarious personality utterly lacking in charm or refinement. He was also a most fortunate man who, while lacking any evidence of common sense, was in fact an outstanding aviator, one who could fly any mission profile and come back with his plane. This was no small thing, a total of 563 Aardvarks had come off the production line and 133 of them, including Richie's carpet bomber, got to test the crew escape capsule and were destroyed, none to enemy fire. Because of the direct nuclear threat still posed by the rapidly disintegrating Union of Soviet Socialist Republics, this skill explained why he remained on active duty.

It was a Friday night and the club was packed, as usual. The senior officers and other gentlemen filled Jandy's pub with small talk in small groups, some including wives happy to escape the children for a few hours of adult freedom. Meanwhile, in the back of the building, the heavily sandbagged Bunker Bar was overflowing with every aviator who was not a squadron commander, plus all the other operations officers under thirty-five. The doors had opened at half past four; three hours later a bus full of nurses from distant Lakenheath arrived on an exchange, they having become bored with the pilots' stories at their base.

Vinnie had been engaged in squadron antics; he'd been playing "carrier landing" and had just "missed the wire" on the table top version of an aircraft carrier landing. Stolen from the US Navy during Vietnam stopovers in the Philippines where it was popular, several four-top tables would be laid out end to end against a longer table and beer poured the length of the surfaces. A candidate would race up to the table to launch himself. A space was left between the smaller tables where the "aviator" would attempt to stick his boots to arrest his slide. Failing to do so would result in the aviator hitting the drink as he sailed off the tables, crashing to the floor as well-entertained spectators threw beer to represent the ocean. Still damp, but enthusiastic, Vinnie was looking for a way to redeem himself in the eyes of his peers who were now haranguing him for his failed flight. He hit the bar, got another beer and asked his side-sitting partner and Weapons Systems Officer, "Wiz," for some advice.

While they were talking, a very fit and very tipsy twenty-eight year old Lakenheath pediatrics nurse, in a tight black-leather dress, was wondering what to drink next. She'd decided against wearing her glasses because her mother had always told her "Your eyes are your best asset." What nobody in the crowded bar could have known was that her biological clock had begun ticking loudly lately; and she was on the hunt for a hubby to give her a baby. Because she couldn't read the labels on the top shelf liquor bottles, she stood on the brass foot rail to bend over the bar to see if she could pull them into view. What she didn't know, but might have been pleased to learn, was that given her presentation and proximity, Vinnie and Wiz thought her "onion ass" was her very best asset. As Vinnie explained later, "Her ass was so beautiful it made me cry."

Each aviator's blood alcohol level was approaching 0.15%, too drunk to fly or drive, but perfect for making a bad decision and carrying it out. Vinnie and Wiz decided it was that time in the evening for "Canadian Rodeo" and gave the required shout which wasn't heard by anyone other than themselves. The human voice is anywhere from 60 decibels during normal conversation to upwards of 90 when screaming. The average bar with crowd noise and a jukebox runs around 88-90 decibels steady, so their call was sucked into the cacophony of ambient noise.

In this version of the "sport," a "cowboy" had to come in from behind and latch teeth on to the ass of whoever was selected as the "cow," a man; or, for something far more interesting, a woman, though one was rarely present. Once somebody hollered "*Canadian Rodeo!*" it was considered fair warning to all that some teeth were on the prowl. Once teeth were sunk, the victim would try to dislodge the attacker who tried at least as hard to hold on for the required eight-seconds, true to the spirit of rodeo. A player was not allowed to use hands either to stay attached or to block any blows. Most times the biter simply snagged some clothing and was spun around the room until he hit something solid.

Emboldened by drink and Wiz's encouragement, Vinnie pushed off from the sandbagged column he'd been leaning against. He slowly moved around until he was positioned at six o'clock, directly behind the oblivious nurse and where her peripheral vision would not detect him as he moved in for the attack.

The young woman had inadvertently obliged Vinnie by standing on tip toes and pushing her butt just a bit further out as she leaned in to decipher the labels. He augured in, exerting all his 120 pounds of biting pressure to secure his place while Wiz shouted "Ride 'em cowboy!" and hit the timer on his watch. Although the nurse was pretty drunk, there wasn't enough of an anesthetic effect so she'd not notice the Neanderthal currently latched on to her ass, because she felt a considerable pain when he chomped down. From bending, she launched upright and turned while coming off the foot rails to shake him off, but Vinnie was not having it and he turned into her turn staying locked in place. She began flailing at his head with her fists and elbows while trying to dislodge him by running into a table, which failed to detach him, but did spill several drinks. The commotion caused the other celebrants to stop what they were doing to watch the ride.

Finally, the eight-seconds passed, Wiz screamed "Time," and a triumphant Vinnie did an emergency "disconnect and breakaway" maneuver, diving low and away to avoid anything that might be thrown at him while making his escape into the crowd of identically dressed aviators. Meanwhile the now extremely agitated and mortified nurse abandoned the club with a cab ride to the base hospital emergency room just down the road. She presented her bitten butt to the Medical Officer on night duty. He called the cops who arrived in short order, along with the alert photographer, who documented the injuries, which were some clear dental impressions that were rapidly bruising and only made worse when seen in a color 8x10. The Chief of Police, a major, happened to be sitting in Jandy's when the radio he always carried went off. He was asked to call the desk sergeant since the event involved two commissioned officers.

After being briefed, the Chief made his way to the Bunker bar where in very short order the names of the culprits had been revealed. A verbal report was made to Larry, who himself had just arrived home thirty minutes earlier. The Wing King was not at all amused, not because of the antic; that was something that just happened. Rather, he was upset that it was becoming known outside of the bar and that meant he'd have to take some form of action. He made his displeasure immediately known to Oscar, who in turn walked back to the Bunker bar, ordered his two aviators out, and to stand by at their homes phones until he decided to call them.

By the time I heard the story on Monday, Dan had already made overtures to Larry that non-judicial punishment under Article 15 of the Uniformed Code of Military Justice (UCMJ), would be the way to go. These punishments were limited to cash fines that go to support the Old Airman's home in San Antonio, Texas, rank reductions (for enlisted only) and/or up to 30 days of jail, or house arrest if a commander thought it appropriate. Lesser responses included Letters of Reprimand (LoR), Letters of Counseling (LoC), or a verbal reprimand. A commander could also exonerate an airman, as many did when they found the charges meritless.

Looking to get in early while deals could still be made, I drove to the Tiger squadron and was greeted by a very nervous Oscar who, so happy to see me, made no mention of me parking my Honda civic wagon in the "Any General Officer" parking slot near the front door. He recounted the events of Friday night and I gave a small thanks for having also left at seven that evening for home and hearth.

Non-judicial punishment is an absolute career killer for any commissioned officer and would be an absolute waste of the millions of dollars spent training Vinnie and Wiz. I knew most commanders would prefer some less costly approach to sanctioning miscreants for boorish behavior. I'd been the Chief of Justice for over a year and I had witnessed the reactions of all the different commanders when presented with matters like these. From seeing their reactions over time, I knew that, in most cases, what they wanted to do was get the attention of the idiot, make sure nothing like the behavior demonstrated would ever be repeated, serve as a warning to any other potential idiots, and ensure appropriate apologies were offered and the hurt parties satisfied. I offered up what I thought would be an amicable solution to address all those needs and societal concerns. After consultations with, and approval by, the Wing King, Vinnie and Wiz reported to Oscar's office standing at rigid attention for some "wall to wall" counseling. The skipper chewed their asses up one side and down the other, expressing his severe disappointment at their childish and immature behavior, the harm they brought to the reputation of the squadron and the wing, how he felt when Larry called to chew his ass, and otherwise displayed his extreme displeasure. Once he'd exhausted his anger, he said, "You can thank Shyster for going to bat for you two dumbasses because here's the deal" and he laid out the punishments to be imposed.

Oscar sentenced the boys to handwrite notes of apology and to deliver those notes while dressed in Class A blues, along with an ostentatious bouquet of flowers, plus a fair amount of "good" chocolate candy. If the nurse accepted their apology, they were to be obsequious in their affirmations that they would never ever do anything like that ever again. He assured both idiots that they would be spending the next fourteen lunch hours at the Equal Opportunity and Social Actions office watching the Oprah Winfrey show, where she would rip on "men who are bad bastards" for one reason or another, with the hope that they would become more sensitive in the process. Since Wiz was simply an idiot consultant and time keeper, he got to pull weekend operations duty for the next two weekends. Oscar then turned to Vinnie, advising him that he'd be spending the next three Sundays caddying for his favorite squadron commander who was saving his dumb ass, when said commander played golf with the Wing King while Vinnie executed a 54-hole walk of shame over those three rounds of golf.

The apologies were offered and accepted, and each man bore his social re-education and rehabilitation stoically, knowing better than to look for sympathy from squadron mates. Each aviator knew the immediate reply to such a foolish plea would be, "You want sympathy? Look in the dictionary between 'shit and syphilis.'" Those two knew it was solely their fault that the squadron was now on "double-secret probation" and any future leadership failures would be dealt with more sternly. I'd previously given thought to posting a sign at the flying ops desks that said:

"This squadron has enjoyed _____ days since the last stupid thing."

I considered at the time the possibility that it could lower unit morale to continue touting the negative, so I benched that idea; but now, as I listened to this latest tale of woe, I wondered if it might not have been such a bad idea.

That Sunday I saw a genuine look of concern, and a bit of fear, on their faces. While the event might have resulted in no more than a slap on the hand in a civilian community, in the rarified air of "selection for promotion and continuation in service," any bad paper in a permanent file was truly "bad." Bad paper meant the difference between a full 20-plus year active duty career with advancement to colonel or even general, or, being condemned to a lifetime of weekend drills and weekdays spent as an airborne bus driver, endlessly flying a regional commercial jet from here to there and back again.

I finished my drink and told them I'd get right on it, but to do me a favor and stand still long enough for me to try and work a solution. I went back home and put my infant daughter into her stroller. I told my wife we were going for a walk to pick wild blueberries that grew along the perimeter barbed wire fence. We wandered down the street filling her little bucket with berries and at the end of the block turned up one more street and found ourselves walking down "Leadership Row," the quiet cul-de-sac where Larry, our vice commander, and the RAF Squadron leader, our liaison with Her Majesty's government, all enjoyed stately homes as befitting their leadership positions.

It was my good fortune to come upon him digging a hole for a new tree his wife brought home the day before. Larry enjoyed the physical exercise because it reminded him of growing up outside of Missoula, Montana, and gave him a chance to be alone with his thoughts (and enjoy a smoke without being chastised by his wife). He'd just pulled out a shovel full of dirt when he spotted us walking towards him, and noticed my daughter's blue lips, evidence that she'd been enjoying the berries.

He snorted, crossed his arms over the top of the shovel handle and asked, "You wouldn't be here looking to work a deal for those six guys in Jandy's, would you?" Seeing no point in continuing the "walking the baby" pretense, I said, "Why, by happy coincidence, I am, and Sir, knowing you're a busy man, I think I have the reasonable solution to the problem." He lit a smoke, that telling me I had until he finished to make my pitch. He took the first drag, exhaled and said, "Go on." Over the next few minutes, I presented a plan that would satisfy his concerns that any punishment be swift, measured, just, and effective, further offering that perhaps there was no need to elevate this matter to something unnecessarily punitive. He listened thoughtfully as I explained my belief that continuing down the excessive paper trail would create additional drama where none was needed. I expressed concern that any administrative action would require extensive interviews with the base commander and his deputy, given they were witnesses to the whole sordid affair.

Once I mentioned those two subordinate colonels, Larry looked at me more closely. He listened while I disclosed that in the course of my representation there would naturally be a need for some interrogation to determine why senior base leadership failed to take any remedial action and make an on the spot correction. I held that it'd be a very sad matter to remark on record and that, but for their lamentable inattention and lackluster leadership, this entire ugly, and most regrettable situation might well have been prevented, or certainly mitigated.

He stroked his chin as he slowly shook his head mulling this over. A faint smile crossed his lips as he said, "Shyster, I think you missed your true vocation, you could have been a hell of a car salesman." He added, "OK, you got the deal of the century, now leave me alone."

On Monday morning every Tiger, including the guy pulling Supervisor of Flying (SOF) duty in the tower, was wearing their blues, squirming uncomfortably while they suffered the reality of a humiliating squadron "down day" where a lecture on officership, bearing, and behavior, was given by each contrite individual present for that evening of infamy.

This shameful day concluded with a lengthy and painful review of USAF Equal Opportunity and Treatment standards delivered to all those officers by the radical-feminist civilian lady who'd been hired for the job. Meanwhile, the enlisted airmen were enjoying a rare extra day off with their families.

That evening, the newly christened "Jandy-6," backed by every other Tiger, delivered a large bouquet of flowers, the customary chocolate, and a bottle of *The Macallan* 18-year-old reserved single malt. These gifts were accompanied by the assembled squadron serenading the now almost giddy Susie Wharton, who of course forgave them for her imagined trespass, while lambasting Phil for not ever bringing her flowers.

79th Tactical Fighter Squadron
**NATO Bold Tigers**
RAF Upper Heyford 1991
Photo courtesy Vlad Shifrin, Esq.

# Fraud Waste and Abuse

RAF Greenham Common, or Greenham as it was known locally, was a former SAC base on the Salisbury Plain near Newberry. Starting life as a golf course, it was sold to the Air Ministry during World War II and lately re-purposed to house ninety-six BGM-109G Gryphon Ground Launched Cruise Missiles (GLCM) and four practice spares without warheads, in bunkers known as the Ground Launched Cruise Missile Alert and Maintenance Area (GLCMAMA.)

The site was always referred to as the "GAMA facility" for *Gryphon Alert Maintenance Area*, as leadership feared using all those initials would no doubt result in the troops calling it "Glick-Momma" not only because that was reasonably phonetic, but because of all the unwanted missiles it could produce and scatter around the country-side. Besides, it didn't sound military enough, lacking the cachet of a *Gamma facility*, a mysterious name that would make a great movie title and provide fodder for those folks who watch late night conspiracy channels. Gamma, the Greek letter for "G" in the phonetic radio alphabet, clarified that this was the **G**ryphon storage facility, to not confuse the casual observer with any other facility containing small, pilotless flying machines powered by a Williams International F107-WR-400 turbofan engine and carrying a W84 150-kiloton variable yield nuclear warhead, if one existed.

Capable of complex aerial maneuvers, the Gryphon flew predetermined flight plans at much lower altitudes than a ballistic missile, typically with a terrain-hugging flight plan. The GLCM was developed to counter the threat of Soviet mobile medium and intermediate-range SS-20 Saber ballistic missiles. The facility sat surrounded by three triple-barbed wire fences. Those were separated by a five-yard clear dirt kill zone, a manned guard tower, and a roving three-man quick-response team driving a HUMVEE with an M-60 machine gun mounted on the roof, consigned to making endless loops inside the wire.

The test run of the Gryphon pretty much won the military portion of the Cold War for the USA. Air Force scientists and engineers filmed a Gryphon loaded with conventional explosives flying 1,316 miles from a site in New Mexico to Eglin AFB in Florida where it flew into the second floor window of a mock-up "Kremlin," destroying the conference room where mock-up "senior leadership" was meeting. This flight path was the approximate distance from Moscow to Florennes, Belgium, site of another Gryphon facility. That film was sent to the Soviets who didn't like it at all because those old Commies knew they now had "skin in the game." Sometime later, on October 11, 1986, at Reykjavík, Iceland, President Reagan and Premier Gorbachov agreed in principle to removing Intermediate-Range Nuclear Force (INF) systems from Europe and to place global limits of one hundred INF missile warheads each.

With no other mission, the Greenham base was slotted for closure in late 1991 as another peace dividend. The installation had been steadily reducing the number of missiles and units on site in anticipation of finally shuttering the base. The Russians would send in observers during each missile removal and those inspectors could be seen every evening in the bowling alley, eating, drinking, inspecting and admiring all their recent purchases at the base exchange (BX).

The old Soviet Union had no bowling tradition and these citizens of the new Russia were excited to learn the sport. They particularly enjoyed the American practice of serving multiple beers in easy-to-carry containers. Each man would pull a six-pack from the cooler, walk up to the cash register, pay, and ask the cashier to open all six bottles so they could drink at their table. Perhaps it was their ingrained cultural concerns about the USSR's historic shortages, but if there were four Russian bowlers they'd bring that collective case of beer back to their table and tuck into plates of hamburgers, hot dogs, french fries, and those hot apple turnovers that spin on a wheel to cook. If it's true that American beer drinkers might not finish a glass of beer if it becomes warm, this was not a concern of those Eastern European imbibers. Each of those four guys worked through his six pack of Budweiser like he was off to rehab the next day. Our guests also raided the BX, buying up the entire supply of Bic disposable razors and ballpoint pens. Those two items were in high demand back home and would be resold for a handsome profit.

That deactivation of Greenham Common also meant a tremendous amount of military equipment would be packed for storage and possible later use at another installation, while excess materials would be prepared for proper disposal and final disposition. Military equipment of low value or items that had been brought into the country tax-exempt would be disposed of by the Defense Reutilization and Marketing Office (DRMO), a place where a good number of British civilians were employed sorting the equipment for further recycling. Items like coolers, screws, bolts, nuts, or plywood sheets were offered for resale to the public for just pennies on the dollar. Tools and other duty-free items were marked "XB-3" and sent to a land fill. If overseas, those items were tossed into a concrete pour on a construction site. It was a cumbersome and inefficient process with staggering amounts of paperwork for little return.

Master Sergeant Kennedy was a slob, which was most unfortunate given he was also the supply custodian for one of those soon-to-be-deactivated GLCM squadrons. Supply custodian was a job requiring attention to detail and careful execution of paperwork because of the military obsession with accountability. Even though the missiles were awaiting removal to the USA for eventual mothballing or destruction, the squadron was required to maintain readiness until that time. This included loading a dummy missile onto its transporter and sending it out to the Salisbury Plain for a week, so the operators could practice getting it ready to launch.

A step in this practice called for taking 4 x 8 foot, 1/4-inch thick sheets of poplar plywood, sheets that cost the US taxpayers $14.48 apiece and strategically placing them around the operator launch station to protect the airman from blast injuries. Just exactly how that sheet of plywood might actually protect the operator from the effects of a rocket launching off the trailer, or a nuclear blast in close proximity, was never made clear to me. I think they said that just to make those poor bastards feel they were protected.

One day, eight of those plywood sheets (total cost $115.84) set the wheels of the military justice system in motion.

It is well known within all the armed services that the one person every unit or organization needs and wants is a "scrounge," that man or woman who can find whatever item is needed at the time it's needed as long as leadership had a "no questions asked" policy about how it was procured. As convoluted and sometimes unresponsive as any large-scale supply system can be, scrounging was a skill highly sought after. Kennedy, born into a family of dirt farmers outside of Mitchell, South Dakota, was one of those natural born scrounges. It was a skill he'd further honed during his previous eighteen years in service to the nation.

On a Friday afternoon in January 1990, Kennedy needed to secure some plywood, eight sheets to be precise, because, somehow over the last few exercises he had "lost" those eight sheets somewhere on the muddy flats of Salisbury Plain. The sheets wouldn't have been stolen or misappropriated; they'd go missing because one sheet of plywood looked like another and, with different squadrons interacting during practice, equipment got jumbled. Kennedy needed to find replacements to mark on his accountability form. Eventually the plywood would be removed from the inventory and sent to the DRMO where some lucky Brit would buy all eight sheets for just one British pound, then worth one dollar and eighty-five cents.

In the ordinary course of business, Kennedy simply would have found the plywood at another squadron and horse-traded for it with the other supply sergeant's need. This year was different because a new squadron superintendent, a senior master sergeant, had just rotated in from the recently deactivated Gryphon unit at Florennes where he'd learned to become a base-closure specialist. He was assigned to Greenham to oversee the final chapter in the life of that installation.

Relinquishing US military installations to a host nation is an intricate business. Not many realize that host nations paid hundreds of millions annually to maintain these installations, allowing our tenure as long-term tenants. As in any leasing situation, the tenants would have moved in the goods and materials they'd need. Now, like any good tenant vacating a lease at its expiration, it was incumbent to leave the place clean and tidy. In a residential lease, that would include not leaving food in the refrigerator. In the case of an airbase, it meant cleaning out toxic materials, like asbestos, various solvents, and petroleum products, including pollutants that had leeched underground, thus finally restoring the environment. Doing any job correctly in a base closure meant a flattering paragraph in the annual evaluation report and a chance to shine when being considered for promotion.

However, as the USAF continued to shrink, so did opportunities for promotion. Evaluation "bullet points," sentences highlighting a significant accomplishment during the rating year, could be the key to future promotions. With nothing left to be purchased, the base contracting squadron closed and its authority transferred to RAF Mildenhall. Just a few months earlier, another JAG named Greg was busy with a legal review on a proposed contact to install a new microwave landing system costing six million dollars at Greenham, the first of its kind for USAFE. Greg knew this system would be bought by US taxpayers, then immediately turned over to the RAF which had no use for it either, since the entire base and flight line were superfluous to their own military needs. The extraneous multi-million dollar radar system would wind up at DRMO and sold to some businessman for a few thousand dollars. Greg flagged the contract, noted his concerns in a written legal review, marked it as disapproved and sent it back.

What he didn't know was that the author of this scheme was a colonel, soon due for promotion to brigadier general, who'd been working this project for the last two years. He'd arrived in England in June of 1987 and became aware of the new system while playing a round of golf with the communications squadron commander who had it on his wish list. The colonel embraced the idea and planned it to be his greatest career accomplishment. What he couldn't know or possibly ever foreseen, was the sudden collapse of the Berlin Wall, the dissolution of the Soviet Union, and subsequent US decision to mothball all three European Gryphon units. The subsequent changes to the geopolitical landscape should have put the skids on that proposed radar purchase but didn't.

The conflict of interest arose because that senior officer, heavily invested in the project, wanted that great bullet point in his file when he would be screened for promotion in just two months. Becoming a general would guarantee he could stay in for another ten Air Force years of being treated very well and collecting full pay after retirement, because generals remained subject to instant recall back to active duty.

Ignoring the legal opinion, this colonel carried on as if November 1989 had never occurred and Greg had never read that contract. He pulled the offending opinion and re-submitted the plan through channels for approval. The colonel didn't realize the airman in the mail distribution room, aware that all contracts had to have a legal review attached, routed it back to Greg who flagged it again, sending it back marked "Disapproved" as against public interest and waste.

Not easily rebuffed, that colonel tried an end run, asking another more senior JAG at Third Air Force, located at RAF Mildenhall, to take a look. Third Air Force is a NAF, a Numbered Air Force, and subordinate to USAFE (US Air Forces Europe). Third was the superior unit providing command and control over the several subordinate wings throughout the United Kingdom, and Greenham was one of those wings. This move was especially poor form since it called into question the competence of the original reviewing attorney. A more senior JAG read the review, agreed with Greg, and directed the Office of Special Investigations (OSI) to interview the colonel, particularly inquiring about his continued interest in a proposal that amounted to nothing more than the waste of government assets, because prevention of "fraud, waste, and abuse" was everyone's responsibility.

The in-person interview with the OSI agent convinced the suddenly terrified senior officer of the error of his ways. His promotion package appeared before the board with little to show for the past two years, since he was unable to laud his considerable efforts on a project that never materialized. A few months later his name likewise failed to materialize on the promotion list, so he retired and moved into a 55+

community along US highway 98, the "Redneck Riviera" in the Florida panhandle. He took up residence in "Air Force Village," an insular community of retired airmen spanning the 100 miles between Tyndall AFB to the east and the sprawling Hurlburt Field/Eglin AFB complex, an area larger than Rhode Island, to the west. Like the swallows of Capistrano, retiring airmen flock there permanently to play golf year round. Every time that retired colonel smacked that small white golfball, he recalled his shattered dream of opening a private executive airport and cargo hub where Greenham had once stood. He mourned never having the chance to draw up brochures offering a microwave landing system to oligarchs coming in their private jets to play golf and stay at his exclusive lodge.

Early on that last Friday afternoon in February, the new superintendent strode through each work space in the realm of his responsibility before leaving for the day. While some supervisors might have undertaken that stroll to shoo workers off to a relaxing weekend, this guy seemed not to register that some of these people worked twelve hours a day. He viewed his exercise as a way of providing cover should some workaholic drop dead over a work bench during the weekend; he'd always be able to testify truthfully, "He was doing just fine last time I checked."

The administrator ambled by Kennedy's work space and stood still, horrified by the clutter and disorganization. He called out the slovenly supply man, admonishing him for maintaining a work space that looked like the wreck of the Hesperus. It didn't help matters that Kennedy's limited attention to uniform wear made him look like he must have washed up in that wreck which resulted in a stern warning. The super told Kennedy an inspector from Third Air Force was coming down from RAF Mildenhall on Monday to take a look around the base, and his office WOULD NOT embarrass the organization. Being senior, the super ordered Kennedy to clean the place up and have it ready for his inspection on Monday morning, then left.

Kennedy got back on the phone with his buddy over at another squadron and concluded the horse trade. He'd give four Igloo coolers and twelve rechargeable radio batteries for the plywood. He then called out to his staff sergeant assistant who'd been in the back organizing the supply cage. The young NCO had been in for just five years and was a quick learner. He popped his head into Kennedy's doorway who then told him to load the traded goods into Kennedy's trunk. Kennedy continued to pack the detritus of his work space into black plastic garbage bags. He toted the bags out to the car figuring he'd store his mess there until after the inspection.

What Kennedy didn't know was the 1991 DoD had an operational budget of $290 billion. It was a time for belt tightening and Secretary of Defense Dick Cheney was looking to cut any way he could. He was retiring two Army divisions and planned to retire another active and two reserve divisions to eliminate135,000 soldiers from the Army. The USAF budget would also get the chop due to the positive political changes in Europe and the death of the WARSAW Pact. These cuts meant the number of air bases, machines and airmen would be significantly reduced. The same was due for the Navy, as we drew down from the bloated six-hundred-ship armada President Reagan ordered built in 1981, to make it a leaner meaner fighting machine.

In an operation as big as the DoD, one of the biggest concerns was "Fraud, Waste and Abuse," where incompetence and criminality routinely resulted in the waste of hundreds of millions of taxpayer dollars. The Inspector General is the office with primary responsibility for these matters and had created a hotline stateside for anyone to call when they saw anything suspicious in that regard. Overseas, the airmen would call the OSI.

Two young airmen who worked in the Services Squadron were getting a start on the weekend after their shifts ended at two. Walking down the street towards their dormitory to catch a nap before heading out to their local pub for a darts tourney, they watched the young NCO carrying two large yellow coolers to Kennedy's car. They also saw Kennedy come out of his office toting two black plastic sacks and slinging them into the back seat of his car. As the airmen drew abreast, they watched the staff sergeant bending over to shove a case marked "batteries" under the front seat of the now packed automobile cabin.

Noting the time, and convinced a theft was taking place, they put in a call to the OSI detachment on base and reported their suspicions.

The two agents on duty, excited that there was a potential crime to investigate, hopped into their unmarked police car and took off for Kennedy's squadron. They pulled up, blocking any possible escape, got out and confronted Kennedy with hands near the pistols strapped to the waistbands of their jeans, just in case he was actually a violent criminal mastermind who might try to resist.

Kennedy, not knowing he was a crime czar, had just finishing stuffing another black bag into the trunk and looked up when he heard the tires. He watched and then tensed as the Ford Crowne Victoria police interceptor rapidly closed in on him. He thought he'd be hit by the car, but it stopped just four feet away and two twitchy guys jumped out at him.

The two agents took his stunned reaction as surprise at being caught in the act. Holding up their credentials and badges, they identified themselves as OSI. Kennedy was aware of the OSI but had never met any member of that agency. The OSI was seen as boogeymen; every airman had heard stories of secret snitches everywhere, which was nonsense, but it worked. Kennedy, a now thoroughly confused and nervous master sergeant, stared at them blankly. Having finished his work for the day, the young NCO walking back outside to head home, saw what was happening and discretely walked back inside.

The cops asked Kennedy if they could look in the trunk of his car, which Kennedy quickly allowed since he knew he had done nothing wrong and had nothing to hide. The agents opened the trunk and saw the black bags full of USAF materials. They also saw books, small tools, and other pieces of specialized equipment jumbled and scattered about. Now suspecting the slovenly NCO was a master criminal who had been looting the supply room, they asked him for permission to inspect his house off base. Still knowing he had committed no crime except possibly "having a messy office," the guileless supply man quickly agreed. He led the agents to his small semi-detached home located in a rural area beyond Thatcham, and just outside the small village of Upper Bucklebury, where he unlocked the door and told them to have at it.

The agents were stunned to see what, to their eyes, was an Aladdin's cave filled with all manner of electrical gear and components. This treasure trove included a still-in-its-original-packing-case parabolic antenna worth over thirty-thousand dollars, casually leaning against a wall, the twin of one they found stashed in the hall closet. Now convinced they had uncovered a major criminal enterprise, they called for help from some agents at Upper Heyford because they knew the inventory would tie up for several days whoever got stuck as evidence custodian. The agents reported by phone to John, the Chief of Justice, a senior captain. John was close to entering the zone for promotion to major. It didn't take long for their infectious enthusiasm to convince John that this was a major criminal operation.

John was very pleased that he might have landed a case of enough import to bring him to the attention of the right folks at JAG HQ in Washington DC. It could be the one that could lead to an assignment as an SJA somewhere, a move he felt might be just the thing to help his faltering marriage. This marital discord came naturally, as he was wedded to the wildly popular CarraLee, from the Berlin troop train escapade.

CarraLee married him because the initial sex was amazing and having two housing allowances let them rent and live in a beautifully restored farm house seven miles away from the base and just outside of the small village of Honey Bottom. A year into the marriage the sexual novelty had diminished, and John's increasing desperation to please and impress his wife was having just the opposite effect, as she began planning her next assignment, one that wouldn't involve him.

Blissfully unaware of her future plans, John oversaw and directed building his "*Case of the Aladdin's Cave*" for eventual prosecution. The Report of Investigation (ROI) wasn't completed and released until the beginning of June as the detachment needed hundreds of man-hours to run down potential witnesses, each and every one of whom had since been transferred to other assignments or retired. This investigation required sending agents to conduct physical interviews and obtain written statements. The final narrative ran over fifty pages, with ten more attached as the required AF Form 52 property receipts, listing each of the hundreds of items recovered from Kennedy's quarters and car. John spent the next month consumed by the thought of getting some flattering space above the fold on the front page of the European edition of *Stars and Stripes*, the military daily newspaper. Armed with his word processor and a vivid imagination, John laid out the charges and specifications until he had over twenty-five charges with multiple specifications including, but not limited to, a copyright violation committed when Kennedy, the technophile, loaded a government-owned copy of WordStar, the DOS-word processing software, on his personal computer, an IBM PC.

What few people then knew, or even cared about, was that in 1986 Bill Gates and a bunch of other smart people created and sold WordStar; making it the second most popular program in a very competitive market. In 1989, after evaluation and discussion at the highest levels, the Air Force went with second best and selected it to become the official word processing program. The floppy disks were put into the supply system and sent to every installation around the globe.

About the time the Air Force was requiring that all members use the program, there was a "long pole in the tent." Holding up the big show, due to those Cheney-directed budget cuts, was that none of the operational units at Greenham had been given word processors capable of running that program. Kennedy, a technophile, read all the bulletins that came out and knew of the requirement to use the program. Tired of waiting for Uncle Sam's supply system, he wasted no time before hitting the BX to purchase an IBM personal computer. He promptly loaded WordStar and spent several weeks learning. When satisfied with his proficiency, he brought the PC to the office and taught everyone else how to use it.

Eventually a shipment of government PCs already loaded with WordStar arrived from Florennes, so Kennedy brought his PC home. Planning to return the floppy discs he'd been using, he tossed them into the whirling paper and scrap maelstrom that was his car's interior and never saw them again.

The charge arose when the OSI agent searching his car found the unmarked white envelopes that held the black floppy discs in the back seat under a box containing the remains of a long forgotten order of fish and chips. The OSI agent was a Luddite who had no idea what he'd found, but thought they were probably "a new type of something." As he held them up, Kennedy shouted "Hey! You found them! I've been looking for those discs; I thought they were lost!" and went on to explain their purpose to the agent who then added them to the AF Form 52.

When they arrived at Kennedy's house, the now better-educated agent asked Kennedy to turn on his machine. As the program loaded, the agent made note that it was a government copy of WordStar which had the copyright statement and FBI warning of the penalty for violations. The government contract said only one set of floppy discs per computer and Kennedy had not deleted the copy from his personal device. When the agent asked Kennedy about the additional copy, he explained that he probably should have deleted it, but he used it to do his work at home in the evenings instead of staying in the office. The agent understood his reason, but seeing a "crime" here, he also understood that a computer wizard like Kennedy probably knew how to delete the program, eliminating any criminal evidence, thus he seized the personal computer and noted it on the form.

John considered the case rock solid, encouraging his boss to refer this to a general courts-martial. If convicted on all of the counts contained in the allegations, the man from Mitchell, South Dakota, was looking at taking up residence for over one hundred years at the Disciplinary Barracks in nearby Ft. Leavenworth, Kansas, where his aging parents could come on visiting days.

The SJA was a major coming up for promotion to lieutenant colonel and waiting for an easy gig as a deputy SJA at some NAF. Once there, he could kill time and kick back until he had three years wearing those silver leaves which would allow him to retire in grade, increasing the amount of retirement money he'd receive each month. While awaiting those orders, he put all his spare and a fair amount of office time continuing to work on the kit car he'd been building for the past two years at the base hobby shop. He was scrambling to complete it before he had to make a PCS move, a permanent change of station, so he didn't have much interest in John's case and provided little scrutiny or "adult" oversight.

In mid-August, John completed the DD Form 458 Charge Sheet and all that remained was for Kennedy's commander to green light the charges and read them to the future defendant. Because of the serious nature of these offenses, an Article 32 investigating officer (IO) was appointed and arrived to listen to the basis for the charges. The IO made note of the evidence and wrote his report to the three-star general commanding Third. In those recommendations, he'd advised that sufficient evidence existed to believe the crimes alleged on the charge sheet could be proved and would result in a conviction.

An investigation is conducted by a JAG officer senior to the accused and is similar to a grand jury proceeding. A prosecutor presents a proposed criminal case to a non-biased panel of citizens to see if they agree that charges should go forward to trial. Finding sufficient evidence to support the prosecutor's contentions, the panel returns a "true bill" of indictment against a defendant. It is often said that a good prosecutor could indict a ham sandwich. That might be true in the civilian world, but the military played hard. If convicted, an airman would be facing extremely harsh punishments when compared to his civilian counterpart, so a more detailed legal analysis of the evidence by a neutral and detached hearing officer worked to protect the interests of all parties.

An investigating officer could recommend sending it back to the owning wing for prosecution at a Special Courts-Martial which had more limited punishments, or even recommend dismissal of the matter, as many did. A base SJA might be upset that the accused's toes weren't held to the fire, but there was no sense in wasting government resources on a case that very likely wouldn't result in a win. Other avenues were available to the SJA for a problem airman, like an administrative discharge board.

All this process and expense was also necessary because, to ensure fairness at trial, witnesses could be summoned to appear from anywhere on the planet. Experts could also be brought in, all at government expense. The accused was given a defense lawyer and, if necessary, another lawyer with more complex trial experience could be flown in to assist. As a result of all this effort, any general courts-martial would cost hundreds of thousands of dollars. Expenses were justified because the Air Force did not tolerate airmen convicted of serious crimes or those who deviated from acceptable standards of behavior. The Air Force closely screened applicants and an airman with criminal tendencies was an embarrassment and stain upon the honor of the service. The key to achieving this "justice for all" was having mature prosecutors experienced enough to understand not every offense is the crime of the century, and smart enough to see the big picture, not just their tiny slice of a rather large DoD pie.

Kennedy, accompanied by his First Sergeant, was eventually summoned to his commander's office one warm afternoon in late August. He stood at attention before his commander as the charges were read to him. John took his stance along the wall, and took stock of his quarry. While the commander read the words, it struck deep into Kennedy that the Air Force, his Air Force, the one he'd faithfully served for all his adult life believed him a thief, and he felt crushed. As the commander's voice blurred into the background, he thought of all the off-duty time and energy he'd devoted to his job. With no wife, other life, or hobbies, he routinely worked fourteen hour days and came in most weekends. Believing in the mission, he rarely took any leave, and each year lost thirty more earned vacation days because members were only allowed to carry a maximum of sixty days on the leave books.

The words "Do you have any questions for me?" from his commander snapped him back to attention. Kennedy looked down at him, realizing this was the first time he'd ever seen him up close, never having any prior occasion to be introduced. Now in shock, he mumbled a "No,

Sir." The First Sergeant led the shamed airman into the outer office and gave him a packet with a copy of the Charge Sheet and a cover letter telling him to contact the ADC (Area Defense Counsel) at Upper Heyford to set up an appointment.

In the meantime, Kennedy was relieved of his duties as supply NCO and transferred to the Services squadron until the matter was concluded. In his new capacity, he supervised the airmen passing out towels and cleaning the gym equipment and maintaining the pool. What he didn't know was that two of the airmen he was now supervising were the ones who called the OSI to drop the original dime on him; which was really okay because they didn't remember him either.

The initial OSI ROI landed on my desk at about the same time and thirty miles away from where the now bewildered airman was finding out his life was about to be ruined. At our first meeting, I listened to his recounting of everything that had happened to result in his making my acquaintance and I recognized a guy who was not a criminal, just a hapless slob.

I drove down to Greenham to visit with Tim, the SJA, hoping to find an alternative to the current plan to incarcerate this sad arch-criminal until sometime into the twenty-second century. I shared my observations with him, adding "What kind of criminal lets the OSI search his home and car without asking for a warrant?" I offered to give him Kennedy's banking statements to show he wasn't stashing large amounts of money and asked him to just talk to the guy for ten minutes to see if this massive prosecution was warranted.

"We both know this case is such a dog it's barking. How about offering Kennedy an Article 15 and take a stripe for him being a putz?" Tim knew that even if the case was a dog it wouldn't have any impact on his career; he'd just heard from a friend that his name had been penciled in for a plum assignment in Hawaii. He listened to me attentively and after a few moments said I had some valid points, but he was going to leave it up to John and see how it all worked out.

Conrad was a lieutenant colonel and SJA from a nearby air base who had been dragooned into service as the IO. An Academy grad who'd gone to law school on the AF dime, he now gave back the full benefit of his education. He was respected as a solid legal thinker and had been a circuit trial counsel in the course of working up the ranks, amassing an amazing record in some heavyweight cases. All this work made Conrad the kind of JAG John had always dreamed of being, except Conrad never lost at trial.

It was mid-September when Kennedy's hearing opened and the government presented its case. Unlike a grand jury proceeding, the accused has every right to be present with his attorney. Jurors may ask questions and make objections to evidence being offered to preserve it for the trial record later, but it was mainly used as a way to get a good look at the government's case. The hearing began at nine on a Tuesday morning and closed at three on Thursday. In that time, the prosecution offered one hundred and thirty-four individual pieces of evidence. This laundry list of purportedly purloined items included six red painted coffee cans containing hundreds of screws, bolts and nuts. While most of those items were loose, some were in sets of five or ten held together on a plastic stripper clip with all but one or two screws missing. A witness testified that those stripper clips resembled those the government bought to eliminate time wasted handing out one such small-item at a time, because it saved money. He added that he'd seen similar cans chock full of nuts and bolts in other places so it wasn't unusual; it just meant not having to get more pieces later. I thought about objecting to this cumulative evidence since this was, at best, just one massive count of theft, it being impossible to determine where each item might have been stolen from. I held my tongue until the last exhibit was presented, an empty cardboard computer paper box. I had to inquire and the IO agreed asking, "Counsel, what's the evidentiary value of that exhibit?"

With confidence born of his unbridled enthusiasm John offered, "Sir, it is the government's contention that this box, found in the defendant's house, previously contained computer paper and is self-authenticating." Like a magician holding a top hat, he held it up to highlight the various markings describing the contents as a box containing tractor feed computer printing paper. To bolster his contention, he advised the court he could call the former supply custodian for the central base supply squadron. That poor witness had just arrived after being flown in non-stop from his current assignment at Yokota Air Station in Japan, just so he could testify as to exactly what that box held.

The IO took a deep breath and cocked his head to the right as he tried to follow and said, "So, your point is what? It had paper in it at one time and the defendant must have used it and that amounts to theft? Does that sound correct?"

John blissfully nodded his head up and down as Conrad continued, "So your contention is that the only explanation for his possession is by theft and it isn't reasonable to believe he might have picked it up from say, the trash can, and put it in his car, figuring he might one day need it to help arrange his assortment of stolen screw-laden coffee cans, something like that?" Conrad continued to be met with a north-south head nod so he looked at me and I shrugged my shoulders as he gave a slight snort and shook his head. He looked down for a minute, made some notes and chuckling said, "Well, this is going to make some interesting reading." With that comment the hearing was closed.

Conrad wrote up his findings on the DD Form 467 and remarked in block 21 that the government's case seemed petty and excessively charged, with some considerable work necessary to prove all the charges, but that wasn't his concern. He found there was sufficient evidence to go forward with a general courts-martial, forwarded the report up-channel, and promptly forgot all about the matter.

As Chief of Military Justice for Third, Major Dave was first to review Conrad's report. A former enlisted man, he had gone to law school on his own dime and gotten a commission. After eighteen years, he'd been told that very day he'd been passed over for further promotion, therefore once this assignment was up, he'd be forced to retire.

He looked out his window and noticed the days getting noticeably shorter, this being life at fifty-two degrees north latitude. For some reason, he remembered that Mildenhall shared about the same latitude as the Canadian Forces Base at Cold Lake in Alberta. Unable to concentrate while he processed the bad career news, he thought about when he spent the winter at Cold Lake on an exchange tour as a radar tech. It got dark early there as well. He watched as the sun went down at just after four and his spirits sagged. He found the thought of leaving the familiarity and comfort of USAFE, and heading into the void of civilian life, disconcerting and disheartening.

Dave switched on a reading light, read the report and the attached AF Form 1768 Staff Summary Sheet the base had sent up. He finished and wanted to say he thought the case was a dog, the charges bullshit and a waste of judicial resources, but at this late date in his career he didn't need to be bothered about that, so wrote that while the charging decisions might have been a bit much, there was enough evidence to result in a conviction. He further opined it was important to go after thieves and passed the file up-channel to Jeff, the deputy SJA.

Jeff, recently promoted to lieutenant colonel, was looking down the road at making colonel. He knew Dave was a drone who'd pour over the IO report because he wanted to get promoted, so he'd be thorough. Once Jeff read the word "enough" he was satisfied and, without reading the report, put his initials on the routing slip. Adding "This is a good case to send a message,"he forwarded it on to his boss, a colonel named Xavier. A name of Basque origin, meaning "new house," it honors Saint Francis **Xavier,** a 16th-century Jesuit missionary who took Christianity to the East Indies and Japan. Colonel Xavier wasn't named after any saint; his mother just had a huge crush on Xavier Cugat, a debonair Latin bandleader at the Waldorf-Astoria. The colonel then put together a one sentence executive summary for his boss, the three-star commander. Reiterating what Jeff and Dave said, Xavier signed off, as he did with all his office memos, with a large X.

X had been very careful as a judge for a number of years, but was nearing the end of a thirty-year career. In less than three months, he'd start his terminal leave, taking all sixty days, never to be seen again. He'd married a local woman while on assignment to Mildenhall years earlier and now spent his days formulating and finalizing his last move to a small cottage fifty-three miles north in Tatterford, a village in the county of Norfolk. He and his wife had purchased the place two years earlier when the pound was very low against the US dollar and together they'd spent many weekends fixing it up and antiquing. He never complained except to regret that, with the thousands of US airmen who had been assigned to Old Blighty since WWII, all the genuine antiques had long ago been shipped to homes in America.

With only nine hundred inhabitants, his new home in Tatterford didn't rate a train station, but a bus came through that could take him to an airport if he ever went anywhere. It also boasted a few pubs including one he chose as his local because it hosted the legal society. X daydreamed of being a gentleman of leisure, owning a tweed jacket and enjoying village life, a life spent downing a beer at his local after a walk in the country on one of the many Roman roads. Winding down his career, he spent the better part of his days on the phone with his old classmates, and now contemporaries, at various stations around the world, keeping up on the internal gossip because information was gold.

The Third Air Force commander liked Xavier. The man knew how to hold his liquor and tell a story, so when Xavier told him the case was important the general took him at his word. He read all the papers and agreed it did look quite bad, so he signed off and asked if Xavier was playing any golf that weekend. Once back in his office X told Dave to assign the case to Bob, the Circuit Trial Counsel (CTC), who was looking forward to a new assignment as the SJA at Howard Air Base in Panama. Bob had spent three years on the road for two hundred twenty-five days each year with nothing to show but a slew of government travel frequent flier miles in his private account as was recently permitted by a change to the joint travel regs.

Foolishly, Bob had told his wife, who was usually stuck home each day with their two-year old son while Bob traveled the continent, about TDY pay. Bob took all the hard cases, not only building an impressive conviction rate, but also air miles. Once she knew the per diem rate for food and lodging and the milage reimbursement, she worked diligently and tirelessly to fill her too often lonely days. Every month she spent right up to his salary plus the projected TDY pay, while she built an impressive collection of Spanish Lladró ceramic figurines, German

Hummel figurines, and any other thing she found exquisite, as well as a Ralph Lauren wardrobe for herself and their two-year old son. This process included her taking frequent flights from London to the Lladró factory in Tavernes Blanques in Valencia, Spain, to spend a few days in the warm sun before visiting the showroom and selecting her newest treasures. Bob learned from this mistake though, and didn't reveal those recent changes to the Joint Federal Travel regulation allowing him to keep and use his frequent flier miles, and from there on out whenever he traveled, it was in the business class section.

Bob was in a bad mood. He'd just returned from running an administrative board hearing which resulted in kicking out an officer from the 7276th Air Base Group in Iraklion, Crete. All officer administrative separation cases required a CTC, and Bob was tasked by his immediate supervisor, Mike, the Chief Circuit Trial Counsel (CCTC). A recently promoted lieutenant colonel, and USAFA grad, who'd also gone to law school on the AF dime, Mike was a serious and focused prosecutorial machine. Bob didn't much enjoy Crete, as exotic as it sounds; it was always hot and dusty, and he had to take C-130 to get there. He asked Mike why he wasn't taking it himself, since the dual-nation island was in Mike's portion of the European circuit. Mike said he was going to be working a hotly contested administrative discharge board at Stavanger in Norway. He explained that he knew Stavanger was Bob's territory, but this would be a tough case and he'd be up against the Chief Circuit Defense Counsel. Plus, the board would be overseen by the Chief Military Judge. The discussion finally closed with Mike reminding Bob that he was a lieutenant colonel and Bob wasn't.

The 426th Air Base Squadron was a two-hundred-fifty person combined unit that provided base level services to the NATO Joint Warfare Center in Stavanger and all DoD personnel assigned to Norway. Four hundred miles west of the capital, Oslo, it nestled in the middle of fjord country on Norway's southwest coast. Stavanger was known for breath-taking scenery with moderate temperatures and is the hub of the North Sea petroleum industry.

When Bob got back from Crete, he checked in with the paralegal who ran the administrative process and began to fill in his travel voucher. He needed to get it approved so he could hustle over to the finance office where he could recover his cash and then hotfoot over to the credit union to deposit it to cover the latest acquisitions from Spain.

Back in the office, Bob inquired about the big show in Norway and the senior paralegal, a master sergeant who was struggling over his sexual identity, looked at him, clearly amused and told him, "I don't think a Tech Sergeant being separated for failure in the weight management program is a big deal. Yours was the much tougher case." The paralegal leaned forward and tugged on the sleeve of Bob's blue AF cardigan and added in a conspiratorial aside, "Didn't you see the new per diem rates for Norway? The chief flew up on Tuesday, picked up a rental car, reviewed the case file on Wednesday and it began on Thursday. By law, local hires can't work past four, and since Friday was a Norwegian holiday: no court reporter. Mike spent the long weekend touring the Norwegian countryside. He finished the board on Monday and returned to Germany on Tuesday afternoon." With a sideways glance as he finished approving Bob's voucher, he added, "Those guys each pulled in three hundred bucks a day just for hanging out and sight-seeing!"

As Bob was fond of telling people later, "That really chapped my ass! He knew Norway was a no-brainer and did it because the per diem in Greece is only $178!"

When Bob had read the OSI report and Conrad's report, what thinning red hair he had remaining stood straight up. He immediately went to Colonel Xavier and asked "Have you read this thing?" Xavier admitted he hadn't and, echoing the notes of his deputy, told Bob the case was winnable and would send an important message to the troops that theft will not be tolerated.

Bob sat back in his chair and looked over at his operational boss. "That idiot at Greenham charged this guy Kennedy with copyright infringement! I am just not able to fashion a rational argument to support a contention that him loading that copy of WordStar onto his computer, and learning how to use it in his spare time, and then teaching everybody else how to use the system, was somehow to the detriment of the Air Force! We bought hundreds of thousands of copies of this program and I'm supposed to suggest that each and every copy has been used and Kennedy's act somehow upset the year-end balance books for Microsoft?" On a roll, Bob continued, "Can you help me make an intelligent argument that would convince the panel that Kennedy stole the now empty box when it was full of paper? I can't!"

The ludicrous nature of the hypothetical struck home and Col X realized that he probably should have dug in a bit further in his review before selling the case to his boss. He'd figured Jeff, the little toad, would burn the midnight oil reviewing it and if he saw a case it was a winner. X knew he screwed up and, if this went to trial and Kennedy got acquitted, the general was going to be asking a lot of questions. He'd wind up looking foolish and the odds of him getting a career-capping Legion of Merit medal would get impossibly long. Anger built as he thought about the next and final performance evaluations he had to write up on his deputy and chief of justice.

His own anger spent, Bob looked at the ruminating colonel and ended with, "I'll tell you one thing, I don't like the way this case smells and, if Sciales makes any motions to dismiss some of these charges, I'm not going to argue against it, and just wait until my closing argument!"

Knowing he was in a bind and realizing Bob was the best trial lawyer in USAFE, X also knew there wasn't another JAG to be pulled in at this late date. He slowly shook his head from side to side as in his mind he rewrote the kill-shot line that would end Jeff's evaluation and career. He looked at Bob now standing in the doorway and capitulated. "Do whatever you think best; I just need some kind of guilty plea so there's no appeal and I don't care about what."

Bob had never had much use for John, his least favorite JAG in all of the UK. Bob always thought John's legal analysis shallow, and he had no ability to distinguish important from frivolous. He'd recently demonstrated this when he recommended non-judicial punishment for an airman after the base librarian sent a letter to his First Sergeant complaining the airman had a long overdue library book about the US Congress. John charged him under Article 134 with "Removing a public record" contorting a library book about Congress into "public record." The maximum penalty for the crime of removing an actual public record is a dishonorable discharge, loss of all rank, forfeiture of all pay and allowances, and confinement for three years.

John didn't consider the intent of the law, which was to stop people from taking reports, statements and data compilations in any form, including classified, from a public office or agency. To come anywhere close to meeting the requirements, that book would have to come from a restricted documents portion of the base library, one they didn't have. John also didn't stop to consider if the missing book would really be prejudicial to the good order and discipline in the armed forces, or even if the librarian's form letter complaint was enough to "bring discredit upon the armed forces." These were all absolutely necessary to get a conviction on the charge, and he'd considered none of it. He just wrote it up and sent it to the airman's commander to serve.

The airman was directed to my office and when I saw the charge, I immediately called John to ask what he was smoking "because you must have been high when you wrote this." In a voice devoid of humor, he maintained it was a valid case and the charges were serious. He added snidely, "Well, if you don't like it, why not remind the accused he could always request a court martial."

And that was exactly what the airman did when before his commander; he leaned over and checked Block 3a, the one that says, "I demand a trial by court-martial."

John was completely thrown by this. He absolutely wanted to avoid a trial, knowing (as we all knew) that he had so rarely come out on the winning side. John quickly put in a call to Bob, asking if he would be the prosecutor for this library book court-martial. Of course, he got a no-go response from Bob, who worried he may have damaged John's ear by the decibels of his initial snort of derision, followed by all-out laughter. With a satirical fare-thee-well of "Good luck with that, Junior," Bob hung up.

Back at my office, and having heard the latest, I called John to ask when we'd be going to court over the purportedly purloined publication; he replied that after talking with his boss, they had decided the court-martial was a bit much. They now were offering him a chance for a lesser punishment by taking the Article 15. To me, this was a variation of the used-car-salesman gag when they say they need to talk to the boss, but vanish to get coffee while letting you stew for twenty minutes. I don't know which stung him more: my own snort of laughter or my reply, "Don't you get it? You can't threaten a guy with a 15 and then, when he calls your bluff by asking for a trial, de facto admit you don't have a case by re-offering the 15, right?" The silence grew heavy on the line so I rang off with, "See you in court."

We never got anywhere near a court room. The entire matter went away when the airman found the book and brought it back to the library.

Next I got a call from Bob who dove right into the matter. "Junior, I think this case is a lot of bullshit so I'll be a man of few words and tell you if you make a motion to drop some of these charges I will not oppose it." I sat back in my chair pleasantly surprised, not that Bob thought the charges were bullshit, that was clear, but rather, the carte blanche to start chopping charges. Before I could even begin to formulate an answer, he picked up the conversation. "I've taken a run through this and just now faxed you a marked up copy where I've lined out all the crap." I heard the fax line ringing and knew my paralegal would walk it in shortly. Bob continued, "I cannot believe what that dummy thought this guy did, but we have to fix this now." All I could do was nod my head up and down and murmur agreement.

My paralegal brought in the sheaf of papers still warm from the printer. I saw only three charges were left, the most serious of them being the allegation of copyright infringement for not deleting the copy on his own computer, plus the lesser misuse of government resources by loading it on his home word processor, and the violation of supply regulations by horse trading for the plywood in the first place.

I shared with my client what had been going on and told him he was going to get something of a beating, but he wouldn't be kicked out, and could still retire when eligible. The matter was set for trial on December the 23rd.

I headed to Greenham the night before trial to avoid the commute from my base; I wanted to be fresh in the morning. I wouldn't be reimbursed for my overnight stay since it was within the fifty-mile distance I'd have to drive to be authorized overnight lodging. I thought it a shame the government put at risk the many people who had to travel this route very early in the morning and very late at night over such a few dollars. A few weeks earlier a JAG in Turkey died while following that rule. Returning to his home station after a trial, late one evening, he died when he missed a curve on a poorly lit road and drove his government car off into a gorge.

I checked into the Greenham Lodge, a Manor House that served as the base hotel and visiting officers' quarters. Built in 1881 by Lloyd Baxendale, it had once been the lodge attached to a golf course. At various times during the second world war, it housed King Haaken of Norway, the Queen of Holland, the King of Yugoslavia, and Generals de Gaulle, Alexander, and Montgomery.

A regular room, fit for a Lord or deposed Balkan royalty, cost eight dollars a night and the large multi-room apartment, fit for a King or Queen, was twelve dollars. I was in a jolly mood to spend the extra four dollars, it being so close to Christmas. Unfortunately, the airman first class manning reception advised me the King Suite had already been booked by another guest, so I made do with the "Field Marshal Montgomery" junior suite. I asked when the small bar in the library opened; the airman smiled and replied, "As soon as you walk in."

After unpacking my bag, I headed back downstairs to get a drink while waiting for Bob. I walked into the lounge and was greeted by the same smiling airman who was now wearing a black vest over his white short-sleeved shirt and polishing a pint glass. He greeted me and asked what was my pleasure. Quickly browsing the impressive assortment of barely touched bottles, I selected a whiskey. While he poured the drink, I took in the bar itself, of highly polished dark wood with scrollwork, testimony to a time when craftsmanship mattered. The library shelves were of a similar wood, not as polished, but further darkened by age and the soot from the thousands of peat fires built in the massive stone fireplace.

I settled into a worn dark brown leather wing-back chair over by that fireplace and looked out into the lobby. I was enjoying watching the peat burning when the front door opened and the trial judge, Colonel Mike, who had presided over most of the trials I'd been assigned to work, walked in. The airman bartender deftly removed his vest as he slipped out the back door to appear back at the reception desk. He checked in the judge and I guessed by Mike's movements that he also had made an inquiry about the King's apartment. His shoulders sagged and he nodded his head a few times, and I knew he was also disappointed.

Mike gripped his overnight bag and briefcase and was headed for the grand and plushly carpeted stairway when he saw me, waved and came inside the bar instead. The vested barman returned and took his order while Mike pulled up a chair. Because Bob wasn't yet present, and the trial was judge alone, we weren't allowed to talk about the case. This wasn't a problem because we had a chance to share whatever recent war stories or items of JAG gossip we had. In an earlier chat Mike mentioned his first trial as an ADC, and I realized that while I was TDY from Mountain Home AFB to a Vietnamese refugee camp in 1975, he was at Mountain Home, representing a young airman who shot dead another young airman because the kid accidentally spilled a beer on him. His client got six years and a dishonorable discharge and Mike got a reputation as a great advocate.

Fifteen minutes later, Bob strode into the lobby and came in to the bar when he saw us there. He called out his order to the barman and took a seat. Mike asked him if he wanted to get settled in first, then during dinner we could talk about the order of the trial and any motions.

The barman had just brought the drink by and Bob took a long sip before answering. His right eyebrow arched and setting down the drink said, "Settled in? I've been here since noon. Hell, I got the King's suite!"

That chapped both our asses.

With the King's suite mystery solved, we sat down to dinner and went through the guilty plea Kennedy would be entering into on the record. Bob explained all of the charges that he'd chopped; then Mike asked how much time we thought we'd need for presentation of witnesses. Bob said he wouldn't be calling any witnesses in aggravation. I had only had two witnesses in mitigation and expected my examination to be under thirty minutes.

Eventually Mike headed for bed, but Bob and I sat up making the barman earn his pay by listening to our war stories. He agreed the best one was the night Bob challenged me in an English pub to down a shot of flaming Sambuca liquor. Bob neglected to tell me to blow it out just before I tossed it at my face, and I could still hear those screams and shouts from some nearby Norwegian tourists as my mustache got a surprise singe.

The dawn broke at the crack of eight the next morning. Part of our agreement was that the court wouldn't convene until ten. I cleared my room, making sure to put the complimentary sewing case, comb and Gideon's Bible into my attaché case, as I'd had occasion to need them all routinely during my career and it'd become a habit. I looked at the Bible and began thumbing the pages and fanning it. The motion caused me to focus my thoughts and served to make the *Good Book* look worn. When I got back to my office I'd go through and highlight some passages.

A paralegal saw me doing that once and, correctly not believing me to be a religious sort, asked why I was doing it. I told him I'd had to make death notifications when I was a cop. It's the worst duty there is. You knock on a door and ruin someone's life as you tell them a loved one has died. There is really nothing you can do or say that will give them any real comfort. That's when people fall to the comfort of religion, even if they aren't religious, and a used bible can go a long way to provide comfort in the knowledge that the deceased had been living a right life.

When an airman dies on duty the Air Force assigns a commissioned officer to perform duty as a Summary Court officer to administer the legal affairs of the dead airman. That officer is authorized to settle any debts the airman might have owed locally, and oversee the packing out of the airman's family and their household goods if the airman was married. The summary court officer alone cleared out the personal effects of single airman, or married ones on an unaccompanied tour.

Only officers with maturity and good judgment were selected under the regulation. That meant tact, diplomacy, and protecting the family and reputation of the deceased from any undue consternation or embarrassment. Summary Court officers have complete and unfettered discretion on what to keep, toss, or give away, and what will go back to the loved ones. There was no review or report of final disposition. Uniforms and civilian clothing had to be cleaned and pressed. Underwear and socks were tossed and, so was any stash of bondage magazines, sex toys and the like. Stacks of love letters from girlfriends, but not the wife, were burned. Playboy magazines, cigarettes, cigars and liquor were passed to barracks mates. Once rid of those items, often little was left to pass along to the bereaved parents; and that was when I started tossing in a worn and marked up bible, hoping it would give them some comfort.

Some circumstances presented a greater challenge. One poor tortured soul hung himself in his room, and I was appointed as the Summary officer. The OSI called me to the scene and the lead agent, a young woman named Susan, closed the door after I came in, asking, "What should I do with this?" She opened the dead airman's wall locker and on display was an impressive collection of slinky cocktail dresses which must have run into a few thousand dollars. They couldn't be returned to his parents; it was clear they would have had no idea of their late son's orientation. The dresses also could not be logged into evidence for any later disposition because that would acknowledge his predilection on paper where it could be revealed. I wasn't about to ask if any of his fellow airmen might have wanted "dibs." I was left with destroying them, but Susan looked at me and said, "Mike, these are beautiful and look at his CD collection, he loved Abba and their album 'Dancing Queen.' His dresses are my size and you know I like to dance. Wouldn't he be happy knowing they worked to finally get somebody laid?" She looked at me with her right eyebrow arched slightly while she waited. Her argument made sense, and it seemed like a right thing to do, so after she took the dresses I tossed a bible into the parent's box after highlighting:

*"For where your treasure is, there will your heart be also."* (Matt 6:21)

The next morning, I met Kennedy while he was walking up to the building and, first, checked his uniform to see how close he got to the mark. Airmen accused of an offense and convinced the system is rigged will sometimes lose hope, which can manifest in less care toward their appearance and less pride in the way they comport themselves. Kennedy was neither a slave to fashion nor grooming, and I'd had him come to an earlier appointment wearing his Class A blues so I could make sure they fit properly and displayed all the ribbons he'd been awarded. This was important because most airmen who worked in non-administrative jobs rarely wore their blues or bothered to attach any new ribbons to their uniform. The nature of the job, out in the field, meant they commonly wore the deliberately durable camouflaged battle dress uniform. Sometimes when the rare occasion called for the blues, an airman might discover a thick layer of dust on the shoulders.

I had also advised him to get a fresh haircut, shave close, and have his shoes freshly shined, reminding him that the ten o'clock court session would begin promptly at half past nine so he wouldn't be late. I wanted enough time to make sure he was squared away before he made his debut on the justice stage. I could see he'd made an effort, because he looked presentable, that is until he took off his blue flight cap. His hair was poking up at all angles as if he'd just awakened from a long sleep. Seeing the problem in a hallway mirror, he licked his hand to flatten the unruly locks, so I opened my attaché case, handed him the plastic comb, and indicated the nearby men's room. He headed there and I made my way into the court room.

I was grateful for the late start since I was feeling the after-effects of the night before. My mood brightened when I realized Bob looked worse than I felt. This was good, because it would also minimize the contrast with Kennedy's appearance when he strolled in.

The trial, no surprise, did get underway at precisely ten. By half-past, Mike, convinced that Kennedy was making the plea voluntarily, accepted his guilty plea. The speed was impressive and we moved right into sentencing.

Bob had no witnesses. My first witness was the young staff sergeant who testified that he had been to Kennedy's house many times before and knew all the gear was there. He'd asked Kennedy about it and was told, "They're just going to want it all back in a few months and if I keep it here it won't get broken or dirty. So I just keep handing them the same old stuff each time, because they never even notice or care."

My second and last witness was a logistics NCO who'd won many awards for his expertise and fine work. I had him share his expertise with the court and had him qualified as an expert on the USAF supply system. I asked if we had the greatest and most responsive supply system in the world and he agreed that we did. I asked him to tell the court about the research I had him do. He pulled out his notes and, looking at the judge, said, "I was asked to put in an order for eight sheets of plywood and note the response time." I asked him to share the response he received. "The plywood is on back-order and has been since I made that request. The system understands that this base is slotted for closure so any requests sit at the bottom of the priority list." I asked him what that meant in regard to this case.

"He could have ordered it and it still wouldn't have been here by today and it isn't likely to get here before the base closes."

I asked the last question, "If you'd had to get some plywood and didn't have a year to wait, what would you have done?"

"I'd have just called one of the other squadrons and traded for it."

It was finally time to argue sentencing. I'd previously seen Bob channel Clarence Darrow; his voice would get folksy and, when he did that, I knew my client was about the get a harsh sentence. Bob would slowly go over every detail, make that panel of officers take note and agree with his recommendations.

Now Bob stood up slowly and, taking a deep breath, tucked his chin on his chest. I was waiting to see who showed up and it was a nice surprise to see that Foghorn T. Leghorn, a cartoon rooster with a pronounced southern accent, would deliver the address. In a very courtly and pronounced fashion, all he said was, "Your Honor, if it please the court, it's a few days before Christmas so the government will defer to your judgment and only ask you to think of Spike Lee and, 'do the right thing,' and that's good enough for us." With that and a short bow, he sat back down.

Mike arched those twin white caterpillars above his eyes and looked at Bob for a long moment before shaking his head just once. He looked at his watch and made a note in his minute record. He sat back, lifted his right hand in a small waving motion, looked at me and said, "Counselor?"

I stood up and asked him for a few moments. He nodded and I looked down at my papers. I could hear the humming of the fluorescent tubes above me and saw the court reporter pull away the face mask he spoke into when he dictated my every word and I waited. I finally looked up and said, "That was thirty-seconds, part of the one thousand eight hundred we've drifted through since you called us to order. For Kennedy that was just a final few of the over twenty-seven million-seconds since the OSI came screaming up on that winter afternoon just as it was getting dark. All through that long countdown, as the days grew longer and the first rose buds appeared, he spent his waking hours and a good part of his sleeping hours thinking about just this moment. During the summer he listened to the mourning doves and saw a parade of evidence that the government now agrees was overcharging, and every day there was no escape for him, no respite. And as the summer faded and the leaves began to turn, he was still tormented and punishing himself, all the while dreading what he knew would be coming."

I turned towards the window as a light snow began to fall, "And now, as the days again grow short and the skies become leaden, it has all led to this time and these few seconds. I'd submit my client has suffered mightily and in a prison he could not escape."

Thirty minutes later he called us back into session. Kennedy and I stood and listened as the sentence was announced: "You are to be reduced one grade to the rank of Technical Sergeant, sentenced to two weeks hard labor without confinement, and a reprimand." He leaned forward. "You heart was in the right place, but we have paperwork for a reason, mindless as it may be sometimes." Reprimand concluded, he declared the court closed and left the bench.

Bob had no notes in front of him, just a piece of paper so he could write down the sentence. He folded it and put it in his pocket. He was putting on his jacket and, while making his way to the door, called out, "Merry Christmas, Junior, I've got to make a phone call and ruin somebody's Christmas at Third!"

Kennedy turned to me and said, "What does it mean?" I told him it meant he'd lost a stripe and hard labor meant working twelve hour days, so the judge was telling him he'd have to work two fewer hours a day. I handed him the sewing kit. The newly convicted NCO got up, shrugged his shoulders and said, "OK, and thanks for the comb and stuff." Without a backwards glance, he walked out of the court room.

Just after lunch, John, as the now former Chief of military justice, spent an uncomfortable fifteen minutes on the phone, a one-way call with an animated Colonel Xavier explaining, in clear and unambiguous language, John's non-existent career opportunities. John flinched when told the punishment for his gross incompetence, being buried alive inside the walls of the National Guard Bureau. This was the USAF version of the "Phantom Zone." If the offense wasn't grave enough to warrant an administrative discharge, a JAG would be assigned to languish there, always ready to be recalled to prove they deserved another chance, few ever selected. Most became fungible, people who could be plugged in anywhere, for any job. Active duty airman often derided them as "Guard bums," people not really in it to win it. This news stunned John, who couldn't imagine how this could have happened to him. In the midst of feeling his career circling the drain, he looked up and saw his wife coming towards him at the quick step and his already pasty features became a lighter shade of pale, when he saw the buff-colored legal-size envelope in her hand.

While Judge Mike stopped in Milton Keynes to find a last minute gift for his wife, and Bob made his way down the now slick single track B1112 towards his home in Hockwold-cuw-Wilton, I was sitting down to dinner with my family while Kennedy sat alone, at home, using that sewing kit to put his new rank on one set of uniforms so he'd be ready for work the next day.

What none of us knew then was that Microsoft had long ago shifted its attention away from DOS, releasing Windows in late 1989, right around the time the Air Force selected WordStar to be its standardized word processing program. This development made WordStar immediately obsolete and by the time Greenham closed twenty-one months later, in September of 1992, every WordStar in the now surplus government PCs took their place in line at the DRMO where they sold for just pennies on the dollar.

+++

# CHAPTER TWO

# Eddie & the Hooker

My three-year accompanied holiday in England concluded and I was recruited by Bob to join him on staff at Howard Air Base in the Republic of Panama where we'd be engaged in fighting the war on drugs that was currently well underway.

Our October move came while Anita Hill was disparaging Supreme Court Nominee Clarence Thomas as a sexist pig who left stray pubic hairs on Coke cans and while a crazy person, one George Hennard, drove his pickup through the front window of the Luby's restaurant in Killeen, Texas, quickly shooting and killing 23 people and wounding 27 others. While these events transfixed the nation, my family and I were maneuvering through the maze that was Atlanta's Hartsfield-Jackson International Airport, from where we would fly south to our new home in the Canal Zone in Panama - the southern-most piece of the United States, at least until December 31,1999, when it would be handed back to the Panamanians under the terms of an agreement signed by then President Carter.

When we arrived, Panama was a country in transition since the recent removal of Manuel Noriega, the long-time despotic ruler and international drug dealer. To maintain order, the civilian government continued a three-hour national curfew from two in the morning until five. Although designed to discourage nefarious dealings and prevent the movements of dangerous people, none of that mattered to us, because it was the law and the US Government respected the laws outside the military installation. The gates to Howard Air Force Base (and every other military installation that ran along the Canal) were closed tight at exactly two AM.

Service members were instructed that if it appeared they were likely to miss curfew, they should "shelter in place" at any casino, restaurant, or hotel until the curfew was lifted a few hours later. Failure to do so — and being arrested by the Panamanian police — would understandably result in a fairly harsh penalty from one's commander. We learned that several Americans had recently been fired upon as they ran through police roadblocks, trying to beat curfew. A dead airman would beget hugely negative press, and the United States was not looking for any international incidents.

Prostitution was legal in Panama, but not on any American military installation. We continually had many people assigned in-country on TDY (**temporary duty**) from various bases in the United States. This was a formula guaranteed to make interesting reading in the weekend police blotter. As the Chief of Military Justice, I reviewed the offenses alleged in the blotter reports to determine if an offense was worth pursuing in a trial by courts-martial or by other administrative non-judicial punishment meted out by a Commander as the sole judge.

These TDY folks were most often aircrews sent to Panama either for a specific and brief mission of a few days duration, or for a longer sojourn and a 90 or 120-day rotation. Incoming airmen frequently lacked critical situational awareness and could easily find themselves in trouble, as they didn't really understand the laws and the ground situation in Panama. A northern tier Air Guard pilot had set a USAF Personal Best record for being robbed and shot in the ass within a half-hour of checking in to the Costa del Sol hotel downtown. He'd just exited his hotel's lobby and was admiring the Cathedral across the street, while waiting for his crew mates to arrive, when the crowds suddenly parted with cries of "Bandidos! Bandidos!"

Panicking people scrambled away from the cries, leaving the pilot standing on the hotel steps but not comprehending why the commotion. The bandit noted him, no doubt, as the sole unmoving object, and swaggered close, pointing his pistol at the flier and ordering in plain enough English, "Give me your wallet!" Many at that moment might consider that a perfectly sensible choice, but the twenty-three year old warrior refused, and as he turned, rather nonchalantly for the circumstance, to head back into the hotel, the bullet hit his ass and he fell. He remembered feeling the tug when the villain pulled out his butterfly knife to expertly slit the left rear pants pocket before fleeing with the pilot's wallet. The victim lived to tell the tale, wallet-less and bullet-less, as the projectile had passed through the right side of the gluteal muscles, exiting promptly enough on the left.

The investigator of the attack, who knew I'd investigated crimes as a civilian cop, consulted me later. She confessed to being confused "whether he'd been shot once or twice" because no bullets had been recovered at the scene by the Panamanian police. She pointed to an 8 x 10 color photo of his ass which showed the small entry wound and the larger gaping exit wound. I explained the distinctions and, to substantiate that, asked to see the pants. She pulled them out of a paper bag. The bullet lost a lot of energy entering through his jeans and hitting his butt, but the return trip through the pants was not to be. Having lost momentum tearing through the previous abutments, the denim stopped it from exiting. So, one hole in the material, one bullet. Case closed.

Eddie was another adventurous TDY guy. A thirty-five year old reservist captain flying C-130 cargo planes on the weekends and during active duty training periods, Eddie piloted an L-1011 Lockheed TriStar cargo plane for a civilian airline in his spare time. He lived in Montvale, New Jersey, with his wife and two teenage daughters. He'd just picked up a ninety-day gig flying C-130s downrange for which he received not only the drill pay and retirement points, but relief of being out of his estrogen-intensive home for a while. The term "downrange" meant anywhere not in Panama, because the DoD had small bases dotted all over Central and South America. Some were quite remote with barely improved landing strips and some were on small islands, like drug-interdiction radar facilities that were part of a radar "picket fence" warning system.

One such island in the Pacific had a crushed coral shell runway and was manned by a dozen Illinois guardsman on a thirty-day rotation. I had finished a job at our air base at Soto Cano in Honduras and was on a C-27 Spartan, a two-engined transport used to get in and out on short, unimproved runways, which seemed to be the norm in Central America. While boarding the aircraft, I noticed a washer and dryer being loaded and a dozen boxes of Anthony's "World" Famous pizza, those from the BX concessionaire. The crew told me they were hauling the stuff to an island with a radar site. We would stay there for a few hours because the crew wanted to do some spearfishing in the reefs. Thanks to an old sunken barge, plenty of exotic fish lived there. We landed and, when the rear cargo doors opened, I saw a man identified by the crew as the French owner and sole full-time occupant of the island. Dressed in worn white linen clothing, he stood next to his one milk cow.

Since we'd be on the ground for three hours, I began chatting with the airman cook assigned and traded him a bottle of Honduran rum plus two hand-rolled cigars for reclining beach chairs and unlimited pineapple juice and ice service for the duration of our business there. I broke out another bottle of rum from the case I'd bought and, along with the two guys accompanying me, sat on the white sand beach enjoying cocktails while the aircrew caught our dinner.

Duty like this meant, to Eddie's great relief, that when not flying, he would be enjoying a nice room at the Visiting Officer Quarters (VOQ), having sole authority over the remote control, not to mention undisturbed time accessing any one of several cable sports channels. In the evening, it was dining and drinking at the officers' club directly across the street. He had a government rental car for use in traveling anywhere he felt like going, all while living inside a secured and safe military installation near the flight line for a short commute to work. And Eddie was an especially happy-go-lucky fellow because he was also scoring a great deal of TDY expense money. The Government Accounting Office is responsible to assess the rate for every country US Forces could be sent. Eddie was currently scooping up $140, tax free, everyday, and from that he paid for his own meals and room which ran about $25 a day. Any amount remaining of the $10,350 he received from the US government for his projected deployment was strictly fun money.

With no shortage of excellent golf courses in the Canal Zone, Eddie played golf anyplace he could drink and drive a golf cart. He hated the jungle and everything that lives there, and saw the value in paying a local guy one dollar per round to chase any of his hooks or slices that entered the ever encroaching darkness of the jungle. His fear was soundly based because just a few weeks earlier, an F-16B two-seater fighter, Tail # 82-1040 deployed with the 179th Squadron, Minnesota Air National Guard, took off one fine Panamanian morning for an "incentive ride" awarded to Staff Sergeant Chris Ford. His superior performance and dedication to the mission that quarter were above all others and won him this prized opportunity. His pilot was the squadron commander, Lt. Col Jeff Dinis; nevertheless, shortly after takeoff the plane dropped off the radar over the triple canopied jungle; it and they were never recovered.

Eddie loved taking advantage of the many fitness facilities and swimming pools during his free time while in mandatory crew rest, but it was Friday evenings when he was scheduled to begin a three-day break that he lived for. Straight from work he'd shower, then hit the barber shop for a hair cut and shave with a "cut throat" razor, one that gave a really close shave, one that lasted two days. Freshly barbered, he'd head to the Club. Eddie routinely wandered into the officers' casual bar to survey the scene. The bar was professionally staffed and had a nice dance floor. One corner held the slot machines; a few tables and quiet booths ran along the wall. The low lighting the club offered was perfect when Eddie was in the mood for a bit of fun.

Prostitutes seeking their fame and fortune in Panama came from all the nearby poorer countries. Since hooking was legal, the prices were much lower than in the USA and the competition for those American dollars, the official currency of Panama, that flowed so easily from the love-starved and often home-sick warriors, was intense. Each night the clubs were filled with many beautiful women filling slinky tight-fitting dresses to showcase their assets. There was a pecking order, and the more attractive women demonstrated their self-confidence by heading into the Officer's Lounge where they could charge more and work less, while others sought success in the NCO bar.

Eddie surveyed the room, settled on a seat at the bar and let the candidates vie among themselves for the chance of scoring an interview to audition as that weekend's "Mrs. TDY Eddie." He'd barely had his first whiskey set before him when a candidate approached from across the dance floor. This process allowed the discerning customer to do a compatibility appraisal for physical attributes, and then, when she was seated, a chance to chat. It took a few drinks to complete the interviewing process and in that short span of time he found himself in the close embrace of a no-kidding Colombian beauty. Tall, with high cheekbones, shiny coal-black hair and eyes like obsidian, her mocha skin was smooth and unblemished. She spoke understandable but heavily accented English, liked to dance and promised to be a great "Spanish teacher." That was the internal USAF term for the prostitutes, because leadership would not use the word "hookers" as it conjured images beyond the missionary-position. With that in mind, it was a short trip to his suite and the final audition for the highly coveted role.

Reportedly, the chemistry between them was excellent and exhausted by their exertion, both fell fast asleep.

### "WAKE UP, LITTLE SUSIE, WAKE UP!"

Around three in the morning, Eddie bolted upright, bathed in sweat, his heart beating like a trip hammer. He realized it was past curfew and he had a hooker in his room, the one he was required to have returned to the main gate prior to the national curfew. He knew he couldn't have a woman stay in his room overnight, so he concocted a fast plan to keep himself out of trouble.

What Eddie didn't understand, being TDY from New Jersey, was while that might have been the notional rule in the USA, nobody in Panama cared if he kept the hooker late, all that mattered was that *US forces* were not outside the base area. An overdue hooker was not an unusual occurrence; the worst that could happen was the cops at the gate would give him some good-natured shit and that would be the end of it.

Just a few minutes later, Eddie and the most-immediate former Mrs. "TDY-Eddie" slunk into the darkened parking lot where Eddie's

1991 white Toyota Corolla rental car was parked. Eddie assured her that it was best if she rode in the trunk until he could transport her to a place where she could safely get off the base. What Eddie also didn't know was that when she had checked in earlier to go to the club, she left her Panamanian National ID card (Cédula) with the cops at the gate; like a library card, she'd get it back when she checked out. The young woman was used to being given a ride or cab fare but, being a good sport, she climbed into the trunk and a terribly nervous Eddie got into the driver's seat to figure out his next move.

Eddie drove slowly down the main street towards the gate when to his right he saw the "Crash Gate Road," a well-maintained concrete road that led directly on to the Bridge of the Americas. This security measure allowed the four-star Commander of US Southern Command to depart his headquarters at Quarry Heights on the opposite side of the Canal and drive immediately onto the bridge; then once across the famous span, he could immediately enter Howard Air Base through the temporarily opened crash-gate, which was then closed and locked behind him.

Panama was a poor country and thus bred burglars who paid visits to all the different military installations with great regularity. My family lived on Albrook Air Station across the canal and realized burglars routinely wandered our neighborhood, some even trying to break into houses that were occupied. I was fortunate: I'd hired a gardener, Pablo, shortly after arriving, for seven dollars a week to keep my small lawn neat and the jungle trimmed back. Pablo asked if he could use our unused maid's quarters to stash his mowers and if I'd allow his crew to use the shower there; I easily agreed. I told them they were welcome to use the washer and dryer there and to help themselves to the mangoes from the tree in the yard. When other families moved, they'd give him any unwanted household items, and I'd gladly hauled those donations, plus Pablo and his buddy, back to their homes in a remote village about twenty miles away, a route he traveled by rickety bus every day. I'd always stop to get a six-pack of cold beer and they'd knock them back on the ride. This small investment of my time yielded a friend who three different times detained would-be burglars and held them at machete point for the cops.

Eddie had no way of knowing that, when burglars visited military bases, they'd slither in from the jungle, often trying to cut the locks on that crash gate to use the road for entry. As a result, a pair of cops were *always* posted there with night vision goggles to watch for villains creepy-crawling their way to "work." Ignorant of this bit of police procedure, Eddie figured he could drive out to the perimeter fence line, letting his date squeeze through the gap where the gates met or, if that didn't work, he could boost her over the barb-wire-topped fence. Eddie knew the road from overflying the base but never imagined cops sitting there in the jungle.

He turned onto the road mindful not to attract any attention. Dappled moonlight coming through the tangle of banyan trees lit the roadway, allowing him to see a bit ahead, so he cautiously crept down the road sans headlights. Not being certain of the exact distance to the gate, but not wanting to run up on it either, he would stop every few yards to squint, trying to see ahead in the darkness before proceeding.

The two young cops heard Eddie long before they saw him; the brakes on his car squeaked when he rode them. Because the sound was coming from the base, the fully alert cops suspected it was their supervisor sneaking up on a post-check to see if they were sleeping. As the white Toyota crept on, Eddie was not thinking to check his right rearview mirror. If he had, he would have seen that his brake lights were casting a red glow that bounced off the silver windshield trim and reflective placard of the parked security police cruiser just a few yards off the road.

The two patrolmen studied the unmarked white Toyota slowly making its way through the dark. They knew it wasn't their shift supervisor because he drove a marked patrol car with red and blue emergency lights on top. Since white Toyotas like this one were rentals put to use in droves by the US Forces, the driver was most likely the shift commander, an officer, on a post check to verify the troops were wide awake and doing their jobs, so they decided to watch further. The Toyota drove a few yards, stopped, then moved a few more yards. Finally the passenger riding shotgun grabbed the radio microphone and called in the blind to "the white vehicle on crash gate road." He got no reply, except from the desk sergeant monitoring the transmission who told him no-one was out on a post check. Armed with that information, the duo called in that they'd be conducting a traffic stop on that white Toyota at their location.

The curious cops started their car, rolled on to the road, snapped on the headlights and hit the rotating red and blue lights. Eddie was looking forward so intently that when the police car headlights flared and he saw the gate only a few yards ahead, he thought he'd accidentally flicked the high beam switch on his turn signal stalk. It was only after a few milliseconds, as his brain registered those two additional colors wheeling off the jungle moss and detritus, that he realized he was well and truly screwed.

The two cops stepped out of their cruiser, neither closing his door. The passenger took up a position behind his car door where he could see everything while the driver turned on his spotlight and added another quarter-million candlepower to the scene. Coming from around his door, the driver edged forward, tugging lightly on the latched trunk lid to see it was secured while looking through the rear window at the empty back seat. Through the Toyota's left rear view mirror he could see Eddie's very pale face looking anxiously at him.

A little more relaxed, the cop approached Eddie, playing his flashlight beam around the cabin to confirm it was empty. Eddie handed up his license and military ID while explaining he was TDY and got confused and that he was very sorry but would be happy to turn around and head back to his room at the Q. The excuse seemed fair enough to the young policeman; the officer looked sober, so there was no reason to keep him further. The cop handed Eddie back his papers and bid him good night. No doubt Eddie was breathing the universal sigh of relief to have passed this hurdle; he was almost outta there. . . but for what happened next. Just as the cop came abreast of the trunk, he heard a few abnormal bumps, as if perhaps there *was* a reason to talk to the officer a bit longer. Trusting his instincts, the cop stepped a few feet back and away from the trunk, put his hand on the butt of his pistol which alerted his partner, who began watching intently.

The cop called politely, but sternly, to Eddie, "Sir? Can you please step out here and bring the keys?" which was a command, not a request. Eddie, now fully engulfed in panic, set the hand brake, turned off the engine, and removed the keys. As he opened the door he thought about how much he missed smoking because he would light one up right then. Eddie stepped back along the car and stopped by the rear tire now wishing he was somewhere, anywhere, not here. The young cop gazed at the man who almost fooled him and said, "Sir, do you have someone in your trunk?" And before Eddie could think of a great answer, both cops heard more pronounced banging on the trunk lid, and a slightly muffled, but heavily accented voice cried, "Let me out, Edddddieeeee, let me out!" The cop looked with a mixture of disbelief and amusement at Eddie and said, "Sir, would you mind opening the trunk, please?" Eddie, knowing he was done, lifted the key fob, depressed the release latch and up popped his date like a hooker jack in the box. Her hair was flattened, her dress was wrinkled and dirty from the spare tire, and her annoyance was not to be dismissed as she screamed "Eeeeeeedddddddiiiiiiiieeeeeee! Why you leave me alone for so long in the car, Eddddddddiiiieeee, why? ¿Por que Edddddiiiiiiieeeeee?"

Eddie, having no good explanation, let alone a rational one, chose to stand mute at this point. Given that he was an officer and a gentleman by order of Congress, regardless of his behaviors tonight, one cop gave Eddie a ride in the back of the patrol car. The other drove Eddie's car and the hooker to the main gate where, after making certain she had been paid, dropped her off before driving the rental car back to the police station.

The cop knew to check because not paying your hooker was a serious business. Two sailors and an airman had recently talked a young woman from Jamaica, who was new to the game, into performing fellatio on all three for twenty dollars, a savings of ten dollars off the standard rate. She kept up her end of the bargain but those cheap bastards gave her a one dollar bill doctored with the "$20" from the corners of four different bills, which they had pasted on each of the four corners of the now counterfeit twenty. The girl discovered the fraud when she went back to the hooker-gathering space in front of the main gate shack. Happily and sassily singing, "I got twenty dollars, I got twenty dollars!" her older sister told her Jorge Washington was NOT on the twenty, Andrés Jackson was. The young hooker was quick to report this offense and all three were charged with counterfeiting and theft of services. They made restitution in the amount of $150 each to the working girl and each was further reduced one rank, mainly for being such cheap bastards. In addition, each was ordered to forfeit one half month's salary and those forfeitures provided another fiscal boon for the old sailor and airmen homes.

At the police station Eddie gave a written statement describing all of his actions that evening, cooperating fully. He was released and told to brief his New Jersey commander within twenty-four hours and not to leave Panama.

On Monday morning, the cops brought the police blotters and incident reports to me for review because I made the initial assessment of the charges based on sufficiency of the evidence, and there were always a myriad of incidents after the weekend. I read the investigation report and after I stopped laughing, took it to Bob's office and read it to him. After he stopped laughing, and looking at the case seriously, we figured it sounded like Conduct Unbecoming an Officer, since Eddie's behavior amounted to "indecorum" which is prohibited under military law. Officers are expected to be gentlemen and having a hooker pop out of your trunk when stopped by the cops would fall under the "indecorous," designation. Clearly, non-judicial punishment under Article 15 was the way to go. We drafted the forms and made our recommendation to the one-star general wing commander, as he was the legal owner of Eddie's ass. The General, a devout Mormon, didn't agree with the behavior, but he understood loneliness on the road. The paperwork was finalized and a copy sent to the Area Defense Counsel (ADC) over on Albrook Air Station across the Bridge of the Americas.

A day later the ADC, a shaky fellow named Bob, casually wandered into my office, intent on learning what we had in mind for his new client. From past discussions ADC Bob, who claimed to have been a policeman in inner city Kansas City, Missouri, routinely squawked about being scared to death of Panama City and anywhere else in

Panama not a military base. His fear grew tortuous enough that he requested and received an early release and transfer from his assignment. The Pentagon understood his fears because many JAGs sought to duck assignments overseas, but, there's always price to be paid. Bob was reassigned to a nondescript joint job at Ft. Meade, Maryland, and moved into a house in nearby Laurel. It was only later he came to realize the population demographics was two-thirds black and Hispanic, which made it virtually the same as Panama only without the benefit of great restaurants and a night life. His wife called back to see how things were going in Panama, and shared a good story with us. One night there was a loud knock on the front door and Bob grabbed a pistol and stood off to one side yelling "Go away, I'm armed!" The voice replied, "I'm your next door neighbor; I have a Fed Ex package that came for you!" His wife bragged that she was only staying in the marriage because she was going to take his pension.

ADC Bob was hoping to make a timely intervention and get a deal for his client, but I told him we'd already passed the matter up to the General and wouldn't be presenting anything except the police reports. It was an open and shut matter and Bob, visibly relieved that he wouldn't actually have to do anything for this client, said he'd pass the information along to Eddie and left. He later told Eddie that by his own valiant efforts and legal acumen he'd stopped the legal office from recommending a general courts-martial and the attending potential jail time, dismissal from service, and loss of pension. Eddie didn't know Bob was full of crap, but he knew a good deal when it came rolling in and he jumped on it. He asked if he could appear that very afternoon as he was supposed to be flying as soon as this was finished and he needed crew rest. USAF air crews are some of the most rested people on the planet. Any time you needed one, it seemed they were on crew rest. Regulations prohibited disturbing that rest absent emergency circumstances. The General agreed to the immediate disposition and had Eddie report to him right after lunch in his service blues. Pilots hated wearing any uniform except for their onesie flight suits. Wearing blues always made them feel uncomfortable, as if they were ordinary people.

The General called Eddie to attention and, in keeping with the USAF aviation checklist culture, went through the form's "Commander's Checklist." Seeing no problems, he accepted Eddie's admission to the offense and ordered him fined one half month's pay for two months for a total $2,643.30, then chewed him out and threw him out of his office. I walked him back down to our office to finalize the paperwork and arrange the payment of his fine, telling him that, Uncle Sam not being fond of installment plans, the money was immediately due and owing. As we drew up to the legal office entrance, he turned to me and said, "Now that it's all over, can I ask you something? Will any of this be sent to my wife?" I assured him our interest in the matter was concluded as soon as the bill was paid.

Visibly relieved as we walked into Bob's office, Eddie whipped out a checkbook that had an L-1011 Lockheed TriStar embossed on each check and said, "Who do I make this out to?"

Leaving the office, the aviator knew his career had taken a serious hit and he'd never get any further promotion, but he was OK with that because he could still fly with the Guard bureau and he still had a great job with Pan Am.

What Eddie didn't know yet was that before he finished his TDY, on December 4, 1991, his employer, Pan American Airlines, after years of losing money, went belly up and would cease to exist.

I pondered the importance of taking the time to make an intelligent plan, since nothing good every comes from hurrying.

+++

---

## Don't Screw The Hired Help

It was morning in Panama and I was safely ensconced behind my aircraft carrier-sized wooden desk, drinking my third cup of coffee and waiting for the phone to ring with something to do. Suddenly, I was the newly appointed ADC and the phone was silent, and it was my own damn fault.

I'd designed and implemented an award-winning legal education campaign since 1988 called "Five Ways Good Airmen Go Wrong" explaining those five most common offenses charged: sex, checks, drugs, alcohol, and being late to work, often cited in multiple combinations. In that briefing, I gave my audience and potential clients concrete, real world examples of each offense. I'd offer that an airman having sex with a fifteen-year old girl in a bar was hosed. Didn't matter that she had fake ID and was drunk when you met her, still guilty. The audience listened and the number of offenses dropped off significantly. The briefing became a part of their record so they had no excuses. That happy result left lots of blank spaces in my daily calendar and I could use my free time to sometimes ride my bicycle across the Bridge of the Americas which symbolically connects North America and South America, or sometimes to ride out past Fort Amador to see the bullet scarred walls where much of the fighting had taken place during *Operation Just Cause* in December 1989.

I'd recently been drafted as ADC after Bob, citing his safety concerns, left early from his assignment and my orders replacing him came as a complete surprise. I'd recently returned from a deployment as the SJA for the 4404th Operations Group in Riyadh, Saudi Arabia, at the tail end of Desert Storm. I'd been recovering from a one hundred-ten day enforced sobriety stint at what was called the "Betty Ford South West Asia Clinic Riyadh, Saudi Arabia chapter." It wasn't that I needed to drink, it was just that as an American, I was offended that I was prohibited from having a drink, should I so desire. So now, back in the land of the happy hour, I'd been taking the cure for my abstinence while working to forget my most recent time abroad. Most Friday afternoons, I drove back across the bridge to Albrook, parked my car at home, and headed to the "all ranks" club one block away for Happy Hour.

Hector, the slender and dapper Panamanian barman, with an iconic pencil thin mustache, had held down the fort there for many years and greeted me with "Hola, Señor Capitan!" With a flourish, he would quickly set in front of me a freshly prepared Cuba Libra (a rum and coke with a lime wedge on the rim). This bar was smaller than others on the base, with just eight bar stools and no tables. Slot and poker machines ran around the wall with a double row of blinking one-armed bandits filling the center of the room, just waiting for suckers. Each betting machine sported a comfortable chair, an ashtray, and a place for your drink. There was no waitress service, and no complaints.

After exchanging the usual pleasantries, I would stroll to a random poker slot in the center group so I could see who walked in and to monitor how busy señor Hector was, if and when I needed a refill. I wasn't a gambler, knowing full well that Las Vegas wasn't built by paying out winners, but I had enjoyed playing video games in law school because it was mindless and provided a chance to unwind. That was always worth five bucks to me, a sum I knew would last at least twenty minutes, which was long enough. One Friday, I was minding my business, as was my habit, when two airmen arrived in the lounge for a quiet drink and set the wheels of change in motion that put me behind the giant wooden desk I was now enjoying in my wood paneled corner suite.

Liquor was cheap in Panama as it was not taxed, so anytime after five, in the golden hour before sunset, I could count on my now former boss, SJA Bob, to get home, change his clothes, and walk on down from his house a few blocks away. We'd often sit outside with a drink until late in the evening at a table on my covered patio. It offered an unimpeded view of the El Dorado district, with futuristic skyscrapers rising amongst the palm trees. The city was a dynamic place, built on the energy spawned being the single largest trans-shipment point of cocaine coming from Colombia. The Panamanian banks, famous for their privacy, were awash with money to loan for building and development from people looking to invest in such an accommodating country.

In a festive mode when we arrived in Panama, the lively alternative to sedate Britain, I'd strung up white twinkly lights around the ceiling of the carport to provide a soft illumination. Bob christened them the "Ziggy Stardust ballroom lights." We'd spend evenings passing the time, sometimes looking over at the house ADC Bob had recently vacated; the one with visible bullet holes in the concrete exterior. Those holes where a civilian wife, standing on her steps at the war appearing before her, was struck and wounded by gun fire on Dec 20, 1989. This could fairly provide some basis for ADC Bob's fears.

The forces of serendipity came into play when those two airmen entered the bar. It was there that their indiscretion first came to light on that Friday at the Albrook club just after my return from Desert Storm. Sitting at those center row slot machines, killing time, I saw ADC Bob and his enlisted paralegal Jane stroll in and take a seat at the bar. They were amidst a lively chat and didn't notice me. I was heading to the bar to say hello when I heard ADC Bob say in low, but clear voice "Listen, what happened in Florida was like La-La land and it's all done now, so we are back to Captain and Tech Sergeant not Bob and Jane."

I knew they'd both gone on leave to the states at the same time. Jane had previously announced her plan as visiting family in Texas. ADC Bob said he was needing some time away after his wife had given birth to another kid, so he was off to visit family in Florida. In fact, the two had flown to Disney World in Orlando for an assignation at the military-owned and operated Shades O'Green resort hotel on Disney property. I kept this revelation to myself, it being no business of mine if he wanted to screw up his life by having sex with the hired help, a practice the Air Force severely frowned upon.

Since fraternization is a no-kidding rule-breaker, those who partake should make sure it's a private affair. Unfortunately, in my experience, fraternization frequently came to light, and always resulted in the harshest disciplinary action for an officer if made notorious. My suspicions, in this case, were further validated when I stopped by his building, not unreasonably unannounced, to return a folding table our office had borrowed. Because my office was responsible for maintaining the courtroom, I had a key to the private entrance. When I walked in I had a direct view into Bob's corner office, since he'd left the door open. On this day, the Fates seemed determined that Bob and Jane's romance be outed.

Bob heard the banging of the table against the door as I dragged it in. I watched as he hurriedly came out from her office to investigate with his light blue regulation shirt unbuttoned and untucked as was his regulation white T-shirt. His hair was as tousled as a military haircut could be and he seemed flustered, asking "What are you doing here?" Not a moment later his paralegal emerged from her office, smoothing her light blue blouse and patting her hair. She froze when she saw me, so it wasn't difficult for me to play connect the dots.

ADC Bob put in for transfer shortly thereafter, citing safety concerns. The safety he was concerned about was his own. If word got out, his career would be at risk, but if his wife found out it would be much worse. He didn't know that Jan already knew all about the affair because the housemaid had long ago ratted out Señor Bobby to the madam; the maid disliked Bob because he was a cheap bastard and had never given her the raise or bonus for long service as was common in Panama.

After I'd been appointed as ADC, there came the matter of this paralegal; normally, Jane would stay on as my paralegal, but I was convinced I didn't need to ever be alone with her under any circumstances that could be easily misconstrued. I asked for a replacement, in particular a young senior airman named Moon. A twenty-three year old black guy, he played football in high school and was currently on the base team. His only flaw was his casual approach to work which earned him the ire of Jackie, the senior master sergeant law office manager, a tough as nails forty-two year old black woman from South Carolina. She saw him as lazy and unmotivated because he'd declared he was only planning to stay in service for four years. That lack of enthusiasm did nothing to endear him to her. Her stated preference was to keep him in her office where she could beat him into shape at her discretion. I felt a kinship with Moon. I'd also had some "moments" when I was an enlisted airman. I knew he could be a great performer with a lighter leadership touch. Jackie complained to SJA Bob about the change and was so vocal in her resistance that I finally had to tell her about the NCO's affair, adding, "I don't need that, thank you!"

The best part of my new job, in addition to being my own boss, was living *and* working on Albrook, and not having to commute across the

Bridge of the Americas each day. The approach to that well-travelled bridge was just one lane, suddenly blooming into two lanes in each direction on the actual span. This engineering created a death-race as vehicles often jockeyed to improve their positions before the return to one lane, thus creating the "*Italian funnel effect*"and many overheated vehicles stuck on the bridge.

During a courts-martial, one juror, a second lieutenant, was late coming back from lunch; Millie, the senior DC Judge, irritated, ordered me to bring him to her as soon as he showed up. A first sergeant waiting to testify heard that and offered that when he was heading back from lunch, he'd seen an officer in blues running on the bridge. A few minutes later, our sweaty and out of breath juror entered the building. I asked him to accompany me to visit the judge in her chambers.The prosecutor came as well and listened while Millie asked the juror for his explanation. The lieutenant told us that, as he was driving across the bridge, heading back to the court from the Airman Awards luncheon, a large truck going in the opposite direction blew past him very closely. This created enough suction to pull his uniform jacket off the hanger behind him, through the open window and onto the roadway. The lieutenant quickly pulled over and ran to grab it. Millie looked skeptical at his story until he turned around and showed us the tire print on his left sleeve and smashed front buttons. She looked at me: I shrugged my shoulders saying, "That's Panama Rules." This time she nodded her head up and down in understanding and agreement...

+++

# Panama Rules

Any time we planned a courts-martial, a judge had to be flown in from DC to hear the case. For people who never left the Enchanted City, as DC was known, and arriving in a place where the United States had recently removed a sitting president at gunpoint was disconcerting. At Howard, when each trial concluded, the judge was required to file a trip report wherein they tended to declare Panama a horror show. Many judges, after reading those reports, deliberately avoided coming to Panama for trials. When this feedback came to the attention of Millie, the USAF's Senior Judge and most senior female JAG, she decided to check out the veracity of those complaints and took the next case.

On the eve of trial, SJA Bob called me and asked if I could go to Tocumen airport to pick up Millie and bring her back to Albrook to check into the guest quarters. Bob complained that none of his guys knew the route and he didn't want her left stranded. I told him I'd be happy to do it and got the flight information.

Tocumen was a worn facility that hadn't kept up with the pace of growth in Panama's past twenty years. Due to some more-than-usual traffic, I got there a few minutes late. I had never met Millie, but coming into the small arrivals area, I saw a pale-faced woman, somewhere north of fifty and wearing a severe frown, sitting alone on a hard-backed chair. She was wearing civilian clothes, and was the right age, but what sold me was her hair. She wore a graying bee-hive arrangement, a style I'd last seen on a court reporter in 1977, so I figured her to be a lawyer. I approached and introduced myself, adding Bob's regrets. I told her traffic had been slow due to a fire on the highway. She looked at me out of the corner of her eye and I just shrugged and said, "Panama rules. Things just aren't quite the same down here. You'll understand after a bit." As we walked out to my car I gave her the standard briefing and admonishment:

Sometimes the traffic lights worked, sometimes they didn't.

If we are stopped at an intersection, please make sure your window is up and the door is locked, or little kids will swarm us and take any watches they can grab.

You will see things you can't believe. Believe.

It was warm and I had the air conditioning on, but Millie opened her window so she could smoke. I drove down the four-lane concrete highway, the car bouncing over the uneven sections, and I made small talk as I noted passing areas of interest. I'd just pointed out Tumba de los Muertos (Tomb of the Dead), the huge cemetery for all the workers who died while the canal project was being built, from 1903 through 1914. It held over 12,000 workers who died building the Panama Railway and 22,000 more who died during the French effort to build a canal. Many of these deaths were due to disease, particularly yellow fever and malaria. It also gave the highway its name, "Camino de la Muerte" (Road of the Dead).

As we pulled up to a traffic light, I spotted the first kid coming up along the passenger side. I told her to quickly roll up her window which she did before the grubby little hand could get inside the cabin. Other kids began to crowd around the car yelling, "Hey Rambo! Give me some money please!" Following the kids, the next wave was the squeegee man. Some poor bastard would make his living with a plastic water bottle and some old newspaper. He'd come up and squirt your window and smear the dead bugs all around and expect you to give him a quarter for his efforts. On my windshield I had a round red decal with a diagonal line running through a squeegee brush that said, "Sin hombre enjugador!" (No squeegee men!) That was usually enough to deter a squeegee man and we were fortunate enough to have the light change before one could set upon us. As we picked up speed, Millie lowered her window again and said, in her droll tone, "You got any other surprises?"

Before I could answer, we crested a rise and beheld a vista that included a raging fire on both sides of the highway, plus in the median. Panama has two seasons, wet where it rains for an hour or so every day around two in the afternoon, and dry when there was lightning, but no rain, and the pampas grasses burned. We were currently in dry season. She rolled up her window and I picked up speed as we sailed into and through the flames. We arrived at Albrook without any further excitement. I dropped Millie at her quarters and I bid her good night.

Before the trial could get underway, there was the matter of choosing the panel of officers who would be the jury. Millie opted to do the initial questioning and asked if anybody had any preset notions on guilt or innocence, and if anybody would favor one attorney over the other; she found no takers. She then asked if any of them had any obligations that might keep them from giving their fullest attention to the matters at hand? That slowed things up because a captain raised her hand and said, "I'm in the master's program; attendance is mandatory or I'll get thrown out, so I need to leave for that at a quarter past four."

I'd been in a fair amount of trials in USAFE and in my experience found the expected answer to this question was, "We will work until we come to a decision, even if it means nights and weekends." If surprised she didn't show it, and Millie did a head nod and asked if anybody else had anything. A lieutenant offered, "I coach my son's T-ball team and a game starts at four-thirty." Millie raised one eyebrow but asked if anyone else had anything else. A lieutenant colonel, the base weatherman, said, "Today is the Airman of the Month luncheon over at Howard and I think most of us have tickets for that." He looked around at the other prospective jurors who were all nodding in agreement. Millie shook her head a bit but said, "And what would be a good time to reconvene today?" The answer came back and half past one was agreed upon by all, with the further understanding that court would recess for the day at a quarter past four.

With no objections from the lawyers, the trial got underway and continued, after the lunch delay, until the end of the duty day when the jury was dismissed. Because it was a jury trial and the jury alone would determine guilt or innocence, and any punishment, it was ok for the judge and attorneys to socialize. We were having drinks in my office and Millie was expressing her astonishment that an Air Force jury would ever ask for time off for anything. In her experience, every juror said they'd work nights and weekends. The subject of Panama Rules came up again and the prosecutor offered that he'd become a believer as well and it was best to just go with it.

The trial ended on Friday afternoon at a quarter past two. Arguments had been made and jury instructions given, so the panel retired to deliberate. We were sitting in my office drinking coffee and having a smoke since tobacco hadn't been banned yet. It was coming up on half past three so I asked if anybody would like a drink. I told them the deliberations would end for the day at a quarter past four, and the closer it came to the end of the duty day, the greater the chance for an acquittal. Millie didn't bother to hide her disbelief, "You're saying it'll be a not-guilty verdict?" I nodded because I felt pretty confident.

What she didn't know was all those jurors lived on Albrook and commuted each day to Howard which meant crossing the Bridge. They knew if they finished deliberating by the end of the duty day, they wouldn't have to drive back to their offices on Howard. That meant they'd not only skipped the morning commute on a Friday, but both ways, no small thing. I shared how I believed if they were going to convict, they'd have done that within thirty minutes because they also knew we moved right into sentencing and that would have trashed their weekend.

Millie's face still betrayed her skepticism, but like a trouper she held up her coffee cup while staring at the bourbon and said, "You're probably right, want to freshen this up?" I filled her cup and we watched as the clock struck four. We made plans to all go out to dinner at Siete Mares (the Seven Seas) seafood restaurant on Calle Guatemala El Cangrejo (Guatemala the Crab Street) known for its crab risotto. At four-twelve Moon announced that the jury was back.

At four-fourteen, the court was reconvened and to no one's surprise the jury delivered the not guilty verdict. Millie thanked them for their service and the court was closed at a quarter past four.

Millie said that she enjoyed the trial and confessed at dinner that she was sold on Panama rules. She decided that all those good old boys in DC were a bunch of pansies and from then on she took every Panama case that came up.

+++

---

# Handsome Henry The U-2 Guy

Another Albrook weekday and I'd just finished drinking my second cup of coffee while watching the morning "Maid Parade" with Moon. My office was twenty-five yards from the Albrook main gate and each morning all the local women who worked cleaning houses would come in. I was struck that all those women wore high heel shoes from home and negotiated unimproved roads and slick clay trails while wearing them, a daily regimen that gave these compact women amazing calf muscles.

My office had previously been occupied by the director of The Inter-American Air Forces Academy, or IAAFA, which was established in 1943 at the request of General Fernando Melgar, Peru's Minister of Aeronautics. The original class was made up of just 11 Peruvian students and was located in my building on Albrook Field in the Panama Canal Zone, then a part of the USA; making it the first US aeronautics training course given in Latin America. Expansion in the 1940s and 50s led to an annual student base of around 400, largely in response to the possibility of increased conflict in the West.

In early 1989, Manuel Noriega decided to flex his muscles and press his political luck. The school had been relocated to the USA and the now empty half of the first floor was turned over to USAF legal services to house the court room and a four-room office suite for the Area Defense Counsel, an office I was happy to now occupy. The two floors above initially held dormitories for students, but now housed TDY Air National Guardsmen. I enjoyed a huge corner office with large windows and custom blinds. Along with a massive wooden desk, I had a leather couch and matching love seat, plus a dark brown mahogany book cabinet where I kept "Don Mello" brand Honduran cigars, Viceroy cigarettes, and a bottle of Cutty Sark whiskey, each being the preferred brand in Central America. Of course, I also kept a bottle of Old Crow Bourbon for when Millie came down from DC to conduct trials. I'd hand-receipted for a full English tea set: cups, saucers, creamer, sugar bowl, and coffee pot. The claims program had paid for the entire set when one cup was broken in a move and could not be replaced. A Persian rug with a large ink stain, partially hidden by a table leg, was in the center of the office.

I was about to fire up the golf game I'd loaded onto my government computer when the back door to the building opened to reveal a guy in a green flight-suit adorned with the silver oak leaves of a lieutenant colonel. He held his blue flight cap in his hand, pausing in the doorway, then leaned on the frame asking, "You the lawyer?"

Six feet tall and fit, his jet black hair and dark brown eyes were accentuated by a chiseled chin and heavy beard that must have needed shaving twice a day, and made me think him a no-kidding poster boy for the USAF.

We made our introductions, then he asked if he could talk to me because he thought he might be in some trouble. I told him I would clear my schedule while shutting off the computer screen and bidding him to sit on one of the two very nice leather wingback chairs El Comandante had also left for me, while I filled out his info card to begin the process.

Any allegation made against a commissioned officer is given serious consideration because the prevailing attitude is that officers are selected after great care is taken in vetting them, physically and mentally. Officers were presumed to be of high moral character and deviations from that standard could have the most dreadful effects on the people under their command, and the reputation of the Air Force, so I paid particular attention as he embarked on the sad tale that brought him to me.

Handsome Henry was a U-2 squadron commander, a critical position. The Lockheed U-2, /TR-1, "Dragon Lady" is a single-jet engine, ultra-high altitude reconnaissance aircraft operated by the USAF and previously flown by the CIA. It provides day and night high-altitude (70,000+ feet), all-weather intelligence gathering. The U-2 has also been used for electronic sensor research, satellite calibration, other communications purposes, and also inspired a rock band.

His was a very important position dealing with operational (flying) matters each and every day. The 24th Wing's mission was to be the "tip of the spear" in the long-raging war on drugs in Central and South America. The intelligence his squadron obtained was critical to performing that mission. As the officer in charge of over 120 officers and enlisted airmen, his behavior absolutely had to be above all reproach; if doubt of that arose, he could be instantly fired by the Wing Commander.

As soon as he told me there was a sexual component, I knew this would be a fun case, because there is absolutely NOTHING in the USAF better than a complaint alleging anything about sex. Illicit, permitted, missionary or kinky, it didn't matter, if sex was connected it would be a big ticket item on the briefing chart.

I got up to start the coffee perking and he followed me, standing by the couch along the window. I wanted to give him my undivided attention because sex injects elements of soap opera and the absurd into the horribly mundane and boring lives of superior commanders. Leadership tended to while away their days in boredom, being subjected to an endless parade of Power Point slides bringing them up to date on the latest status of everything operational. Those slides revolved around maintaining aircraft readiness rates above 85% and any changes in the twenty-four hours since the last briefing.

Henry handed me the package he'd been given by his immediate superior, the Operations Group Commander, a colonel. The cover letter informed him that a Commander Directed Investigation (CDI) was being opened into an accusation of his having engaged in sexual relations with several-to-many married women, wives of subordinates, none of whom were his wife. These CDI are unstructured investigations which can provide a commander with information useful in evaluating any complaint that needed to be discreetly investigated for veracity before going further and ruining lives. The skills of the appointed IO are vital, so either lawyers or senior officers are appointed to the task by a commander.

I was shocked by the nature of the allegations. I'd known pilots who were "players," those good looking, fit and trim young warriors in their green onesie flight suit, who'd roll up their sleeves and saunter into the bar, always on the make for a good time and a few laughs. Players could be married or single, but in my entire life experience I never met one who ever went through the Officer Wives' Club phone roster and made multiple successful snake passes. Making a play for another guy's wife or girlfriend was usually reserved for when a guy was TDY somewhere for 179 days, not while everybody was home.

These peccadilloes were *actually* only frowned upon if they were indiscreet and the affair became public knowledge. Even then, the parties would typically be ordered to "knock it off." The idea of him sexing up a bunch of wives, all known to each other, stretched the limits of credibility. I was expected to believe evidence existed that he'd "run the table" with eight different women, one of whom, Lucy, I discovered was not only a lovely woman, but was deaf from birth so he'd have had to have learned sign language to charm her into bed.

I poured the coffee and nodded at the bottles in the cabinet, which he declined. As I thought of some immediate lines of questioning, a grin spread over my face. Handsome Henry asked me what I was thinking; I told him, "Sheeee-it Henry, if it was me I'd be so flattered I'd plead guilty just for the bragging rights." His faced drooped so I shared the story about the two very old guys who run into each other walking on the beach in Miami and one says, "Murray! I haven't seen you in more than five years and suddenly here you are; I cannot believe it! Where have you been?" Murray shrugged his shoulders and replied, "I was in jail." Stunned, the friend says, "Jail? You? What were you in for?" "Rape" came Murray's laconic reply. The friend shouted, "Rape? That's ridiculous, look at you, you're an old man over eighty, that's crazy!" "I know" said the friend, "but I was so flattered I pled guilty anyway."

Henry cocked his head and said, "Huh?" I told him they had nothing and this was just a bullshit fishing expedition to see if there was something there, and I began to dial the phone for the legal office.

Maybe it was the tropical heat and humidity that made some people so certain other people were having sex. If a man and a woman were perceived as laughing a bit too loud, or talking a little too close, or talking to each other too often, it wasn't long before some frustrated person would gossip to someone else that the two must be having an affair. An "innocent" remark such as that often spreads in a not so innocent way.

This archaic and chauvinistic attitude manifested one day when a very attractive female staff sergeant came into my office complaining that she'd just been counseled by a squadron commander that her friendship with a male married airman was the subject of a complaint and she needed to knock it off. The NCO was upset because she was happily married, and while she liked talking with the other guy because they shared an interest in photography, she absolutely wasn't interested in having sex with him. Not only highly insulted, she was worried that the baseless allegation would become known, spread and take on a life of its own. She was also angry because it wasn't her squadron commander who counseled her, it was *his* commander, who had chosen not to contact her male friend. She sat across from me fuming and complaining how men always took the blame directly to the woman.

I asked her the name of the offending commander, who turned out to be a sanctimonious guy I knew was one of those "born again and better than you" types, and I put in a call to him while she sat in her chair. When he came on the line I verified that he had in fact counseled her and he did acknowledge it. I asked if he had first procured any evidence to support his beliefs and he sermonized that it was his personal belief that something inappropriate was going on and he wanted to nip it in the bud. I decided to dive straight to the heart of the matter:

"So if understand correctly, sir, you think those two are fucking?"

After a sharp gasp of air when he heard "that" word, he replied, "Well, I don't know about that, but it seems inappropriate."

"So you do think they are fucking?"

"I'm really uncomfortable with you using that word."

"Well, sir, I'm really at a loss for putting it any other way. You clearly think they are fucking because you called her in and told her to knock it off and that must mean you think they are fucking because fucking somebody not your spouse is a violation of the UCMJ, so I have to determine if you think she's guilty of fucking this guy."

"I don't know about any of that..."

"So we are agreed; there is no video of them fucking and nobody ever peeped in a window and saw them fucking, and neither party confessed to fucking, does that sound about right? I'm only asking because the charge of adultery requires some proof of two people fucking, or going down on each other or fucking up the ass, and we don't have any of that, do we?"

The line was silent so I continued, "Sir, the problem as I see it is you abused your authority by calling her in, a person not under your command, without any legal basis, to accuse her of unlawful fucking and possibly ruining her professional reputation. It could be viewed as conduct unbecoming an officer because we are expected to have our shit together before we go about casting aspersions and accusing people of unlawful fucking around. She's pretty upset and I'm trying to get her to reconsider making a formal complaint to the Inspector General, because that could get pretty ugly pretty quickly."

He was still silent, but I could hear his breathing had become labored, so I concluded with, "Sir, can we agree that she wasn't fucking anybody and put this all behind us, with perhaps a written apology to her? I think that would go a long way to settling this matter."

For no other reason than to get me to quit saying the word "fucking," he agreed and asked me to please tell her he was sorry and he'd follow up with a letter exonerating her.

I hung up the phone and looked at the young woman who was holding her sides and asked if she was satisfied. She surprised me by saying, "Fucking A' sir."

With this in mind I got on the line with Bob regarding Handsome Henry's case. Bob assured me in no uncertain terms that his office had nothing to do with any of this and, as no one had consulted him, this debacle was solely owned by the Ops commander. He wished me good luck.

The complaint consisted of a single handwritten letter to the Ops commander complaining that Henry had been engaging in "numerous affairs with several of the wives" in the squadron and proceeded to name them. When I got to Lucy, the aviator looked shocked and surprised, asking, "Is that the deaf lady?" and sank back into the fine leather Chesterfield sofa where I would ordinarily take my fifteen minute afternoon combat catnap.

I took his cup to freshen it, nodded again at the bookshelf and produced the bottle of Jim Beam. This time he nodded back. I found it was much easier to get people talking about the matter they were jammed up over if they'd had a drink to loosen their deep inhibitions. Henry was no different. He had graduated with an engineering degree from the University of Nevada, and taken an ROTC commission. He knew he was a poster boy and admitted he loved flirting with women, and said he did in fact flirt with all of those women, although he couldn't remember flirting with Lucy, other than to smile brightly at her.

I produced the copy of the poison pen letter and handed it to him to read. When he was done I said, "Do you recognize the handwriting?" He said he didn't. I looked at it again. The flowing cursive was a practiced hand, suggesting an educated woman wrote the missive. I began to read it out loud and as I did I noticed that the sentence structure was not quite right and realized the writer learned English as a second language. I asked him how many of his officers were married and had brought their wives with them on this tour. Henry had no idea, but a call to his orderly room revealed there were nine wives. He asked the airman to read each name, and he noted a new name, which was not one of the women listed in the complaint.

I asked Henry if he recognized the name and he said he did; she was a Panamanian woman who'd married a squadron officer a year earlier. Like every successful flirt, Henry's "psycho" meter was fully calibrated and he'd gotten enough of a hit off her that he had deliberately avoided being around her. The ability to recognize an unbalanced person of the opposite sex who would either make your life very interesting or ruin it was an important one because sometimes unsuccessful players wound up in the morgue. As a twenty-two year old security policeman, I attended my first autopsy in November 1975. It was conducted on a twenty-one year old airman who died in the shower. Sadly, it was his girlfriend's shower and he was shot dead by her jealous husband who came home early.

Henry's judgment about this particular woman had previously been validated after he heard stories from squadron social events he'd missed where things became "animated." This innocuous term actually denotes quite a dust-up which might involve arguments, objects being thrown, or violence visited upon a spouse, and many of these moments presented at children's birthday parties. At one memorable birthday party for a five year old, an NCO's wife beat her husband with the piñata stick, that had just been used quite safely in the birthday game. She'd just found out from another wife at the party that he was teepee-creeping with a neighbor's wife while the cuckold husband was TDY downrange. Those reports had re-enforced Henry's belief in the accurate calibration of his psycho meter, because it registered as "Full-tilt Batshit Crazy" when they'd first met, and he had made every effort to avoid being around her.

After some discussion, we came to the only conclusion possible: this woman had gotten pissed off by Handsome Henry *not* lavishing his attentions upon her, because she was a beautiful Panamanian, not some Colombian dog, and she'd written the letter to get revenge for his perceived slight. I called Bob and offered my theory of the case. He laughed and said I was probably right but that the Colonel had the authority to order the investigation and it would all come down to what the IO found during the course of that investigation.

A few days later the commander of the Services Squadron, a lieutenant colonel in charge of dining halls, transient quarters, pool and fitness facilities, all morale and quality of life matters including "weeds and seeds" was appointed as the IO. He set Henry's interrogation to begin immediately following lunch, a quiet time when there would be a break from all the complaints he ordinarily received, like "the popcorn machine broke at the theater." A career Air Force officer, he'd never been appointed to anything like this before and he wanted it held in the court room, to either lend weight to the proceedings, or more likely because Jeff, the civilian court reporter, told him he didn't want to move the recording equipment from the courtroom.

When we walked into the courtroom for the examination, I noticed the IO'd set up two chairs across a table from one another so I grabbed another one for myself, placing it next to Henry. The hearing officer set his attaché case on top of the table, opened it, and began thumbing through files until he finally found what he was looking for, the list of questions to ask. With a gravitas that would have made Senator "Tail Gunner" Joe McCarthy, a virulent Commie hunter from the 50's, proud, the investigator reviewed the questions he'd prepared, his head bobbing up and down as he re-read them silently. Satisfied that he knew the first question well enough, he looked at Henry over the top of the open case and asked, "Did you have sex with Mrs. X?" Before Henry could answer, I interjected "Sir, my client is not going to answer that question."

Undaunted by my legal rebuff, the novice interrogator turned to the next question. "OK, well, answer this. Did you have a sexual relationship with Mrs. Y?" Again I interjected that my client was not going to be answering any questions that amounted to him admitting guilt to something that never happened and he never did.

The IO became frustrated at this point and said to me "Captain, I am trying to find out what is going on here and, if you keep answering for him, then I won't be able to ask my questions."

I agreed with what he was saying and told him, "Yes, sir."

"Well, will you let me proceed with asking my questions without your interference?"

The enormity of that response stunned me for a moment. Clearly, this was an investigator who had no idea of what exactly a lawyer was for and I was reminded of watching Lieutenant Colonel Oliver North getting grilled during hearings in front of the Joint House-Senate Iran-Contra Committee. Chairman Daniel Inouye suggested that North speak for himself and admonished North's attorney, Brendan Sullivan, for constantly objecting to the questions posed. Sullivan responded, "Well, sir, I'm not a potted plant. I'm here as the lawyer, that's my job."

I decided to take that same approach, so I offered, "Sir, I am not a potted plant. I'm here to represent my client, not make your task easier."

That turned out to be a show-stopper. The investigator hadn't prepared any questions that didn't involve a confession to every allegation, so he stood silent for a few minutes while he figured out his next course of action. Tired of this useless exercise that was wearing my patience and interfering with my afternoon, I finally said, "Sir, I don't know what pinhead ordered this investigation, but unless you have some actual questions for my client, I think this interrogation is at an end."

The hearing ended on that sour note and I thought no more about it because there was simply no competent evidence to support the ridiculous contention of marital infidelity. I told Henry the matter was going to die from a lack of evidence and went back to my office to continue playing the video golf game that the useless hearing had interrupted. I heard no more of any investigation regarding the case and a few days later Bob called to tell me the matter had been concluded and Handsome Henry was officially off the hook. He admonished me to remind Henry, "The legal office had nothing to do with that goat-rope cluster-fuck."

A week later, I was walking out of the Wing Command section after the weekly staff meeting I attended as a guest of the Commanding General. He felt there was no reason to exclude me from having the same information as any of the other units assigned, plus he valued my observations as an "outsider" not beholden to him for a rating evaluation, the one person who could "speak truth to power." At one meeting a supply officer discussed some of the unusual items the government was getting ready to dispose of as no longer needed, including a doughnut making machine. When the Security Police Chief reported an increase in burglaries in the warehouse section of the base I proposed giving the doughnut machine to the cops and let them open a doughnut shop in the center of the crime zone as that would insure an adequate police presence in the area. The top cop was not amused, but the general was.

As I walked towards the stairs and passed by the Operations Command offices, the colonel who'd ordered the investigation drew up along side of me and said, "Captain, I want to talk to you." His tone suggested this wasn't a request for my company and wouldn't be because he wanted to sing my praises. I followed him inside and watched as he went behind his desk and took a seat while I stood in front of him.

Sitting behind a desk lets that person project power and authority and this is especially true with people who lack confidence in their actual authority and powers. I wasn't intimidated because my desk was twice the size of his and gave me confidence even when not sitting behind it, as I'm certain it did for El Comandante all those years ago.

Direct and to the point, he leaned across his desk and with great intensity growled at me saying, "I don't like your goddamned attitude and I'm going to see you get reprimanded." This was no small threat, the USAF was undergoing a reduction in force and a letter of reprimand for an officer was a career killer.

I'd always hated bullies and knew they tended to talk out of their ass, so I likewise leaned forward and replied, "Sir, you don't have to like my goddamned attitude, but you really need to respect my fucking position."

He looked stunned as I turned on my heel before being dismissed, adding, "Sir, if you have any more threats to direct at me due to the performance of my job I would strongly encourage you to speak directly with my supervisor." And with that I was out the door leaving a clearly enraged colonel behind me.

I quickly made my way downstairs and was just walking into Bob's office when his secretary buzzed saying, "The Operations Group commander is holding on the line for you."

Bob looked up at me on the other side of his desk with his finger poised over a line with the angrily blinking red light and said, "Anything I need to know about this?" I told him "I think he doesn't like my goddamned attitude and wants you to reprimand me."

Bob shook his head, quietly chuckling, knowing this would be his most interesting call of the day, and punched the button while cheerfully saying, "Colonel, how can I help you today?"

For the next few long moments, I heard the not quite audible comments coming from the outraged commander as Bob held the phone away from his ear. When the colonel calmed down, I listened to Bob's end of the conversation. "Yes, sir, he is certainly out of control and I wish somebody would get on top of him. No sir, I'm not in his chain of command. In fact, there isn't anybody on this installation in his chain of command because he reports to a colonel in DC, who reports to the President. It's the nature of the independent judiciary demanded by Congress."

The conversation wound down rapidly. Bob rang off and hung up the phone. He was now grinning as he said, "You really pissed him off" and I told Bob I hadn't a clue as to why. He leaned back in his chair and said, "I think it might have been when you referred to him as a pinhead."

Lesson of the day? I learned to never put anything down on paper you wouldn't want your worst enemy to read in open court.

+++

# Harold's Having Babies

L iving and working on Albrook afforded me an extraordinary amount of quality family time with my wife, Laurie, and kids, especially our youngest daughter Maggie who had just turned three as we arrived in country. Laurie left every morning at seven for her job teaching English at the Department of Defense Middle School in nearby Curundú village. I didn't have to be at work until a quarter past and the day care was only two buildings away from my office, so we'd ride my bicycle in together, she in her little bike seat.

Some afternoons and on weekends, we'd just idle around outside while Maggie played in the splash pool and enjoyed the day. It was on such a fine afternoon that we were watching some US Army UH-60 Blackhawk helicopters, a part of 1st Battalion, 228th Aviation Regiment "Winged Warriors," as they engaged in exercises known in bulk as the Fast Rope Insertion Extraction System (FRIES). This is a technique for descending a thick rope to deploy troops from a helicopter in places where the helicopter itself cannot touch down.

My three-year-old daughter had been growing up watching *"Thomas the Tank Engine,"* a fictional steam locomotive on the Island of Sodor who was always looking to be "a really useful engine" while having adventures with other "useful" machines, including a helicopter named Harold. Hearing the sounds of the helos approaching she became very excited. I held her up in my arms as she pointed to the now-hovering machine shouting, "Daddy! Harold the helicopter!" Of course, we kept watching, she being fascinated by all the noise Harold was making which he did not make on TV. Even though a couple of hundred feet distant it seemed as if he was right on top of us.

Suddenly a rope flew out of the port side hatch and soldiers were sliding down to the grassy infield of the unused runway. Maggie became very exited, pulling on my collar and shaking me shouting, "Daddy! Look! Harold is having babies!" The soldiers descent went on for some minutes. They slid down and dropped to the ground, the helo landed, picked up "the babies," circled, pulled up, dropped the rope and continued the drill. Now the third iteration, and the Blackhawk was hovering around thirty feet off the ground, holding until the infiltration was complete. This maneuver demands the pilot manually hold the hover and that isn't easy, depending on the weather and winds. The crew chief monitors the rise and fall and calls it out to the pilot, because the machine tends to drift up and down, so any troop fast-roping must prepare for a slightly longer or a slightly shorter experience. The helo is also most vulnerable while hovering, presenting an easy target for a rocket-propelled grenade, so the training incorporates that same urgency in practice, dropping the ropes and soldiers as fast as possible to get out of the kill zone.

One of the soldiers stepped off the airframe and was about halfway down when his rope broke and he fell the remaining distance into the thick mud and grass on the verge. My daughter banged on my shoulder saying, "Daddy! Look! The baby fell!" as the helicopter immediately dropped down, scooped up the injured soldier and headed to Gorgas Army Hospital about two flight minutes away. As the sounds of those two General Electric T700 turboshaft engines faded, she looked at me and held my cheeks to keep my attention, asking "Is the baby okay?" I told her I'd check.

It was Monday. We'd had our coffee, watched the maid parade, read the newspaper and the phone simply wasn't ringing. It had been one of those weekends where no episodes of sufficient criminality came to the attention of the authorities, so the most I could expect were small matters that would come in the mid-week, notices of proposed nonjudicial punishment actions for some infraction. Until that time, there was scant to do but get ready and go for a two-hour bike ride at mid-morning. Bike riding was a penchant of the then-Secretary of the Air Force Sheila Widnall, she being a long-distance bike rider, and so biking became the"latest and greatest" method of measuring fitness.

Mondays were my day to ride out past Fort Amador, the scene of some of the most bitter fighting during the "Operation Just Cause" Christmas invasion and regime change in 1989. I was getting ready to change into my biking clothes when Moon buzzed and told me that an Army private was wishing to talk to me. I had an informal arrangement with the

Army defense JAGs at Ft. Clayton that if they were swamped or conflicted, I could take some of their case load. The same was true for the Navy at Rodman Naval Station, in their case because the nearest Navy defense lawyers were at the bases of Guantanamo in Cuba or Roosevelt Roads in Puerto Rico.

Moon ushered the private inside. He was nineteen if a day and quite slender. His uniform appeared loose on his frame and I could see the white sling supporting his left arm which was in a cast. He came before me, stood at attention, and saluted with his good right hand. I returned his salute and told him to take a seat. I reviewed his intake card which had only the letters "ROS" written on it. A Report of Survey provides procedures by which a military member may be held financially liable for lost, damaged, or destroyed government property. I put the card down and said, "Now, tell me all about what the Army thinks you did and how I can help you."

He sat erect in his seat, put his cast on the wooden armrest and leaned forward. "Sir, I'm not certain if I can trust the Army guys, them working for the Army." This was a common perception among airmen I'd counseled, an idea usually started by some "barracks" lawyer who needed to believe that all the "good lawyers" got jobs on the outside and only poor ones came on active duty These "school of hard knocks" airmen-barristers would then proceed to offer their own non-legal advice to the airman which usually involved telling the commander to stuff it. Advice like that is how a number of my clients wound up in my office with an Article 15 for being late coming back from lunch instead of getting a simple butt chewing.

When I was serving as the defense counsel at RAF Upper Heyford, an airman sent to me on a matter told me he'd been advised what to do by a guy in his dorm. The advice was absolute nonsense which wouldn't help the airman's cause at all. I got the name of this unauthorized practitioner of law, a guy who worked maintaining aircraft. I called maintenance ops and found out exactly where his plane was parked, put on my all-access line badge and drove out to that aircraft. I got out, opened some panels and started poking about the plane's innards. When the maintainer noticed me messing around, he strode over to me saying, "Sir? This is my plane, you can't be doing that." I looked at him and said, "I don't know the first thing about airplanes, do you mind if I grab a wrench? I think I know what to do." He looked at me, confused, and started stammering. Now that I had his fullest attention, I said, "I'm the designated area defense counsel and you aren't. I don't work on your plane and you don't practice law. Got it?" He did.

I now quickly disabused the private of his concerns regarding the Army lawyer's fitness to practice, but since he was sitting in my office, I told him I would listen as he explained his situation then direct him as needed to resolve the problem. He cleared his throat and began, "Sir, I was fast-roping out of a Blackhawk when the rope broke..." and I interrupted saying, "Its *you*! The falling baby!" Of course, he looked at me in confusion and I immediately said, "Sorry, never mind, I saw that accident. I was watching the drill from my house and saw you fall."

Visibly relieved that I wasn't crazy, he gave me details of the accident: how the rope had been looking frayed and he reported such to his platoon sergeant overseeing the training, but had been told to "shut the fuck up and soldier on" so out the door he went. He said he'd lost hold of his M-16 rifle during the fall; it had been attached to him by a ten-foot rope for just such a contingency. When he hit the ground, the mud took up a lot of the impact force and only his arm broke.

At that point I didn't understand what his problem was and asked him. He said, "Sir, I got knocked out and didn't know much until I woke up in a bed at Gorgas, but when I came into the unit today my First Sergeant handed me this." He passed his copy of the DD Form 200, Financial Liability Investigation of Property Loss. According to his first lieutenant company supply officer, the private owed Uncle Sam $586 for a brand new M-16A2 rifle. It noted the old one was destroyed when the "soldier was grossly negligent by failing to retain positive control of his weapon resulting in the destruction and loss of government property."

I looked up and asked, "Now exactly how did you do this?"

He said, "That's just it, sir, I didn't! The rifle landed near me and the tire of the Blackhawk landed on it when it set down to pick me up and it broke at the upper receiver."

It only took the briefest of phone calls to his Orderly Room and a discussion of the safety requirements for fast-roping with the battalion legal clerk, especially the part in the Army Field Manual that said:

> 6-7. FAST-ROPE INFILTRATION/EXFILTRATION
> SYSTEM (FRIES)
> Before conducting a fast-rope operation, a thorough
> inspection of the fast rope is necessary.
> a. Inspection of the Rope. The rope must be laid out to
> inspect the entire rope. The rope must be checked
> along its entire length for fraying. Snags in the
> rope from normal use will not significantly
> weaken the rope. However, *a rope with fraying of
> several strands in one particular spot must not be
> used.*

He agreed and asked me to send the private to him and said he'd take care of it. He told me he knew this officer from a recent assignment in Germany at the Chiemsee Army kasserne, a recreation center run by the Army as a resort for the troops assigned occupation duties. The lieutenant wanted to punish a soldier by putting him on bread and water for three days. The paralegal explained that bread and water was a navy punishment limited to people embarked or attached to a vessel and thought no more about it.

A few days later, on a cold autumn afternoon, the paralegal was running around the lake and saw a heavily dressed figure hunched over in a small aluminum rowboat a few yards out on the lake eating white bread and drinking water from a canteen. The paralegal grew curious and asked the guy who explained his company commander had sentenced him to three days bread and water. He'd just started the punishment that morning and had been given five loaves of white bread and five canteens of water. The paralegal called him in to shore and the Battalion commander counseled the junior officer to use more sense.

This wasn't an isolated case. I had a Navy Petty Officer from SEAL Team 4 come in with an ROS wanting to charge him $480 for a Colt Model 1911 semiautomatic pistol he'd lost while "down range" on a mission. Not wishing to become involved in the particulars of this highly classified mission, all I asked was if he lost the weapon during a sanctioned US operation and he said he did, so I followed by asking if he was running at the time of the loss and again he agreed. I finally asked him "If you'd gone back to recover the pistol would that have endangered the success of your mission?" He looked at me and said, "Depends on if being dead was failing." After his command was made to understand a trial would certainly involve the release of a lot of highly classified compartmentalized information, and one .45 pistol would not effect the outcome of democracy in Central or South America, his OIC agreed the loss was probably not negligent and the sailor released from liability.

After thanking the clerk, I hung up the phone and let the private know his matter was happily concluded.

I went to the daycare to pick up my daughter and when she came running out saw a Blackhawk going past and pointed saying, "Daddy! It's Harold!" I grabbed her up and said, "Do you remember the baby who fell out of Harold?" She looked at me with solemn blue eyes and nodded her head up and down while I told her, "Good news sweetie! He only hurt his wing a little bit, but the doctor said he'll be just fine."

She hugged my neck and kissed me.

+++

# Unknown Naval Engagements We Lost

## POPEYE AND BLUTO

It was a Tuesday morning, shortly after my first cup of coffee but before the maid parade, when Moon ushered in two US Navy Petty Officers Third class. Identically dressed, they stood in front of my desk in long-sleeve blue chambray shirts, white T-shirts, blue bell-bottomed dungarees, while nervously twirling their white "dixie cup" caps in their hands. The intake card identified them as Hull Technician Jones and his partner and co-defendant, Engineman Jones.

I invited them to sit and share with me their tale of woe. Hull Tech and Engineman, both assigned to nearby Rodman Naval Station, had just been offered a "Captain's Mast," navy-speak for "non-judicial punishment,"or NJP. The term was a holdover from the old days; when a sailor was charged with an offense, he was brought before the Captain to stand at the main mast so all could watch and be witness to the verdict and punishment. This location had made it easy for the crew to set up the gang plank should the crime call for "the walk," or the ropes for "keel-hauling," where the condemned sailor would be tied to a rope and tossed overboard. His mates would then haul him below the keel and around the other side. This process took several minutes and the body was dragged across barnacles attached to the hull. Few ever survived this punishment. Even today, sailors are brought to the bridge for this process, although the gang plank and keel hauling are fortunately no longer available options.

The NJP action was being brought by their commander, a lieutenant with Special Boat Unit 26, the only Special Boat Unit located outside the United States. This unit brags a long and storied history going back to the Swift Boats in Vietnam. Its members included Senator John Kerry, a highly decorated Swift Boat officer who actually jumped off his boat to chase down and kill a Viet Cong fighter who'd fired on his craft.

The current mission profile was the defense of the Panama Canal Zone and the dispatching of Mobile Training Teams downrange to Central and South American countries. Elements of this included inserting Navy SEALS on covert missions anywhere those low-draft boats could travel. This sizable fleet included several Mark III patrol boats capable of infiltration and exfiltration, thanks to their ultra-modern encrypted communications systems and state of the art radar/sonar navigation equipment. Armed with machine guns, a 40-mm grenade launcher, plus a slew of small arms and ammo, these small craft brought an astonishing amount of firepower to whatever marshes, creeks, inlets, or swamps these riverine gunfighters merrily sailed to. These patrol boats are of all-aluminum construction with their pilot house offset to starboard providing maximum deck space for weapons and equipment. The craft has a low radar cross-section and quiet engines for clandestine operations and with a mission duration of up to five days. They also cost a heap of taxpayer dollars.

The petty officers' problem had erupted the previous Friday when both sailors had been assigned to repair and maintain one of the three 8V71T Detroit Diesel Engines that boosted the boat's speed to better than 45 knots (50mph). This tasking entailed disconnecting some length of pipe that passed through the hull below the water line. The guys had been working hard in the hot, tight, and humid confines of the engine room when their progress was interrupted by two important things: a missing part and their noticing the little hand on the four and the big hand on the three, ergo: the weekend had begun. Time to head to the club to enjoy their liberty; this job would wait until Monday. They cleaned up, secured the vessel and ran down the dock. They enjoyed a fabulous weekend that included several glasses of ice cold cerveza and meeting some recently arrived Colombian Spanish teachers.

Bright and early Monday morning, the two returned to their duties where they realized, to their surprise, that their commander, the installation commander, the safety officer, and a host of other senior members of the command staff, whose names they were about to learn, were all on the pier. The officers were at the berth, quite interested in a

US Navy Mark III patrol boat resting several feet below the water line and leaving just the upper half of the wheel house visible.

Soon the boat was raised from those briny depths but the electronic equipment, while water resistant, was not *waterproof*, and was now destroyed by its lengthy immersion in salt water. An investigation revealed the sailors had disconnected an exhaust line and installed a wooden plug they'd taken from their Navy issue plugging kit. This might have been a satisfactory fix but for a couple of things. It was really the job of Hull Tech to do this sort of work, given the hole was in the hull, but as Engineman had been closer and said that he'd plug the leak, a plan OK'd by Hull Tech, who was eager to get out of the stinky, dank and nasty confines of the engine room. At that point, Hull Tech left and Engineman banged that plug into place for all he was worth. When he saw no leaks, he called it a job well done and beat a hasty retreat.

If Hull Tech had been watching this procedure, he no doubt he would have noticed that Engineman had not availed himself of the Oakum spun tar which the kit provided to effectively seal the plug. As a result, this omission, sometime over the course of the weekend, allowed hydrostatic pressure to pop the plug and the good ship began taking on water. The automatic bilge pump did a heroic job but was simply unable to keep up with the volume of water flowing into the engine locker. Once the water had fried the electronics, the pump died and the ship slowly settled below the gently lapping waters.

The Navy JAG office prepared the paperwork, the sailors were called in and served with the written notice of NJP action by their commander who directed them to beat feet to my office.

I finished reading the investigation paperwork and gave them their options, which included refusing to accept non-judicial punishment and taking a chance on a courts-martial with the possible loss of all rank, pay and privileges, or a dishonorable discharge and a lengthy term of confinement at Ft. Leavenworth. As their faces dropped, I continued to explain that they could accept non-judicial punishment asking their commander for mercy, given the most he could do was take one stripe and half a month's pay for two consecutive months, plus confinement in the brig for not more than fourteen days, which really wasn't such a big hit for sinking a US Naval vessel.

They sat solemnly processing it all and looking to me like I was supposed to make up their minds, so I reminded them, "You do understand that you two sunk a Navy ship, right? I think the last time a Navy vessel was sunk was during combat in World War II." Adding, "I'm actually surprised that you two guys aren't headed to a general courts-martial." That energized their more rational thought process and they decided to accept the punishment and head back to Rodman. I asked if they wanted me to call the ADC at Gitmo or Rosey Roads to see if he or she might have different thoughts, but they declined politely, thanked me for seeing them and trudged off to learn their fate.

A week or so later, I was having a few drinks with the Navy Staff Judge Advocate and asked him what punishment had been awarded to my ship-sinking specialists. He told me they'd each been reduced one grade from Petty Officer Third to Seaman First, and ordered to forfeit one half month's pay for two months (which) further enriched the Old Sailor's home. I shared that I was pretty amazed at the light sentence. He explained that the Navy currently had a particular interest in maintaining its own reputation. That interest in sparing departmental embarrassment meant a few people who should have gone to jail for their dereliction of duty didn't, so the Navy made up for it by preferring to prosecute people for more administrative offenses like DUI, adultery and bigamy.

This SJA was a commander who had been in the Navy for twenty years, serving in a variety of assignments. As he didn't like to tell "stories" to the two lawyers on his staff, and this being Happy Hour, he opened up to telling me legal war stories. At one point he mentioned being assigned to Holy Loch in Scotland a few years earlier, so I told him the story of my experience at Holy Loch, when I happily parked in a very nice space marked "Any Captain." Being an Air Force guy, it didn't occur to me that the sign was intended for an 0-6 Navy Captain. My rank faux pas so annoyed the only captain on the station that, the next time I visited, the sign had been amended to read "any NAVY

Captain." That was a darn good story, but the SJA shared a better one from Holy Loch.

## GO BIG OR GO HOME

In 1986, the USS *Nathanial Greene* was a James Madison-class nuclear-powered fleet ballistic-missile submarine, part of the nuclear triad consisting of land-based, aircraft, and submarine-launched nuclear warheads. Each Trident carried fifteen warheads and the *Greene*, then assigned to the Royal Navy submarine base at Holy Loch, in Scotland, was suddenly retired from service, returned to the USA, removed from the Navy list on January 31, 1987, and scrapped. The press release at the time said the decision was a unilateral action undertaken by then President Reagan to demonstrate to Soviet Premier Gorbachev the depth of American commitment to satisfying the SALT II restrictions on nuclear weapons. That news was well-received by the Russians and Gorbachev.

What Reagan could have never known was that Mikhail Sergeyevich Gorbachev would be the eighth and final leader of the Soviet Union. A lawyer by training, he headed a delegation to Canada in 1983 to meet with then Prime Minister Pierre Trudeau. In his memoirs he remarked that he realized Communism could not win when he visited a Canadian grocery store and saw a fully stocked meat aisle dedicated to nothing but bacon.

Knowing there would be more to the story, I offered, "Well, that sounded easy." The SJA told me "If only it had been that reason." According to him, that sub had been traveling submerged in the depths of the Irish sea, confined to a large defined exercise area and in the midst of an Operational Reactor Safeguards Examination (ORSE). This evaluation was conducted during an underway period, typically towards the end of a deployment. The inspectors review all of the ship's records from the date of the previous ORSE while the engineering department takes a written nuclear engineering competency exam. After the review, a battery of intense simulation drills begins and each of the three watch sections stands a single drill watch: one as a casualty assistance team, one as drill monitors for a third watch, with the fourth watch for catching up on sleep amidst all the horns and alarms announcing drills and exercises. This drill period can last up to twenty-four hours.

After the drills, oral interviews test the engineering department's level of knowledge. Additionally, there are monitored evolutions to evaluate a department's ability to perform selected maintenance items. A typical ORSE lasts for three days and the various ship's departments get little, if any, sleep during this grueling exam. The consequences for failure are severe, including firing the ship's Captain and Engineer/Reactor Officer, plus any other standout screw ups, so the Captain relied on all of his officers and sailors to exceed standards. Typically he selects a junior officer to perform the role of "conning," or directing ships operations for him, and serving as "officer of the deck" (OOD). This officer stands a four-hour watch in the Operations compartment control room and carries out the Captain's commands. The OOD may give the conn to a junior officer for training purposes, and when the OOD and the conning officer are not the same person, the OOD retains responsibility for the ship.

The OOD assigned a newly promoted lieutenant junior grade (jg) as conning officer. The duty navigator, an experienced quartermaster, was the enlisted sailor responsible for navigation and always knowing the exact speed and position of this undersea behemoth. These requirements were demanded for missile accuracy if ever a launch was ordered by the National Command Authority. The ship's performance was monitored after each patrol by the Johns Hopkins Applied Physics Laboratory (APL) under government contract. Excellence was expected and everyone knew the cost of failure. The *Greene* was equipped with a hovering system to manage the trim more effectively when firing missiles, and this increased the missile rate of fire from one per minute to four per minute during a nuclear missile launch when minutes counted most.

During patrols, the crews were tested on their ability to launch by random exercises. These exercises always included conducting simulated launches on a no-notice basis. The Joint Chiefs of Staff cared very deeply about that performance, needing the submarines as an effective nuclear deterrent against the Soviet Union, so the pressure on the crew was tremendous. Driving a sub in deep water is only made possible by sonar systems that provide a three-dimensional electronic view of the black world surrounding it.

While an important mission, not every sailor particularly selected for duty in this "silent service" remained as committed as they might have been, once they'd experienced a few 90-day cruises locked in a can with a bunch of smelly guys. That was certainly true of the lieutenant jg with the conn. He'd graduated from the Naval Academy three years earlier, having gone not so much for love of country, but for the excellent electrical and nuclear engineering education he'd received with no student-loan debts. He knew he could snag a job as a civilian contractor for the Navy and start bringing in the big money the day he left service. He was trying to hasten that process by eating his way out, since weight was the other DoD obsession, along with non-missionary sex. All military members were required to maintain a healthy weight as determined by insurance actuarial tables. If you grew beyond the maximum, it was *"Thanks for your service,"* an honorable discharge, and a happy meal.

At the other end of the happiness spectrum lay the Petty Officer First Quartermaster, a sailor who loved the Navy and loved his job. This devotion was reflected by the gold-threaded insignia he wore on his dress uniform, thread that silently, but proudly, attested to over twelve years of good conduct and outstanding performance. The "quartermaster" is in charge of watch navigation and is responsible for the maintenance, correction, and preparation of nautical charts and navigation publications. He is also responsible for navigational instruments, clocks, and the training of ship's lookouts and helmsmen. He performs these duties under the control of the ship's OOD.

On the *Greene,* the quartermaster was a qualified navigation electronics technician (NAV-ET) who was additionally responsible for electronic systems that dealt with navigation, internal communications, atmosphere monitoring, ship's entertainment systems, re-circulatory air systems (ventilation) and remote valve indication or manipulation. It was a big job, a demanding job.

The preceding six hours had been nothing but SCRAM drills, a term derived from old English slang for "leaving quickly." This involves the rapid shutting down of a nuclear reactor, usually by rapid insertion of control rods, either automatically or manually by the reactor operator. Since it was such a very big deal, the crew was largely focused on what was happening in the back of the boat. The OOD, a lieutenant commander, had wandered off to see what was happening and the lieutenant trainee was bored because, as he later admitted, he didn't care at all about any of it and secretly hoped they'd fail.

The quartermaster station had a back-lit chart and the electronic systems would send up a blip of light marking the sub location on the map, while also working as a depth sounder. The quartermaster asked the conn if he could go to the toilet, he having suffered a disagreeable meal a few hours earlier. With permission, he left the compartment. The lieutenant was now responsible for keeping an eye on the sub's position. Fatigued from the constant excitement of drills and bored by his life in the Navy, he wandered about the compartment with his cup of coffee and paying no mind as the *Greene* quietly departed the defined space of the undersea training area, entering an area were seamounts existed.

A seamount is a large underwater mountain, usually conical in shape and rising at least 1,000 m (3,280ft) above the ocean floor. Seamounts are usually isolated and are volcanic in origin. Many are charted, some are not, but when an area is known to contain them, the area of "discolored water" is annotated on the charts.

The quartermaster finished in the toilet and was making his way back to his station when he decided to get a cup of coffee from the thirty-cup pot kept in the sonar room. It was empty so he made a fresh pot. He was just adding the milk to his steaming cup while chatting with another sailor when the collision-jarred *Greene* came to a complete stop. Unprepared sailors went flying as did anything not bolted down. The Captain ordered an emergency main-ballast tank-blow, forcing high-pressure air into its main ballast tanks. The high-pressure air forces water from the tanks, quickly lightening the ship so it can rapidly rise to the surface. The ship popped up in the Irish sea and all hands were ordered topside and told to prepare to abandon ship until the damage-control parties could verify the exact extent of the damage.

The quartermaster returned to his watch station and checked the charts, then raced topside, glanced around at the shore and declared "Yes! This is exactly where the map showed us to be!" Happy that his own calculations were confirmed, he was not then realizing the blame buck was going to stop with him.

The *Greene* had struck the top of an unobserved seamount while the quartermaster was away from his station. If the lieutenant had bothered to check the charts, he'd have noticed the *Greene* departing the exercise area. If the *Greene's* depth had been a few feet higher, she would have missed striking it, and upon his return, the navigator would have noticed the error and suggested the appropriate course corrections. If the coffee pot had contained some coffee he'd have returned to spot the problem, but none of that happened, and the *Greene* suffered a serious crack in its outer hull. Fortunately there was no damage to the pressure hull and the boat was able to return to port.

Submarine accidents are not an unusual occurrence. Subs are routinely involved in collisions and the Navy continues to hate admitting these things happen. On Jan 17, 2017, after 43 years of being classified Top Secret, it was finally revealed that in November 1974 the SSBN *James Madison*, armed with sixteen Poseidon nuclear missiles, was heading out of the US naval base at Holy Loch, thirty miles north-west of Glasgow. Shortly after leaving port, it turned suddenly and was struck by an unidentified Soviet submarine which had been sent to tail it. Both submarines surfaced and the Soviet boat subsequently submerged again to make its way thousands of miles to home port for necessary repairs while the Madison limped back to Holy Loch.

Once the amount of damage became clear, a financial analysis determined it would be cheaper to take the *Greene* out of service two years earlier than scheduled and the political decision was made to make "lemonade out of lemons." This bit of political theater meant they didn't need any publicity from legal proceedings, so the decision was made to relieve the Captain citing a "a loss of confidence in his ability to command." The lieutenant received a punitive Letter of Reprimand effectively ending his career and his resignation was accepted. Not unhappily he went to work for General Dynamics a few weeks after being released from service. The quartermaster went to a Captain's Mast, where in addition to forfeiting one month's salary, he also lost a stripe and had to remove all the gold-threaded insignia on his dress uniforms, and replace it with red-threaded insignia, a massive stain on his reputation.

I'd represented airmen who had broken or destroyed government property worth under $1,000 get hit with some serious jail time, so I learned that if you damage something, make sure it is so big that nobody wants anybody to know anything about it and you'll be just fine.

+++

## Mandatory Briefings

P anama offered a fantastic opportunity to immerse yourself in the local culture and travel to exotic locations and points of interest. So many officials found it necessary to visit Panama, we had a series of set places to show them and a list of first-class restaurants to entertain them.

In 1994, the Deputy Judge Advocate General and Senior Paralegal came to Panama on an inspection tour required by Article 6 of the UCMJ. Congress mandated a visit to every facility with an assigned JAG, wherever they serve around the globe, to see how things were going. In the ordinary business of overreacting, stateside units spend months preparing slides detailing all of the relevant metrics regarding every part of the legal office operation. Every courts-martial, government claim, environmental issue, or operational matter undertaken and completed are documented, quantified, and slapped into a briefing slideshow with particular attention paid to the shade of colors green and red for the easy-to-understand arrows denoting unit performance.

The guests arrive in the morning and the show starts at eight after a thirty minute "getting to know you" session over coffee and Krispy Kreme doughnuts. The lights go down for two hours of "death by powerpoint" with a twenty-minute break, then more slides until lunch at the club. Reconvene at half past one and finish at four. The DJAG would give the troops a Washington brief, then whole affair wrapped up with a potluck before the visitors drove themselves back to the airport.

It was a little different overseas. In England we met our bosses when they arrived on the base and enjoyed hosted drinks in their suite before dinner in a nearby pub. We had our lunch at the officers' club, then, after the briefing, and as a salute to England, the entire office went to a Medieval dinner theater at a nearby castle. In the morning we saw them off with coffee and pastries.

In Panama our guests enjoyed Quarters 11, on Albrook. This three-thousand square foot open-floor-plan hacienda grande had a view of the Bridge of the Americas and a fully stocked bar along with a "mother-in-law" suite for his executive assistant. The visitors came into the base on military air so we could pick them up plane side and, returning to Albrook, treating them to a ride across the bridge, then checking them into their quarters. When settled, the DJAG invited us all to have a welcoming drink with him. He eventually came to regret this practice, as I'd been the project officer and doubled up on the miniature bottles after taking requests from all seven staff attorneys. Generals are given a generous entertainment allowance, and an airline size bottle only cost fifty cents, but we still managed to exceed his daily allowance.

Any welcome dinner was held at Bob's house where he'd arrange a large buffet dinner complimented by a variety of red wines. After dinner, Bob's wife introduced them to Nicaraguan-style rum cake which sat floating on the rum it could no longer hold. This was all concluded over brandy, rich Honduran coffee, and hand-rolled cigars I regularly picked up at the Air Mobility Command (AMC) quonset-hut terminal and gift shop at Soto Cano air base in Honduras.

We knew this "Welcome to Panama" formula was a winner because a few months earlier we'd had a visit from the colonel at Air Combat Command who came to see what we did for a living. The colonel was purportedly a tea-totaler and notorious for being hyper-critical, high maintenance, and easily bored. We had the regular rum cake, and a pseudo cake just for him, at the morning coffee and we made a note of pointing out the distinction and accommodation to him. Bob sat next to him and watched as the colonel accidentally forked Bob's cake, took the bite, then, switched plates with him. At the mid-morning break, our visiter just went straight for the loaded cake.

We got him kitted out in a flight suit with his name on it and took him on a two-hour helicopter patrol across the length of the Canal. All this attention, plus a big dinner later, resulted in his glowing closing remarks in which he declared this his best trip ever. I'd known we do just fine when he asked me to bring him a big glass of bourbon.

For the DJAG, our morning briefing was held over breakfast at the club, one served on china by waiters, with a break at half past ten for coffee and another rum-soaked cake. To the relief of all concerned, there were few questions from the Deputy. He already knew things were fine from the pre-briefing he received before he even got on the plane. A slide show worked to let him see the talent in the field while each briefer stood to present. The formal portion of the visit finished at half past eleven, so it was off to lunch on the officers' club veranda at Rodman Naval Station because of an amazing view of the Canal and Bridge of the Americas. The Navy requires wide spaces to maneuver their vessels. This wide-open scene of the Bridge of the Americas, framed by palm trees swaying in the breeze, made the luncheon a relaxed affair and gave the DJAG a chance to get to know some of the attorneys.

Everyone later changed to civvies for the upcoming schedule of events which included an installation tour and visit to the Mira Flores control center for the Panama Canal. This was always included because it gave every important visitor, or anybody hanging around who wanted to do it, an opportunity to operate the mechanism to close or open one of the locks that let a ship in or out. It made a great, "There I was" photo for the den. Before dinner, it was back to Quarters 11 for cocktails and another opportunity to break the general's daily hospitality allowance, and soon we would be heading to the city for dinner.

Dining was often a memorable adventure in Panama. The nights are usually balmy with extravagant jungle greenery, a variety of architectural styles, and menus from any cuisine you could imagine. One Friday night, Laurie and I went with another couple to have a drink at one of the large hotels in the city center. As we walked along a popular tourist street we passed a basement joint with "The Bunker Bar"on a hand-painted sign. This had once been a favorite venue of soldiers stationed at nearby Forts Clayton and Amador. It sported rope netting covering the front windows and doorway, a late 1989 design modification after some pro-Noriega supporter threw a hand grenade inside it.

A few yards ahead we came upon a policeman engaged with a crowd of about a dozen unruly young people. Panamanian law prohibits insulting policemen but cries of "Gordo" and "Oy chuleta" were shouted. Calling a fat man a gourd, or referring to him as a pork chop, was not the way to make friends among the national constabulary. Having had clearly enough of the upbraiding, and benefiting from lax rules, and, with few limitations on the use of deadly force, the hefty cop put his hand on the revolver's butt and cautioned the students. At this point, our wives decided it might be smart to hurry inside for a drink at the Holiday Inn less than fifty yards away. As Gordo pulled the pistol both women exercised their options to rush up the driveway and vanished into the hotel lobby.

Ivan was the hospital administrator, but at this point, more importantly, a black man from inner city St. Louis who'd seen these situations play out too many times before. He began backing up towards the driveway and tugging on my sleeve. I wanted to stay. I knew those kids weren't armed or they'd have shown their heat by now, and besides, if the cop was going to shoot anybody, it wouldn't be us.

The crowd became more agitated and angrier as they disparaged the policeman; some were shouting horrible things, including that his mother had sex with dogs. At that, the cop had had enough; he pointed his pistol in the air and fired a shot. Despite this unambiguous warning, and accompanied by his verbal commands to leave, a slender young man wearing oversize glasses and hair in loopy brown ringlets, took two steps forward while yelling "¿Qué vas a hacer? ¿Dispararme?" (What are you going to do? Shoot me?) The policeman mulled that challenge over for a nanosecond while I wondered if we should have left with our wives. How far could this escalate? Decision made, the policeman slowly lowered his weapon until it was lined up correctly, then pulled the trigger and shot the poodle-headed agitator in the left thigh. The kid went down sideways like he'd slipped on some oil, but it wasn't oil, it was his blood pouring onto the street. Ivan now insisted we leave and I agreed, hearing whistles blowing as cops came running into the area.

We talked about it over drinks to let our wives know what they'd missed. When we came out an hour later the street had been hosed down and it was like the earlier event had never happened.   +++

---

# Where's A Good Place To Eat In This Town?

**D**inner tonight with our visiting general was scheduled at El Cortijó, one of the finest restaurants in all of Panama and rated "Two AK-47s" on the legal office restaurant guide. The weapon's rating had nothing to do with the quality of the restaurant's food, which was uniformly excellent, always cooked to perfection and served with a great flourish by tuxedoed waiters gliding through the large dining room. Instead, it was about the establishment's security.

The large dining room's pastel pink walls provided a muted background for the wall-length tapestries from Spain that covered them, depicting scenes of centuries long past. For private parties there were three smaller rooms. It wasn't unusual to see American military bodyguards standing outside a door as leaders in the war on narcotics dined inside and the next night tall Peruvians in ill-fitting suits showing bulges where guns awaited use, stood watch as cartel people met for dinner.

The restaurant at that time had enjoyed a "one-shotgun rating" meaning the doorman carried a sawed-off double barreled shotgun as a deterrent against would be robbers. Now considered "quaint" in modern day Panama City, management hadn't redesigned security as the criminal situation was changing. The restaurant was a neutral location and had always been a place where all were welcome. They'd never heard of the "Strip and Git" bandits, a four-man robbery crew that was terrorizing the good citizens and cash rich customers of Panama City. Those bandits would disarm the guard at a high-end establishment and take over the building while demanding the customer's valuables. To make sure nobody was hiding anything they'd also have everybody strip down to their skivvies. As a result of this it became routine for Laurie to leave her engagement ring at home, and put on the faux Rolex watch I'd bought for ten bucks in Saudi. We also always wore clean underwear when going out on the town, just in case.

On the night the shotgun ratings changed, the Strip & Gits hit El Cortijó, easily overpowered the doorman and got the drop on the Peruvians standing outside a private room. They corralled all of the bartenders, waiters, and kitchen help into the main dining room. Two of them worked the collection of goods while the other two went into the small dining room. The host, a patrón (employer) from Cartagena, Colombia, was a man not easily ruffled. He saw them as "malparido" or badly born. As the two pistoleros scanned the room, their eyes settled on the old man. He looked back at them through dark eyes and asked, "Plomo o plata?" (Lead or silver) and adding "¿Sabes quién soy?" (Do you know who I am?)

The robber drew up and looked at the fastidiously groomed man sitting at the head of the table. "Silver or lead" was the Colombian way to make someone an offer he couldn't refuse. The bandito jefe looked hard at the dapper gentleman and wondered if he should know him. He saw a man in his early fifties and wearing a very expensive looking Rolex, plus other pieces of expensive gold jewelry. His girlfriends were likewise dripping heavy metal, as were some of the other men now all looking anxiously at their jefe.

The bandit was twenty years old and had only recently formed this gang. An orphan, he'd hit the streets when he was just seven and was now at the top of his game. During this spree he'd knocked off rooms full of politicians, military officers, and lots and lots of rich people; they all said the same thing, "Do you know who I am?" The young Bandido didn't ever know and didn't ever care; all he saw that night was an old man who thought he was the shit. It was time to go to work. He sneered at the old man saying, "Si,culo, ¡Ahora quítate toda esa ropa!" The man he had just called an asshole nodded, and the entire party began to strip.

The bandit wasn't smart and he had a limited attention span. He had been unable to take the meaning of the way the old man responded to him. The narco hadn't said, "Plata o plombo." (Silver or lead) instead the old man had asked him the opposite, "Plombo o plata?" meaning, "You threaten me with lead while robbing me?"

The bandits collected their best haul to date, then fled into the night and back to their lair in the barrio. Embarrassed and worried about a bad review, management immediately retained the services of two AK-47 toting off-duty members of the National SWAT team and business went back to normal.

Two weeks later I was having coffee in a cafe along Via Argentina, an avenue loaded with outdoor cafes, and I saw the back page of the Saturday edition of La Prensa, a popular national daily. There were so many murders in Panama that photos of unidentified corpses were routinely posted in the quest to identify the remains. This time was different because there were four corpses laid out together with card board signs near where their genitalia had once been, and saying in Spanish, "We were the Strip and Git Bandits."

+++

## Where Do You Want To Go Next?

Because he was a brigadier general, when heading off base the security folks insisted we use government transportation driven by sober airmen, and somber personal protection officers (PPOs), each carrying a fanny pack hiding a small MAC-10 compact .45 caliber machine pistol with folding stock. These PPOs would check the area; once cleared, they would stand outside the restaurant throughout the meal, with one inside, guarding our private dining room. This left us with no responsibilities, so we could fully enjoy ourselves. As we began to flow into the room, Laurie and I made our way to the rear since I was not assigned to the JAG office and was considered an independent. This was Bob's show and an opportunity to let new people meet the brass.

Tables were pushed together forming a square with the center open. Bob saw me pulling out a chair for Laurie and he waved us up. He directed us to a seat where we'd be ten feet across from the general and his executive officer. I started to protest but he told me "Junior, Pete remembered you from England and thinks you're funny as hell, so make 'em laugh."

I'd met Pete, now a colonel, when he was a lieutenant colonel and the SJA at another base in England where I'd visited as an IO on a matter. We'd cemented our friendship during a week-long course and networking opportunity in Garmisch-Parkenkirchen, in German Bavaria. After class we all headed to the different bars in town and usually closed them. It didn't hurt that this was also when Karaoke was the rage and everybody had blackmail photos of drunken comrades singing off key with one eye half closed.

The dinner progressed and, as the courses were changed, the general made inquiries to learn about each attorney's ambitions. This was a great opportunity to lay out your career path and work an assignment with the one guy who could absolutely make your dreams come true. I had given some thought to another overseas assignment because they were the real deal. I was in the operational world and an operational lawyer who enjoyed being in the field on real world assignments. I couldn't imagine what possible attraction could lure me to the Pentagon, an assignment long considered a "must do" part of career progression. Once inside the Emerald City that was the Military District of Washington, politics dominated; it was the survival of the fittest to move up the chain, scratching and clawing as needed to get to the top.

I didn't want that. After I had returned to active duty, and midway through our seven-week officer orientation school, we were flown from Maxwell AFB, in Montgomery, Alabama, to DC for a military version of "rushing" prospective associates. The glamour not only wowed the new guys, but it gave senior leadership a chance to look over the talent. Our commander regaled us with his ability to have whistled up a McDonnell-Douglas VC-9 from the Special Air Mission folks at Andrews and directed it flown into Maxwell and haul us to a four-day "Grip and Grin" weekend in DC. Salesman that he was, he made it sound like he'd pulled powerful strings to provide us this executive transport. By this he also implied that, as JAGs, we'd be traveling first-class-deluxe like this routinely.

What we didn't know was the plane also flew the AF band to their myriad engagements and the only reason we got a ride was because one of those engagements was in the local area. Otherwise we'd have been sitting sideways in the nylon strapping web seats in a C-130 Hercules. The executive jet, with all first class leather seats, would be flying us back to Maxwell only because it had to pick up the band on Sunday night.

Booked into a nice hotel in Crystal City, we were to meet the next morning in the lobby for breakfast prior to a tour of the Pentagon. As we were dismissed that evening, one of our group, Howard, an attorney with no prior military experience, asked what to wear the next morning. The lieutenant colonel giving the briefing said, "Howard, wear anything you like, just be comfortable." Most might have interpreted that as a uniform choice between wearing a tie or going open collar. The colonel was visibly surprised, if not stunned, when Howard presented himself for breakfast the next morning wearing his hotel bathrobe and slippers, but not any more stunned than Howard would be when he was encouraged to return to civilian life after just shy of six months.

Once we reached the Pentagon, our military tour directors wandered us through the different offices where today it was the job of those senior officers to impress us new folks with the important work they did. They finished the tour off with heavy hors d'oeuvres and happy-hour prices at the club. I saw the same things there that I'd seen at a party at our law school dean's house just a year earlier: a lot of guys working the room. The highlight was when a new hire named Todd was in a group talking with a two-star general.

About the time Todd pulled a Swedish meatball off a toothpick and began to chew it, someone told a joke. Todd could't help laughing and tried to cover his mouth, but a fair-sized speck got by him, landing on the general's right shoulder board and in the gap between those shining silver stars. The general didn't see it as he was looking at the guy who told the joke. Quick as a mongoose, Todd reached up with his left hand, angled it high and outside then dove in to flick the bit right off with such deftness the general never noticed. After the perfect flick, Todd continued the moving arc of his hand to stroke the back of his head while smiling at me. I admired his move and knew I could never compete with that. Not many could.

Now, a few years in, I still had no desire to take any assignment in the District because I'd seen too many guys who got sucked into the vortex. I'd pass through on occasion when sent back there for a course and, while there, visited old colleagues. I'd listen to their horror stories of two-hour commutes, houses costing far more than they could ever afford, high taxes, and inclement weather. In my evenings, I could go to museums or walk around the Mall and enjoy the sights while my colleagues were driving home, and then I went to restaurants while they went to sleep. I just didn't see the benefits of an assignment there when it was so much better as a tourist.

Since the general's offer, I'd given a lot of thought to taking an assignment in Asia, a part of the world I'd never seen. I could have been a short-notice volunteer for Korea, but Laurie informed me of her desire to return to the valley I'd taken her from six years before. This was where she and our daughters could reconnect with her family and friends. My direction from her was to secure an assignment to Mountain Home, Idaho, known as *"The airbase time forgot."*

Built as a B-24 training base during WWII, it closed three years later. It was re-opened and briefly enjoyed a build up in 1950, thanks to the Korean War, and then lay forgotten by the budget people. I knew this because it was also the assignment that first brought me to the Gem State in 1974. The base seemed old then, the infrastructure evidenced a quarter century of subsistence-only maintenance, and with no new missions on the horizon. I'd popped in for my commissioning physical and didn't note any great improvements. As an additional unhappy sales point, it was located fifty miles east of Boise, Idaho.

The room had just hit a silent moment when Pete asked, "So, Mike, any thoughts on what assignment you'd like next?" He'd caught me off guard and I'd forgotten the guy sitting next to him was the Deputy JAG. I was focused on Pete and didn't see the general lift a glass of whiskey to his lips as I said, "I'd like to work the assignments branch at JAX so I can send people I don't even know to places I can't even spell."

The DJAG shot the liquor back out his nose, snorting and coughing and I saw my career arc moving in the wrong direction. Then he started laughing and coughing while wiping some tears from his eyes. He waved a hand at me and said, "Name it."

I looked at my wife, and asked for the job.

For the second time in my career I was assigned to that base time forgot, the 366th Wing at Mountain Home AFB, Idaho.

+++

# CHAPTER THREE

## Rub My Belly Like A Puppy

The US Navy liked to brag that they could bring a carrier group to anywhere in the world within 72 hours. The planners at Air Force staff levels saw that claim as a direct threat to funding and declared they could have planes flying and fighting anywhere in the world within 48 hours. It was to that end that the "composite wing" at Mountain Home, consisting of F-15 and F-16 fighters, as well as some B-1 bombers and a KC-135 refueling aircraft, was cobbled together and served to demonstrate the viability and utility of such an organization.

An organization like that needed a special kind of JAG, one who understood the nature of operational work in a foreign environment and, given my overseas service, I was named the Chief of Military Justice, with additional duties as the "operations law" attorney. This meant I was consigned to deploy anytime the composite wing deployed. Before any of that could happen, I realized I had landed in the uncomfortable position of working for a "bad bastard" in the form of a USAFA grad and failed pilot candidate turned lawyer, who was the Staff Judge Advocate for the wing.

It is a well established rule that officers could not fraternize, or engage on an informal basis, with enlisted personnel in their charge. The rule acknowledged that personal friendships could interfere with an officer's ability to carry out any mission. The analogy frequently given is that, should a dangerous mission come up, and a friend was fully qualified as most capable of completing that assignment, one might be tempted to pass it off to another, less qualified person in order to protect the favored airman. Fraternization can also lead to undue familiarity and a reluctance to follow orders, but more seriously, it could also lead to sexual encounters, as in the case of Panama's fearful ADC Bob, where an enlisted airman might feel compelled to submit to a sexual relationship that one might ordinarily not have, but for the rank and authority of the superior officer.

This SJA was physically intimidating. A weight lifter, he looked like a Russian olympian, barrel-chested, squat and powerful. He had the self-confidence and arrogance that comes from expertly gaming the promotion system and, as his career progressed, he took every educational opportunity that came along. He even snagged a highly coveted all-expense-paid one-year-assignment to obtain a masters-at-law in constitutional law from a prestigious university. Despite never finishing the course work, and failing to secure the degree, he deftly maneuvered the byzantine labyrinth that was the JAG assignments system. After finally obtaining enough seniority, paper qualifications and checking all the right boxes, he was given control of a legal office with seven attorneys, twelve paralegals, and five civilians.

Possessing zero people skills, coupled with his coming from the Academy, an educational system that encouraged bullying behavior, this SJA rapidly beat his staff down by unceasing criticism of any work product that came across his desk. If the claims shop processed all matters within the allocated time standards, he'd tell them they could do better and scold that the air force standards "were just the acceptable minimums." He'd warn them he expected "better performance" the next month. This had the effect of demoralizing the office and put all the airmen assigned, both officer and enlisted, in fear for their careers, since he was also famous for writing unflattering performance reports. He'd already killed one NCO's career by remarking on his evaluation "continue to supervise," effectively telling the promotion world that the airman had climbed the ladder as high as he could.

Naturally people wanted to avoid getting on his bad side, and when a young and very attractive female staff sergeant was assigned to process the administrative discharge packages, he simply couldn't contain himself. He began to flirt openly with her, visiting her office and inviting her to stay in his office after meetings concluded to have coffee. A hard-ass, his demeanor softened noticeably whenever she was around him. Unbeknownst to the rest of the office, he'd talked her into beginning a secret affair, which was well underway when I reported for my assignment.

I sensed something was wrong even before I arrived. I'd called up from Panama and spoken with his deputy, a guy I'd known from my time as a defense counsel in Europe. Brian was a jovial sort, famous for having arranged the karaoke machine during that Bavarian conference, as well as being the life of any party. Yet, when I talked to him, he sounded guarded and even a bit curt.

Now on station, I saw airmen in a state of perpetual anxiety. If an exercise was scheduled to kick off at midnight, he'd call the staff a few hours before to wake them up while admonishing them that the exercise would kick off in several hours and they'd best be on time for the recall, alert and ready to go. When a riot control exercise was scheduled, he asked about what order should be given to disperse the rioters. I shared my experience from my early enlisted days, when the security forces practiced riot control, that the usual routine was to give the crowd an order to disperse, cite the authority for the order, then give the crowd a set time to clear the area before action would be taken against them. Not satisfied with my answer based upon prior training and experience, he detailed a young attorney to stay late and call Air Force bases around the globe to see if there was a better answer. When I came in the next morning, the sad and exhausted young lawyer told me the tale and there wasn't a better answer to be found.

If an attorney was preparing for a courts-martial, this SJA would insist on hearing the closing argument and proceed to shred it, with no aim other than to increase fear. This anxiety manifested itself in several ways. One lawyer began to lose his hair, another was diagnosed with irritable bowel syndrome, and a paralegal developed high blood pressure.

With no oversight from the Wing Commander, or Numbered Air Force SJA, there was no impetus for the SJA to improve his managerial style. By Christmas time, I was so tired of his bullying behavior and maltreatment of subordinates, I gave serious thought to punching out and beginning a civilian practice. I shared this with that young staff sergeant when she came in to brief me on the status of that month's discharge actions. She saw I wasn't as gregarious as I normally was and asked me what was wrong.

The holidays were upon us and in the previous six years, every legal office I'd ever worked in or visited, went to a "reduced manning" status with a different attorney and paralegal manning the office each day so everyone could enjoy some rare down-time with families. As the ADC all I had to do was check the answering machine each afternoon at three. This would not be the case here. The SJA wasn't married and had no family in the area, so he had no sympathy or concern for the welfare of his staff's families. As a result, the office would be fully manned, even though the rest of the wing was on reduced manning and wars never begin over Christmas. Two new attorneys had just arrived; when they were introduced to the SJA, he made inquiries as to their marital status. One lawyer had just enjoyed the birth of his fourth child and was looking forward to the holidays. The SJA shot down any ideas he had by brusquely telling him during this first meeting, "Don't get too attached to the kid, we have a deployment mission and you won't be seeing much of him."

I passed the holiday season with a sense of dread and foreboding. Laurie noticed the change in my personality and urged me to just get out, saying more than once, "Why would you work for a company that values assholes over professionals?" I had no answer for her other than it was a life I knew and had always previously enjoyed. Her viewing the Air Force as a "company" concerned me. She'd lived in England and Panama. She'd lived in some tight-knit military communities. She'd always come for drinks on Friday nights, made friends and traveled with other wives on trips in Europe. Military people were each other's family; and, everyone knew that every other soldier, sailor, airman or marine, always had each other's back. They were the people you shared special memories of good times and dire circumstances with. The transient nature of the profession, always moving, coupled with the gloom of being away from family, and our unique American culture, all led to that bonding. In Europe all those war games and exercises were a constant reminder of some stark realities, and that adding to the intensity of the connection. Military communities always had plenty of celebrations. Laurie received her own and also attended many baby showers. This was in addition to the never-ending, birthday, promotion, retirement, block parties, shared holiday dinners, and sadly, more than a few funerals.

When Maggie was born, my boss, Dan and his wife, Sue, were right there, along with Maggie's de-facto Godmother, Jeri. Later, when Sue got sick and couldn't go to a fancy dinner at a snobby British hunting club, Dan invited Laurie, but she also passed because Maggie was running a fever. Moving from a safe date, Dan's next best choice, one fraught with professional peril, was Jeri. She was a subordinate and he ran the risk of being accused of favoritism. The fact that Jeri was the smartest lawyer on staff and could carry on an intelligent conversation, useful qualities the other female staff members lacked. Most impressively, for a little bitty woman, she could hold her own drinking in the bar against all those fighter pilots. While these were valid and legitimate considerations, he knew it would be the fact that she was beautiful that would be the genesis of any complaint by any other staff attorneys.

Dan didn't have to ponder this conundrum for very long before realizing she was back in the States attending a course on contract's law. Left with no viable female options, he asked me to be his "date." I was the ADC when I accepted; I wasn't under his supervision, so there could be no claim of favoritism. I accepted, but only after he agreed to get me a wrist corsage instead one for my chest. From moments like those, Laurie knew very well what it was like when working relations were cordial and collegial. She kept on, "You remember when you guys did that skit at the Christmas show? You put those lines on your face so you looked like a ventriloquist's dummy and sat on Dan's lap? It was a scream!" Finishing up her tirade against my bully boss, she heaped her scorn by comparing his approach to leadership with Dan's. "How about when Dan held the bus for you when your trial was running late and we had to get to that medieval dinner theater? You think this jerk would ever do that for anybody?" She looked at me and made her position clear, "You've got options, you don't have to put up with this crap."

A part of me knew I didn't have to put up with that crap, and another part remembered the advice my late brother-in-law, Ted, had given me two decades earlier, "Never let the bastards win." I also remembered all the leadership training I'd had in the Army reserves while going to law school. I learned every good leader puts the troop's morale and welfare ahead of his or her own, and leadership is about staying the course and not quitting. I knew I couldn't quit, but I just didn't know what I was going to do.

Karma took care of this problem on the first workday Monday after New Years. I'd just returned from lunch when several OSI agents, including the detachment commander, a major, walked rapidly past my office, heading towards the SJA's office. As the Chief of Military Justice, I knew their habit was to come to me with any matters under investigation, so this breach of protocol gave me pause. I followed them down the hallway to let them know he wasn't in, his habit being to leave for the gym at half past eleven and not return until well after one in the afternoon.

The agents stopped at the door and, trying the doorknob to the vacant office, discovered it was locked. The commander briefly cursed that fact, turned to me as I walked up, asking, "You got a key?" He snapped his fingers adding, "We need to get in there right now!" I told him to hold up a moment and asked what they wanted inside the vacant office. Visibly annoyed, he opened his notebook, held up a piece of paper he said was a search authorization for the SJA's office, returned it to his notebook, closed the cover; again holding out his hand for a key. Knowing this was something big, I told him I'd have to see that authority and he reluctantly handed it over. The authorization allowed the OSI to search the office for any evidence of sexual activity and any papers evidencing an illicit sexual relationship between the SJA and this female staff sergeant. I could barely contain my excitement thinking, "Could this possibly be the end of our nightmare?" I reached into my pocket for the master office key and offered "You guys need any coffee?" Realizing I wasn't intimidated by the SJA, they all relaxed as they walked into the office, breaking out the UV lights and additional forensic gear while other agents began pulling open drawers in his desk.

What none of us knew was that over the holidays this staff sergeant had made a routine appointment with her gynecologist and, while waiting to be called, struck up a waiting-room conversation with a young lieutenant, an Academy grad on her first assignment. The staff sergeant noticed the small bump, and, in congratulating her, learned the lieutenant was a few months pregnant. She excitedly shared that having this baby would spur her boyfriend, the SJA, to man up and finally marry her. She was also excited because being pregnant gave her a reason to wear a beautiful new dress she'd bought, rather than her mess dress which no longer fit, to the base New Year's Eve party.

Processing this discovery of her relationship as actually being one of "side-girl," the staff sergeant remained calm. The next time she saw her boyfriend, on the last afternoon of the year, and while he was entreating her to "rub his belly like a puppy," she broached the subject of marriage. He smiled and told her wanted to be married to her in the worst way, but she had to wait a year and a half until he could put in his papers and retire at half-pay with all the benefits. He assured her that once free from the prohibition against such relationships, he would make an honest woman of her. He explained this was also the reason he couldn't take her as his date to the New Year's Eve party being held at the Officer's Club, she not being an officer.

Sadly, he didn't know she knew about the other woman, or he might have spun a better lie. He didn't comprehend the anger that arose from her humiliation at being treated so casually and used as a living sex toy. Knowing she was competing with the pregnant lieutenant sparked an anger that only grew as she cried away the lonely minutes to midnight on that last evening of the year. On the first Wednesday of the new year, she walked into the OSI offices and told her tale.

A complaint against a sitting SJA was a big matter and one that meant the OSI couldn't come to me for advice on the matter, so they consulted with the SJA at 12th Air Force located in Arizona. The allegations were presented in a report and the three-star general commanding Twelfth authorized the search of the SJA's office. That search resulted in a considerable amount of forensic evidence of office trysts, forever rendering his couch and conference table, despite professional cleaning, as "never looked at the same way again."

The SJA was relieved of duty, temporarily labeled a "special assistant to the wing commander" and sent off to hand count grapes at the commissary while he awaited his fate. Brian got the chop as well, under the theory that as the deputy he "knew, or should have known," about the illicit affair, which labelled him complicit and causing the Wing Commander to lose all confidence in him. I was appointed the SJA on an interim basis while a temporary replacement could be identified to hold down the fort until a permanent replacement could be found. Meanwhile an IO was flown in from Arizona to conduct the investigation which resulted in a substantiation of the charges. A few months later, a general courts martial was convened with officers senior to the SJA flown in TDY from different bases within 12th Air Force to serve as the jury.

What I didn't know, or fully appreciate, at that point in my career, was that the Academy is nothing if not loyal to its own. Twelfth Air Force sent a major as a temp while the replacement decision was pondered at the highest levels. A few months later the replacement arrived, another USAFA grad. On a fast track, he'd served as a military aide to a Congressman and needed this assignment in the field as a "touch and go," staying long enough to get a great performance report to become eligible for a better job. To facilitate his re-assignment after this hardship tour at the base time forgot, he made a "drug deal." This was shorthand for a secret agreement, with a former USAFA classmate in Arizona, who worked it with another USAFA classmate in the assignments section at the Pentagon.

The accused would be allowed to plead *not* guilty *and* have a jury trial. If convicted, the agreement limited the approved punishment to not more than one month confinement, but would allow a dismissal if so ordered. It also allowed an appeal of the sentence.

There was nothing unusual with pre-trial agreements; they were a matter of routine and usually given in return for an accused waiving the right to trial (which saved the government time and money) and forfeiting any rights to appeal. But *that* wasn't the deal in this case. The disgraced SJA would go to trial and hope for an acquittal, knowing full well any penalties would be limited. He'd been given a major advantage and was in a no-lose situation.

The time came and it was the word of this staff sergeant against a career poster-boy who shamelessly paraded his new lieutenant wife on the stand where she tearfully shared the sad tale of how their son had been born with a heart condition. She pleaded that to convict his father would mean the child would no longer receive the medical benefits he needed. This shallow contention was later rebutted when the prosecution (also from out of town) brought in a witness from the personnel office who testified that the SJA, prior to getting married, had paid a visit to his office asking if there was any other way he could get the kid listed as his dependent without having to marry the mother.

It took the panel less than an hour to convict him on the charges of fraternization and conduct unbecoming an officer. After a short recess the sentencing phase of the trial began. In this portion the accused is entitled to call witnesses on his behalf who could testify to any previous good character and offer any other reasons to show mercy or at least a reduced sentence for his transgressions. At this time, the prosecution is also allowed to present matters in aggravation to get the maximum punishment.

Although this man was guilty of maltreatment of subordinates, the staff was still so cowed, and so afraid of his potential acquittal, and the possibility of his return as an SJA on a future assignment, that none would give throat to the abuses they'd routinely suffered in the two years prior to the trial. That same fear made them decline to testify at the sentencing, all claiming they hadn't really seen anything.

I'd seen and heard plenty and was happy to get on the stand and provide "impact" testimony about how his behavior had affected the office in terms of morale and unit cohesion. I'd testified in a number of trials as a civilian police officer and knew full well the value of speaking directly to the jury. I walked them through the atmosphere I discovered when I arrived, the pervasive nature of the hectoring and bullying and told them how his behavior had reduced mission readiness. I told them how he trumpeted words like "integrity" and "honor" and acted with neither.

I shared how he was a rigid disciplinarian and described one incident. A lieutenant at the supply squadron was a "banked" pilot. There weren't always enough slots to put every qualified pilot into an operational aircraft. The AF had spent a lot of money on training him that far, so they put their investment aside and let the pilot gain some practical experience in another career field before moving into the cockpit full time.

Meanwhile, the banked aviator had engaged in a relationship with a young enlisted woman, and the matter become public knowledge when she became pregnant. She was allowed to separate and became a civilian; once relieved from the prohibition against fraternization, they married. The SJA pressed for a court-martial; but the squadron commander, remembering what it was like when he was an undergrad in Ohio, declined to follow that counsel. He opted for a letter of reprimand, chewing out the young aviator but not including it in his permanent record. The airman was allowed to take his assignment, and the couple moved to Florida. Not satisfied with that outcome, the SJA had directed me to call the gaining unit to see if they were aware of this matter. I declined and told him the fellow was off our patch and not under our chain of command. His face got red and tight as he grew angry, more at my resistance to his suggestion than concern for the future pilot. Without any justification to order me to call, he simply stomped off.

I also told those officers that he was a chronic bully and seemed to be one of those guys who liked hiding in the dark while directing the spotlight of justice on everybody else.

The panel deliberated for a little over an hour before announcing a sentence of six months confinement, a massive fine, forfeiture of all pay and allowances, and dismissal from service. It was at that time the judge informed the panel, the prosecution, and the gallery full of every member of our legal office, of the secret agreement limiting his jail time to one month's confinement. We all then watched as the disgraced former JAG was led from the courtroom in handcuffs and sent to the jail until he could be transferred to Ft. Leavenworth in Kansas. According to the prison guards they'd had convicts from every Air Force Specialty Code (AFSC) or job title, except a 51J4, SJA, and now their board was completely blacked out like a pathetic bingo card.

After talking to some of the airmen who were incensed about the sweetheart deal he'd gotten, I went outside and headed to my car. As I unlocked the door, one of the officers who'd served on the jury came up and asked if he could talk to me, now that the trial was over. He had wondered if there were other things that hadn't made it into the charging documents. I spent a few minutes going over the litany of abuses, all of which were outside the statute of limitations. This included credible information the OSI obtained that, while this convict had once been assigned to a remote base in Alaska, he'd been notorious for having sex with young enlisted women by using his rank and position to get it. I also filled that pilot in on a discussion I had with a colonel I met at an environmental law conference in Seattle who'd been this criminal's roommate while he was in the same masters at law program a few years earlier. That colonel shared with me that the now disgraced former leader had come home on several occasions bragging about how he'd solicited prostitutes who would submit to "golden showers" allowing him to urinate on them. The colonel, having heard about the scandal, added, "I hope they nail that sick son of a bitch."

All the while the pilot was nodding his head and, when I finished, said, "We all thought there was something more to the story and a couple of us thought six months wasn't enough. Too bad he got that deal."

The convicted officer mounted his appeal which dutifully went up the chain, but it was rejected. The Secretary of the Air Force signed off on his dismissal when he had nineteen years and six months in service.

He lost his pension, and his wife, after she heard the testimony from the personnel office witness, divorced him.

+++

## In A Place As Strange As Cairo

Every other autumn, Bright Star, a joint, and combined, multinational forces exercise is held in Egypt. This valuable exercise demonstrated American support for the Egyptian government. It also brought in a lot of much needed cash and 1995 was one of those years. This was the first time the "composite wing" would deploy to fully demonstrate these unique capabilities. As the ops lawyer, I'd be dispatched with the first wave, an advance team, to prepare the way for the main body which would later deploy for the main two-week long exercise. One part of my brief included overseeing "bartering with the natives" as contracts were let for basic goods and services. These negotiations were as varied as each different country.

Earlier that summer we'd loaded up our wing and flew off to a Canadian force air base in northern Alberta, two hundred miles north of Edmonton, to practice the concept. We arrived in mid-August and as we were off-loading our equipment were met by the Canadian customs officer who offered, "You better enjoy it, Yanks; this is our one week of summer." By the time we left two weeks later, there was frost on the ground when we got up in the morning. My sole bartering experience was of buying cigarettes at their small market.

Now it was early autumn and the first contingent of the advance team packed up and made their way east. I hadn't been tasked with going early, so I assumed somebody else got the tasking and I'd go over with the main body in another month. I was disabused of that notion when I was sitting in my office two days after the first wave left and my First Sergeant came wandering in. He often came into my office, comfortable with shooting the breeze because he knew my enlisted background and so relied on my judgment in matters of discipline as balanced and rational. On this day he came in carrying two cups of coffee. I took the proffered coffee and, after some small talk about the weekend, he brought up a new topic. "The deployed commander noticed you weren't on the plane when they arrived in Cairo." I shared that I hadn't been tasked and, if they thought I was, it was news to me. He just smiled and shook his head knowing he'd have to go chew out some admin clerk for leaving me off the deployment roster. He asked me when I thought I'd be able to make the trip and I offered that I had a few things going on at the office but I supposed I could be cut loose and ready to go in about two weeks. His grin got wider as he said, "How does leaving tomorrow sound to you?"

Bags packed, I got on the charter and, after a thirty-hour trip that involved picking up a few airmen and soldiers at other stations, we found ourselves doing a tight "cork-screw" landing (to practice avoiding enemy shoulder-launched missiles) and were immediately engulfed in a severe sand storm. The brown haze roared up as we taxied; when I made my way down the stairs I was greeted by the colonel commanding the operation who handed me a pair of goggles and said, "Glad you could make it, Judge."

Bright Star would have over five-thousand participants and a base camp was being erected. Row upon row of general purpose (GP) large desert tan tents were set up in neat rows running in both directions from the center of the compound. A large concrete slab had been poured and a dining facility capable of serving all those hungry troops was set up on that spot.

Meanwhile, contracting specialists were meeting with local vendors to provide goods and services. This always presented a challenge because bribery, known locally as "backsheesh," was an integral part of the Arab business world and that custom ran into direct conflict with the applicable DoD and other federal regulations. I had learned about it during my time in Riyadh, Saudi Arabia, and when sent on jobs around the Gulf. This bribery was subtle, no bags of cash would pass hands. The bribery would begin with an offer of dinner, usually at some fantastic five-star hotel, or if available, a Michelin-starred restaurant. The night would progress to drinks at a discotheque where a lovely escort would be introduced and, from there, to the hope that the evening would culminate with the award of an inflated contract for goods and services. Those Egyptians knew their business and understood that the young contracting officers, many of them first lieutenants on their first deployment overseas, had the sole authority to sign off on sales of one million dollars or less on just their signature, no reviews required and sales of less than five million were rarely questioned. That was one of the reasons the commander wanted me there sooner rather than later.

One my second night on the ground, while still jet-lagged, I came across our two young contracting officers wearing civilian clothes and heading toward the entry control point where a black Mercedes sedan awaited them. I asked them where they were going and they told me they'd received a dinner invitation to the Mina House, a fancy hotel in Giza near the pyramids, from one of the Egyptians looking to obtain a contract to provide livery services for morale tours. These tours would be offered to the airmen who would soon be arriving. I recognized what would follow and instructed them to wait; I'd change clothes and go with them. The two lieutenants hemmed and hawed, explaining that the invitation was only for them and they didn't think bringing along another person would be a good idea, their host might get upset.

Knowing the host would be more upset at my telling him he'd lost any hopes of the contract, I waited until the two decided that maybe it was better if they put off the dinner and saw the contender during normal business hours. Dejected, they walked back to their tent while I sent off a message to their commander asking that another, more seasoned, contracting officer be sent over to ride herd on them; my only goal being to prevent Uncle Sam from being taken for any more than was absolutely necessary to accomplish this mission.

+++

# The Free Camel Ride

The 13th Amendment to the US constitution prohibits slavery, but is inapplicable to troops on active duty. Twelve to fourteen-hour days were the norm. Lazy weekends spent watching football and drinking beer were just a hazy memory. The Air Force was not completely heartless; even the hardest charging boss knew that troops needed time off every seven days to recharge their batteries. This largess had nothing to do with compassion or sympathy; it had to do with maintaining, or improving, performance. The Services Squadron did its best to help the troops pass the time between work cycles. They shipped an entire gymnasium full of weights and fitness machines to compliment the library, education office, and outdoor movie theater they had built erected on the fortified concrete wall of an abandoned aircraft parking revetment.

Despite all those "comforts of home," leadership also knew that, with the Egyptian air base being so close to the pyramids, it would be insane not to offer the troops a chance to visit one. Vendors were selected after a competitive bidding process, and thanks to no discernible legal issues arising, I was pressed into service as the morale officer and quality assurance person. My job was to make sure the USAF got complete performance on the contract from the vendor, while also trying to keep the troops from being too badly hustled by those Egyptian entrepreneurs who would swarm the bus at every stop, hoping to sell the Americans a few trinkets.

Every other day, three buses holding one hundred-twenty first-time visiting airmen would depart from the airbase to visit the pyramids, rug factories, perfume shops, and the Khan el-Khalili, the giant bazaar — a collection of hundreds of small shops all located under one roof and covering several acres of land.

It's hard for a first-time visitor to understand the "hustle" being thrust upon them by local salesmen at any given moment. More than once, I had to calm a situation where an airman discovered he not only wasn't getting a genuine item of Egyptian antiquity as claimed, but was also paying way too much for the privilege of buying a "sacred scarab beetle" that was actually made in China.

It was mid-day when we arrived at one of the Seven Wonders of the World, the Great Pyramid at Cheops, the largest of the three pyramids in the Giza pyramid complex. The Great Pyramid was closed that day, but one of the others was taking visitors. My group was composed of a number of Chicago police officers fulfilling their Army reserve military commitments as part of a logistical support unit attached to our base and this was their big day out. They entered the pyramid, and because the ancient Egyptians were much shorter than people 2,500 years later, each and every adult had to bend over while walking up an incline to avoid bumping heads on the low stone ceilings while making their way to the ancient burial chamber.

Located in the center of the pyramid was the vault where the mummy's remains were held. What we didn't know was any interesting items of antiquity had long ago been brought to the museum in Cairo. What we did learn was the importance of spacing while ascending. One guardsman on point was behind a group of German tourists and let out a scream when the gentleman immediately in front of him passed gas not one foot from his face.

We entered the burial chamber and discovered that any mummified remains had been removed, leaving a bare altar. In their place sat a deeply tanned, and eerily mummy-looking-woman, named Carol, on her two-week vacation from sorting mail at the post office in Sedona, Arizona. Sitting in a lotus position; with thumb and index finger touching and pointing upward, Carol offered how she'd come to Egypt a week earlier and was satisfying a long-held desire to meditate inside a pyramid. She came here each morning, bribing the harees (guard) to let her in early to secure her space on the altar. All this was in the hope of either reaching a higher consciousness, or talking directly to the aliens.

From our brief discussion, it was never made quite clear to me, which was okay. After a few moments of looking around the empty burial vault to give the German tourists some lead time, we walked back into the sunlight. There was a quarter hour break to take souvenir photos, and mill about, until the busses returned to haul us off. Our next stop would be where the Sphinx had been also been patiently waiting for us these many thousands of years. This would also allow the airmen a chance to eat some "American food" at the Burger King and KFC which so strangely stood nearby, and just out of the photo line.

An old Egyptian man wearing a dirty white dishdasha, that looked like a worn nightgown and, leading an equally worn-looking camel, approached our group. In broken English he asked who wanted a picture taken while sitting astride the beast. He implored the group to take up his offer saying, "Ride the camel for free! Special friends ride free!" I immediately thought back to a night long ago in old Mexico.

I'd first enlisted in 1971 and was trained as a security policeman. Our academy training was conducted on the west side of Lackland AFB, near San Antonio, Texas, where all USAF basic training took place. After basic, it was just a short bus ride to our new homes. We always had weekend liberty, and one Friday afternoon three of us took off for "Boys Town," a zone of tolerance just 160 miles west, and right outside of Ciudad Acuña, Mexico. Unique in concept, prostitution was legal in this zone and that made it irresistible us.

It was long past eleven when the old man in a serape wandered up, thin white hair poking out from under a sombrero. The peasant ensemble he wore was made more authentic by a thin white linen shirt, worn white pants held up by a rope belt, and open-toed sandals. I couldn't help but notice his hump back as he came up and without introduction asked simply who of us was the most macho.

Tom, the Texan who had brought us to this place, begged off because he was nuzzling the neck of a bright bottle-blonde young woman who'd become rather attracted to him. Our other companion, Danny, was extremely drunk, so by default, I told the old man I was his guy. He smiled and said, "Señor, I will bet you one dollar you cannot hold these two pieces of wood for five-seconds." In the dim light provided by a candle on the table, I saw the dark shapes of two wooden handles each attached to a wire; but, being drunk, I failed to notice those wires were running under the leather serape. I had no idea what his game was, but, like the rube I was, handed over a dollar bill and said, "So what now?" He said, "Please, take this one and hold it tight." I did as he instructed. He then said, "Now please, grab the other one and count to five and if you still hold, you win." Fair enough, I thought, as I put my drink down on the table and grabbed the other handle.

I should say, "I tried" to grab the other one. I'd no sooner grabbed that wooden peg when I was shocked just about senseless, dropping both pegs instantly and falling back onto the padded naugahyde seat. The old man was wheezing with laughter; waving his index finger at me, and turning to the left so I could see his back. He flipped up the serape and I saw the Sears brand Die Hard 12-volt battery, and I knew the "*Forever Battery*" had just kicked my ass. In my defense, the wooden pegs had been painted dark brown so the groove that had been cut to allow the wire to wrap around it wasn't visible in the dim light. My hands had been damp from holding the drink and, once I touched that other peg, I closed the circuit and let the current flow along an uninterrupted path in an instant. He won his dollar fair and square and that cheap lesson taught me to look at every angle before committing to a bar bet.

With that memory in mind, I decided I would just watch for a while. One Chicago cop finally took him up on the offer. The old man, features wizened from decades spent out in the sun, made the camel kneel and the reservist climbed aboard. When the owner uttered a few words, the camel stood and the rider's friends took happy snaps, while making rude and mildly obscene comments. The photo-shoot ended and the rider said he was ready to come down. At that point, the camel owner happily told him, "Five pounds, please." The indignant policeman, shot back, "You said it was free" to which the camel owner replied, "Yes, free to ride, but five pounds to get off."

I heard the Mexican battery man's words and was chuckling because this dilemma brought to mind the business legal maxim touted by my business law professor, Mark Anderson, "A deal's a deal and it's your own damn fault." In the present matter, clearly, this chump on the hump hadn't thought it all the way through. The soldier was also not realizing it was only a buck in US dollars, not much to dicker over since how many times can you get a photo atop a camel? Besides, this was guaranteed to be on the "There I was" wall in his man-cave after he retired.

My amusement turned to astonishment as the now obviously enraged policeman yelled, "Well, fuck that!" He yanked his hat off his head and swatted the camel's rump, generating an immediate and unintended outcome. The camel raced off at a speed that even surprised his handler. The rope lead flew from his hand as the now screaming policeman grabbed the hardwood saddle pom and held on for dear life. He was last seen traveling at high rate of speed as the galloping camel lit out for the open desert and destinations unknown.

I was now faced with not only this dilemma: a vanishing American who would soon no doubt be tossed from that camel and injured. But, I also had a very upset Egyptian screaming "El Ameriki stole my camel! El Ameriki stole my camel!" I didn't know what the penalty was for camel theft in Egypt, but I was pretty certain the last thing we needed was any sort of international incident. While the Egyptian wailed on, I could see the camel growing ever smaller, then losing sight of it when its course turned beyond another pyramid as he and his reluctant jockey made their way into a vast empty region.

On top of all this, the three tour busses had arrived and couldn't be delayed, so I found a capable looking senior NCO. I told her that she was now in charge of the expedition and I'd stay behind to work the current camel issue. The busses were loaded and took off for the next stop on the tour, while I tried to calm the agitated camel owner who was busy telling me quite forcefully that his camel came from a long line of highly prized camels and had won many races. His camel was well known for his beauty and sired many children and was valued more than gold. Happily, within several minutes, two policemen atop their own camels arrived. When the vendor explained his complaint, they immediately tore off in hot pursuit.

The next forty minutes passed slowly, and I was wondering how to frame the report I'd be certain to have to write, when I saw the trio coming back towards us. Upon arrival, the group was met by the once-again hysterical purveyor of camel rides who was lamenting the fact that this Ameriki had not only absconded with his prize breeding camel, but, by Allah, the poor beast was not walking normally and the giant had made it so. This foreigner had so abused his poor camel, which had been raised as a member of his family, that the beast was now lame. He would lose his livelihood, and he and his wife and many children would be forced into the streets, all because the Ameriki did not respect the laws of Egypt and had taken advantage of his good nature.

The Egyptian cops and I knew those histrionics were all an act for the benefit of the rube astride the dromedary, but the rube appeared genuinely concerned because as far as he knew, he might well be on his way to "compare and contrast" the Giza municipal jail with the Metropolitan Correction Center back in the Windy City. This was a prospect that caused the color to drain from his face as he looked down at me for guidance.

I asked the outraged vendor if fifty pounds (ten dollars) would be fair payment for revenue lost while the camel was "free ranging," with a few extra dollars for all of the inconvenience. I knew the old man would be doing very well if he pulled home sixty dollars in any month. This was about the same amount an Egyptologist with a university degree wound command. That ten dollars would go a long way to supplementing the household budget. He knew it as well, so feigning further indignity, but looking to resolve the matter, the camel owner gave a command, the camel knelt before him, in the process dumping the rider onto the sand. A ten-dollar bill passed hands to seal the deal. The Chicago cop's *Lawrence of Arabia* tour was finished, as was his welcome on this particular trip. A cab driver was hired to take him back to the airbase after dropping me off at the Sphinx where the busses were loading for the next stop at the carpet souks.

+++

# The Ugly American

It is a sad fact of life that most Americans aren't able, or choose not, to travel internationally, but perhaps it's just as well because, from my experience, many, when they do hit the road, tend to expect that every convenience or delight they enjoy at home will await them in the country they are visiting. When back home in the USA, first-time international travelers frequently report their astonishment to discover that not everyone speaks or understands English, regardless of how loud it is shouted, and the US dollar is not a universally accepted form of currency.

The main body of the wing, a couple of thousand airmen, arrived a few days in advance of the beginning of the exercise and a part of that contingent was the new SJA who flew in for what would be his second-ever deployment outside of the Pentagon. His present assignment to Idaho was his first. He was tall and thick, a physically impressive man with a solitary passion which was food, but not just any food, only American food. He was also incredibly cheap. When going out to dinner with his family, he'd ask the server if there were free refills. When told there was, he would order water for his wife and three kids and let them sip his drink.

A product of the institutional indignities suffered as a "Doolie" during freshman year at the Academy where he was made to understand that he was in fact lower than whale shit. He was later imbued with a confidence that could only come from spending the succeeding three years being assured he was, in fact, now among the very "best and brightest" America had to offer.

Like so many others from that institution, he fully believed he'd earned whatever perks and bennies he could grab, owing to his particular educational experience. Within two days of his arrival on station, I'd been approached by the two counter-intelligence OSI agents assigned to the deployment who asked me if I could somehow rein him in. His continuous efforts to get free items from prospective vendors was running counter to the established contracting rules, and would soon be considered by them to be solicitation of a bribe. I promised to do my best, but given the "bull in a china shop" approach he'd presented in the short time he'd been assigned to our unit, I thought it unlikely and told them they were certainly free to do their duty as they saw fit. I idly wondered how many more years it would take for the assignments section to dig up a boss who was an ROTC grad with a lick of sense.

A tour was bound for the grand bazaar — the Khan el-Khalili — located near the Grand Mosque in Cairo. This bazaar had been in the same spot for centuries and was a collection of hundreds of small shops (souks), each selling a vast assortment of foods, clothing, baubles, bronze figurines and curios, all in the glow of colorful lights. My younger daughter had asked me to find a "golden" horse to bring home to her as a gift so I began my search of the various souks. Moving deeper and deeper into the khan, I noticed the ground went from pavement, to cobblestone, and finally to hard packed dirt. The new guy tagged along with me and, as we went deeper and deeper into that rabbit warren, his apprehension grew and he expressed his concerns for our personal safety. As his fear became more animated, I finally had to advise him that the odds of a terrorist waiting for us to stumble into his den in the back of a souk were extremely small. He continued to whine and squawk, but I kept on until I finally found a small bronze statue of a horse that I thought would fulfill my daughter's request.

Walking back toward the front of the bazaar, I was treated to a continuing line of questioning, which amounted to the myriad ways one could say, "Are you sure we can get out of here?" Relieved when we could see the entrance and he felt we'd made it out safely, his fear outwardly seemed to dissipate, and his obnoxious self-confidence returned. I paused at a small kiosk with a few tables in front to order an espresso. I asked him if he'd like one but he maintained that he only drank Coca-Cola, which was regrettable because the vendor didn't sell cold beverages. The fellow did sell baklava, a delicious pastry loaded with honey and pistachio nuts, a popular middle eastern dessert, and my wife's favorite. I ordered two pieces and offered him one. He shook his head, waving away my proffered treat as he asked, "How do you know it's not poisoned?" I could not believe his question. Exasperated I replied, "Do you honestly imagine some Egyptian baker would get up in the morning and make poisoned baklava in the hopes that some American might come by and order some?" Seeing he was still skeptical, I added, "I don't know your business experiences, but it seems a poor model to make a product for sale that would kill your customers and ensure no repeat business." He didn't budge so I gave the extra piece to a little Egyptian kid who'd been eyeballing me hopefully since I'd bought it. He took it, giving me a big "shukran!" (thank you) before scampering away.

The rest of the tour group showed up and we all piled onto the bus, heading off to a food court in a nearby mall so everybody could get a "taste of home" at some American franchise. I wandered around the area, keeping an eye open to make sure nobody wandered off and got lost. My boss had decided to broaden his cultural experience by ignoring the packed KFC and entering a Chicken Tika, the Egyptian answer to KFC, lured solely by a large sign that offered one liter of Pepsi with the purchase of a large chicken dinner. As I walked up to the shop, I could hear his angry voice and saw him yelling at the counterman as he pushed away a soft drink cup. I asked what was going on and the counterman told me that his customer ordered a smaller meal and was given the twelve-ounce cup of Pepsi that meal deal called for.

Egypt is a poor country where the profit margins are thin. While Egyptians are a warm and gracious people, they are also proud and, if they believe they are right, they will stand their ground. That was the current situation. The SJA turned to me, complaining that he'd been ripped off, while the Egyptian was telling him that the giant Pepsi only came with the big dinner.

Sensing the big American was not going to leave, the exasperated chicken-seller bent over and grabbed a one-liter bottle of Pepsi. He angrily slid it across the counter while uttering a string of what I could only assume were unkind words about this unhappy customer particularly and Americans generally. I also knew that he would take this small international incident home, where it would be the subject of much discussion with his family, his neighbors, and his friends.

Satisfied that he'd gotten the better of the vendor, the SJA strode out of the restaurant, cradling the liter bottle like a Heisman trophy winner as he made his way back to the tour bus. I had done my best to apologize on behalf of the stereotypical "ugly American" and the Egyptian nodded his head indicating that he understood. When I opened my wallet and handed him fifty Egyptian pounds, his demeanor instantly changed. He smiled at me and pulled out another liter bottle but I waved him off while offering him thanks and shaking his hand as I left to get on the bus.

+++

# The Night Of The Flying Marilyns

The AF likes to practice new and innovative management and leadership techniques. Every few years, some colonel at the Pentagon sells the latest and greatest idea to make the USAF even better. In the grip of an ever-changing and diminishing force structure over the years, the motto had been to "do more with less." To help us achieve that goal, in 1994 leadership bought into James Covey and his best-selling "Seven Habits of Highly Effective People." This book's proffered regimen was touted as having exactly what the Air Force needed to adjust productivity to the increase in tasking.

Unfortunately, the concept never took root and shuffled quietly away after three painfully long years of never-ending meetings with hundreds of powerpoint slides on precisely what words to express our unit Mission Statement. After a year-long collective linguistic soul-searching, we finally arrived at, "Prepare mission-ready Gunfighters to fight and win today's war and the next." The USAF had been doing that successfully since inception in 1947, but it was important to spend a couple of hundred man-hours to sum up that effort in fewer than fifteen words.

A big part of this colossal failure was the process of developing metrics to determine where an organization was in the spectrum, how it well it was achieving whatever it was they did, and how it could improve. As one master sergeant explained in a briefing to the Wing, "Total Quality Management means you never do anything perfectly, because you are always looking to improve." A lieutenant colonel approaching retirement commented, "You know that's exactly what the Communists said, 'The revolution is never finished,' so is this some kind of commie indoctrination?"

As TQM was spinning up, one suggestion was after-hours team activities to provide an opportunity to bond. This is what the clubs were for but with an increased emphasis on getting people to quit smoking and drinking, attendance fell off. People were still smoking and drinking, but now went off base to socialize. Leadership soon recognized this and decided mandatory team-building events were the answer.

Our first event was flogging water at the base airshow, *"Gunfighter skies!"* Air shows have been popular ever since the Wright brothers and the services routinely offer these performances not only to demonstrate the capabilities of the military, but more importantly, as a recruiting tool to locate and captivate the next generation of warriors. For the different base organizations, the airshow provided a way to raise funds for squadron events instead of having to nickel and dime airmen. Every year the different squadrons set up booths to sell food, memorabilia, and anything else they could conceive of.

Volunteers manned those booths and "flogged," or offered, their wares to visitors. Because I'd sat on various club boards of directors I was made the legal office morale manager and the guy responsible for coming up with a plan. I'd taken a marketing class as an undergrad, and the one thing I learned was "simple sells." I invested all our coffee fund money and bought cases of one-liter bottled water from the commissary. Each bottle cost a dime and we'd sell it for a dollar. One paralegal brought a blow up pool that we filled with ice and hundreds of bottles of water. Several parents brought their kids and little red wagons as our sales team. Our sales approach was simple. We had the kids make hand written signs and we coached them on how to sell their wares. We practiced having them look sad, almost on the verge of tears and, if anybody asked, they were to tell the adult that their mom had a mean boss and nobody could leave until they sold some water. One little seven year old girl was great at making her lower lip tremble and could even pull a tear on demand. We'd launch them with full wagons and few made it more than one hundred yards before coming back empty, pockets stuffed with dollar bills. We cleared over nine hundred dollars.

The next big event was for our office to take in a baseball game. It was late May and I was waiting to get my next assignment. I lived in Boise but all the other folks from our office had to drive the sixty miles to the stadium in Garden City where they'd watch the Boise Hawks take on the guys from some other small town in the Class A-Short Season

Northwest League. The entertainment usually consisted of the wildly popular "Race Ernie the Keebler Elf" where some little kid would be brought onto the field to race Ernie around the bases. If the little tyke beat him, he'd win a year's supply of cookies. The kids never lost; I once saw a kid fall rounding third so Ernie also took a dive. Tonight's entertainment would be even more exciting: At the game's end, the "Flying Elvises," direct from Las Vegas, would be dropping from their plane to the field.

The SJA was still a cheap bastard. He bought the cheapest tickets, those along the first base line. He wanted to make sure there was enough money available for a pizza party, because he could eat a lot of pizza. He forgot those tickets were being paid for out of the office slush fund we'd generated flogging water at the air show. Those tickets would have been OK for a night game because they faced dead north, but for us on that late on that warm summer afternoon, the scorching afternoon sun would pretty much blister the left side of your face if you didn't bring sun block. The better seats, with the low sun at your back, were along the third base line, but they each cost two dollars more and would have taken an extra forty bucks from our office fund, money he felt would be better used to pay for that pizza, so we sat where he put us.

The second big surprise, after realizing we were consigned to be broiled, was that all the groundskeepers were wearing long iridescent green cocktail gowns and blonde wigs. Despite fishnet stockings, the long slit up the side revealed a forest of leg hair on the nearest one. The announcer explained that the "Flying Marilyns" were substituting on short notice for the Elvises, who it turned out were then attending a funeral for one of their own who augered in at a Monster Truck rally near Yuma, Arizona two days earlier.

The innings played out and somebody won just as the sun was dropping below the horizon. We could hear the sound of the nearing airplane and watched as the grounds-crew Marilyns struggled to lay out the large white cloth **X** over center field, muscular arms with tufts of shoulder hair looking oddly out of place under spaghetti straps. The announcer directed our eyes skyward to watch for the smoke as the skydivers jumped, popping smoke canisters attached to their legs.

Right about that time, the plane cut its engine and a stick of men abandoned the machine and those Marilyns headed to earth. What none of us could have realized was that a cold front was screaming into the valley. As the winds rose, the aspen trees began to shimmy and shake. Innocent of the weather event rapidly approaching and wanting to dazzle their fans, those Marilyns deployed their chutes at seven thousand feet so all could see and appreciate the smoke patterns as they wove in and outside of each other, one Marilyn even standing atop the canopy of another. The crowd lapped it up as the announcer struggled for adjectives, but it shortly became clear that those Marilyn's got caught in the weather front, and instead of appearing larger as they came toward us, the smoke trail showed they were  beginning to sail west.

Not a one made it to the field, but we read in the paper the next day, one landed at a backyard barbecue. The cops spent most of the evening responding to calls of Marilyns dropping all over west Ada County.

It really was a perfect ending to a less-than-stellar tour and prepared me for the next stop on the journey.

+++

# CHAPTER FOUR

# Be Ready To Fight, Tonight!

Testifying against my former boss helped to get him properly sentenced for his salacious and illegal affair. I was glad the court also found him to be no gentleman and dismissed him from service. It was only after that when leadership in DC finally realized the scope of the problem and began to assess the damage done to our office. A decision was made to offer a permanent change of station (PCS) to those who wanted to leave this mess behind them. I was one of those more than ready for an early departure to get out of what had been an incredibly toxic office. I'd been selected for promotion to major and since a major had recently arrived on assignment to the legal office, and was on orders as the deputy, it was time for me to hit the road. Once again, I put in for a "short notice" world-wide vacancy.

In late spring, the good folks at the assignments branch were kind enough to remember that they always had a hard time filling slots in Korea, so much so that some officers chose to retire rather than take a tour there. When I said, "Send me anywhere, as long as it's overseas!" the used-car-salesmen in assignments realized they had a short notice volunteer for a remote tour. Short-notice volunteers for hard-to-fill remote tours were rare as hen's teeth and my orders were cut a few days later. I was the new Chief of Military Justice for Headquarters, 7th Air Force, Pacific Air Forces, Osan Air Base, Republic of South Korea (ROK). Seventh was most noted for having baseball great, and future Mr. Coffee pitchman, Joe DiMaggio, assigned there when he was in uniform during World War II.

People came to Osan from all across the Air Force and for a variety of reasons. While I was deliberately fleeing a bad assignment, others like Joe were paying off an "in-residence" school tour, and more than a few volunteered because it was the last "wild west" assignment with some semblance of the old Vietnam era days. The saddest were the ones who'd simply been caught having never served overseas and had run out of excuses.

Like the French Foreign legion, or federal prison, it was best never to delve too deeply into how somebody came to be in Korea; they'd tell you if they felt like it. Korea was a "no judgment" zone and like Vegas, what happened in Korea tended to stay in Korea. Unless you were intemperate enough to come to the attention of the authorities, and then it could get very ugly, very rapidly. Up and until then, there was no end to the parties, dinners, and other events where groups would form based on common interests and go from there.

Seventh consists of approximately ten thousand Air Force personnel located primarily at the 51st Fighter Wing at Osan and the 8th Fighter Wing at Kunsan, along with five other smaller operating bases scattered throughout the Republic. Air Force personnel stationed there fly and maintain the General Dynamics F-16 Fighting Falcon and the Fairchild Republic A/OA-10 Thunderbolt II combat aircraft, and perform a myriad of intelligence, logistics, planning, communications, and liaison duties. The US Forces Korea motto was "Be ready to fight, *tonight!*"

Part of "being ready" was my liaison duty which included being the bag man for our annual Chuseok (harvest holiday) visit to Korean prosecutors offices. I'd fly to Seoul with the Commander on his dedicated Black Hawk helicopter when he had a meeting up there, during which time I could purchase ten bottles of Chivas Regal from the General Officer liquor store. This meant no taxes or other add-on costs, so each 18-year old bottle cost nine bucks instead of seventy. In the afternoon when he finished his meetings we'd fly back to Osan. Later, during the holiday, we made formal office visits in suits to deliver the hooch and improve our relations with the South Korean prosecutors. This was helpful when the occasional airman would run afoul of Korean law.

Although a combat-ready command, Seventh also provided assistance to non-combatants and civilians within the region. Rescues at sea, typhoon evacuations, and medical assistance were typical of those missions. Together the two wings were part of the "speed bump defense" positioned to withstand any attack and hold back the entire might of the Armed Forces of the People's Democratic Republic of

North Korea in the event the (then) evil Kim Jong Il (not to be confused with either his evil son and heir, Kim Jong Un, or his dead Dad, Kim Il Sung), launched an all out offensive to remove the Yankees. The goal was for North Korea to achieve reunification through *Juche*, or "self-reliance." Juche is the official political ideology of North Korea, described by the regime as Kim Il-Sung's "original, brilliant and revolutionary contribution to national and international thought." The idea states that an individual is "the master of his destiny" and that meant the North Korean masses were to act as the "masters of the revolution and construction," whatever that means.

The USAF contracts with private airline companies to haul its forces from here to there on a circuit. Korea-bound planes with a load of new troops departs out of Los Angeles, with a stop in Seattle, to pick up more troops before heading up to Alaska and then on to Japan and then Seoul. Sometimes being an officer has its perks and I was seated in the business class section where I met my seat-mate and future wingman, Joe. Another major, he was an A-10 pilot coming to Osan to do a tour in the planning shop. He'd just finished taking Air Command and Staff College in residency, one of three professional level courses all officers are expected to take during their careers. Most do it by seminar, but a lucky few get to take a year off to attend the course as full-time students and graduate with a masters degree. Of course the Air Force extracted a heavy payment, in this case a "non-volunteer" assignment to Korea, and Joe was unhappy at the prospect of spending a year away from his young family.

After arriving at Osan, I reported in to my new boss, Col. Tom Tudor, who'd had prior Army service in Vietnam some twenty-six years earlier as a young JAG. He was from a distinguished New England family that included ancestor Frederic Tudor, who founded the Tudor Ice Company and became Boston's "Ice King" by shipping ice to the tropics from many local sources of fresh water including Walden Pond. With patrician features suggesting his English ancestry, he spoke with a clipped tone ending many sentences with "my good man."

I saw an old portrait on the wall and asked if that was a Korean thing and could I hang a picture of my grandfather on the wall? Somewhat taken aback, he explained the subject was his great grandfather many generations removed. He was a man the Continental Congress had seen fit to appoint as a colonel at the young age of twenty-five, Harvard graduate William Tudor, the first US Army Judge Advocate General. My new boss then focused on the portrait while the conversation hung in the air which I took as my cue to leave. Our office staff was small, just his deputy, two NCOs who handled all of the pesky papers that came in, and me. I was shown my office, a cave with no windows that had been an unheated storage room, while the Boss and Deputy had windows and wall heaters. Even the lobby of the office had windows for the admin troops.

The best one could hope for in Korea was to be finished with your tour before the balloon went up and a war happened. I always believed any attack from the North would stall as soon as the lead tank found the first Burger King. The average North Korean combat troop gets about 1,600 cals a day, while our exercise physiologists estimated it takes over 3,500 calories a day for any kind of sustained combat operations. I believed any invasion would be halted when the invaders ate those Double Whoppers with cheese, large fries, large chocolate Oreo milk shake, and Dutch apple pie, ingesting 2,510 calories in the process. This massive caloric overload would render them instantly sleepy, causing the attack to stall.

My scenario did not take into account the fifteen thousand artillery and mortar tubes pointing south. Until such time as I rotated or got to "fight tonight" and get killed, I simply had to do my job monitoring the various criminal and other nefarious activities coming to the attention of the Security Forces; while also serving as the legal representative for the targeting committee, a vital function because wars don't get fought on the fly. Targeting teams work to identify all military targets in any hostile country. Those targets consist of leadership, command and control (C2), logistics hubs, and individual units. My job was to make sure if we targeted a radio relay station, that the North Korean People's school for Blind Children wasn't inside the blast ring. If it was, we needed to put a different and less destructive weapon against the DPME, the Designated Point of Maximum Effectiveness. If the engineers opined that no other weapon could do the job, I'd put a note in the file restricting any attack to nighttime when school was out.

Most weeks my job consisted of reading accounts of commissary goods being sold on the black market. This explained the excessive amounts of rice, ox tails, Parliament cigarettes, Pinch whiskey and Crowne Royal on offer at the commissary, BX and liquor store, since they just happened to be the most popular brands in Korea. Even though rationed and controlled, every week hundreds of thousands of dollars worth of these exotic and Korean duty-free goods flowed from the various BXs and commissaries and into the trunks of dependent ID-carrying Korean spouses. They'd hit every base between Osan and Seoul on a daily basis to purchase their daily quota of goods in an illegal, but highly profitable, procedure called "race-tracking."

I'd also review arrest reports from the weekend, highlighting any of particular immediate interest to my boss, Colonel Tom, who was the legal advisor to the three-star general who commanded Seventh. The subordinate bases handled the discipline; really all we did was look for anything that might "blow up" and become significant. We had some difficult cases, like the young enlisted creep who was sexually abusing deaf-mute Korean orphans because he figured they wouldn't know what he was doing was wrong and even if they did, who could they tell? Turns out a visiting Mormon missionary with a deaf sister was fluent in Korean Hangul written, spoken, and signed. When he visited the orphanage he uncovered this shocking situation. The pervert got twenty years at Leavenworth.

There was always something of interest after a long weekend in South Korea, given those ten thousand airmen assigned to the peninsula at that time, each of whom considered it a land of enchantment. In Korea, the drinking age was eighteen, alcohol was cheap, and "juicy girls" worked to make a living while giving comfort to a lonely GI.

"Juicys" were farm girls from the provinces. They'd borrow five thousand dollars from a mama-san to get set up in the town and get a job hustling pineapple juice as overpriced "champagne" to GIs who were looking for a little company. A good drink hustler could settle her debt in a year, saving a fairly substantial amount of money before time and gravity spurred her to settle down and cull a GI from the herd. She would marry and let him take her to the "land of the big BX" as the United States was known globally.

After spending a day in-processing and getting oriented, I went to the Club for lunch and was pleased to run into Buck, an old friend from my tour at RAF Upper Heyford. Born and raised in Charleston, South Carolina, he possessed a masters degree in bio-mechanical engineering but found his passion in flying. Despite this advanced education, he believed in the supremacy of Clemson football, the nutritional value of Moon-pies, and the acting ability of Pamela Sue Anderson. He also considered himself a "parrot head," a die-hard devotee to Jimmy Buffet and all things "Margaritaville."

Buck had the central party room up in field grade quarters directly above the club. They'd originally been single rooms but sometime earlier in the decade the center wall was taken out and the quarters expanded into 400-square feet, suitable for field grade officers, vice the 200-square feet allotted to junior officers. This gave him a nice sized kitchen, long hallway, bathroom, lounge, and bedroom. An important part of his shipped baggage was a Presto brand "GranPappy" Electric Deep Fryer and Jimmy Buffet-sanctioned off-white and lime green "Margaritaville Bahamas Frozen Concoction maker." Buck was a man who believed everything should be deep fried and enjoyed with a frozen drink.

He introduced me to a number of his friends from past assignments including Mongo, a captain and 'recovering former Navy guy' who lived on the top floor. Being a junior officer and a former Navy guy, he was stuck in a corner room which had about as much space as Anne Frank's hideout in Holland. He'd arrived a few weeks earlier and was also assigned to the plans shop in the basement. Mongo took the lead in showing me around and introducing me to the guys with whom I'd spent the bulk of my off duty time with. My new comrades were guys with names like: Axe, Stretchee, Welder, Cream, and DA-Veed, all of whom would share in the fun in the "Land of the Morning Calm." Korea is more fairly described as the "Land of Morning Jitters," because the ROK guys lived in a very tightly wrapped culture with a fondness for strong coffee.

+++

## What happens in Korea, stays in Korea

July and August marked the assignments season, a time to move when school was out and those children were easier to uproot and plant elsewhere. For that reason, the bulk of rotation in and out of the Korea Peninsula occurred then. You'd meet the new people at least three times; waiting for the same charter flight you were on, again during in-processing, and again during the first commander's call, so friendships would form based on repeated exposure.

The traveling nature of the operational world also meant the odds were good that you'd meet somebody from a past assignment and that was a quick connect to all of their friends. Through them, you met others and pretty soon you knew pretty much every other officer by face and certainly had enough companions. An important component of warrior bonding is seeing just what a person is made of and the quickest way to find that out was to take a new arrival out for a soju experience.

Soju is a fermented beverage derived from a combination of rice, sweet potatoes, and maybe a few other available starchy ingredients, which are then brewed to make a molasses which is fermented, distilled, bottled, and sold. Some premium brands were said to offer a super-soju which is distilled multiple times to further refine the taste. In my sad experience, no such efforts had been made to improve the soju I'd imbibed during my time in Osan in 1996. The once-filtered soju we enjoyed was served either straight up or adulterated with kiddie cough syrup (guaifenesin DM) providing the "cherry flavor, *children love!*"

This national drink of Korea could also be served in a large plastic "ammo" bowl full of ice and red Kool-aid, then mixed with yogurt so it could be touted to the unwary as a "health drink." The liquor was traditionally drunk sans straws by dropping your face into the ice and carefully sipping, while avoiding aspirating, until your nose got numb.

One popular pastime was taking the early Sunday morning blue bus to Yong-son barracks in Seoul to catch brunch at the US Army-run Dragon Hill hotel and resort, located adjacent to the Itaewan shopping district. This was the premier Army resort facility in Korea, the place where spouses and kids who came to see mom or dad would stay during their visit. The Dragon Hill offered the soldier an opportunity to enjoy quality time with his loved ones while shielding them from the gritty realities of an assignment in a land where the war never ended. The paused Korean war is actually just a truce, a ceasefire and subject to being resumed with no notice.

Dragon Hill was also famous because for just ten dollars you could enjoy an "all-you-can-eat, made-to-order, world-class brunch" with unlimited complimentary champagne as we did at least once a month. We'd arrive at nine and leave around one to go shopping in Itaewan for fake Rolex watches and shoes large enough to fit Young Jim, a former B-52 weapons officer. Six and a half feet tall with size fifteen feet, he was thrown out of more than a few stores after being called "Goemul!" (monster) by the frightened proprietor, thinking a monster had come in her small shop.

Since this was a combat zone at the tip of the spear, the focal point of any outings or activities was the Club, where peer pressure, plus the thought that the balloon might in fact go up, made for some remarkable evenings. The bartender, Sammy, was a Korean woman who'd started off life as a juicy but eventually landed a job at the club and, with her smarts, soon enough became the head bartender. She knew what everybody drank and a cold one was always sitting on the bar before a high-tipping and thirsty airman could even put in the request.

Osan Air Base generally, and 7AF HQ particularly, were THE high priority targets for the eleven thousand North Korean special forces (NKSF) in their four hundred Colt AN-2 prop airplanes. Those old Soviet-era wooden airplanes were simply designed, had a range of 500 miles, and a low radar signature. Each could carry a dozen highly trained NKSF assassins who would jump out and rain down death from above. This threat was such a concern that every evening the ROK Army posted hundreds of guards armed with Mistral anti-aircraft missile launchers and 2,760 missiles, to listen for propellers droning southward and to shoot as needed. Knowing these realities sped up the evening decision making process, an analysis consisting of "Do I stay and continue to party, or go home and read the autobiography of Kim Jong Il and wait to die?"

The club sat at the bottom of Hill 180, famous in the annals of American warfare as the site of the last US-led uphill bayonet charge during the Korean War. Captain Lewis Millett, commanding Company E of the 2nd Battalion, 27th Infantry Regiment, led his men in an assault on an enemy position atop the hill. When heavy enemy fire pinned down one platoon, Millett took another platoon forward, then joined the two groups, leading them up. Wielding his bayonet while throwing hand grenades, Millett yelled encouragement to his soldiers throughout the hand-to-hand combat. At the top of the hill, his men stormed the enemy position, forcing the North Koreans to withdraw. Although wounded in the shin by grenade fragments, Millett refused to be evacuated until the position was secured.

Historian S.L.A Marshall described the attack as "the most complete bayonet charge by American troops since Cold Harbor during the Civil war." Out of about fifty enemy dead, twenty were found to have been killed by bayonets, and the location subsequently became known as Bayonet Hill. For his leadership during the assault, Millett was awarded the Medal of Honor after previously being awarded the Army's second-highest decoration, the Distinguished Service Cross, for leading another bayonet charge earlier in the same month.

Above Buck's condo sat the "Crack Houses" for the junior officers. Built on the side of a steep hill meant the engineers were constantly dealing with the effects of the heavy rains washing down the slope each year. The cracks were large, but assurances were given that the building was safe and habitable. Given it was the nineties, amid the current USA "crack"cocaine epidemic, the commanding general was not amused by the nickname which in turn only reinforced its use.

Also built into the side of Hill 180 was the Joint Operations Center, or JOC, a massive battleship-gray concrete structure, with pine trees painted across it to blend into the real trees that surrounded it. The JOC is the single point where any air battle would be directed should a war start. Manned by senior-ranking American and Korean military leaders, including my three-star boss, this meant we were definitely on the "kill them first" list for any decapitation first strike. Thanks to nobody ever vetting the Korean guy who ran the commercial photo store on base, the North Koreans probably had pictures of every airman assigned and, because the receipt usually included the customer's duty phone and assigned organization, the enemy could figure out what jobs each performed, which made identifying high priority targets easy.

Although the JOC was camouflaged, I just assumed the North Koreans would simply target the one place on the base that didn't look like a building but had driveways leading up and into it. Resigned to the eventual obliteration of anything and anybody in the vicinity of the JOC thanks to those 15,000 mortar and artillery tubes pointed south, I felt pretty comfortable working in a three-story office building next to the number one target on the Peninsula. I still felt reasonably safe, unless the North Korean targeting systems were not quite right, or I was in the wrong group photo being distributed to those NK spec ops killers.

As is the culture at isolated and remote installations, going to the Club on Friday night was a given. The duty day ended at half past four, but with the stressful nature of my job (making slides for the commanding general on how the troops were doing regarding criminal matters), I felt the USAF would not unduly suffer as a result of my early departure from my assigned duty station, having never experienced any genuine Friday afternoon emergencies, not counting Michael Jackson.

+++

## Who You Gonna Call?

It was 4:14 on an early autumn Friday afternoon and I was clearing my desk in my perpetually chilly wall closet/office with every intention of heading out the door and down to the warmth of the club. While rubbing my fingers to restore circulation, I heard the trill of the office fax machine activating and knew a message would be dropping into the receiving tray. Thinking it must be some urgent tasking (the only reason for anybody to send a fax on a Friday afternoon) I walked over and picked it up.

I saw the small cartoon and recognized it as an image of Michael Jackson performing his signature "moon walk." Glancing at the body of the letter, I saw in large, attention getting type:

## This is a Michael Jackson Emergency!

The sending phone number was Japanese and the writer, Jackson's manager, explained that MJ was on a tour of Asia and his three Russian An-124 "Ruslans" cargo planes, chartered to haul the all the gear necessary for his show, were denied landing at Kimpo Airport which had cited a lack of space. The manager was requesting that we clear some space on our ramp to accommodate these three oversized transport planes and in return MJ would put on a special "thank you" concert for "the Army at Yong-Son barracks" when he concluded his sold-out performances in Seoul, if time permitted.

Recognizing "if time permitted" as weasel words that would let him blow off any complimentary concert and sensing this was something I'd want to run by my boss, I brought the paper into his office, and disturbing his afternoon meditation, showed it to him. His brow furrowed as he scanned the request, and he finally looked at me accusingly saying, "Is this a joke, my good man?" I assured him it wasn't and asked if he thought I should bring it to the attention of the general for his approval or denial?

Before he could render an opinion, the brigadier general who served as the deputy commander strolled into the office. Originally from somewhere in the hill country of central Texas, Pat was a Vietnam vet and former A-10 pilot. Gregarious in nature, he'd already started his weekend and was now brandishing an icy cold Heineken he'd pulled out of the small refrigerator he kept in his office. He was a believer in "work hard, play hard" and no small part of that was shooing people out of their offices on Friday afternoon while admonishing them that their work would still be right where they left it on Monday morning. He popped into the doorway with a quizzical look on his face, asking, "What in the world would keep you lawyers here when a whole universe of fun is waiting outside these dull confines?"

I took the paper from Tom and passed it to Pat while he was taking a long pull from the dark green bottle. He finished his drink and held the paper up at arm's length, mute testimony to eyesight no longer as sharp as it once was. He studied it for a second, then snorted in derision before handing it back and asking me, "Is this some kind of a joke, partner?" I looked at my boss to see if he'd take the question but he nodded so I told him this was most certainly on the level and asked what he thought about it.

He took another pull on his beer while he thought about parking availability on the ramp and said, "Let me get this right, he wants us to do backflips through our collective assholes late on a Friday afternoon so he can come and maybe put on a show for the *Army* at Yong-son?" I nodded and he just shook his head and said, "Well, I don't think we have enough room, and his not offering to do a show right here makes it even less attractive, so I'll leave it to you to share the bad news." With that pronouncement and a wave of the hand, he was out the door and making his way down the stairs.

I wrote, "Unable to accommodate" and scribbled my signature underneath it, then sent that answer back to MJ before heading out the door. MJ still did manage to perform that weekend; it seemed there actually was space at Kimpo; his manager had just balked at the amount of money the airport authorities were going to charge for parking.

I ambled on down to the planning vault in the basement where those architects of mayhem, Mongo, Buck, Joe, and the rest resided. More often than not, they'd left a few hours earlier to shoot a round of golf, calling it their "personal physical training time." This check was important to make sure they didn't get some last minute critical tasking I might need to share with my boss. Regardless, all I could do was encourage them to secure their work efforts, fasten the vault door, spin the lock, and hasten down the street to get a seat at the bar before it filled up, Friday being half-price drinks and heavy hors d'oeuvres.

The early crowd at the bar always included Old Bob, the civilian guy. Nobody really knew what he did, some job that involved moving papers and that explained why he drank. Seated next to him was Tim, the OSI counter-intelligence guy, another perfect-attendance award holder. Tim was a retired Secret Service agent, but picked up this CI contract to help defeat North Korean intelligence services. Mainly Tim liked to reminisce about his years as a bodyguard for former President Ronald Reagan until just two years earlier when that poor man's Alzheimer's could no longer be denied. Tim's face was a map of Ireland, but he was fluent in Korean. He choked on his drink when I mentioned that the unvetted photo shop guy might be from North Korea. That was also the first time he ever left the club before the free snacks were served.

Our stool time was overseen by Sammy who, despite being somewhere past forty, didn't look it thanks to her artful application of makeup, but it was her skills behind the bar and snappy comments that made her popular. She'd never date an American, though plenty asked. She explained it succinctly one night to her most persistent last-call suitor, Sphinkster, saying, "Listen to me, You don't shit where you eat" adding, "and neither do I." She also provided a corollary to "all the girls get prettier at closing time" by adding, "the horny drunks get more pathetic."

Sphinkster's real name was Tommy and his nickname was inspired by the sphincter, that circular muscle which normally maintains constriction of a natural body passage and orifice, then relaxes as required by normal physiological functioning. Sphinkster was a "Whizzo," a backseater, the weapons guy on an F-15E Strike Eagle. He was so chronically uptight that his nickname was permanent and most likely on his official record instead of a last name. On any given Friday evening, after several stiff drinks, Sphinkster would be working his failed mojo with Sammy. Even though unmarried, he was way too uptight to go visit Mama-san to make a date with a working girl; he knew that path was fraught with exposure to disease and unsavory types. Upon reflection, he might have had a point there.

The bar had plenty of seats, but also sported a brass rail for folks who preferred to lean. Beyond it were square tables for four and a couple of round ten-seaters; which were usually filled by groups from the larger squadrons, like the 31st Special Ops Squadron detachment who flew "Pave Low" HH-53 helos. Those machines were armed with port and starboard side mini-guns capable of firing several thousand rounds a minute and protecting the front and sides of the bird. Another gunner manned a .50 caliber machine gun on the rear ramp to shoot up anything approaching from behind.

There might also be a gaggle from one of the two flying squadrons: the 25th, A-10 drivers known as "Assam Dragons," and the 35th, F-16 pilots known as "Fiends." The small dance floor had a spot for a band, but that was never used, unless Mongo and the Steel Wool band made a special appearance. That house band usually performed at the "Black Cat Loungee," the haunt of the U-2/TR-1 spy plane "Dragon Lady" community.

Along the far wall and near the dance floor was a Star Eagle jukebox that held 100 CDs, and unlike the halcyon days of my enlisted assignment in the Portuguese Azores, it was no longer twelve songs for a dollar, just two songs for buck and the machine didn't take quarters. Paulie, the Club Manager, didn't seek, or respond to member input, so the songs that came with it when the jukebox was new were never changed. During the year I was there, I learned all the words to "*LaBamba*" and "*Crazy.*"

Paulie was a retired chief master sergeant who had been the club manager for as long as anybody could care to recall. Every once in a while, he'd show up in the lounge to either launch a promotion and special pricing for some liquor that wasn't selling, or to make comment about some concern he had. One evening a drunken aviator dropped a glass while in the bathroom and Paulie shut off the jukebox (a serious social faux pax), and admonished the collective group that he expected better behavior out of us. This occurred late enough in the evening to cause the assembly to rise en-masse and make their way to the men's room where several dozen glasses were hurled against the wall to give him something to really complain about.

The last time we saw Paulie in the lounge was when he came in on a busy Friday afternoon to announce that despite Osan being located at the epicenter of any war on the Peninsula, and the vast majority of folks being assigned there on an unaccompanied basis and missing their families, he was considering making the bar a "non-smoking" facility. Smoking was currently permitted inside and outside, an allowance given as we were on "the tip of the spear" and most likely to die first, as the exercises constantly reminded us. You'd think he might have guessed it, as his proposed unilateral action resulted this time in both glassware and food flying in his general direction, along with threats of his immolation, or solo flight over the patio ledge to the street twenty feet below. This time, the price of his ambition was too high; he ran out of the bar, never to be seen again for the duration of my tour.

If the weather was nice, there was a patio with tables and chairs and every Friday the club would set up the "Membership Appreciation Night" free food line, offering hamburgers, hot dogs, fries, coleslaw, and pickles, but really it was a trap to catch all those cheap bastards who loved drinking at the bar but not paying dues. Thanks to peer pressure and shame, lots of people took advantage of the sign-up table right before the line. Membership was twenty dollars a month, and paid for itself because you could charge broken glassware replacement as well as food and drinks on your card, which came in handy if you lost at liar's dice or accidentally wearing your hat inside the bar and had to buy the house a round of drinks.

+++

---

# Ajima

A jima, is Korean for "middle-aged lady, eligible for marriage or married." That might be the official definition, but that's baloney. Truth is the ajimas are widowed or divorced old ladies who decided "enough is enough" and determined to spend the remainder of their days out of the shadows, doing exactly whatever it was they wanted. Many found work as housekeepers for the Americans where they could run things as they saw fit and not be bothered, because the military people were here and gone in no time, paid their bill promptly and didn't speak Korean, something completely different from their former lives.

An entire network of self-regulating ajimas operated under a seniority system. The younger ajimas cut their teeth using short-handled brooms, sweeping up the exteriors of buildings. In America, broom handles tend to be at least four feet long and facilitate upright handling. For a reason never unearthed except the possibility that they cost less with short poles, Korean brooms were just two feet long, forcing the operator to bend over while sweeping. This explained the number of stooped ajimas, who had spent years bent over to sweep. Eventually, they hoped to get a position indoors, owing to the attrition of more senior ajimas, either through death or catching an American husband who saw nothing wrong with a forty-year old woman who already knew how to cook and clean; and, as a bonus, spoke very little English.

If an ajima could get work inside one of the office buildings, they knew they'd be spending their days in warm comfort while swabbing out toilets and mopping floors. The best move was to get into a dormitory because that was the top of the heap for good jobs. Each ajima ran half a floor with twenty rooms and each resident using her services paid sixty dollars a month for those services which included washing dishes and clothing, dusting, making the bed, polishing boots, and ironing uniforms. It was a great value for the money and most people took the deal. Sphinkster was a notable exception, he being incredibly cheap and convinced every ajima was a "flower girl," one of many mythical North Korean "sleeper agents." Reputedly, the flower girls' twofold mission was, while young, infecting unwary GIs with incurable sexually transmitted diseases, and, when older, taking up positions as room ajimas where they would work until ordered into action by Pyongyang, then slay every American while they lay sleeping.

Until being murdered while you slept, having an ajima also meant your room was instantly cleared after the briefest inspection when leaving at the end of the assignment. I'd met my ajima, Mrs. Yoon, on the day I was assigned my room. During the incoming room inspection, the movers brought in my pitiful collection of three boxes containing all the clothing and possessions I'd need for the year tour. All five feet of her came barreling into the apartment saying, "OK, you new guy. I take care of you!"

Having concluded her interview and taking employment with me, we were sitting at my table drinking coffee while the room was checked out as ready for occupancy. The Inspector was a tall fellow from Texas. He checked the bathroom and yelled, "Ajima! The fan over the toilet has not been cleaned!" She yelled back, "I just a little old Korea lady!" He then told her he'd do it for her this time while she looked at me and winked.

I started trying to put things away when she took my arm and gently, but firmly, led me to the door while saying, "Go now!" I did and when I came back that evening, as if by magic, my uniforms were ironed, starched, and pressed as if they'd been to a laundry. My black leather boots were polished brightly and all of my civilian clothing was pressed and hanging neatly as well.

Mrs. Yoon was a stout woman, powerful from years of hard work and she wore her graying hair short and unkempt. She liked me because I brought her three oranges and three candy bars each week. Of course these small gifts were against all the regulations for fears of fueling the black market, since all foods were rationed and only US Military assigned to Korea could shop in the commissary store. I also let her use my telephone to call her "bad" son and "terrible grandchildren," whom she decried as having no respect for her, but she called them anyway.

To combat race-tracking, a security policeman was positioned at the entrance to the commissary. The cop would check your ration card when you came inside. You had to show the ration card again to the cashier when concluding your purchase. Certain items, like liquor, cigarettes, rice, and meat were rationed and your card was marked. The Korean cashiers always demanded to see my ration card and one time I said, "Do you honestly think I got on a plane, flew here and dressed up like this for a package of hot dogs? Why aren't you guys checking that Korean lady's card? She's buying four fifty-pound bags of rice and twenty beef oxtails!" She looked over at the load of goods piled on next checkout stand conveyor belt and said, "No, she's OK, *we know her.*"

I happily broke those rules because, while I knew she was a sweet old lady, I could never fully discount Sphinkster's constant warning of "flower girls." Sphinkster speculated that many of those flower girls were still out and about the base and most would be somewhere in their sixties and not unlike my very own dear Mrs. Yoon. After that, I felt oranges and candy were a prudent investment to make sure that if that terrible day came, she would come by my room and, after wiping Sphinkster's blood off her combat knife, shake me and whisper, "Go hide under bed now!" while marking me off the list as killed.

+++

## Les Nessman And Rich The Naked Dancer

Having a perfectly clean room all the time made it much easier to use my free time in the pursuit of more enjoyable pastimes like reading and listening to the radio since I had decided to forgo television for a year. Most evenings I'd go out for a walk around Song-tan village outside of the entertainment zone and browse all the different businesses and lives being led. I'd see Korean kids coming home from school in their uniforms and passing by later I'd see those same kids working in their parents' shop. I never saw any Korean kids just hanging out being bored because Koreans know the value of education and hard work in that highly competitive society.

I especially enjoyed walking through the markets and experiencing all the items presented for sale or consumption, including some of the ugliest, most disgusting-looking fish I'd ever seen; I was further horrified to learn that those ugly fish were something people ate. When the winter set in, the soup stalls became popular as did the soju tents where you could buy bootleg soju for little money. That would be the stuff that wasn't filtered or subject to any governmental quality standards. You could buy it cheap in the tent or pay more for the same foul beverage in a bar. Curiously, the soju tents were "off limits to GIs" but the bars weren't. That fermented rice liquor had the power to make the most stalwart heart stone-stupid and incapable of intelligent thought.

It was still early in the autumn, before "Chuseok" (Korean for "the great middle of autumn"), a major harvest festival and a three-day national holiday celebrated on the fifteenth day of the ninth month (September) of the lunar calendar, during the full moon. It was during this holiday when Rich, the naked dancer, made his "DiMaggio" mark in the annals of Seventh Air Force lore.

Rich had only recently arrived and he missed the immersion into the large permanent change of station (PCS) crowd that came during the summer months. While he might have missed the big group, he did manage to come in with Les Nessman, who in reality was a female major named Crystal, originally from Puerto Rico.

Les was nicknamed after a male character on a popular TV show "WKRP in Cincinnati," less for any physical resemblance to the character, for she chose to wear big red glasses, a style favored by brassy TV talk show host Sally Jessy Raphael. Rather, she was named after "Les Nessman" for her behavior. In an episode of that TV show, a frustrated Les, wanting the privacy of an office, but working in a common area, laid out tape to create an imaginary office he could enter and exit through an equally imaginary door. Likewise, our Les was assigned work at some mind numbing job in the JOC with a desk in an open area, lacking even a privacy shield. This was most unfortunate since her desk was also located near the coffee pots.

Les was tormented and frustrated by the constant foot traffic passing through what she considered her office space, because it certainly wasn't used for anybody chatting her up. Along with an abrasive personality, she lacked any regards for tact and diplomacy. Routinely lashing out at offenders, Les quickly killing any shot she might have ever had at a "Miss Congeniality" award, if the USAF supported that sort of thing, which it didn't.

One can only imagine the collective surprise that Monday morning when men and women arrived at their work station. Those hungover warriors, seeking a restorative jolt of early morning caffeine to chase away the last remnants of that weekend's poor decision making, were surprised to see yellow and black caution tape on the floor across their usual path. Being hung over, they all just kept on walking. After a few episodes of this outrage to her newly declared privacy, Les had clearly had enough. She stood up and in her loudest voice advised all the people assembled in the area that her office space was to be respected and to find new routes to get their java fix. She declared this clearly delineated space was her private office which they could not enter without her permission; which she was not ever inclined to give.

That pronouncement led to an immediate return-volley of crumpled up paper, pens, and random food items, all of which inspired Les to quit the field and scurry away. Her attempt to control the environment failed. The very next Wednesday, the naming committee, composed of anybody who was at Happy Hour, decided from that day forward she was to be only known as Les Nessman.

Meanwhile, given Rich's own profound lack of social skills, it didn't take long for Les to set her sights on this "only port in a storm" while Rich subscribed to the more philosophical, "beggars can't be choosers." In no time at all they were an item and each other's exclusive wingman.

It was finally Chuseok and all of Korea was on the move. This national holiday was a time for families to be together and celebrate in the manner much like our Thanksgiving weekend, so virtually all businesses and restaurants were closed. The restaurant closures were not good for us, but did cause us to imagine how Jews must feel on Christmas Day when they went to the always-open Chinese restaurants and a movie. Our only option was drinking at the few bars that remained open. The various rounds of beer and ammo bowls were ordered, drunk, and later passed, sometimes in the bathrooms, or sometimes against a wall just outside because the toilets were too small for the crowds these places generated. The excessive amounts of ginger consumed at most meals made the urine stink so bad the bar owners would throw buckets of ice into the urinals to try to reduce the odor. This made little difference, hence it was way better to go outside and lean against a wall to piss directly into a binjo ditch, a concrete sluice that took it away.

As the curfew approached, some might engage in taking one or more "for the road," then wander happily back to the base in the secure embrace and care of their wingman. On this particular evening, it had been Rich who decided it was his turn to find his upward limit on soju ingestion. The DJ at Club Batman put on the Macarena for a nice holiday treat, a popular dance song that, with only eight moves, was easy enough for then-President Clinton to dance to. Once the first few notes sounded, Rich exploded from his chair, racing to join the rows of drunken airmen trying to recall the correct sequence of the eight moves.

Most of the dancers seemed not to have processed the instructions given as the song began, but were determined to show their talent, with Rich doing his best just to stay upright. When it became evident that Rich needed to hit the road, he had to be helped by Les and another brave soul because soju drunks were known to suffer projectile vomiting without warning. They had their work cut out to avoid the stumble that would take the three of them into a binjo ditch. Les stuffed some still hot yaki mandu down Rich's throat and that pain got Rich straight enough to walk unassisted through the gate check.

"Mandu" means dumpling in Korean. In most places, traditionally it was fried golden parcels filled with rice noodles, cabbage, tofu, eggs, toasted sesame oil, spring onion, and seasoning. In Song-tan, mandu chefs liked to step it up for the airmen. When staggering back to beat curfew and needing it, this super-yaki consisted of any vegetable laying around dipped in thin batter, dropped into a wok full of hot oil and stirred until hot enough to form a blister on the roof of the mouth of anyone foolish or drunk enough to eat one before it cooled. They came in three different sizes, 800, 1,600 and 2,400 wan (one, two, and three dollars) "best friends size." These sizzling morsels came wrapped in old airmen performance reports, or any other official documents, that were given earlier to a Korean contractor to destroy, who instead sold them to the street vendors. One guy found his dumplings came wrapped in his own first draft evaluation report, but it worked out OK, because the oils tended to make those papers illegible after a few minutes.

To see if the yaki had cooled enough to eat, I'd offer one to a passing drunk and listen for a scream. It was a double bonus if I got rid of the one green hot chili pepper Mrs. Kim would always toss in for fun. Once at the gate, the theory went, if you could walk those twenty feet past the cops unassisted, you could walk all the way home. At the base entrance was a cab stand which always had lines, but never had cabs, because the guys who lived at the far end of the base tied them all up for their long haul home.

Rich lived closer, on the bottom floor of the geriatric dorm, the one where field-grade officers resided who couldn't get a room in field-grade officers' billets above the club. I lived on the third floor, but Rich was a bottom dweller, living across the hall from my part-time wingman, Joe. Once they were inside the gate and Rich made it successfully up the small hill leading home without puking, he was deemed fit enough to make it the rest of the way. The other helper peeled off, leaving Les to help steady him for the final two-hundred yards. They staggered into the dorm, making their way down to his room. Rich wasn't any help because he was in a soju stupor, that point of intoxication where one is clearly aware of everything going on but powerless to make a coordinated movement. He was still trying to hum the Macarena and attempting a few feeble dance steps, so Les fished out his key, unlocked his door, and spun his dancing self inside. She kindly hung the key on the hook, popped the lock button, and left, heading back uphill to her room in the crack house.

Les had just passed the club when she realized she still had Rich's ID card and had to go back. Regulations demanded you have your ID card with you at all times because you never knew when the balloon might go up and you'd be killed by North Korean special forces; it was critical for graves registration's ability to rapidly identify who you were. When she returned to his room, his door was locked and he didn't answer her knock, so she headed down the hallway to ajima's room. Ajima came out with her copy of the room key (which would make her job killing the tenant much easier when the balloon went up) and uncomplainingly walked down to his room where she unlocked the door. Les pushed open the door and turned on a light. These rooms were small and sliding doors compartmentalized the bathroom and bedroom for privacy, but as everyone lived alone, those doors were usually left open to make the rooms seem bigger. Upon entering Rich's "spacious" abode, Les and the ajima were treated to the sight of him laying face down on his still-made bed, stark naked and with his clothing strewn about. This was nothing new for an ajima. She playfully spanked his butt a few times, and then, as was her habit, began picking up the mess to get a jump on the next day's work. Les stood silent, holding the ID card and wondering where to put it.

Joe heard the knock at his door and thinking it was somebody looking for a nightcap or a last cigarette, opened it to see a grinning Les motioning him to quickly come join her in the hallway. Joe stepped out of his room and Les, who was now trembling with suppressed laughter, tugged him by the shirt sleeve and brought him into Rich's room.

She'd delicately placed the ID in the crack of his ass, his face photo clearly visible above the butt line. Joe was the witness required to share this tale at the next mid-week happy hour.

The naming committee forever declared him "Rich, the Naked Dancer."
+++

---

# The Tailor

Korea offers an opportunity to immerse yourself in the local culture and experience the traditions and mores of the local community. For the folks stationed at Osan Air Base in 1996, it meant going off base to the Song-tan section of Pyeongtaek City, a village that had been entertaining American airmen since the Korean War began some forty-three years earlier. The 'ville had grown up around the installation, with buildings and businesses butting right up against the fence line. When you walked out the front gate and immediately turned right, you ambled past a series of shops. Mr. Kim, the shoe maker, surprisingly seemed to stay in business. According to legend, you ordered shoes, you paid in advance, and Mr. Kim would say, "You come back in two weeks, ready then." A guy named Razor who came to Korea two years earlier had just been re-assigned. In packing, he found a forgotten old slip from the shoe shop and headed down to Mr. Kim's to collect his shoes. He presented the chit to Mr. Kim who barely looked at it and said, "Come back in two weeks, ready then."

Shops also sold knock-off purses from Dooney and Bourke, and Coach, which were made in local factories under license. Thanks to my other wingman, Buck, I learned more than I could ever want to know about women's hand bags. More than trying to please his wife, his percularities resembled a man with a deep fetish, especially since his wife never seemed to receive the purses he purchased. I also never understood his crush on Pamela Sue Anderson and his making me watch "Barb Wire," the second worst movie ever made. In fairness, his taste in movies was simply awful because he also made me watch "Escape from LA," the worst movie ever made, which involved Peter Fonda surfing a giant wave through downtown Los Angeles.

Next came the artists' shops where for a few dollars you could give one of the many starving Korean artists a chance to create your portrait in oil. Just give them a photograph and come back in a few days for the finished product. The only problem was Asians have an epicanthal fold in the eyes, thanks to a 35,000 year old gene mutation known as EDAR. Africans and Europeans carry the standard version of the gene, but in most East Asians, one of the DNA units has mutated. As a result, the painted eyes were never quite right, because all of the American subjects in the painting wound up looking vaguely Asian, which would account for the statistically significant number of portraits that were never picked up.

A few steps down were the tailor shops and it was my habit to stop in to visit my own tailor, Mr. Oh. I was there one fine Saturday morning in early autumn, just to say hello and have a few drinks with him, as drinks were mandatory for his visitors. He liked Crown Royal and, liquor being so very expensive, I kept a bottle at his shop which made life easier; I didn't ever want to offend him by turning down an offer of soju. Mr. Oh spoke perfect English with only the slightest hint of an accent. I'd asked him how he managed to learn it so well and he smiled when he told me "Armed Forces Radio and Television Service plus Voice of America."

On this particular day, several Japanese tourists came into the small shop and gave a greeting to Oh, who sat silently while looking at me. The potential customers hailed him a few more times then gave up and left the store. I was curious about his behavior because Oh was the most polite man I'd ever met and he'd deliberately snubbed those tourists. I had to ask him: "What was that about?" Oh poured himself a large glass of whiskey, took a big sip, set the glass down and told me the tale.

Oh was born in 1936, the 25th year of Korea's occupation by the Empire of Japan. Although they considered the Koreans "cousins" and considered Korea a "protectorate," the Japanese regularly visited great cruelty upon the Koreans who actively resisted the occupation, and Mr. Oh bore witness on many such sad occasions.

His family lived next door to the Japanese Chief of Police when then five-year-old Oh was selected to be the playmate for the Chief's five-year-old son. One day, as is the habit with small children, the two lads got into a quarrel which became a physical dust up, with Oh getting in some licks before the Japanese child ran home crying. A few minutes later, a very angry Chief of Police showed up at Oh's house demanding Oh's father punish his "impudent son" for daring to lay hands on his betters. Oh's father knew that to refuse this demand would mean deportation to a slave camp or a date to dance on the end of a rope at the "hanging tree" on what is now the Osan golf course. The only tree to survive the massive defoliation of Korea to provide wood for Japan during the occupation, it had two thick lower limbs that were about ten feet off the ground and each could support hanging five Koreans.

With tears in his eyes, Oh told me how his father had to punish him with enough severity to appease the furious Japanese officer. To reach that satisfaction, Oh's father struck and beat him, lightly at first, but as the policeman exhorted him to be firmer, the force of the blows necessarily increased. All Oh could do was curl up in a ball while his father exhausted himself, flailing, punching, and finally when he couldn't hold his arms up, began kicking until Oh passed out from the pain. As a result, Oh lay in his bed for over a week before he could get up again. With tears streaming from his now-aged eyes, Oh looked at me and asked, "How could a father be made to do that to his son? As a child I could not understand or appreciate the danger my entire family was in. All I knew was my Dad was prepared to kill me if it meant my family would live. This was a hard thing for me as a child and it broke my father."

He looked down at the glass in hands now trembling. As he took another drink, he looked straight ahead at the wall and told me the worst part. His father was eventually drafted into the "Service of the Empire" and died, along with thousands of other Koreans, during WW II. In a small voice Oh said, "I hated him for what he did to me and, even when he was leaving our home for that last time, I could not forgive him, and now it's too late."

We sat silent for a minute until his memories cleared. He sat up a bit straighter in the chair and leaned in towards me saying, "And that's why I hate those fucking Japs!"

+++

---

# The Ville

After leaving Oh's shop, it was only a few more meters until you'd hit the main street in Song-tan, a street full of nothing but bars of all genres and clientele. Theme bars including disco, soul, rap, country, and Goth, a charming subculture that was born in August 1979 with the band Bauhaus's first single, "Bela Lugosi's Dead." Bars featuring a specific style of music were supplemented by karaoke bars, with names like UN Club, Upstairs Downstairs, Dragon Club, Club Scandal, Friend's bar, and many others. My favorite was the Club Batman where some smart guy purchased the computer screen lights from the TV Show "Voyage to the Bottom of the Sea," and wired it up. Consisting of nothing more than a large panel of opaque colored squares that lit up in a constantly changing sequence, this backdrop showcased female entertainers performing a mid-Twentieth century interpretive folk dance.

This ritualistic performance involved lighting large candles and spinning them about while dripping hot wax onto their bare breasts. All this to the thunderous applause and, shrill whistles from a more than enthusiastic, and hormonally charged, crowd of lonely GIs. This in turned spurred juice sales and better tips for the juicys. Those bars ran on either side down the length of "Song-tan Special economic zone" which was actually more the "Song-tan Korean Male exclusion zone" because young Korean males were not permitted inside.

Upon arrival in-country, you are considered just a sprout, young, fresh, and new, and were taken out for your "green bean" tour of the zone which introduced the Soju experience. At the end of your tour, you are a brown bean, old and worn out, and not much good for anything. Song-tan was lively every night of the week, but especially on the weekends. Then, hoards of airmen and soldiers stationed at the various small installations scattered about the area, but still in close proximity of Song-tan, would come into town for a bit of fun.

That fun would manifest when some poor drunken eighteen-year-old soldier, fresh from Picabo, Idaho, population 200, would come in to the 'ville freed after a week living in field conditions, otherwise known as camping in the mud. That always reminded me of that recruiter from so many years earlier who delivered on his promise of, "Clean sheets, good coffee and air conditioning" while preparing for a war nobody ever wanted to re-ignite. We all knew that if the "balloon went up" the chances of surviving were pretty small, since US Forces in Korea were simply considered a speed bump dedicated to buying time until the US could marshal sufficient forces to join the war.

Exercises and drills were routine simulations of the balloon going up. When an alarm went off, you had to hustle to your office while security would be establishing ID check points at various strategic locations, like the route to my office. Walking with another major one morning, we came upon a very serious security cop who demanded our IDs to make certain we weren't North Korean infiltrators. Meanwhile, South Korean airmen walked by, unchallenged by our interrogator because he couldn't speak Korean, which was OK since they weren't part of the exercise anyway, as they had their own exercises. The other major, a black man, had finally had enough of being delayed. Exasperated he looked at the young airman while pointing at me and said, "Do either one of us look like we could be remotely Korean? You ever seen any Koreans come in these shades?"

In those clubs, I'd watch as some sad sack, lacking buddies, would walk into the bar and sit at an empty table, where in very short order a juicy would show up, plop herself into his lap, and grind her butt into his crotch, producing the desired effect within twenty to thirty-seconds. Those young girls from the provinces didn't want to be a farmer's wife, so they took a chance by heading to the big city to make a lot of money and start a wonderful new life. Bar owners would give them a five thousand dollar stake to get set up hustling drinks. Once they paid off that debt, they'd save for plastic surgery to get breasts, lips, calves, and buttocks enhancement to increase earning capability.

Once her mark consented to buy her a drink, she would run her hands up and down the guy's biceps and shoulders, remarking on his strength and masculinity. The GI, having already put himself on the hook for ten bucks, would naturally expect something a bit more for his investment, but the juicy would patiently explain that she could talk to him only while the three-ounce glass of pineapple juice was full and then she must find another patron....unless the strapping and handsome, maybe even "sexy, sexy," GI would buy her a "fishbowl," a genuine plastic fish bowl full of ice, pineapple juice and a very healthy dose of soju. If the handsome stranger went for that, she could stay much longer and would begin to run her hands up and down his inner thigh for added emphasis. The now-hormonally supercharged GI would gleefully whip open his wallet to pull out 80,000 wan ($100) to fuel his hopes of a "Dear Playboy, this happened to me in Korea…" kind of night, which sadly, would never happen at all. Instead, after his drink was delivered, the juicy would excuse herself to go the toilet, which allowed her to make a pass around the room looking for another customer to hustle. She might return, but only long enough to take a pretend sip, then run her hand up his inner thigh once more. Then, while giving that thigh a gentle squeeze, she'd say she had to go talk to her friend for just a minute, and did he want to try the juicy? The GI, now in a low hover due to the endorphins and adrenalin coursing through his veins, would agree to enhance his experience with the rapid ingestion of the pineapple-flavored soju "GIs love!" Then, with fused eyes staring happily at both of her, and oblivious to everything else, he would begin his wait for her return. This "catch and rev" scammer would then proceed to victim number two, and go on for longer than I ever cared to stay in any one bar, so I'd leave and make my way to the street after hearing some short-haired teenager pleading, "I don't have any more money, I thought you liked me…" and realizing the truth, that he was just another customer.

+++

---

## Long Time Or Short Time?

It was a balmy evening in early October and I was in the upstairs part of club "Upstairs-Downstairs," playing darts with my wingman, Joe. Soft spoken and steady, Joe was assigned to the headquarters like I was, but like every other planner, he worked in the secured vault in the basement preparing war plans. A conscientious fellow, he rarely saw daylight, so when the weekend hit, he wanted and needed to get off-base as fast as he could. Those speed-walks provided him the only fresh air and daylight he'd get during the work week.

Our opponents that evening were Buck and "Bugs," a tall and lanky lieutenant colonel with bright red hair who was taking one last tour before retirement. Bugs's given name was Bruges, his grandparents came from that city in Belgium, but pronounced his name with an anglicized "*Brugs*" which to his eternal dismay became "Bugs," which he hated. Bugs planned on operating a tourist helicopter service in Las Vegas once he'd punched out.

Meanwhile, his pal Buck was wearing his latest acquisition, a white Formula-One lightweight bomber jacket sporting an obscene number of

NASCAR racing patches touting every automotive supplier and driver in existence. Made in Korea by the same guys who knocked-off everything else, sometimes a word or two was misspelled, but I never saw "Talladega" spelled correctly, ever. While shopping one day, Buck was outraged to find that a winter-weight jacket in the garish orange of his alma mater, Clemson, had become "*Climson*." Thinking through his outrage, Buck decided that at only twenty dollars, his teenage son would never notice.

Bugs, being close to sober on that October night, spent a good chunk of time lining up his shot, but still missed. This led him to complaining about the lack of quality control on Korean darts which were just "not quite right," a phrase that applied to virtually everything in Korea. In one of the more dangerous instances of this lack of quality control, stair-steps seemed universally not quite right; made by hand, some steps would be taller or shorter depending on the worker's levels of skill and sobriety. This lack of uniformity throws off your muscle memory and can cause a stumble and, of course, this effect is magnified once soju is involved. When not tossing their own not-quite-right darts, Buck and Joe talked of opening a "Mississippi mud-hole," an unimproved area of swampy land where off-road enthusiasts could slip and slide to their heart's content. They dreamt of this wonderland being located somewhere near Evergreen, Alabama, Joe's home town, and also apparently home to some serious four-wheel driving, mud-loving folks.

That night, I found myself just gazing out the open window to the street scene below. Night had fallen and the street vendors were setting up shop. There was "Miss Lee Hamburgers" serving a hamburger with fried egg on top. Miss Lee wore a McDonald's knock-off hat and apron to lend authenticity, but still…not quite right. Another stall, closer to the
gate which was the preferred location, was the chief mama-san selling

yaki to the streaming hordes of warriors in various stages of "inebriation plus hunger."

In the midst of all this humanity, I spotted the figure of the mama-san who operated the bordello which was located just off the main street, down a short alley, behind a faded jade green door. All the bordello doors were painted the same pastel green, thanks to the release of the first full-length porn film, "Behind the Green Door." Commercially released in 1972 it starred former Ivory soap-ad baby, Marilyn Chambers, all grown up and doing dirty, nasty things. Naturally the Korean mama-sans wanted to let the world know that they offered the same services, so they reasonably painted their entry doors green.

I remembered Mama-san from a few weeks earlier when I was walking back to the base with Buck. That night she saw us and offered her pitch, "You want a young girl?" I was in a playful mood so I said, "Sure! Show me some beauties!" I was, after all, the Chief of Military Justice for the Korean Peninsula and held my own Korean national police ID card identifying me as a high-ranking police official not to be impeded! I needed to know what sorts of temptations our fine young airmen might run into when looking for love in all the wrong places and she seemed to be the person to interview. Despite his protests and concerns, I insisted Buck come along. His reluctance caved once Mama san said, "What? You no likee girls? You likee little boys, maybe?" Buck's southern pride and manliness would not tolerate any more scandalous aspersions cast upon his sexual orientation, so he fell in step and off we headed.

We walked down that alley, turned into a small courtyard and beheld a faded green-iron door. She pushed it open, bidding us to come through, and we entered a small and poorly lit garden area. All along the walls were wooden doors leading to the many small bedrooms. She pointed to a woman standing in the shadows a few feet away who'd been hidden from our view until Mama closed the entry door. I judged her to be somewhere between forty and sixty, it being difficult to see clearly in the low light. I was confident she was certainly much closer to crone than teenager. This was confirmed when she opened her mouth to smile, reminding me of a poorly carved Jack-O-Lantern. Reluctant to go any further with the charade, I simply waved my hands saying, "Anyo, Anyo" (No! No!) while began backing towards the door with Buck close behind. Mama seemed to take offense and said, "Why you no likee? You likee him?" She thrust her jaw out toward Buck, the contempt clear on her face. She thought him gay, which was not a good thing to be thought in Korea, ever.

Wanting to continue my exit, I decided to explain why I was rejecting her kind offer. I turned to her saying in my most lawyerly way, "Now see here, Madam, I'm a lawyer and your employee over there appears to be a direct violation of the Magnuson-Moss Warranty Act of 1975, a US federal law governing consumer product warranties and requires manufacturers and sellers of consumer products to provide consumers with detailed information about warranty coverage. In addition, it affects both the rights of consumers and the obligations of warrantors under written warranties. As you offered me a "young girl" and clearly, this woman is somewhat older than my grandmother, you are in direct violation of this law and thus we must take our leave of you with the sincerest hope you mend your ways! Now we will bid you good night."

That Act had absolutely no bearing on the matter at hand, it was just something snappy I remembered from Professor Macintosh's Uniform Commercial code class and, with that, we were away through the green door and heading back home.

Now, here I was, sitting on a perched on a barstool at the open window and looking over her kingdom; watching as she hustled the GIs who were wandering the streets, looking for adventure and a way to get rid of all that excess money they were supposed to be sending home to Momma and the kids back in Nebraska. Deadbeat Daddies in Korea were a terrible problem. If a US based airman hated his wife and life, he could sign up for a remote, in effect taking a year of marriage off. If we received a complaint from a wife, along with a judicial notice of arrearages, the USAF would simply garnish the husband's wages until his arrears became current. His First Sergeant, like a military Godfather, would also give any fiscally irresponsible airman a clear and unambiguous reminder that his continued employment, and salary, were contingent on him never again failing to meet his familial obligations or otherwise becoming a pain in the ass. The threat of an administrative discharge, with no pension, usually worked to eliminate recidivists.

As any male approached, Mama-san would make her pitch and, when she got a nibble would say, "You want long time, short time?" Short time was thirty bucks for thirty minutes and longtime was sixty for sixty minutes. This is where self-confidence met fantasy, because no young guy would ever want to admit to not being manly enough to ride a woman for an hour, especially if he was with some of his fellow warriors. Succumbing to pressure, many opted for "long time," paid the money and vanished behind the green door. I decided to take note of time-elapsed from the moment the customer agreed to the terms, and again when he came back outside with a new spring in his step while tucking his shirt back into his pants. Over the course of the evening, I counted a mixed group of young soldiers and airmen, twenty-three total: ten white, nine black and four who looked Hispanic. Fifteen elected to go long time and the rest were either cheap or more self-aware. The average elapsed time was thirteen minutes.

Many nights I'd be waiting to throw a dart and would verify my observations. Over time I found the actual elapsed time remained consistent. It occurred to me that when one party expects a break from the routine to enjoy an hour of skin to skin contact and intense physical pleasure provided by his dream date and, the other party is only interested in getting that guy off and out the door as fast as possible, the girl is always going to win. The guy will never admit it, or complain to anybody, not to the Mama-san and certainly not his buddies.

One evening I was again walking back from a shopping trip with Buck, who this time was looking for a purse he hadn't seen before, which meant we were really just taking a walk, when we ran into Mama-san, big and beefy, standing squarely before us, asking "You want young girl?" Clearly all Americans must look alike because it seemed she didn't recognize us from our first engagement with her. She was insistent in the charming way only a Mama-san can muster: "Hey! What's the matter? You shy guy?" I hemmed and hawed and Mama seemed to take that as a sign that I had some special itch that just needed to get scratched. Her experience told her that would be worth a few extra bucks. She kept hitting me just below the shoulder saying, "What the matter? You want two girls? (tooth suck) Oh! You bad man!" (tooth suck) and then she punched me again. Finally I looked at her, then looked down and said, "I want a young boy. How about it, you got a young boy?" Then she did the big tooth suck, strong enough to pull the saliva off the walls of her mouth so it made a slurping noise, and she walloped me once again, "Oh, you bad man!" I feigned embarrassment as I started to leave with Buck in tow, but she grabbed me and said, "OK, OK, I get you young boy!" I turned back towards her, but looked hesitant. I waited a few moments before stammering "I want a boy with no legs."

That stopped her cold for about five-seconds, before she punched me in the shoulder, sucked in a bunch of air and smiling, she said, "Oh, you very bad man!" Again I started to leave when she said, "No, wait, I get for you." This gave me serious pause because Korean children who are not perfect or are the children of a mother who remarries but the husband won't take them, are sent to a state-run orphanages where the children are left to their own devices and fates. Many fall into prostitution and slavery. In that instant, I had the most terrible image of some ten-year-old Korean orphan yelling "No Mama-san! NO!" as she merrily trimmed him to stumps. I started waving my hands and moving away from her saying, "No, no, never mind. I am leaving for America. I don't want." I wasn't leaving for several months, but I certainly didn't want her mutilating some child on my account. Happily, there were never any reports of boys abducted for this purpose.

+++

# Kaygogi

It was a Wednesday night in late autumn and the winds of winter were not far off. I decided to stop reading *"With The Century,"* a farcical autobiography by the late dictator, Kim Il Sung, just as he was describing a double rainbow and a glowing new star appearing in the heavens to herald the 1942 birth of his son and heir, Kim Jong Il. I put the book down just as he was describing the birth taking place on North Korea's cherished Baekdu Mountain, even though Soviet records indicated he was born in the Siberian village of Vyatskoye, in 1941. Knowing this story would keep, I decided to nip on down to the Club for a bit of society.

Just a few people were there, some Fiends at the bar shooting their wrist watches as they described feats of aerial élan, while a couple of civil engineers, with pants covered in mud and muck from the runway repair work they oversaw, sat quietly sucking beers at a table. They were USAF Combat Engineers assigned to one of the seven Rapid Engineer Deployable Heavy Operational Repair Squadron Engineer (RED HORSE) squadrons deployed globally and were the USAF's heavy-construction unit much like the Navy SeaBees.

The USAF issued each unit location a no-kidding giant statue of a Red Horse. Naturally, other squadrons would routinely attack the horse with washable paint making it a Zebra, or coloring in the stallion's giant penis, but the trick was to not get caught. When the RED HORSE at Malmstrom AFB Montana got done up like a Zebra with a red penis, the infuriated Wing Commander ordered a formal investigation, which sadly failed to reveal the culprits. Having served as a cop when I first enlisted out of high school, I had a pretty good hunch about who the culprits were, but it wasn't my investigation. In mid-2000, on my way out the door to my next assignment, a senior SP NCO confirmed my suspicions that the cops had done the deed. They'd waited until dead of night, closed the front gate and, declaring a robbery drill was underway, set up patrols to divert any traffic that might be out and about while they took a photo of their handiwork.

That night in Korea, Buck was at the bar with Mongo and Da-Veed, an F-16 guy who worked in plans. His name was David, but he got that name from the efforts of a crazy Korean woman named Sonny who was desperate to capture his genes for no other reason than Da-Veed had long legs and she wanted those genes for her offspring. It also helped that Da-Veed had slightly almond-shaped eyes and thick, straight black hair. Every Friday night, despite nobody signing her in, Sonny magically appeared in the bar. She wore a red leather jacket with the collar turned up, making her look like "Ming the Merciless" from the old Buck Rogers serials, but not quite right. Sphinkster made numerous passes at her, but she only had eyes for the tall American and would cry "Hello Da-Veed! It's Me! Sonny!" as if he didn't know. The Koreans are not opposed to eugenics and she kept up her attempts to capture his genetic material until he finished his tour and safely returned to the states.

On that same evening those three were then joined at the bar by Stretchee, an F-15 guy also assigned to plans. He was a fraction under five-foot-five, which made him just eligible for a pilot slot, although he looked like he should still use a phone book to see over the cockpit glare-shield. He got his name when some wag remarked "Ooooh, you gotta stretchee long time to see over top!" and the name stuck. The four of them were rolling dice playing "four, five, six," a game of chance with three dice, with the intent of wining big bucks and doing great financial harm to their buddies.

As they played, Stretchee was in an animated discussion about college sports teams with Welder, a Navy guy attached to Seventh who also worked in the plans shop. Welder got his nickname when his A-6 Intruder came in hot for landing, with the anti-brake system not working. When he applied the brakes they fused, welding the calipers to the brake pads, while igniting the magnesium wheels, hence the name: Welder. A proud Navy Academy grad, he chafed at the requirement that he wear a PACAF patch on the right pocket of his flight suit. Unhappy with that, he had a new PACAF patch made by Mr. Kim that changed the "Pacific Air Forces" written in gold thread below the crest to say, "Go Navy beat Air Force." It was six months before anybody noticed.

Meanwhile, Young Jim, a recovering B-52 navigator with a hang-dog rubbery face that always made him look dour, was talking with Bugs. B-52 guys always dealt with the real possibility of being directly involved in a nuclear scenario with low survivability rates, and empathy was not a strong suit. Young Jim gesticulated freely and gave unfiltered and animated responses to any discussion. Those two were my best option for intelligent conversation, so I pulled up a seat and ordered a soft drink because I liked to confine my alcoholic intake to the weekends.

It wasn't but fifteen minutes later when Françoise, a thirty-five year old Canadian civilian contractor who worked on Black Hawk helicopter avionics systems, ran into the lounge in an apparent state of near hysteria shrieking "Kaygogi! Kaygogi!" Thinking she'd been injured somehow, we jumped up, led her over to one of the seats while somebody brought water and a double brandy. Françoise shot the drink, lit a smoke and, after a few moments, was calm enough to tell us her tale of woe.

Françoise lived off-base in an efficiency apartment that was part of a larger house. It was really a closet with single bed, hot water kettle, shower stall, and a view of the back of other buildings. The Korean owners, Mr and Mrs Kim, were friendly enough, but nobody in the family spoke any sort of English so the relationship was one that relied on smiles, hand gestures, and some pigeon-English /Korean "Kor-engrish," all having worked quite well for some months. The Kims were nice people, happy to have a tenant who worked for the American government because that allowed them to charge exactly whatever the maximum governmental rent allowance was. As a bonus, they even had a happy and lively little white Pomeranian dog. Each day when Françoise would come home after work, the dog would greet her excitedly. She asked Mr. Kim the dog's name by pointing at it and he replied "Kaygogi." Every day when Françoise returned from work, she would greet little Kaygogi happily, as she had become quite smitten. She brought him little treats and eventually was able to teach him several tricks (with English commands) as the dog was quite clever. Kaygogi reminded her of her own pup that she had to leave with her Mom back in Edmonton.

This evening however, when Françoise came home she wasn't greeted by Kaygogi. In fact, there was no sign of the little dog, only his leash hook and open collar sitting on the floor, the leash loop run underneath a table leg. Worried, Françoise called out to Mr. Kim who was busy stirring a large pot of soup he was preparing for the evening meal and asked after the dog's whereabouts. "Mr. Kim! Where is Kaygogi?" Sharing a bright smile, Mr. Kim lifted the wooden spoon from the broth and, using it as a pointer, directed her gaze to the rapidly boiling pot while he said, "Kaygogi!" and, in that one terrifying moment, Françoise understood that little Kaygogi was no longer a pet, but on the menu for supper. She fled the house for the Club where she could share her pain and find consolation from the horror she'd just experienced.

The effect of sharing her trauma was cathartic and Françoise regained control of herself, until Young Jim broke the silence when he said, "Well, what the hell did you expect? It's pronounced *Gaegogi* which is Korean for dog stew!"

+++

## Total Quality Management

"This isn't some damned football game."

- General Bogan, *Fail Safe,* 1964

I n late November the weather had turned damp and cold, bone-chilling cold. The brochures all said Korea had a climate like Virginia. If cold and rainy springs followed by hot and muggy summers and short autumns leading into bone chilling winters were what the "State for Lovers" had to offer, I knew I'd not soon be looking for a place in Richmond.

I was staring out the window musing because I'd just read a report in the *Stars and Stripes* about yet another scandal involving a bad courts-martial in Europe, this time at Spangdahlem air base, home of the 52nd Fighter Wing. There had been a series of seemingly never-ending scandals in each of the services in the 90's following Desert Storm. That was the period when the last of the Vietnam era guys who knew how to "*fly, fuck, and fight*" without making the news, began hitting retirement, leaving only all-volunteer Cold War-era warriors who had never experienced a war-time mission. The armed forces lost that focus after the Soviet menace went away.

Desert Storm didn't qualify as much of a war because, at one hundred hours, it didn't last long enough to have an iconic song written about it, whereas the Vietnam War and its draftees spawned loads of albums, movies, and hit TV shows. The USAF experienced another draw down after Desert Storm, a global reduction in forces (RIF) when many fine officers with excellent combat records, including some JAGs, were being told their services were no longer required, given a stipend, and shown the door. Closing bases and decreased manpower requirements taught many of the new guys that being a ruthless sycophant was the way forward in a career. One of them called to thank me for all my help getting him promoted. I had no idea who he was but I could tell he was merely reading a script and assumed he was dialing every JAG senior to him with the same speech, in hopes of getting some continued support in his climb up the ladder.

I'd just learned that a defendant in a criminal case had committed suicide on the morning his trial was set to open in late October, and blame was zeroing in on the over-zealous prosecutors who had made it happen. It was just another sign of a disturbing trend and attitudinal change within both the JAG department and the USAF generally. I'd noticed the new JAGs coming in were all graduates of the "top ten percent of the top ten law schools," unlike myself, upper fifty-percent at a bottom fifty-percent ranked law school. Very few of those direct commission appointees straight out of school had prior military, or general-life experience, and they thought every offense was a courts-martial offense. Their approach to charging crimes seemed an "intellectual creativity challenge." Many saw their win tally as a badge of honor, and some immature jerks even made bets about who could have the most courts-martials, obviously having no thought or concern about those airmen, or their families, they would unnecessarily toss into the justice grinder and bring before the bench for some metric. Instead they chose to treat justice like a football game with winners and losers, and they would not be on the losing side.

This belief was bolstered by new guidance from higher headquarters encouraging prosecutors to avoid losing a case by charging "everything including the kitchen sink." The concept was overloading the defense in the hopes that with enough charges, something would stick. In early 1996, at Mountain Home before I came to Korea, I'd overheard my then-SJA and another, both Academy grads, make such a bet while we were all TDY to a course at the JAG school at Maxwell AFB, Alabama. When I got to Korea a few months later, the other SJA was at one of the subordinate bases and had indeed conducted a greater than average number of courts, and more than were conducted at Mountain Home, winning the bet. He was promoted and assigned as the SJA at a NAF in Europe, while the loser was promoted and sent to Alaska.

I'd become aware of this new mindset beginning in England in 1988 when I was assigned, over my objections, to charge and prosecute an airman with rape and adultery for having consensual sex with a woman married to another airman in the squadron. The wife testified the sex was completely consensual and confirmed she'd told the young man, "Shush! Don't wake my husband," who was passed out drunk and sleeping on the bedroom floor.

The young airman was acquitted of the rape, but convicted of adultery. He was stripped of his rank and sent to jail for two weeks, a punishment even my somewhat reserved wife, Laurie, thought wildly excessive. The trend towards harsh morality-justice continued as USAF prosecutions for adultery globally went from sixteen in 1987 to sixty-seven in 1997. Between 1989 and 1996 the Air Force courts-martialed three hundred eleven airmen for adultery; two hundred eighty-six of them male, as conservative religious fundamentalists became more engaged and sufficiently emboldened to impose their personal standards on others while on active duty.

It became routine to hear "And I'd like to thank my Lord and Savior Jesus Christ" during a change of command ceremony. Some people began adding Bible verses to their email signature blocks or putting large, ostentatious crucifixes on their desks and asking other airmen if "they'd found Jesus." They pushed their religious beliefs freely and those beliefs colored their ratings of officers under their command.

In 1996, the 104th Congress passed, without debate or publicity, the *"Honor and Decency in the Military Act,* amending title 10, United

States Code, and thereby prohibiting the Department of Defense from selling, renting, or otherwise providing sexually explicit material to any individual." So now adult war-fighters serving the nation in remote locations like combat zones, or aboard ships, could no longer buy a Playboy at the BX to look at the centerfold and dream about who and what they were really fighting for. Airmen now had to get themselves off base to buy a bit of smut along with those folks who chose not to defend and protect America, while the base BX lost customers and revenue.

+++

## Unintended Outcomes

On May 17, 1995, inside a hanger belonging to the 52nd Equipment Maintenance Squadron (EMS), thirty-five year old Tech Sergeant (TSgt) Thomas Mueller, a seventeen-year veteran assigned to the 52nd EMS, along with TSgt Bill Campbell and another airman, finished a repair job on an F-15C Eagle fighter, registration 79-0068. The plane had come in a week earlier requiring scheduled "back shop" maintenance, work that couldn't be done on the flight line, so the bird was brought into the hanger for the repairs. Campbell reattached a pair of flight-control rods to two hookups that relayed the pilot's tug on his control stick to the movable ailerons and horizontal stabilators that control the plane's flight. Mueller double-checked the work using a mirror and flashlight, then signed off as completing the task. Born in Germany, he emigrated to the United States and became an American in 1977. Mueller married a Texan and had two sons, Daniel, fifteen, and eleven year old Marcelo. He was well regarded by his contemporaries and the aviators; as one wrote, "I'd feel completely comfortable" flying any F-15 Mueller had fixed.

On May 30, 1995, Major Donald Lowry, a thirty-six year old family man originally from Key West, Florida, and then assigned to the 53rd Fighter Squadron, completed his walk-around inspection of the plane, got into the cockpit and went though the preflight checklists that included "stirring the pot," moving all the flight control surfaces under the watchful eyes of the aircraft marshal who was connected by an intra-phone. Recorded communications indicated that Lowry realized he had some kind of a problem, yet elected not to abort the takeoff. The Eagle is a plane that wants to fly because it can climb to 30,000 feet in one minute and move out at 1,875 mph. Lowry "lit the can," igniting the afterburners, and those two Pratt & Whitney F100-PW-100 turbofan engines, each producing 25,000 pounds of thrust, shot that fighter down the runway. The nose began to lift, but after gaining just thirty feet of altitude, rolled sharply to the left and crashed onto the golf course a short distance from the runway. Lowry died upon impact.

A safety investigation showed that during that routine maintenance, the mechanics had crossed and mis-connected the control rods which meant that Lowry, while pulling up on the stick and to the right to gain altitude to clear the runway, had actually turned the nose down and left.

Further inspection revealed this same error had occurred twice before in 1986 and 1991 and had been caught by the marshals during preflight. The solution was to color-code the rods to prevent this from occurring, but for reasons unknown that information was not "cross-fed" globally. This was unfortunate because this was also during the time when General Ron Fogleman was appointed Chief of Staff, the senior Air Force officer.

### A CULTURE THAT DEMANDED ACCOUNTABILITY

A 1963 academy grad, Fogleman was an experienced multi-mission combat pilot. Shot down over Vietnam in 1968 while piloting an F-100 Super Sabre, he was rescued by clinging to the skid of a two-seater AH-1 Cobra attack helicopter that landed at his crash site. He had a Silver Star and Purple Heart among his numerous awards and decorations. Fogleman was a very tough guy and an excellent pilot who had also been an F-15 demonstration pilot for international air shows.

He was also a humorless professional who expected the same from all under his charge and he brought that iron discipline everywhere he went as he rose to the top. As the 7th Air Force commander in the early nineties, he closed the on-base massage parlors and made them, and all the soju tents and some bars off-base, off limits to airmen. That didn't stop anybody from going to those places, but now they did so clandestinely and at risk to their careers.

His tenure began on Oct 26, 1994, and he inherited a large mess from his predecessor, Gen Merrill McPeak, most famous for deconstructing and redesigning the entire AF during the great RIF of '92. McPeak kept everybody off balance by making radical changes to the uniforms. Those changes created a hue and cry from the airmen; while they were complaining about that, he implemented major organizational changes.

The current issue consuming Fogleman's time was the April 14,1994, downing of two US Army UH-60 Blackhawk helicopters. A pair of Eagles had, on a bright and clear morning over Northern Iraq, misidentified the Blackhawks as Iraqi Mi-24 "Hind" helicopter gunships. The two F-15 pilots, call signs Tiger 1 & 2, were also from the 53rd Fighter Squadron. For these missions they were under the operational control of a USAF AWACS aircraft providing Battle Space management for the no-fly zone which was imposed after Desert Storm.

This northern Iraq "no fly zone" had been in effect above the 36th parallel since the end of the fighting two years earlier, and no Iraqi helos had flown during the preceding thirteen months. Those Eagle drivers hadn't studied the training silhouettes posted on every toilet cubicle door of every flying squadron or they would have known an M-24 Hind retracts its landing gear during flight, and the Mi-8 Hip troop transport has tricycle landing gear, while the Blackhawk is a tail dragger.

Those doomed Blackhawks were engaged in supporting *"Operation Provide Comfort,"* assisting Kurdish refugees in northern Iraq. The fighters made two passes to visually confirm the helos as Iraqi. Tiger 1 said, "Tally (I see) two Hind." Thirty-seconds later Tiger 2 confirmed with "Tally, two Hind."

Satisfied they had Iraqi Hinds in their sights, Tiger 1 launched a radar-guided AIM-120 AMRAAM missile; thirty-seconds later Tiger 2 fired a heat-seeking AIM-9 Sidewinder missile. Both Blackhawks were destroyed, killing 15 Americans and 11 foreign officials. They were:

- **US Military:**
- SSG Paul Barclay (SF Commo NCO)
- SPC Cornelius A. Bass (Eagle-1 Door Gunner)
- SPC Jeffrey C. Colbert (Eagle-1 Crew Chief)
- SPC Mark A. Ellner (Eagle-2 Door Gunner)
- CW2 John W. Garrett, Jr. (Eagle-1 Pilot)
- CW2 Michael A. Hall (Eagle-2 Pilot Command)
- SFC Benjamin T. Hodge (Linguist)
- CPT Patrick M. McKenna (Eagle-1 Pilot Command)
- WO1 Erik S. Mounsey (Eagle-2 Pilot)

- COL Richard A. Mulhern (Incoming Co-Commander)
- 1LT Laurie A. Piper (USAF, Intel Officer)
- SGT Michael S. Bobinson (Eagle-2 Crew Chief)
- SSG Ricky L. Bobinson (SF Medic)
- Ms. Barbara L. Schell (State Dept. Political Advisor)
- COL Jerald L. Thompson (Outgoing Co-Commander)
- **British Military:**
- MAJ Harry Shapland (Security/Intel Duty Officer)
- LTC Jonathan C. Swann (Senior UK Officer)

- **French Military:**
- LTC Guy Demetz (Senior French Officer)
- **Turkish Army:**
- COL Hikmet Alp (Co-Commander)
- LT Ceyhun Civas (Laison Officer)
- LT Barlas Gultepe (Liaison Officer)
- **Kurdish Partisans:**
- Abdulsatur Arab
- Ghandi Hussein
- Bader Mikho
- Ahmad Mohammed
- Salid Said (Linguist)

To compound matters, there was confusion over who "knew what they knew and when they knew it" with fingers pointing in all directions. Calls for a Congressional Investigation and hearings were started, but Fogleman refused to let the subpoenaed witnesses appear and the hearings ended with no conclusion.

Command knew somebody had to be made to pay for this, and Capt Jim Wang, USAFA grad and lead supervisor aboard the AWACS, was selected. In his report, the Article 32 IO recommended five counts of dereliction of duty for failing to alert the pilots that the Blackhawks were American. Wang was acquitted at trial and Maj. Gen. Nolan Sklute, the Judge Advocate General later commented, "Justice was done. An incident like this does not necessarily mean that the conduct of all those involved rises to the level of criminal culpability." Sklute was the last TJAG to feel that way.

Fogleman ordered a career-killing administrative LoR placed in Wang's personnel jacket and the jackets of five other officers, including the F-15 pilots, and three members of the crew on Wang's plane. None of the others ever faced criminal proceedings because this was not a criminal act, but a tragic accident, one that never would have happened if safety protocols had been followed. All these prosecutions did was reduce confidence in the USAF leadership. Morale eroded and the retention rate for pilots and mechanics plummeted as these highly trained technicians took their valuable training and experience over to Delta and other airlines, for more money and fewer work hours, with no risk of going to jail over such tragedies.

While the Blackhawk matter was still on the front burner, Lieutenant Kelli Flinn, a USAFA grad and the first female B-52 bomber pilot, was again back in the news. She'd originally come into the national spotlight when she broke this barrier. This milestone was celebrated when then Secretary of the Air Force, Dr. Sheila Widnall took a flight with her. The AF loved doing things first and a female piloting a nuclear bomber was big.

This time Kelli was making national news because word of her having an open and notorious affair with a married man became public.

The cuckold wife was an enlisted airman who went to her First Sergeant after finding love letters from Flinn to her husband. The First Sergeant approached Flinn, asking her to knock it off, but she disregarded his warning. She was charged with adultery for having sex with the married civilian and fraternization for a two-day tryst with an enlisted airman a year and a half earlier. Frank, her lawyer, was a retired JAG who'd spent his life in the defense world; broke with long standing tradition and started trying these cases in the "court of public opinion" while the press obliged. The USAF wasn't ready for this because until then keeping matters out of the media had been a gentlemen's agreement. Sadly, for the Air Force, the defense attorney understood the salacious nature of the entire episode was a huge media draw, adultery not being a crime prosecuted outside of the military.

What all those senior JAGs in DC didn't know was that Frank *knew* most of the JAG leadership were a bunch of philanderers. When *60 Minutes* did a piece on Flinn, her lawyer, Frank, complained about JAG leadership being philandering hypocrites. There was a lot of scrambling to find a JAG spokesman who could honestly say that he was unaware of any adultery going on with any senior JAG officers and then deny that the prosecution was solely because she was a woman.

In the end, a not-very-well-known colonel, a conservative Mormon who didn't smoke, drink, curse, or run around on his wife, was selected. He'd spent his career in acquisitions, which absolutely guaranteed he wouldn't have the first clue about any of the open and notorious goings of some of his colleagues in the E ring. This made him the perfect department spokesman since he could honestly say he knew absolutely nothing about the peccadilloes of his fellow JAGs.

Leadership had no choice and had to use him, inexperienced in media matters as he was, because it was well known that most of the senior JAG leadership had either engaged in extra-marital relations or knew of others who had. One now silver-haired senior Colonel, as a young captain instructing at the USAFA, got dressed after catching a nooner with the wife of another instructor and ignorantly came back to work wearing one of the blue uniform shirts belonging to the cuckold husband, as noted by a sharp-eyed paralegal who saw the husband's name tag.

As this first-time spokesman read his prepared statement issuing denials and took questions, sweat poured off his forehead under the glare of the lights. The Osan bar was crowded and, when the aviators saw that lawyer sweating profusely, they shouted "Weasel JAG! Weasel JAG!" while throwing popcorn at the TV.

While JAG leadership stumbled around, Fogleman, frustrated by the repeated inability of bases to deliver accountability, made his displeasure known. Subordinate commands echoed his sentiments to wings and their staff judge advocates and those new generation JAGs were happy to prosecute with predictably bad results.

As a result of this edict, Lt. Col. Karen Tew pinned the ribbons to her dress uniform and packed a suitcase for jail. She knew she could be facing up to ten years behind bars once she entered her guilty plea, and wondered what would happen to her two teenage daughters and her elderly parents. In court the forty-one year old career officer apologized for bringing disgrace to the Air Force saying, "No words can describe the shame and humiliation I feel as a result of my actions." The jury gave no jail time but sentenced her to be dismissed from service. Barely a year short of retirement, she would lose everything -- her job, her pension, her benefits, and the only way of life she had known as an adult, all because a lonely middle-aged woman had an affair with an enlisted man. Nobody gave her a knock-it-off warning, nobody thought to give her a second chance. Discipline and accountability demanded command make an example of her as a warning to others who might fall to the temptations of the flesh.

Five days later, while taking a shower, she felt the lump in her right breast had grown larger, and knowing her medical benefits and $450,000 life insurance policy would end with the impending signature of the Secretary of the Air Force, Karen waited for her parents and children to leave for church, then put a shotgun between her eyes and pulled the trigger.

Now this new breed of sangfroid prosecutors brought charges against TSgt Mueller for those crossed rods, and the lead circuit trial counsel selected to prosecute was a *Kuhfeld Award* winner. That award recognizes the active-duty officer in the grade of major or captain selected as the most outstanding judge advocate of the year based on demonstrated excellence, initiative, devotion to duty and stellar resume. In the mid-90s, five past winners were assigned to USAFE headquarters at Ramstein Air Base, Germany, and two came to physical blows in the hallway over some legal analysis, each believing they were the smartest and best JAG in the room. A non-Kuhfeld winning lawyer witnessed the purported donnybrook later telling me, "It was like watching kittens bitch slap each other."

Now looking to gain a psychological edge on the defense, the prosecutor spread 8 x 10 inch color autopsy photos of Major Lowry out for display on her table in the court room before the Article 32 hearing started. She did this just so Mueller would be certain to see them, an inexcusable and despicable tactic, but not beyond what a weasel will do. She also intercepted, reviewed, and did not disclose, privileged materials sent to the defense counsel, later claiming she'd seen a hole in the envelope and thought maybe the documents weren't really meant for the defense.

The Article 32 IO reviewed the evidence and recommended both NCOs face a general courts-martial prosecution for negligent homicide. Although her original thought had been to charge them with murder, she knew she'd never prove Mueller had planned on killing Lowry. With those changes announced, the two career airmen were looking at total loss of rank and pay, three years in prison, and dishonorable discharge.

Mueller's trial was scheduled to begin on the morning of October 3, 1996, which also happened to be his seventeenth wedding anniversary. When his wife woke up alone, she called his father who had come for the trial and, together with the security police, search parties went out looking. Mueller's car was found parked near a stream in an area where he liked to take his sons to fish. There was a hunting stand nearby, and Major Dee Mills, the Security Police Chief, started to climb the ten foot ladder while calling for Mueller to come out. As she neared the top, she heard the gunshot.

Mueller left a note written in his blood on the glass, "Rosa, I love you. I was not negligent."

TSgt Campbell was awaiting court-martial but, in light of the tragedy, command dropped the charges and administratively discharged him before he could retire and collect a pension. For her own highly improper behavior, the prosecutor was offered non-judicial punishment and, in a previously unheard of decision, the SJA for a Numbered Air Force was appointed to represent her. This JAG happened to be the same hard-ass prosecution crazy SJA from Korea who had made that stupid bet at Maxwell. He was now temporarily appointed her defense lawyer, despite never having worked as a defense counsel, and suggesting the "fix was in." He made the Article 15 go away, but she was given an LoR, fired from her job as a circuit trial counsel, and sent to Randolph AFB in Texas where she gained enough weight to get her sorry ass thrown out.

+++

## Kylie Minogue and the dancing 4X beer cans

I'd managed to get home for a short Christmas leave, and it looked like I'd be staying on the Peninsula until my rotation date the coming July. Serendipitously, the wheel of fortune turned on a raw and overcast morning shortly after I came into the office. I was watching the daily "slip and fall" show on the icy driveway into the JOC, all choreographed by the early morning wake-up music of the ROKAF fifteen-minute daily aerobic workout. Someone in Korean leadership had attended a course in the USA and became a devotee of Richard Simmons, the exercise guru. Now, every morning, at a quarter to eight, the loudspeakers would spew songs designed to get your heart racing and blood pumping.

My reverie was broken by "Michael, my good man! Have you got a minute?" and with that hail I topped off my coffee cup, headed into Col. Tom's office and got the news. "You have been selected to be the 7th Air Force legal representative aboard the US Navy Command vessel *Blue Ridge*, departing from Hawaii and sailing to Australia as part of Exercise Tandem Thrust '97." The plan was for me to fly commercial to Hawaii, then join the ship at Pearl Harbor. With sailing time plus the exercise, I could plan on being gone for a month. The happy thought of thirty days off the Peninsula during a cold and wet spring, and heading to warmer climes on an all-expenses-paid cruise aboard a navy ship, was just the tonic for recovering from a brutal winter. Over the years, I'd entertained idle thoughts of what might have happened had I gone into the Navy JAG program, and here was just the opportunity to scratch that itch.

I went back to my room to start packing my cabana wear for my upcoming voyage. Ajima had just gotten off the phone and was telling me about her rotten grandchildren when the phone rang. My boss explained that the General didn't want his Justice Chief off the Peninsula for that long; so, instead I was being sent to Hawaii with orders to report to Special Operations Command Pacific (SOCPAC) at Pearl Harbor and would receive further orders there.

Two weeks later I stared out the window as the 747 made a slow pass by Diamond Head and all those hotels and beaches leading the way to Honolulu International Airport. Until that moment, everything I knew about Hawaii was gleaned from watching *Hawaii 5-0,* a 1960s television series set on the island. I later met up with the SOCPAC representatives, two Navy Seals who brought me into a small room to "read me in" on the nature of the exercise and what they did for a living. They also had me sign a standard non-disclosure form prohibiting me from discussing techniques or procedures and I was suddenly a member of the Special Staff. I was now part of an advance team going down to a Royal Australian Air Force (RAAF) base in Townsville, Queensland, on the East coast. We were to coordinate and execute the small Special Operations portion of a very large exercise.

During World War II, a Japanese naval force grabbed a foothold in the Coral Sea in an attempt to conquer Australia. They failed and Australia remained independent. Taking the lesson, planners wondered, "What if another power was to attempt such an invasion?" The United States and Australia were determined to be ready, so every two years US and Australian forces gather to rehearse projected scenarios in a bilateral exercise called *Tandem Thrust*.

I met up with my boss and the other two members of the Special staff, a public affairs officer and a medical logistician. For this job we were led by an Army Colonel, Pat, who was wearing a First Special Forces Group flash on his beret. He welcomed me, asking, "Are you as good as Harmon Rabb?" a reference to the hugely popular TV show "JAG," the story of a handsome former fighter pilot who had to become a lawyer after his night vision went. He was usually accompanied by a smoking-hot female Marine lawyer and together they operated out of the JAG headquarters in Virginia. They worked under the direct supervision of The Judge Advocate General, a former SEAL and action figure who would sometimes go out on adventures with them, assuring the show bore zero resemblance to the actual JAG world. I knew right there it would be a fun trip.

Colonel Pat "read me into" my piece of the exercise, which was to evaluate the need for lawyers in Joint and Combined special operations. They needed to know whether to put JAGs into advisor slots or pick a commissioned officer special operator and send him, or her, to law school and generate their own little Harmon Rabb in three years.

Special operators are often referred to as "snake-eaters." This nickname imbues them with a certain dangerous cachet, and they enjoy the sobriquet. It came to being thanks to a Special Forces habit serving snake meat at the Gabriel Demonstration Area on Ft. Bragg, in North Carolina, for visiting VIPs, the press, etc. For me this meant I'd be an observer going out with various groups of special operators on an array of missions to gain a better understanding of the exact nature of the work and legal issues arising. This part brought me no particular joy. I'd served as an engineer in the US Army reserves while working my way through law school and we'd spent two weeks each summer in "the field," living and working amidst the pines and Juniper trees. I didn't much care for the life, which is why I joined the US Air Force, where people, on any deployment, slept in tents at fixed locations because aircraft need concrete.

In the very early morning hours of March 3, we loaded all our gear, equipment and selves aboard an aging C-141 Starlifter and took off for RAAF Townsville, having only a brief stop scheduled for refueling at Anderson AFB, located on the northern coast of Guam. Arriving there a few hours later, we deplaned and were ushered into the transient waiting lounge while the maintenance and refueling was attended to. We were not permitted to leave the confines of the lounge, but plenty of vending machines provided a diversion while we waited. We were still there, working on "diversions" until midday when a string of blue USAF busses pulled up in front and Col Pat directed us all onboard, offering only, "They said something was broken on the plane and we'll be stuck for a few hours, so we'll get some rooms at Billeting." The procession drove around the base, finally arriving at the billeting office only to find out there were no rooms available on the base, but rooms could be found at the Hyatt Regency two miles away.

Now happily aboard the bus, off we rode to this fabulous and no-doubt expensive hotel; as a bonus we were treated to a tour of the island, a place that bears an astonishing resemblance to US Highway 19 along the rural gulf coast of Florida. We checked in and got receipts for our rooms. I was issued a roommate, a Special Forces reservist whose other job was as a Diplomatic Security Special Agent, a point he reminded me of no fewer than six times saying, "You know, DSS agents are credentialed federal officers, like the FBI."

Having been a cop in a past life, I understood what he was saying and why. In the world of law enforcement, the term "credentials" immediately brings to mind the FBI, the top agency in the hierarchy of law enforcement, and leads to inferiority complexes hovering around other agencies without the same "brand" recognition. And this causes other of the lesser known agencies to share their "authority," so others would not think of them as just federal security guards.

It was shortly after two when we finally checked in, so while my credentialed roommate visited the bar, I visited the lobby, then ventured outside to dip a toe in the Philippine Sea, then went back to the room to take a shower and catch a nap. The Special Agent came back to the room around six, terribly inebriated having spent his daily per diem on sweet drinks with umbrellas. He sat on the edge of the bed, took off his shoes, and fell back into the mattress, asleep.

Thirty minutes later, the phone rang and we were ordered out of the rooms and back on the busses to get on the plane which would be ready to go as soon as the maintenance guys replaced the broken white navigation light on the tail of the aircraft. This was not insignificant since the most vital aircraft lights during flight are colored aircraft navigation, or position, lights. The port (left) wingtip light is red, while the starboard (right) wingtip light is green. The final navigation light is located on or near the tail, and is white. These are required to function so the aircraft can be spotted from any angle and, if coming up from behind, can tell a pilot if he is to the right or left of the aircraft in the lead.

What none of us knew at the time was that on March 2, 1997, Cyclone Gavin had formed in the Pacific and was traveling south and east; the outer edge of that cyclone was hitting the island of Guam about the same time our maintenance guys finished the repair. Gavin was responsible for at least eighteen deaths and caused over $23 million worth of damage, as it hit the islands of Tuvalu, Wallis, Futuna, Fiji and New Zealand. Due to the unusually severe impact of this storm, the name Gavin was retired from the tropical cyclone naming lists.

While the outer edges of that monster storm bore down on Guam, we were waiting it out in the transit lounge we'd left but a few hours earlier to wait for the word to board. Now watching as the black storm clouds drew closer, I sensed we wouldn't be going anywhere. The winds soon picked up to above forty knots sustained and the airfield was closed until Gavin passed. Now instead of a nice soft bed in a room with a balcony view of the Philippine Sea, I was sitting on a hard-backed plastic chair designed to make a person uncomfortable within twenty minutes to discourage loitering, and surrounded by several sleeping soldiers and my own hung-over DSS agent extraordinaire.

Daylight came and the weather cleared. We dragged ourselves to the aircraft and boarded. We flew further south and finally, as the sun went down, we arrived at RAAF Townsville to begin our job.

We deplaned and made our way into the customs hall. I processed through and was waiting with the other members of the Special Staff when Col Pat came chugging up. His face was a bit tight as he said, "Hey JAG, the customs guys want to see you." My immediate thought was some bonehead must have to tried bring in some meat, fruit, or other prohibited item. I walked up to the booths and made an inquiry of a senior customs guy. "You guys were looking for the lawyer?" He looked up at me, asking, "Are you the JAG?" and I told him indeed I was, hence the following conversation took place:

Him: "Hey! Have you ever landed an F-15 on a heaving carrier deck?"

Me: "No, the F-15 is an Air Force plane, it'd be an F-14 Tomcat, but I'm not currently night-qualified."

Him: "How do you disarm a nuclear bomb?"

Me: "You cut the red wire."

Him: "Where's your Sheila?" (Girl) A reference to his very amply endowed work partner.

Me: "I left her home, this is no place for a woman."

He laughed and ordered the line shut down, so all the inspectors and customs folks and I could get into a group picture. While the other specials watched with some consternation at not being lionized themselves for being special, I enjoyed the moment with my new friends and realized that some days it pays to show up when a TV show about your job is #1 down under.

After clearing customs, we went to the airbase, got our room assignments, and met our Australian hosts, in this case the highly vaunted Special Air Services Regiment (SASR) whose mission was not classified:

> "...Providing unique capabilities to support sensitive strategic operations, special recovery operations, advisory and training assistance, special reconnaissance, precision strike and direct action."

The SASR is primarily structured to conduct covert long-range reconnaissance and surveillance in small teams in enemy-controlled territory, while commando units are utilized to conduct raids in larger groups. In addition to war-fighting during conventional conflicts, the regiment is also tasked with maintaining a specialist counter-terrorist capability. Other jobs include training local indigenous forces, recovery of kidnapped Australian citizens, humanitarian assistance, and counter-insurgency operations. They also kill an awful lot of bad guys. This is all remarkably similar to our own US Special Operations, but I can't comment either way because a signed and countersigned form exists in a file somewhere.

We met our counterparts and mine was a charming Army lawyer, a terribly sensible fellow as we began by going to the Officer's Club for lunch which included drinks. There we rapidly finished our coordination on the interoperability of our Rules of Engagement and spent the remainder of the day toasting bi-lateral relations.

The Australian SAS folks were extremely well-trained and very engaging. As joint planning meetings were undertaken and capabilities shared, the days passed and after the weekend the field work portion of the operation would begin and expand when the main body and command vessel Blue Ridge came steaming into port sometime in the next week, dependent on Cyclone Gavin's track.

Meanwhile, I was considered JAFO, short for "Just Another Fucking Observer" and taking it all in: going out on night operations and ambushes, searching for areas of any legal concern, and developing training scenarios which included ethical hypotheticals designed to make the students think through the analysis, and not simply looking to find a written order to paste against it.

This was the most hazardous duty I'd ever been assigned, as everything that can sting, bite, or kill you lives in Australia and most of those critters come out at night on an airbase that essentially sat in a swamp. On my last evaluation assignment, I was observing a night extraction. Snake-eaters get dropped off in one place and often have to change locations to reach the extraction point. This effort is directed by a Tactical Air Control Party or TACP, a combat air traffic controller. We were getting ready to take off in his pickup truck, heading for the extraction point at a remote edge of the airfield when I asked, "Is your radio working?" The Tech Sergeant, a consummate professional, looked wounded and frostily assured me it was.

We drove out to the far end of the airfield and, when he decided we were in position, parked and shut off the engine. After a few moments, I realized I was hearing a persistent humming and asked if we'd parked near some power lines. He assured me there weren't any nearby. It soon dawned on us that the now threatening sound were mosquitos (locally dubbed "mossies") looking for dinner. Quickly, I rolled down my sleeves, buttoned my shirt's top button, and pulled down the flaps to my BDU patrol cap, covering any exposed skin I could. We finally heard the sound of the MH-53J, *Pave Low* in the distance and got out of the safe confines of the cabin and into the mossie-filled darkness. The NCO set the radio down, turned it on, and called out to the helo, but with no results. The cigarette I'd lit was holding the swarm away from my face, but I started thinking about the medical briefing we'd gotten about Dengue and Ross River Fever. The controller changed frequencies and started cursing the gear. He finally got them on a hand-held radio, lit an infra-red strobe, and called for the extraction.

The MH-53J was a part of the 31st Special Operations Squadron at Osan and had been flown down to Australia inside the belly of a C-5. I didn't have night vision googles and couldn't make out the huge machine as it descended because I had to bury my head in my arms to avoid the detritus blown about as the over-one-hundred miles per hour rotor wash turned grass stalks into missiles. I didn't mind though, because it absolutely got rid of the mosquitos. The airman led me aboard and sat sulking in a corner over his equipment failure. He didn't get that I wasn't an inspector; I wasn't there to grade him. I was simply an observer there to see how to improve their capabilities and make it easier for the war fighter to do the necessary legal evaluations in the field. I would, however, add a note about the comm failure; a failure like that would cost lives in a real world situation and should be an immediate mission kill and recall.

I had also been declared the unit morale officer for this exercise and needed to conduct research into the availability of entertainment of various kinds on the local economy, and what host nation laws the troops had to obey when they had some time off.

I was happy to report to Colonel Pat that prostitution was legal in Australia, because I knew those guys would be looking for hookers. I spoke with the managers of several brothels and determined all the sex workers were checked routinely for health and enforcement of proper sexual hygiene, and all the businesses proved very professional in their operation. This meant none of the troopers would get in trouble looking for love in all the wrong places and possibly creating an international incident. Gambling was likewise legal and casinos and slot rooms were many and easy to find. Drinking was legal over twenty-one and drunk driving was strictly prohibited, so arrangements were made with taxi companies.

Townsville enjoys tropical weather and is a pleasant place that has enjoyed a long history with visiting American forces, starting with the February 1942 arrival of the 22nd Bombardment group. On one occasion, thinking I'd buy a little something for Laurie, I visited an opal shop, Queensland being one of the few places on the planet where opals are found. The shop was run by two lovely elderly woman and when I said hello one brightened up, asking, "Are you an American?" When I replied, "Why, yes I am" her eyes got a little bit distant and she said in a soft voice, "I remember when your dads all came down here during the war. God, they were lovely fellows."

I also learned some of those Special Forces snake-eaters were always very concerned with operational security. The Navy SEALS covered every window in their section with newspaper to maintain operational security. They also didn't like to have their pictures taken or otherwise be identified, which also added to the mystique of the outfit while keeping their faces off a terrorist bulletin board on the internet.

With the weekend upon us, our hosts wanted to show us another side of Australia, the one not focused on hookers or slots. The decision was made to take us to a professional rugby match. The Townsville Cowboys would be playing the Penrith Panthers, who were up from Sydney, some 1,300 miles south, there being a couple hundred thousand square miles of pretty much no other competition except for Brisbane and it was 830 miles south. The SAS Public Affairs guy had worked it out with our PA guy and all of us were off for a real treat. We had seats right down by the pitch, best seats in the house, and we were settling in for two forty-minute periods and a ten minute half-time break which would include the special treat of Kylie Minogue, live and on stage!

We didn't have any problem getting beer. I'd learned from the local TV that, "Australians wouldn't give a Castlemaine 4X for anything else." It also helped that you couldn't swing a dead cat without hitting a sign or poster declaring the same. This might have either been incredible marketing or possibly was due to the fact that they had the only brewery in Queensland, but who can say for certain? This relentless psychological pressure to only drink a 4X gave me no pause for concern, because it was also the only brand they carried. I stepped right up to the counter to order. The guy looked at me and said, "You a Yank?" and remembering how it'd worked well with the customs folks, I channeled my best inner John Wayne, replying, "Why, yes sir, I am!" The delighted barman said, "Put your money away Yank, drinks are on us." It was this random act of kindness that convinced me that if the apocalypse came to the States, I was moving to this country. Nice folks, free beer, and some recently observed drive-through liquor stores, made Oz seem an excellent place to ride out the end of times. If I had any hesitation, it was about to be put to rest with the half time show.

I don't recall an awful lot about the game. Perhaps it was the beer, or the whiskey a very nice SAS major had thoughtfully brought in a flask. Originally from Wales in the UK, he enjoyed a Welsh accent not unlike the actor Richard Burton's, slightly gravelly, clipped, and very clear. We'd struck up a friendship, he also enjoying Marlboro lights, my brand at the time. We'd taken the habit of sojourning to the club for drinks after work; he was an animated and entertaining story teller.

We were about thirty-five minutes into the contest when he'd leaned over to share a particularly good one.

> "One time in New York City there was this fellow and he was in a terrible state. He was sitting in a lounge at the train station having a rather large whiskey. A friend of his was passing by and asked, 'What's wrong with you, you look terrible.'"

> The man was greatly upset, "I've had the most awful morning. My wife is mad at me and has stormed off. We're supposed to be going on a trip to Pittsburg, Pennsylvania, for our anniversary. When we got to the ticket window, I saw this very beautiful young woman with very large breasts who was selling the tickets. I was flustered by her beauty and when she asked what I wanted, what came out was 'I'd like two pickets to Titsburg' and now I'm in trouble."

> The sympathetic friend shook his head in commiseration. "It was a Freudian slip, I'm certain, and everybody makes a slip like that now and again."

> The man looked up hopefully, "Really? Has it happened to you?"

"Certainly" came the reply. "On the last day of my marriage, I wanted to ask my wife to pass me the strawberry jam and it came out 'You ruined my life, you bloody awful cow!'"

I started laughing but had to cut that reaction short, when I heard the stadium announcer say that the Townsville Cowboys were very pleased to welcome the visiting American Army Special Forces and the Australian Special Air Services. He then directed the audience to look over on the home team side of the pitch. The Australians are nothing if not patriotic and wildly supportive of their armed forces. The shouts, applause, and whistling began. Turns out those SAS guys also hated having their photographs taken by strangers. My friend turned away and shouted something at the Australian Public Affairs Rep who was smiling broadly at the fine work he'd done. The announcer was fairly well demanding we stand up to receive the adoration of the crowd. While the others all looked down at the ground, or pulled their ball caps tighter, I stood up, took off my hat and waved it at the crowd. I motioned the other two "special staff" to jump up as well and let the near hysterical crowd capture our images. There was no threat to us. As we'd been so often reminded recently, we were really just *ersatz*-special operators, nameless faces in the crowd.

For all we know, somewhere in several houses in Australia and on terrorist bulletin boards abroad, photos identifying us as Australian SAS members might still be hanging. It was just another case of inadvertent misidentification, the previous being when Welder, Mongo, and I were invited by our Korean friend, Mira, to attend a dinner

honoring Korean-Italian friendship. These invites were extended so the Italian Ambassador to South Korea wouldn't be the only European-looking guy at the dinner. A photographer for the *Chosun Ibo*, a Korean national daily, took our photo; the next day it appeared in print with the caption, "Three distinguished *Italian* gentlemen were in attendance."

Meanwhile, back at the stadium they hadn't missed a beat as the action moved on to the half-time entertainment which would be none other than the then world-famous Kylie Minogue. The announcer fairly screamed, "You knew her from *Neighbours*, but she's all grown up now!" Kylie had been a "goody-goody" on the longest-running soap opera down-under and she was looking to shed that image. To that end, she'd also taken up with a French photographer and began her "Tres Bizarre" stage, one that had her reveling in her newly released sensuality. For tonight's performance under the lights her backup dancers were four bright yellow Castlemaine 4X Beer cans.

Kylie came rolling into the stadium standing on a stage attached to a forty-foot low-boy trailer. Waving to the crowd as her beer-can dancers jumped off, she launched into one of her songs. It was clear she was lip syncing, but nobody was paying much attention. The folks in the stands, reminded by the dancing beer cans, were busy getting their own beers refilled. I was enraptured, not by Kylie, but by those dancing beer cans.

It has just got to be tough to dance in a beer-can suit. It really sort of comes down to hopping and hoping you don't hit another can to your right or left, or even worse, lose your balance and go rolling off to one side. The cans were obviously game, but no match for the gyrations of a then still fiery, albeit faded, superstar desperately singing and dancing her way back to the top and out of that backwater. The singing went on for several long minutes, in the midst of which one of the cans sat down on the pitch and lit up a cigarette. Yeah, if there was an apocalypse, it'd be OK to wind up here.

Meanwhile, the Blue Ridge, my original assignment, finished sailing in and around Cyclone Gavin's edges all the way to Australia while enduring some very rough seas in the process. I went aboard and met with the AF guy who caught the voyage. He cursed the Navy for existing, and the AF for sending him on the job, as he'd been seasick for two weeks. That told me enough to scratch that itch and remind me I'd made the right choice years ago.

In my after-action report to the Commander, SOCPAC, I opined that it'd be much better and easier to send some snake-eaters to law school than try to train a JAG.

+++

# Rocket Man

After my year in Korea, I sat in my office at Malmstrom Air Force Base, Montana, watching the snow fall, just as I'd done for more days in the last two and a half years than I cared to remember. This base was named for Colonel Einar Axel Malmstrom, the son of Swedish immigrants, who was shot down during his fifty-eighth combat mission in 1944 and spent the remainder of the war in Stalag Luft One, in Barth, Germany. He'd been the vice Wing Commander, but died in a plane crash on Aug 21, 1954, so the base was renamed in his honor. I was dreaming of warmer climes and a more interesting assignment, but I'd been sent there as the Deputy Staff Judge Advocate, which was to groom me for a position as a Staff Judge Advocate and my own office.

The base, originally known as Great Falls Army Air Base, was created early in WW II and performed operations in support of the "Lend-Lease" program with the Soviet Union where the US would lend equipment to allies, in a sort of "rent to own" scheme. Bell P-39 Air Cobras, Douglas C-47 Sky trains, A-20 Havocs and B-25 Mitchell bombers were flown there, then transferred to Soviet pilots who in turn flew them to Siberia. During the program a total of 1,717,712 pounds of cargo containing aircraft parts, tools, miscellaneous equipment, explosives, and medical supplies were shipped through GFAAB. These shipments became one of the greatest technology transfers (and espionage operations) in the history of the world. The plans for the atomic bomb, hundreds of tons of nuclear weapons materials, strategic intelligence reports, and the plans for much of the most advanced aviation, electronic, and heavy industrial technology was transferred to Stalin in sealed diplomatic containers. Dozens, if not hundreds, of Soviet agents also entered the US through Great Falls as part of the Soviet Lend-Lease delegation and staff.

After WW II, the Strategic Air Command (SAC) surged into prominence. A massive command with global reach that accounted for half of all AF assets, it being the organization directly responsible for bringing nuclear destruction to the Soviet Union should the need ever arise. Malmstrom sits a little over one hundred miles from the Canadian border and, in the paranoia fueled 50's, it was just the place to station B-52 bombers ever ready to launch within the required three minutes. The planners gave little thought or concern to the weather. Great Falls sits on wide open plains, bordered by the Rockies to the West and nothing but prairie running east until Wisconsin. The bombers left years earlier, another peace dividend. The flight line was closed, the control tower demolished and this ultimate deterrent against foreign aggression continued to function, but with little or no surface activity to distract you from the ever present wind.

It was currently home to the 341st Space Wing comprising three missile squadrons, each owning fifty LGM-30G Minuteman III missiles. Each missile was fitted with three W-78 warheads with a yield of 335 kilotons of TNT. These rockets were scattered around the 20,000 square-mile range complex, along with multiple Military Alert Facilities, or MAF, each responsible for launching their assigned missiles to any target designated by the President. A MAF consists of a buried and hardened Launch Control Facility (LCF), and a Launch Control Equipment Building (LCEB) topside. In addition, each MAF has a helicopter landing pad, a large radio tower, a large "top hat" High Frequency antenna, a vehicle garage for security vehicles, recreational facilities, and one or two sewage lagoons. The entire site, except for the helicopter pad and sewage lagoons, are secured with a fence and security personnel. About a dozen airmen and officers are assigned to a MAF. The wing prided itself on being like Domino's Pizza, guaranteeing those warheads would "be on target within thirty minutes or the next one is free!"

Montana is "Big Sky" country and that means you can see the weather coming at you from great distances, so you'll be able to hunker down in time. The snows fly starting anytime after October 25 and it can snow as late as Memorial Day in May; but, keeping everyone on their toes, it has snowed in Great Falls during every month of the year including August. It never really gets hot, but it certainly does get brutally cold, and parking meters bear electric plugs so you can plug in your engine heater to keep it from freezing. On particularly cold mornings, the tires on my car would be flattened on the bottom and hardened by the sub zero cold, so it took a few minutes of bouncing along on out-of-round tires to warm them up and back to round.

Great Falls itself was an insular city of fewer than 57,000, with a decreasing population, and dwindling business community. Methamphetamines proved popular to help locals power through the two or more minimum wage jobs they needed to keep a roof over their heads. It was the sort of town people left and never returned to.

A knock at the door interrupted my reverie. A paralegal brought me the orders telling me the assignments people came through and I was being assigned duties as the Staff Judge Advocate for the Office of Military Cooperation in Kuwait (OMC-K). I knew something about Kuwait because of Desert Storm a few years earlier, but never knew such an office existed and had no idea what they did. The job required Top Secret clearance and Special Compartmentalized Information (TS/SCI) access which I already had, so it was adiós to this frozen land and off to sunnier climes.

What I didn't know was that I was about to become a part of Foreign Military Sales as an international arms dealer.

+++

# CHAPTER FIVE

## Kuwait

*"Living large at the edge of the Empire"*
—Osama Bill 2000

# Tales From The Desert Kingdom

The assignment was diplomatic. Starting on July 1, 2000, and for the next three years I was detached from service with the USAF and attached to the State Department and seconded to the Kuwait Armed Forces (KAF) as a lawyer and advisor. The government of Kuwait was forever grateful for US involvement in the liberation of their country from the oppressive and brutal Iraqi regime under Saddam Hussein ten years earlier and had adopted US equipment and doctrines to make certain this never happened again.

I'd watched it unfold on TV in my rooms at the King Haaken suite at Greenham when the Iraqis attacked Kuwait on August 2, 1990. They'd planned the attack during the height of summer when most citizens were on holiday abroad to escape the searing heat that would get as high as 120°F. I watched Iraqi helicopters fly past the iconic Kuwait Towers, and so did the Kuwaiti leadership.

To make certain it never happened again, this country of fewer than two million people purchased in excess of eight billion dollars ($8,000,000,000) worth of US arms and equipment: F/A 18 Hornet fighters, M1A2 Abrams Tanks, Apache and Blackhawk helicopters, Patriot missile batteries, patrol boats, and all the others "pieces-parts" needed to create and maintain a modern military force capable of defending the nation.

All of these individual needs and requirements were rolled into one large international agreement simply referred to as "*The Case.*" That much business required a staggering amount of governmental approvals, international agreements, and contracts, so a lawyer was needed to ride herd on all of that, while also providing a legal liaison between the government of Kuwait (GOK) and the USA. I was that liaison.

There was also the matter of the sixty or so military and civilian advisors who, as a part of the case, offered expertise and advice in their area of expertise. We had an F/A-18 guy, a Navy guy, several tank guys, academic training guys and others, all having responsibility for a piece of the Kuwait Armed Forces (KAF) pie.

The Kuwaitis were fantastic hosts and paid all the costs of the Americans which included: housing, vehicles, fuel for those vehicles, school for the kids, all the salaries, and contributions to social security and medicare. Our family lived in a 5,000 square foot, four-bedroom, five-bathroom flat which took up the entire floor in an apartment complex complete with a pool and a fitness room. I drove a brand new Jeep Grand Cherokee as my personal vehicle. My flat was actually one of the smaller sizes; an NCIS civilian agent lived in a 10,000 square foot place with an indoor waterfall.

The KAF would fly us home once a year for a vacation and paid to have those kids attending US universities fly into Kuwait for a visit. All of this amounted to some of the $262 million annual costs package that included two National Guard battalions totaling roughly 1,600 troops who came to "train where they'd fight." Those guys lived in warehouses converted into open-area dormitories on Camp Doha, a post culled from a former book warehouse complex located east of Kuwait City. This same $262 million also provided full support for the USAF squadron of A-10 "Warthog" tank killers kept "at the ready" at Ahmed al-Jaber air base south of Kuwait City and C-130 air cargo operations conducted out of Ali al-Salem air base to the North.

The OMC-K offices were located within the US Embassy, which is sited on a prime location next door to the Emir's (King's) 1,100 room official palace at Bayan, and across the street from the Emiri "diwan," a regularly held men's gathering where ordinary citizens can talk directly with senior leadership and be heard. Kuwait is a constitutional emirate with a semi-democratic political system led by the Emir, with a Crown Prince as designated successor. There is an elected Parliament and a council of Ministers, who are selected almost entirely of members of the Royal family. The Royal family is from the al-Sabah tribe and leaders are selected from one of the two main groups, the al-Jaber and al-Salem in rotation. Those smaller tribes are each led by a Sheikh (prince).

Entry to the Embassy chancellery building was gained by placing the right hand on a biometric palm reader. Magnetic locks released the bullet-proof outer door, then through another set of lockable bullet-proof glass doors which led into the atrium area where a Marine security guard on duty in a booth behind more bullet proof glass would monitor the people's comings and goings. OMC-K resided underneath the first-floor executive offices where the Ambassador and his deputy, the "Charge d'affairs," had their offices. Getting into our hallway involved punching in a code on a cypher lock, which secured a very thick reverse-mounted wooden door, which opened to a hallway, which led to a door with a heavy-dial combination lock, which finally offered entry to the offices. Once inside, it was just another government office designed by some uninspired architect on loan to the Government Accounting Office (GAO) from the Post Office.

The office is headed by a general officer from one of the services. After getting a quick briefing from the guy I was replacing, I met my new boss, an Army brigadier general, in passing; then again when I attended my first staff meeting on July 11, a little over a week after arriving and before my jet lag had fully cleared up.

The relatively small conference room had a long table with seats for thirteen people, a screen for power point slide shows, and chairs lined up along both walls for overflow crowds when other groups used the room. As a lawyer, I was again considered "special staff" and reported directly to the General. This status provided me a wide level of autonomy, so important for me to do one of my jobs, which was to visit every work space and facility, watching closely enough to make sure the GOK was getting full value for their money and that all of the contract terms were being honored.

Because I could read, write, and make power point presentations, I was eligible for other jobs as a back-up since we only had one person in any slot. Owing to my augmentation to the intelligence shop during war-time exercises in the UK, I became the backup Operations/Intelligence officer, and because of my police background and long association with the OSI, the backup counter-intelligence officer. In addition to those critical slots, the Army lieutenant colonel security chief, "Osama Bill," (a name he earned by bearing an uncanny resemblance to the Iraqi dictator) and I were routinely employed as both VIP drivers and human door stops. Our job was to open and hold the doors so any visiting dignitary could walk without delay into our offices. In addition to duties like those, every officer was eligible for VIP escort duties and miscellaneous other tasking, included doing anything considered "too hard" by any of the three colonels assigned.

Most of the people assigned to Kuwait worked in the field, spending every work day, starting at six, with the various Kuwaiti army and air force units at their camps and facilities. This hardship was off-set by a duty day that ended at two every afternoon and included a mandatory lunch at the KAF club, a huge buffet with waiters to pour the tea and lemonade. A small staff of twelve senior officers and NCOs were assigned work in the Embassy office. Nine of them were assigned desks in cubicles out in a large open area; but, being a lawyer and working with privileged and confidential communications, I got one of the three private offices with a door. This was no small thing and highly coveted if for no other reason than the ability to set one's head down for a combat cat nap before the next briefing.

Now I was sitting in on my first meeting. Although I was a major, I was still junior in rank to all the other officers present and thus took my seat at the chair furthest from the head of the table and closest to the screen. This worked for me as I could see all the faces of the other staff members, as well as the boss, without turning my head. The general entered and the meeting began with an intelligence briefing from the operations officer who brought us up to speed on all US and coalition forces in the area.

Desert Storm ended in 1992, and "no fly zones" had been established over Iraq to monitor their forces to assure Saddam wasn't up to any tricks. An embargo on Iraqi shipping meant the US Navy always kept a carrier group in the Arabian Gulf as a show of strength and to catch any boats trying to run oil to foreign customers. Any vessels captured trying to slip the embargo were taken as "prize vessels" and towed to a holding area where the oil would be sucked out by a Kuwaiti tanker and the ship sold for scrap to India. The cash generated would be deducted from the eleven billion dollars the Iraqis owed the Kuwaitis for breaking their country in the first place. It was hazardous duty and two American sailors, Petty Officer First Class Vincent Parker, 38, of Preston, Mississippi, and Petty Officer Third Class Benjamin Johnson, 21, of Rochester, New York, drowned while trying to close some sea cocks that a desperate ship's captain opened to flood the captured smuggling vessel in order to destroy evidence.

When the ops briefing finished, the general began asking the attendees individually for any other matters needing his consideration. An army colonel assigned to ground forces mentioned that the Kuwaitis, in the form of their four-star wearing Chief of Staff, had been calling him to insist that we tow or otherwise get rid of the hulk of a C-130 Hercules cargo plane that had been heavily damaged in an accident a few months earlier. The KAF Chief complained it was spooking the Kuwaiti C-130 pilots who had to walk past it everyday when they went to their own planes, some complaining it was a ghost ship and haunted by evil spirits. The general pondered this for a few moments, then looked around the table, stopping when he got to me. He said, "You're in the Air Force, right?" I nodded my head up and down confirming it while saying, "Why, yes sir, I am. I'd be your lawyer." He smiled a thin smile and said, "Well, good to know. You're now my Air Force lawyer project officer in charge of getting rid of that plane. Make it happen."

+++

---

# The Ghost Ship

On December 10, 1999, a few minutes before two in the morning, a C-130E Hercules, call sign Flash-07, tail registration 63-7854, piloted by Capt. Darron A. Haughn, his co-pilot, 1st Lt. Karina DeGarmo, navigator, Capt. Russell Hedden and flight engineer, TSgt Jeffrey Morgan, plus eighty-six passengers who had just arrived in country a few hours earlier, lifted off the runway, retracted the landing gear and departed Kuwait City International

Airport (KCIA). The flight plan called for a ten-minute flight to Jaber Air Base south and east of KCIA. The crew was from the 61st Airlift Squadron, at Little Rock Air Force Base, Arkansas, and was flying only their second mission together, having themselves just arrived in-country a few days earlier. The aviators welcomed the opportunity to log some flight time to become oriented and familiar with the air space. They'd received no briefing from either the US or Kuwait ops guys about any special flying procedures to be used in the Gulf. A weather report published one hour before take-off said visibility was one mile at the airport. Another check just before takeoff showed that visibility had increased and during the flight they would see the airport lights from miles away, but there were some scattered foggy patches in the area.

In pre-flight planning, the crew considered using an ILS (instrument landing system) approach for landing which was available if they came in from one direction, but they elected a VFR (visual flight rules) approach, so the base control tower instructed the plane to land from the opposite direction. The plane began its final approach despite, as the accident board found, "The pilot never recognized his landing picture and failed to transition to a normal visual glide path for landing." This meant he could not see the runway and everybody on the flight deck would have been looking for the approach lights. While looking for them, the crew took their eyes off the instruments and the aircraft was now descending "well below the glide slope," meaning the descent was too steep. At 125 feet above the deck, Flash-07 entered previously unseen fog.

TSgt Morgan screamed *"go around"* and Capt Haughn slammed the throttles forward. Those four Allison T56-A-7 turboprops were spooling up to 4,200-shaft horsepower and began clawing into the air, but it was too little too late to arrest the sink rate. Inertia carried the plane lower, drifting down until it slammed into the ground some 2,895 feet short and about forty feet left of the runway centerline. Capt. Haughn, aided by Lt. DeGarmo, acted quickly trying to pull up the plane, but they nonetheless felt a thud that rocked them in their seats. Capt Haughn later told investigators, "I felt like the airplane had hit something." Lt DeGarmo reported, "We entered the fog bank ... it all happened pretty quick and we hit the ground."

At impact, instead of splaying out as designed to do upon an impact, the landing-gear shafts burst through the plane's metal skin and instantly killed three military passengers who were strapped in their seats above the wheel wells. The airmen killed were A1C Benjamin T. "Travis" Hall, 24, from Hiawatha, Kansas, and assigned to the 90th Transportation Squadron at F.E Warren AFB, Wyoming; A1C Warren Willis, 21, of Council Grove, Kansas, assigned to the 55th Transportation Squadron Offutt AFB, Nebraska. Sitting across from them, and alone atop the opposite wheel well, was Capt. Michael D. Geragosian, 66th Rescue Squadron based at Nellis AFB in Nevada. An airman sitting across from the two airmen watched those fatalities occur and was so severely traumatized he required hospitalization. At impact the lights went out and the emergency lights came on while dirt and cold air came blowing inside from where the wheel wells used to be. The Hercules struck a ground-based Instrument Landing System antenna before those propellers found purchase, and while the plane retook the skies, body parts mixed with red hydraulic fluid, which was leaking under pressure from the damaged right horizontal stabilizer.

Despite the horrendous conditions amidst the roar of those engines, after some initial pandemonium, the training kicked in. The crew attended to the aircraft while the passengers showed the value of constantly training in wartime skills, as they performed first aid and buddy care on their injured comrades. Once the plane, minus it's landing gear, achieved straight and level flight, the crew declared an in-flight emergency, and began dumping fuel over the Arabian Gulf while waiting for the fire department to foam the main runway at KCIA. When everything was ready, Capt. Haughn came in low and slow and crashed a second time. As soon as the plane came to a halt, every living person evacuated and left everything behind. They never came back.

My first challenge was to find out exactly how you get rid of a heavily damaged aircraft. The USAF provided phone books with listings of organizations on all the Air Force bases globally, but despite my best efforts I couldn't find any place marked "aircraft chop shop." I thought back to when I'd worked as a claims officer in Panama. The airbase at Soto Cano, in Honduras, sent down some Reports of Survey for my review and they included the final disposition on some C-130 propellers that had gone missing.

A lot of stuff went missing in Honduras, like when the USAF issued new full-sized refrigerators for the hooches, and the airmen were told to leave the old ones outside to be collected by engineers who would destroy them, as required as a condition for not paying Honduran import duties. That evening one airman saw what looked like a giant square white beetle running down the road, when a group of eight soldiers lifted one excess refrigerator and hightailed it back to their area because the Army did not give their people refrigerators. It was removed from the accounts and the disposition written as "stolen by persons unknown."

The survey officer located those propellers in a depot at Warner Robins AFB, one hundred miles southeast of Atlanta, Georgia. Named for Brig Gen Augustine Warner Robins, the Air Force's "father of logistics," it's the home of the Air Force Materiel Command's Air Logistics Center, the worldwide manager for a wide range of aircraft, engines, missiles, software, avionics, and accessories components including propellers. A few phone calls later and I'd found the USAF's chop shop, the 653rd Combat Logistics Support Squadron.

I explained the nature of my request and emphasized how the host nation was anxious for this plane to be removed and this effort was of vital importance to the diplomatic interests of the United States. The voice at the other end said I could expect a team as soon as possible and right after they finished the job they were currently on. I agreed to be responsible for getting them country clearances, plus arranging the "care and feeding" of those airmen, which would be easy since our office handled country clearances for all military and civilian visitors coming in by military airlift. The five-star Crowne Plaza hotel, just a few minutes from the Kuwait airport, would be able to accommodate any and all guests for as long as they were in-country, thanks to an incredible friend of the USA, Hassan, the Syrian-born, London-bred general manager. His cooperation and assistance were vital when we had to respond to short-notice requests for billeting of large groups, like the military personnel supporting White House visits. For his service to the mission, and our nation, Hassan was a permanent guest, welcome at our happy hours on either Monday or Wednesday, a privilege more valuable than gold, given Kuwait was a "dry" country and alcohol was prohibited and our embassy bar was legally in America and "wet."

I gave my progress report to the General who looked up, said, "OK, thanks" and then went back to some papers he was reading. Feeling there was more to be done, I called the base at al-Jaber to ask who owned the plane, and was directed to the wing in Little Rock, Arkansas. I called the Staff Judge Advocate's office there and was surprised when an acquaintance from several TDYs to the JAG school, and who was now the SJA, came on the line. We exchanged some pleasantries and a bit of gossip before settling into business. In the years before cellular communications and social media came of age and since knowledge is power, the only way to have stayed up on the scandals and gossip was by calling and chatting. I told him what was happening and he asked if I'd called Air Mobility Command (AMC) Headquarters at Scott AFB, Illinois, to fill them in. When I said I hadn't, he said he'd take care of it.

The next day I got an e-mail from a staff lawyer at AMC headquarters advising me there was now a "JAG hold" on that plane and nobody was to touch it until they'd had a chance to review the situation. They'd be back in touch when they decided what they wanted to do. I'd never heard of a "JAG hold," which sounded like something he heard growing up and watching Harmon Rabb on that hit TV show, JAG. I put in a call later that afternoon; because of the seven hour time difference, they opened when I was closing for the day. I asked for the lawyer who wrote the email. When he came on the line, I introduced myself and asked what was all this business about a "JAG hold." He told me that the news of the Kuwaitis wanting the plane removed was unexpected and they hadn't yet decided on what form of action to take against the aircrew. This was a bit surprising and somewhat disappointing, as the accident had taken place seven months earlier, and the accident investigation and safety board, concluding in late March, had attributed the causation to pilot error.

He explained they were building a criminal case to charge Capt Haughn with negligent homicide and dereliction of duty, and criminal charges for the rest of crew, as well; but, they needed to appoint prosecutors and cut orders for them to come to Kuwait to review the scene of the crime. After that, they'd appoint an IO to conduct the Article 32 investigation and to prepare a report which would have to be reviewed by the convening authority. After charges were preferred, the plane would have to be made available for inspection by any defense counsel appointed to represent the air crew. He ended by telling me it would take at least six months and I could tell that to the Kuwaitis. I thanked him for his time and said I'd be in touch.

I got up and went into the break room to make a fresh pot of coffee. I watched it brew and, when it was done, I filled my cup and sat back down at my unclassified computer to type out an email response to that phone call. I wanted to memorialize it, should questions arise in the future. I informed him that I'd conducted a "conflict of laws" analysis on the international jurisdiction issue and, while I was certainly sympathetic to their problems, the wreckage was in Kuwait and no less a personage than the four-star KAF Chief of Staff wanted it gone. I offered to wait two weeks for them to get their act together before the plane was considered abandoned. After that, it would be their choice of a disposal site: some junk dealers in Kuwait or the USAF "boneyard" at Davis-Monthan AFB outside of Tucson, Arizona. I also told him that in the interests of judicial economy and fairness I'd be calling Legal Defense Services at Ramstein Air Base in Germany, since their lawyers were responsible for providing criminal defense services for our region. I pressed "send" and left my office to get a cup of coffee with Hassan, since he would be securing all the necessary rooms for the inbound airmen. My direct line was ringing, and I knew who it was, as I closed the door behind me.

It appeared that the AMC folks were pissed that I'd countermanded their "JAG hold" with my "JAG release" but they still sent two prosecutors. I met them at plane side two days later, when they arrived on a C-5. They asked to be taken directly to the aircraft. We drove down the ramp, passing silver and white KAF C-130s, until we parked in front of the broken plane. They got out, took photographs of the exterior, then entered the cabin and I went with them.

At first the inside looked like any other C-130 interior. Pale institutional green primer coated the interior airframe and an equally unappealing pastel green fabric insulation was pressed up against it while exposed conduit pipes ran the length of the ceiling. A few tiny portholes provided interior light. Red cargo-netting passenger seats along both walls and a double row running up the middle of the plane made all the passengers squeeze in together while siting sideways. But it was "the things they left behind" that told the tale of terror those eighty-six passengers experienced during the confusion after impact.

Hot winds whistled through the shards of twisted metal, remnants of what had once covered the wheel wells and made the airframe creak and groan. On the metal floor lay backpacks, magazines, books, military equipment, and other detritus, including a dark blue Timberline ball cap with its brown bill stained red from hydraulic fluid. There were other, darker reddish puddle stains on the floor, remnant bloodstains mixed with hydraulic fluid that had been absorbed by dirt and grit.

Flies buzzed about, never minding us as they got on with their business. I understood why the KAF wanted it gone; this was a death ship and, even with that hot wind, it felt cold. When the prosecutors finished taking photos and making notes, I drove them down to al-Jaber air base. They did a terrain walk there and talked with the same commander who'd been there when it happened in December. The group finished up after an hour and I drove them back to KCIA and left them at the military terminal where that same C-5, heading back to the States, would return them to Illinois. They'd been on the ground less than five hours.

Two days later, a circuit defense counsel flew in from Germany on Lufthansa and I met him on the civilian side. I took him to the plane and watched him make notes. When I called the air base commander at al-Jaber to let him know we were coming for the defense lawyer's terrain walk, he informed me that he would not let the defense lawyer on "his" base. I explained that all sides needed equal access, but he was firm for reasons he was not inclined to share, and which I could not question; although, I suspected those two over-eager prosecutors had advised him not to let any defense lawyers onto the base where they might muck up the government's case.

Annoyed, I gave the defense counsel that bit of news, then drove him to al-Jaber anyway. What the al-Jaber commander didn't appreciate, was as the SJA, I was obligated to offer impartial assistance to all the parties in the matter, and I resented it when prosecutors tried to stack the deck and so impede the work of defense counsel. I always believed the faceless government could afford to err on the side of complete disclosure of all evidence to let a court decide believability. I also believed while a government loss is mildly embarrassing to some lawyer's ego for an afternoon, that loss should not result in anyone going to jail and having their life ruined, like poor TSgt Mueller.

What the American commander didn't know was that I was also a major in the Kuwait Air Force and could enter al-Jaber through the KAF gate to go anywhere I pleased, and I did. The ADC conducted his terrain walk and left that evening, despite my offer to show him around. In fairness, the daily temperature was over 110°F.

USAF leadership was eager to hold someone accountable for those three deaths. On July 17, 2000, charges of dereliction of duty and negligent homicide were preferred against Capt Haughn by the 43rd Airlift Wing Commander. An Article 32 investigation opened on July 24, 2000, to investigate those charges.

I contacted the voice at Warner Robins who told me the plans were finalized and the fifteen-member team would be arriving by military air on October 12, 2000. I told him that transportation would be waiting at plane side and the team had been booked into the Crowne Plaza, just a few miles away. I also shared that it had several fine restaurants, an olympic swimming pool, and a fitness facility.

+++

# Unanticipated Outcomes

In 1998, the US Congress put together its budget providing funding for the DoD. Due to fiscal constraints caused by an effort to balance the budget, the funding for one expensive-to-maintain-and-operate combat store's supply ship was deleted from a budget line somewhere, leaving twenty-five similar ships to provide a secure replenishment and provisioning point for Navy vessels scattered about the globe. The Navy made a command decision to pull the oldest vessel from its station in the Gulf of Aden and retire it because there were ample qualified providers of goods, services, and fuel at Aden harbor, in Yemen.

When October 12 came, the weather had finally broken. We noticed some semblance of an autumn, the daily high only going into the low nineties. This was a good thing since we would all be attending an Oktoberfest garden party and BBQ hosted by our new Chief of the OMC-K. Jeff was a recently promoted Army brigadier general who came to us from an assignment in Germany. He was a Chinook pilot and had spent most of his career in the 160th Special Operations Air Regiment (SOAR) *Night Stalkers*. Famed for operating at night and at low altitude, their missions included flying special operators on attack, assault, and reconnaissance missions anywhere on the planet. He'd been on the ground in Kuwait for just a few weeks and was still learning the ropes. Now he wanted to introduce us to his family, a wife and two teenagers, who were joining him on this plum assignment. The party was just getting underway. Laurie and Maggie were sitting at a table chatting with Jimmy, the OSI guy and his family. I was just waiting for a call from KCIA operations to let me know when the plane carrying my crew of scavengers was on final approach.

What none of us knew, as the brats started to sizzle, was a few hours earlier, at half past nine, the *USS Cole* (DDG 67), whose ship motto was "Glory is the Reward of Valor," docked at Aden harbor to begin replenishment operations. Refueling started at half past ten and all was going well until forty-eight minutes later when a small fiberglass boat carrying explosives and two suicide bombers approached the port side of the destroyer and exploded, creating a forty-by-sixty-foot gash in the ship's port side, killing seventeen sailors[3] and wounding thirty-nine others. The destroyer's rules of engagement (ROE), as approved by the Pentagon, prohibited the gunners mates standing security watch from firing upon the small boat (which had not yet been known to be loaded with explosives) as it neared them, without first obtaining permission from the *Cole's* Captain or another officer.

Shortly after one, just as the brats were reaching perfection, we received first word that the *Cole* had been attacked and our security posture was being raised to Force Protection Condition (FPCON) level **Delta**, the highest level. There are five FPCONs:

FPCON NORMAL indicates no current terrorist activity.
FPCON ALPHA indicates a small and general terrorist threat that is not predictable.
FPCON BRAVO indicates a somewhat predictable terrorist threat.

---

[3] The dead were:
Hull Maintenance Technician 2nd Class Kenneth Eugene Clodfelter, 21, of Mechanicsville, Virginia
Chief Electronics Technician Richard Costelow, 35, of Morrisville, Pennsylvania
Mess Management Specialist Seaman Lakeina Monique Francis, 19, of Woodleaf, North Carolina
Information Systems Technician Seaman Timothy Lee Gauna, 21, of Rice, Texas
Signalman Seaman Cherone Louis Gunn, 22, from Rex, Georgia
Seaman James Rodrick McDaniels, 19, of Norfolk, Virginia
Engineman 2nd Class Marc Ian Nieto, 24, of Fond du Lac, Wisconsin
Electronics Warfare Technician 2nd Class Ronald Scott Owens, 24, of Vero Beach, Florida
Seaman Lakiba Nicole Palmer, 22, of San Diego, California
Fireman Joshua Langdon Parlett, 19, of Churchville, Maryland
Fireman Patrick Howard Roy, 19, from Keedysville, Maryland
Electronic Warfare Technician 1st Class Kevin Shawn Rux, 30, of Portland, North Dakota
Mess Management Specialist 3rd Class Ronchester Manangan Santiago, 22, of Kingsville, Texas
Operations Specialist 2nd Class Timothy Lamont Saunders, 32, of Ringgold, Virginia
Fireman Gary Graham Swenchonis Jr., 26, from Rockport, Texas
Ensign Andrew Triplett, 31, of Macon, Mississippi
Seaman Craig Bryan Wibberley, 19, of Williamsport, Maryland

FPCON CHARLIE indicates a global terrorist attack has occurred, or local terrorist activity imminent.
FPCON DELTA indicates a terrorist attack is taking place or has just occurred in the immediate area.

Because of the immediate threat of terrorist action against military personnel and locations world-wide, all US military personnel were restricted to their installations. While this did not apply to the OMC, it did apply to the airmen who were inbound, as confirmed by a telephone call I'd received moments after the notice of the attack. I left before those sausages came off the grill.

The C-5 Galaxy lumbered down the taxiway and stopped as directed by the marshal. Coming from a BBQ, I was wearing civilian clothes, a Hawaiian shirt I'd had made in Korea and tan khakis. The forward crew hatch opened and a folding stairway was extended. I came aboard and showed my Embassy credentials to the loadmaster who directed me upstairs to the passenger deck. I climbed those stairs and was looking into the wide open eyes of fifteen airmen who were either jet-lagged or had never been greeted by a guy in a Hawaiian shirt before. The flight engineer handed me the microphone and I told them about the *Cole* and the change to FPCON Delta. *That* really got their attention. I then broke the news that, unfortunately, due to the threat they wouldn't be staying at the Crowne Plaza as advertised, but instead would be brought to Camp Doha, a secure *Army* installation twenty miles away, where they would be safe and sound. A collective groan arose from those passengers because Air Force is the only branch of service that promised clean sheets, air conditioning, and good coffee, so lodging with a bunch of grunts in a warehouse suggested that none of those comforts would be forthcoming. Much to their chagrin, they'd find out later there was no espresso machine either.

This group was led by a Master Sergeant Deutsch, a dour-faced senior NCO who hadn't slept in an open bay barracks situation since he'd gone to basic training in 1986. He wasn't fond of listening to several hundred soldiers, snore, pass gas, play loud music, and otherwise interfere with his sleep. On the second day, he gathered his airmen together and made an announcement that the sooner they got out of Kuwait and back home to Georgia, the better it would for everybody.

With that admonishment, his crew set to working twelve-hour shifts, starting in the cooler evenings. Those scavengers had that plane disassembled and ready for transport in a little over thirty days, whereas if they'd been booked into the five-star Crowne with all those amenities and daily per diem, the disassembly probably would have taken two or three months.

All of the flight surfaces, wings, tail, stabilizers, and those four heroic and undamaged Allison engines were labeled, stuffed inside the dead bird's cargo compartment and prepared for shipment back to the Georgia. The team used a sixteen-inch metal saw and jury-rigged a wheeled axle to prepare the fallen Herc for loading. With only the nose and fuselage intact, those wheels made the air frame resemble a clown's car in a circus. The only question remaining was how to transport those remains. Deutsch told me a C-5C, a specially modified variant that could accommodate extra-large payloads was being tasked for the job. There were only two such aircraft in the fleet and it was coming from Germany to pick up the parts and his crew the next day.

The next morning was Friday, the religious off-day, when all good Muslims went to the mosque to pray and hear a sermon. I was out shopping with Laurie when I got the call saying the big plane was inbound, so, together we headed to KCIA to see exactly how this process would work. Laurie was interested in seeing what had been occupying so much of my time, having believed my work generally involved sitting in an office, reading dull papers all day.

The giant aircraft parked on the tarmac and opened its massive doors to receive the remains of Flash 07. A steel cable was attached to the front landing gear. Ever so slowly and carefully, the airframe was winched up and into the belly of the Galaxy, which now made it look like a giant fish was eating a clown car. The tow  was nearly finished when an airman came to me saying we had a problem. Deutsch needed me inside, so I walked up the cargo ramp and saw him on a platform. Ordinary C-5s had a 50 passenger deck above the interior cargo floor and at the same height as the crew compartment but, in this C variant, that deck was removed. I climbed the steps and joined him. He pointed to a spot centered just above the cockpit windows, explaining that we had a few too many inches of airframe pressing up against an interior wall and the transport's massive doors would not close and secure. I asked him what he thought the tech solution was and he offered, "I can take a sledge hammer and put in enough of a dent to make those few inches, but I'd be damaging government property that might be needed later as evidence, and I wanted to make sure that's OK."

I admired his commitment to ensuring no further damage occurred, but immediately relieved him of that burden. I explained my reasoning, assuring him that, "This plane has crashed twice and that airframe will never fly again, so I think you'll be forgiven for putting another dent in it; go ahead." He still looked hesitant so, "leading by example," I took the sledge hammer and wailed on the indicated point until he told me I'd made a big enough dimple; the hulk was now winched in those final few inches. The loadmaster signaled that the doors had been closed and sealed, so the big plane was ready to take off.

Laurie and I watched as the engines spooled up and the beast began to slowly roll forward and down the ramp until finally turning on to the runway. I listened for the familiar higher pitched whine of the four General Electric TF-39 engines, each generating 43,000 pounds of thrust, vaulting that 380,000 pound airframe, plus the 75,562 pounds remnants of Flash 07, into clear November skies. We watched it vanish into the blue.

I was back in my office on Monday when the phone rang. It was the SJA from Arkansas asking for an update on the project. I filled him in and the subject turned to the legal matters in the works. We both felt a court-martial was sending the wrong signal but, if higher headquarters pressed he was going to have to send a witness request for the KAF air traffic controller on duty in the tower that morning. I responded with a Korean tooth-suck to get his attention and he asked about my concerns. I explained they were two-fold. First I'd have to get the Kuwaiti government to permit their airman to travel to America to testify in the proceeding, and that wouldn't be too hard.

The difficulty would be when I told them the defense counsel would lay the blame squarely on that Kuwaiti controller, just like the USAF did with Capt Wang in the Blackhawk shoot down. That defense would paint the airman and the entire Kuwait Ministry of Defense as incompetent and legally responsible, which would certainly lead to an acquittal and embarrassment for all concerned.

While he took that in, I further assured him that scenario wouldn't happen because, once I told my boss, he'd have me brief that four-star-wearing KAF Chief of Staff, who would be disinclined to accommodate our request. If the KAF witness wouldn't come, then the defense would complain of government interference by denying them the opportunity to question him in Kuwait when they visited and that would certainly result in an acquittal, so they might as well save some civilian lawyer earning another big commission.

Remembering the lessons from the Panama, and the *USS Greene,* since the issue was big enough and potentially embarrassing to our host nation, I offered him a shot at making lemonade out of lemons. I told him they could offer non-judicial punishment and hope he'd take it, but concluded with, "Frankly, I'd give the guy a medal for his airmanship. Yes, he screwed the approach, but he recovered and not only saved the aircraft, but all those passengers and crew. On top of that, he also crashed again, this time knowing he was crashing, and nobody got hurt. The pressure on him was enormous. I wouldn't burn him for a manufacturing design defect."

A little over a year after Flash 07's last powered flight, on Dec 16, 2000, the 43rd Airlift Wing commander announced that he was **not** recommending a court-martial for Capt Haughn, and the matter was closed.

+++

# Merry Christmas From The Maid's Prison

Thanksgiving came and signaled the beginning of the American holiday season, as noted by the appearance of Filipino workers in the Sultan supermarket wearing pilgrim hats and costumes. Many Kuwaitis attended universities in the USA since the 70s brought back those American traditions they enjoyed, adding them to the schedule. This year, the run up to Ramadan saw folks partying like the Catholic Lent's "Fat Tuesday," the last big party period before Ramadan. Starting on Monday, November 27, 2000, Ramadan, a holy month of fasting and reflection began. This annual event was looked forward to with a mixture of anticipation, and some dread, by everybody in Kuwait, and not just the Muslims.

Ramadan is observed during the ninth month of the Islamic calendar and commemorates the first revelation of the Quran to the Prophet Mohammed, peace be unto him (PBUH). It's a time of strict fasting and all restaurants are closed from sunrise to sunset. Anyone, regardless of religious beliefs, caught smoking, eating, or drinking in public is subject to a large monetary fine and possible detention, until a detainee signs a good conduct pledge of no further departure from the rules.

Laurie and I were shopping in a grocery store in the fashionable Salmiya district, an area popular with ex-pats working in Kuwait. We noticed a European man drinking juice from a can as he walked about looking at the groceries on shelves. As he passed by the meat counter, the butcher yelled "Haram! Haram!" (It's forbidden!) The European sneered at the small man and continued browsing the beef selections. His air of contempt faded after the old man vanished into the back, reappearing moments later with a very large, very angry-looking guy who spent his day carrying sides of beef to the table saw. He walked up to the now frozen European and snatched the metal can from his hands, crushing it while saying menacingly, "HARAM!"

Ramadan is also a time for spiritual reflection, personal improvement, increased devotion and worship, very much like Lent, that forty-day period, when practicing Catholics are expected to focus on simple living, prayer, and fasting, in order to grow closer to God. Owing to the rotation of the moon each year, Ramadan begins eleven days earlier than the year before. Everyone prefers the winter Ramadan: it's easier to maintain a fast when the days are shorter and the weather much cooler. For practical purposes, this month-long experience inspired old people, studying for their "finals," to drag their grandsons off to the fajar prayer; which begins at *subh saadiq* (true dawn or morning twilight) when the first morning light appears across the full width of the sky and ending when the sun rose. This prayer time is not popular with children.

Friends told me stories of camping and having their grandfather briskly waking them for this prayer by shouting and giving a swat or two. Muslims are required to wash their face and feet before they begin prayer. It is cold at night in the desert and, when the boys got to the wash basin, they saw a skiff of ice had formed. Not eager to get any colder, they splashed water on the ground to fool the old man. He was not amused and they caught a beating.

After those morning prayers, it's a personal choice whether to pray the midday Dhuhr or afternoon Asr prayers and many people nap or watch soap operas in between prayers. Everybody makes it home by sunset, in time for the Maghrib prayers. This is important because that's the time to break the day's fast. From Fajar and through to Maghrib, the faithful are prohibited from eating, drinking, smoking, or having sexual relations. As a result, the highway is a dangerous place come sundown because hungry, thirsty, and nicotine deprived drivers are anxious and irritable.

I was waiting at the KCIA Royal VVIP (Very, Very Important Person) Terminal for such a guest to arrive and chatting with the other drivers, all of whom were provided by the Kuwait government, when I heard a click as the imam at the nearest mosque turned on the loudspeaker to begin his "call to prayer," which lasts several minutes. Tradition dictates the next step: taking a drink of water and eating a date to break your fast, slowly bringing up your blood sugar before heading off to pray. Nicotine addiction would always reveal several lighters igniting and cigarettes firing up before the first words were uttered.

After the fast is broken with a bit of food and drink, the faithful are off to Isha'a, the night prayers which begin after the last of the red light has left the sky. When that was finished, it was a time to offer family and any guests the very best food your kitchen could prepare. An abundance of extra food is prepared by those who can afford it and much is later delivered to the less fortunate. This is a time for great charity, as well as impressing your friends with your wealth, generosity and the skills of your kitchen staff. As a result, it is just about impossible to get a bad meal during Ramadan, and most Kuwaitis admit to gaining an average of eight pounds over that holy month.

This holiday results in a remarkable shift in behavior. Schools move to a ten o'clock late-start and classes are held for just a half day. Businesses also shorten the work day, opening at ten and closing by two, but then reopening after dark. Government services opened at ten and staff were "required" to stay until four, although nobody did. These short operational windows were further adjusted by the personality of the holder of the office you were seeking to do business with. At that time, most men in Kuwait smoked cigarettes. Some smoked expensive Cuban cigars, but many enjoyed the traditional water pipes called nargilla. Americans knew this as "hubbly bubbly," an observation on the sound made when the smoke is drawn through the water.

The pipe uses tobacco cured in fruit syrup which is placed in its small clay bowl, then covered with aluminum foil. The tobacco is shaken and a toothpick is used to make a dozen holes in the foil. Burning charcoal, glowing red, is placed on top of the foil, its heat cooking and slowly burning the tobacco. The smoker draws in smoke through a tube attached to a pipette. This negative pressure sucks the smoke through the holes in the bottom of the clay pot, down a carburetor and into the water chamber on the bottom. Uneven air pressure makes the ball bearing in the carburetor bounce around, producing the bubbling sound. This water-filtered smoke comes down the tube, out the tip and into the lungs. Lacking any additives, nargilla is not supposed to be physically addictive like cigarettes, but can be psychologically addicting.

The scale of nicotine dependency and withdrawal was problematic during Ramadan. This became abundantly clear when you had to conduct any business with someone who might be feeling bad or cranky during the oral fixation withdrawal phase, just as cigarette smokers craving nicotine do. Despite the posted hours, most people showed up no earlier than ten and conducted an average of just twenty-eight minutes of business before closing their office door to turn on one of the cooking channels, or soap operas, both very popular when you've nothing to do all day except wait to pray again. If you hadn't caught someone by half past ten, you weren't going to do so that day, and the ones you did catch tended to be cranky and irritable. Every office in the KAF had a large TV mounted on the wall, ostensibly to keep an eye on the latest news and developments in the region, but most days they were tuned to a cooking channel.

One day, during that holy month, a KAF colonel asked me to come to his office to discuss a problem he was having with some French patrol boats the government had purchased a year earlier but had yet to sail from their moorings in Marseille. Seeming to divert his attention from the matter at hand, he looked at the TV chef making eggs Benedict and said, "We are having a problem with the cookers, what should we do?" I advised him that was a warranty issue and the French Defense Attaché was the guy to run that problem past. He shook his head and said, "No, you don't understand. I mean the cookers, the guys who make the food." He explained that two times before they'd flown a couple of Pakistani cooks to Marseille and each time the cooks failed to show up at the docks, having seized the opportunity to vanish into the local Pakistani community. I told him to try sending a navy crewman with those guys the next time.

Now it was December 19, a Tuesday, and I was at home. There were four apartment buildings in our compound and OMC employees occupied all but two flats. These buildings were surrounded by a high wall with locking gates and an Olympic-sized swimming pool filled the center common area. The landlord employed a harees (gate keeper) to unlock the gates in the morning so the children could queue up for the school busses and deliverymen could make their rounds. Our harees was named Mershak and he was from Egypt. Very short, but sturdy, and very friendly and accommodating from behind he looked like a small bear. The younger children had trouble pronouncing his name and called him Milkshake, and I hired him to wash my Jeep everyday. He asked for only fifteen dollars a month and I thought it well worth it because the State security people were always going on about checking vehicles for bombs and such, even issuing us telescoping mirrors so we could check each morning that our cars hadn't been turned into killing machines. I'd read the reports on those events and it seemed the bad guys always used a mercury tilt-switch. A simple trigger, the mercury is level and if tilted it will complete a circuit and the bomb explodes. This is why people are urged not to move any suspected explosive devices. For car bombs, the driver getting in would cause enough of a tilt to activate the switch.

Every morning Milkshake would climb up on the hood and on to the roof where he'd shake the hell out of that car while he dried it, an action that reassured me no explosives had been attached to the frame. I also paid the Sri Lankan dry-cleaning runner across the street ten dollars a month to keep an eye on my Jeep during the evening. I promised him a one hundred dollar bonus if he ever saw somebody messing with the rig and called me. He lived at the dry cleaners, sitting outside all day and night on a broken old couch. He would deliver a customer's laundry to their car for tips. My added payment was significant, since the average median household monthly income in Sri Lanka was eighty-five dollars; and, the workers who'd come to Kuwait sent most of their pay home to their families. He waved at me every day when I came outside, giving me the "thumbs up" while dreaming of catching a potential terrorist planting a bomb.

There was a knock at the front door. We weren't expecting guests but weren't concerned that it'd be some maniac come to kill us. I'd opened the door before to find the French-born wife of our Charge d'Affairs looking for a different flat and even had the Canadian Ambassador show up accidentally once. More likely it was the Bangladude Coca-Cola soft drink vendor with our standing order. From Bangladesh, he spoke no English and had only a few teeth. Wearing a purple one-piece zip-up coverall and a dirty sweat-stained light brown turban that bore mute testimony of his toils, he'd smile his Jack-O-Lantern smile and say, "Croaka Crolla? FAN-ta?" looking to fill our order. He'd show up at odd times, but anybody willing to lug cases of soft drinks up three flights of stairs was welcome to show up whenever they liked.

But this time, it was a small Indian woman wearing a tan maid's work uniform. Her long black hair was tied in a prim pony-tail and her black eyes shone wet against her dark skin. She introduced herself as Fernanda and asked if she could talk to me. I ushered her in and she asked if I was a lawyer. I told her I was, but not in private practice. She shook her head and said, "No sir, I want to make sure you are the lawyer who works for the OMC. I am the maid for Mr. Joe and I am afraid I am going to be sent to the maid's prison for a long time because I do not have a work visa."

That took a moment to sort out. People who seek employment in Kuwait were required to get work visas before they arrived. A governmental agency issued and monitored these visas because there was always a huge demand for expat workers to do those jobs Kuwaiti citizens were not inclined to do. In Kuwait, yearly an airline pilot makes $61,000, a university professor, $32,000. At the other end of the pay scale, a maid will make $1,500, a baker $3,600. Also on that end were bus drivers, porters, mechanics, road crews, fast food employees and so on. These service sector jobs are filled by expats from India, Bangladesh, Sri Lanka, Pakistan, the Philippines, and elsewhere in Asia. To them the pay is good, and enough that they can send money home to their families.

The expats tend to cluster in certain jobs for certain countrymen. Indians work in administration, Filipinos will commonly have nursing, electrical and carpentry work; Hungarians find work as physical therapists; but, Bangladeshis were always at the bottom of the government employment pool. You'd see them sweeping roads by hand with small brooms, planting trees along the motorway, and maintaining public flower beds, easily identified by the yellow zip-up coveralls they wore regardless of weather and temperature. Speaking English and Arabic was the minimum requirement for a "good" job; as was a university degree, so these poor souls, speaking only their native tongue, were relegated to the most menial jobs.

Any job aspirant from a foreign country would pay a local employment agency one thousand dollars or more to find employment in Kuwait and make all the arrangements with a Kuwaiti employment company that matched a worker with a position. In addition to that, any employer was required to purchase a work permit visa for that employee and this cost two hundred Kuwaiti dinar, about six hundred and fifty dollars. The visa was good as long as the employee stayed with their employer. If the employee quit or was fired, the visa expired and the employee was required to leave the country within forty-eight hours, or risk being jailed and owing a ten dollar per day fine levied for each day overstayed. That fine was due and payable immediately upon detention; if a person could not pay the fine, they were sent off to a debtor prison until such time as they could raise the money. When the facility became overcrowded, the government would thin the population, putting the longest serving prisoners on an aircraft bound for foreign shores.

Many Americans employed foreign maids, which worked out well for each side. Because most maids were live-in, they would keep the house tidy for about $100 per month. As live-ins, they only worked eight hours a day at most, could eat whatever they liked, would be taken for medical treatment if necessary and had Sundays off. All of the flats leased for Americans had a small maid's room off the kitchen with a small bedroom, a shower and toilet. To a person from rural India, these rooms were luxurious because they not only had private wash facilities, but clean water on demand, electricity, air conditioning and access to food. This allowed them to wire their entire salary home each month. Most maids were younger women who had gotten married in India, had a child, then could leave the child with her mother to care for and raise while she earned money to send back home to India. The American monthly salaries and benefits were considered excellent, since the going rate paid by Kuwaitis was eighty-three dollars a month and the maid had to buy her own food.

I'd first learned of these significant wage disparities while assigned to a base in Saudi Arabia during Desert Storm. Pete was the senior dining-room worker and self-appointed drinks waiter for the officers' tables. He knew what drinks everyone preferred and your glass or coffee cup was never empty. Pete's birthday was coming up and he would be leaving for a holiday trip home to Bangladesh. Every two years, his company gave him a ticket to Chittagong for his unpaid one-month vacation, as required by law. We ordered a cake for him and passed around a card to sign, with a suggestion that each person toss in five bucks as a tip. When the day came, we gave him the cake and the envelope containing two hundred and twenty dollars. He opened it, screamed, and passed out. When he came back around, he began crying and weeping, as we learned we'd just given him a year's wages.

Domestics worked six days a week with one day off, usually Sunday. Since most servants were from Goa, a part of India colonized by Catholic Portugal, they could attend church services at the Cathedral downtown. Kuwait subscribes to freedom of religion. In 1911, an American missionary doctor, Dr. C. Stanley G. Mylrea, restored the eyesight of a favored granddaughter of the 7th Emir, Mubarak Al-Sabah, who invited the Reformed Church of America to open a medical center in Kuwait that became known as the American Hospital. Convinced those Christian doctors and nurses were people of good will and true followers of the Book, he allowed them to build a larger hospital, a church, and later a Catholic cathedral. While not as fond of the Hindu multi-deity beliefs, the Kuwaitis did not prohibit their free practice of religion.

Because of our diplomatic status, we didn't have to go through any employment agency, and employment residency visas could be transferred to any of us but we were still required to pay a two-hundred dollar administrative transfer fee. Everyone assigned to the case and their families, were given diplomatic passports and enjoyed many privileges, including diplomatic immunity. Of course this immunity could be waived by the ambassador if a host nation made a complaint of a criminal nature. All Embassy personnel understood this and, for military people, it also meant that, while they might avoid local trouble, there was always the potential for prosecution and punishment under the UCMJ if they did anything to get themselves kicked out of country.

Fernanda told me she first had been working for a Kuwaiti man, but that he had transferred her visa to an American, Joe, for whom she had been working now for over two years. He recently told her that he was getting ready to leave Kuwait to return to the USA for another job. When he gave her passport back to her, she saw that her visa was two years expired with no new visa in its place. She brought this up to him, but he'd just told her not to worry; that he had a lot of "wasta" (influence) and this wouldn't be a problem. He said he'd have to drop her off at the jail, of course, but that would be a temporary concern. It sounded to me like dropping an unwanted puppy at the pound. He told her he had cleared everything through the Kuwait civil authorities, so she would only be there for one or two nights before she was put on a plane for India. She was no dummy, and didn't believe him, so she consulted with another maid who worked for Jimmy, the OSI guy; that maid asked Jimmy what to do, and was told to come talk to me.

Of course, this was indeed a problem. According to the law, if she was arrested by the police, she'd have to pay $7,300 dollars to get out of jail and only then could she be deported. There was zero chance of that payment being made, so she was looking at becoming a prisoner in the maids' prison until she'd been kept for enough years to have been imprisoned long enough so she'd finally be put on a plane for India.

 This problem was exacerbated because her employer was an American who did enjoy diplomatic immunity while on this assignment. America has been a global champion of human rights and the story of a diplomat engaging in human exploitation would not make good reading in DC. Because Joe was a civilian employee, we had no criminal jurisdiction over him[4] and the Kuwaitis would simply not be interested in the matter of some foreign maid and some foreign employer. I told her I would work on this matter and get back to her within the next two days. I instructed her, that until this was resolved, it'd be best if she stayed with Jimmy's maid.

The next morning I went into the office, knocked on the General's door and asked if he had a minute for a matter. He looked up and sighed as I closed his door, an act he associated with bad news to follow. I briefed him and watched as his face went slack and his jaw dropped open. He asked me to repeat the problem, and I did while he sat there shaking his head side to side. No need for any discussion on this one; he just looked at me and said, "Take care of it and take care of her. If you have any problems, call me." This was important because, since I'd arrived four and a half months earlier, all I ever heard about this particular employee was that he was very connected and "great friends" with the ambassador. I was warned that a person who got on his bad side could be declared "persona non-grata" and sent back to the USA, which I recognized as a variation on an old theme.

As a young airman on my first assignment at MacDill AFB in Tampa, Florida, I'd stopped a car for speeding on base and the driver admonished me with "Do you know who I am?" I confessed that I didn't, so he told me he was great friends with the base commander. I

---

[4] The September 2007 murder of 17 Iraqi civilians by employees of the private security firm Blackwater spurred the Federal Government into action. The result was 18 U.S.C 3261, The Military Extraterritorial Jurisdiction Act (MEJA) which applies to certain felonies committed by those employed by or accompanying the Armed Forces abroad. The current dilemma came under Section 3271, that deals with peonage and slavery. The first time I ran into this jurisdictional issue was when a retired Army Master Sergeant named Sands was living in Saudi and running the cafeteria at the US Military Training Mission. He got tired of being hectored by his wife, so along with his butler, murdered Mrs. Sands, dismembered her and packed her in several small boxes for his butler to bury. The butler called the police but the Saudis said they had no interest in prosecuting since no Saudi blood had been spilled after all. The US wanted to recall him to active duty, but that was overruled by the courts, so Mr Sands got away with murder. I learned this when I got briefed by the OSI while assigned to Riyadh Air Base during Desert Storm. The agent told me this and pointed to the boxes I was leaning against as containing the remains of the late Mrs. Sands.

figured there was a good chance he was lying, so I directed him to follow me to the commander's office assuring him if the colonel asked me to let him go because he was a good guy, I'd do just that.

What he didn't know was that I routinely delivered the police blotter to the commander's office where I'd flirt with his secretary, and recently she'd introduced me to the colonel who now knew me by sight. We entered his office and I explained why we were there. The colonel just looked at him and said, "Who are you?" The man offered they'd met at a BBQ and, face slightly reddened, he shuffled away a few minutes later, holding the citation. After that, when somebody asked me if I knew who they were, I'd reply with, "No, but I'm certain you're going to tell me anyway" as I wrote up their citation.

Recognizing rain-making when I saw it, I went upstairs to the executive offices and, popping my head into the ambassador's office, asked if he knew the employee and if I should back off looking into any complaint of wrong doing. He looked up and said, "Who?" I now had all the guidance I needed.

The personnel office confirmed that the weasel had already administratively processed out of the organization and was scheduled to leave later that very evening on a charter back to the USA. The clerk told me his tour had been up since the beginning of December but this guy had been "taking his own sweet time out processing" while shopping for items to send back to the states. I called the AMC terminal and got hold of a captain who was in charge of the military air terminal. Passengers were required to check in six hours prior to the flight to get manifested and he confirmed my guy was in the terminal. I explained the problem and asserted that he needed to deny boarding to this guy because we needed to talk to him. The officer complained that Mr. Joe was already manifested and couldn't be taken off the flight and cited AMC regulations, even though the plane not scheduled to arrive in Kuwait for another five hours.

What he didn't know was I was actually familiar with AMC passenger regulations since my assignment to Panama, where plenty of AMC aircraft transited through on almost a daily basis and I had to become familiar with all of them. I knew he was fabricating that purported "regulation," and I knew why. He didn't know that, during my interview with Fernanda, she had told me that Mr. Joe had a gentleman friend who spent his weekends sleeping at Mr. Joe's, and who had a silk bathrobe he kept there, this at a time before homosexuality was accepted by the USAF. She had read his name tag on the uniform that she had been regularly required to wash and iron when he stayed overnight and had written down the name of this mystery guest; who, coincidentally enough, was that captain who was bent on keeping Mr. Joe on that plane. He also couldn't realize that I'd seen him leaving the building early on a Friday morning a week earlier, while I was enjoying my morning coffee on the balcony and watching Milkshake dry my car.

I confronted him with this information and reminded him that I was conducting a commander-directed investigation and any refusal to cooperate fully and in compliance with the law would not go very well for him down the road, especially since lying to me was a criminal charge, as well as conduct unbecoming an officer and gentleman.

He understood my meaning and told Joe he was under orders to not let him board the flight until he called me. Joe called to ask what was going on. I explained he needed to get back to the apartment complex because Fernanda's situation would be resolved before he went anywhere. I reminded him that his diplomatic passport was expired and his contract completed, so he was effectively an illegal tourist who, in very short order, might find himself a guest of the Kuwaiti government. Left with no choice, he agreed to come back and settle things.

Meanwhile, with the concurrence of my boss, I'd secured the services of the third most senior officer in our shop, an Army colonel, to serve as a mediator to arrive at an equitable solution for all the parties concerned. No doubt the civilian owed the maid some relief. It was just a question of fashioning that relief. An hour later, Joe arrived at the apartment complex. Gone was all his starch and air of self-importance. All that remained was a guy who knew his bluff had been called.

I led the discussion, describing his keeping Fernanda employed without renewing her visa and failing to pay her the last few months' salary. I offered the mediator that this was a case that would, in a Federal court, be violative of the 13th Amendment to the Constitution, by whose power Abraham Lincoln freed the slaves from involuntary servitude. This comment was not lost on the African-American hearing officer. I told him how much her fine would be, then brought up the matter of Fernanda's outstanding back pay. I offered that including an additional amount for her inconvenience needed to be considered, due to the employer's failure to follow the law, seemed reasonable. The colonel agreed and the amount of restitution was set at $8,300 due and payable immediately in cash, Kuwaiti dinar preferred, but US dollars welcomed. When Joe claimed he didn't know what to do, I gave him the Western Union account number I'd set up for her so the money could be transferred to India, and put into a bank account so she wouldn't have to carry such a large amount and risk robbery before she could pay her fine. Our sad business concluded, everyone signed off on the memorandum recording the agreement. I reminded Joe that there was still time to make the flight, but he needed to hurry.

He returned in under an hour with the receipt from Western Union. It was fortunate that he still had cash on him after emptying out his Kuwait dinar and dollar bank account the day before. He was then allowed to return to the airport where he made his flight.

I now had to work Fernanda's surrender so she could pay any fines and simply be allowed to depart Kuwait. Part of my brief involved making friends locally and one of those friends just happened to be a Kuwaiti major in the Ministry of the Interior (MoI), the Kuwait National police. We'd met at the pistol range and struck up a friendship. He was an excellent shot and I'd been on pistol teams as a young enlisted airman, so we'd challenge each other and then go to a cafe for coffee and sheesha. He spoke English with a slight Boston accent, the result of having attended Boston College for his undergraduate degree. Since I didn't know who else I might have to deal with, I was accompanied by my volunteer translator, Akef, (The Hook), a Palestinian guy who worked in the housing office.

We visited the MoI just before the end of the day with a very sympathetic major. He checked into the matter and verified that she did currently have a fine due and owning in the amount of $7,300. He snuck a glance at his watch. It was getting late; soon it would be time for Maghrib prayer and he wanted to beat the traffic. People racing for home before sunset were aggressive and reckless during Ramadan from not having eaten all day and accidents were more frequent. The major was also feeling the desire for a cigarette. The yearning begin to tap into his conscious thoughts, just as it had been with increasing regularity over the last six hours. He was getting antsy and simply wanted to conclude this matter as rapidly as possible.

He sighed and leaned across his desk, absently patting his left breast pocket on his uniform, feeling for the cigarette pack and thinking how good it was going to taste. He also thought that it was Ramadan after all, a time of prayer, reflection, and good deeds. He took note that oil had just passed thirty-seven dollars a barrel, up from seventeen a year earlier, and so it was also a time for generosity. Agreeing this matter was a great pity, and really in everybody's best interest to avoid potentially embarrassing all parties, he announced the fine would be *waived* and Fernanda deported as soon as she'd been processed.

I explained this to the newly wealthy Fernanda and she agreed to surrender to the authorities, but not until after I took her to the Western Union so she could release the money to her mother. It took a few days, but Akef and I visited her every day, bringing food and cigarettes that she could trade if needed to make her stay a little more comfortable. Late Christmas Eve afternoon, I got a phone call that she would be going out on that night's flight to India and we could go to the observation deck at KCIA to watch her go through immigration departure control. My mandate from Jeff was clear so I called Akef to tell him I was going out to the airport to watch the proceeding and make sure she was on the plane, and I thanked him for his help. His silence surprised me because I thought he'd be happy to know the job was finished. Ramadan had just ended; tonight was Eid al-Fitr, a time for celebration and he could be home with his family. His reply sounded like he was wounded: "I work with you and you don't want me to see the end of this story?"

And that was how we both wound up leaning against the railing on the airport observation deck at sunset, just in time to hear the muezzin calling the faithful to Maghrib prayer. I knew Akef to be a devout Muslim and told him to go and pray, I'd watch for the group. He declined, while lighting a cigarette, his first of the day. He shook his head and told me it was his kind of luck that he'd be praying while she was run through the airport by the cops. He figured Allah would approve of him missing a prayer for this purpose and besides, he could make it up later. He told me his wife and extended family had all been following this little soap-opera quality drama by cell phone text message updates. They all wanted to be in on the happy ending and he had to be able to tell them himself.

It was quiet on the floor below as the business of traveling slowed down while folks made their way to the prayer rooms to pick up whatever extra spiritual help they could muster before boarding a flight. Akef was leaning back and resting his elbows on the polished metal railing. We'd had some discussions about the Middle East and he'd try to explain things so I could understand some of the enormous cultural differences in the region, a region that appeared homogeneous to most Americans. He'd been just as angry as anyone when the *USS Cole* was attacked because it was cowardly. The Hook had worked for us since the OMC was created in 1992 and would tell anybody who'd listen about how fairly the Americans treated him and every other foreign-born employee. He'd developed friendships with many of the people who'd been assigned and still kept in touch with some of them. He enjoyed pretty much everything American, and he'd even put in for a green residency card in the immigrant lottery. (The US at that time admitted 600,000 immigrants each year. These green cards were distributed using a State department algorithm for most in need of immigrating and the balance distributed by a lottery — like a raffle for a new car.)

### DO YOU KNOW WHY THEY HATE YOU?

He pushed off the railing, and leaning in towards me said, "Do you know why they hate you?" I was caught off guard and shook my head saying, "Sorry?" He smiled and repeated, "Do you know why they hate you?" He thrust his jaw in the direction of a guy wearing a dishdasha that instead of falling to just above the ground, rose about four inches off his ankles, exposing his bare feet clad only in sandals. This Gulf Arab fashion faux pas, plus his long and unkempt beard, defined him as a fundamentalist Muslim, the kind of guy who doesn't like foreigners or progress and looks forward to going back to the seventh century, when things were clear and the path easy.

Religious fanatics came into prominence in Islam in 1979 after zealots seized the holy city of Mecca, in Saudi Arabia and demanded the royal family return to, and promote, a pure (and absolutely no fun) fundamentalist Islam. This zealotry had spread throughout the Arabian gulf, down into Africa, and east into Java, Indonesia, and the Philippines. Although less of a concern in Kuwait, plenty had bought into the fervor.

Now understanding what he meant, I shook my head saying I hadn't the first clue as to why. Akef looked evenly at me and said, "They hate you because Americans are the chosen people and everyday you point out their hypocrisy." He'd finished his cigarette, crushing it out on the floor while he looked at me and continued. "Everybody thinks the Jews are God's chosen people, but they aren't. It's the Americans." I was astonished by his declaration, but he kept on. He started counting off his fingers, "There are five pillars to Islam — *Shahada* which is faith, *Salat* which is prayer, *Zakāt* which is charity, *Sawm* which is fasting, and *Hajj*, which is a pilgrimage to Mecca." He ticked off each one saying, "Faith. You Americans are a religious people and most Americans I've met are Christians. You have faith, you believe in the one true God, Allah, you just don't accept Mohammed, peace be unto him, as his prophet, but that's OK, because you believe."

He touched his index finger saying, "Prayer. You are the most prayerful people I've ever seen. Somebody sneezes, you say, 'God Bless you.' You pray before you eat, you offer blessings to everybody and often say, 'Well, bless your heart!' for no reason, just because you do. You guys pray way more times in a day than most Muslims." He touched his middle finger, "Charity? Whenever there is a disaster anywhere in the world, the first people to show up are the Americans.

You never ask who needs the help, you don't care what their religion is, you just come and you help. Fasting? You guys are always fasting, I read all about finding spiritual peace and happiness on some new diet plan, and when you are here, even though you are not Muslim, you honor us by joining in our fast and respecting our views." Finally, he came to his pinky. "The Hajj, well, you don't go to Mecca, but the hajj is about renewing your spirit and fighting Satan, working to become a better person. Your libraries are full of self-help books on how to become a better person. You guys are always asking for feedback and writing performance reviews to improve. You guys are making those long beards look like hypocrites every day and THAT is why they hate you. You point out all their failures just by your example and you guys don't even know it."

I was touched by his comments, and I couldn't disagree with him. He continued, "The Americans are God's chosen people and I know this because he has given you the most wonderful bounty of good land, minerals, water and more, and you people don't just keep it, you share it with the world. I see the news reports and watch as food is delivered to starving people, people who would die except for the Americans. You send men to the moon and the bottom of the oceans. You invent medicines that cure people. You have freedom of speech and thought. The long beards will hate you, but that is their problem, because all of us who know you guys, and all those people who watch the news see this and know this. *That* is why fundamentalists hate you and also why they will never win."

We turned back to look down on to the terminal floor while I contemplated the weight of what he said, the cultural insight he'd shared. A minute or so passed quietly, and then we were rewarded with the sight of, maybe, fifty maids, each handcuffed to another as they walked through the area, escorted by the police. I'd given Fernanda a small bright orange nylon wallet and asked her to hold it in her hand when she came to the airport so I could spot her and be certain she was OK. I saw her in the first group of twenty or so. She was looking straight ahead, knowing her freedom was just a few yards away. She never saw us and she, like the rest of the women, proceeded toward her freedom, and vanished from our sight.

Akef went home to his family and told the tale to a rapt audience. I came home and saw the artificial Christmas tree, brightly lit and on display in the living room, and I thought about the devout Muslim who gave up time with his family during this special season to help an Indian woman he did not know get home to her family for Christmas.

+++

---

# Sparkle

It was a Monday evening in March, just half past seven, another ordinary midweek "hump day." I'd stopped by the lounge for the Wednesday happy hour and free pizza night. That ended at six so I was back home watching an old black and white Egyptian comedy on TV when the phone rang. Answering, I heard a familiar voice ask, "Do you know who this is?" Of course I did, it was my boss, Jeff, a voice I'd heard plenty of times in person, on the radio, via cell phone, and office intercom. Without waiting, he continued, "I need you to report to the MoD hospital and standby. I want you to take charge of things there and report back to me by landline, no mobile phones. You'll understand when you get there." I grabbed my identification badges and hustled to the dark blue Jeep Grand Cherokee.

While I was getting ready to drive the ten miles to the Armed Forces hospital, a UH-60 Blackhawk Army Medevac helicopter was lifting off from OP 10, an observation post somewhere on the Udairi Bombing Range and forty-five miles north of Kuwait City.

Just half an hour earlier, a Navy F/A 18C fighter, call sign Lion 71, and flown by Commander David Zimmerman, a highly decorated 3,000-hour pilot and squadron commander of VFA-37, had been involved in fratricide. His squadron was deployed aboard the aircraft carrier USS Harry S. Truman, CVN-75. The F/A 18 Hornet is an all-weather jet aircraft used by both the US Navy and Marine Corps as both a fighter and an attack platform. In its fighter mode, the Hornet is primarily an escort and for fleet air defense. In attack mode, it is used for force projection, interdiction, and close and deep air support, which includes the dropping of bombs on targets.

Zimmerman was on the range as part of a night Close Air Support Exercise (CASEX) and preparing to drop three MK-82, 500-pound bombs. He was being directed by Staff Sergeant Tim Crusing, call sign Havoc 20, the TACP combat air controller from the 19th Air Support Operations Squadron, Fort Campbell, Kentucky, but currently assigned to the 332nd Expeditionary Air Support Operations Squadron (EASOS). TACPs can be individuals or teams of airmen attached to conventional and special operations units to provide precision attack guidance for US and coalition close air support aircraft, artillery, and naval gunfire. They establish and maintain command and control (C2) communication; and advise ground commanders on the best use of air power.

Another controller, Staff Sergeant Jason Faley, was also assigned and acting as the observer, but Crusing was the senior controller. OP 10 was atop a long ridge-line running east to west and a mile and quarter south of the target area. It was marked, per regulations, with a circle of chemical sticks, a visible white strobe light attached atop their Humvee's antenna base, and an infra red (IR) strobe placed on the top front of the vehicle. Since this was a live ordinance exercise, three soldiers from the 707th Explosives Ordinance Disposal (EOD) unit, on ordinance clearing duty, came to OP 10 for safety. They were joined by four army special forces soldiers and another soldier from a nearby training camp who had been observing. The Green Berets brought along a New Zealand SAS officer, Major John McNutt, the only Kiwi assigned duty in Kuwait. Six KAF soldiers from an artillery unit were waiting for training to begin later in the evening, and they were standing at their cars a short distance from the group waiting to watch the show. Six vehicles parked nearby. The weather was fine, visibility was ten nautical miles with scattered clouds and a light breeze out of the Northwest. The temperature was a balmy seventy-five degrees Fahrenheit.

Zimmerman was accompanied by a wingman, but also in the immediate vicinity was a Navy F-14B, an American supersonic, twin-engine, two-seat, variable sweep wing fighter and the same kind Harmon Rabb flew on the hit TV series *JAG*. Using call sign Latch 41, it was piloted by Lieutenant Patrick Mowles accompanied by Lieutenant Andrea Powers, the Radar Intercept Officer (RIO). Together they were the Forward Air Controller Airborne - FAC(A) and a part of the training exercise.

Havoc 20 and Latch 41agreed that they would share responsibility for control of Zimmerman's in-coming strike aircraft. Latch 41's Mowles was responsible for Lion 71 checking-in and orally providing target area orientation, talking to help Zimmerman locate both the friendly position at OP 10 and the target. Meanwhile, on the ground, Crusing would maintain "Positive Direct Control" observing and controlling the attack. He also retained "Final Clearance Authority" for Zimmerman to release the bombs.

Lion 71 flew over the range at about 10,000 feet, getting ready for the run, and it was then that a series of most unfortunate errors were made, beginning when Zimmerman mistakenly identified OP 10, then one mile ahead of him, as his intended target. He overflew the area, banked, and began his bombing run while calling for the target to be illuminated or "sparkled." That task fell to Staff Sergeant Faley, the observer.

Faley used a laser pointer to "sparkle" the target for Lion 71. When Zimmerman called for that sparkle, Havoc 20/Crusing briefly took his eyes off Lion 71 to see if Faley was illuminating the correct target. This caused him to lose his visual on Lion 71; so, when he turned back, he saw the three aircraft, the F-14, Zimmerman's wingman in an F-18 and Lion 71 and asked Zimmerman if he was inbound. Mowles in Latch 41 had orally guided the Hornet, telling Zimmerman he had "good nose position," which in turn gave him a "warm fuzzy," and false situational awareness as to his location in space relative to the target.

Zimmerman now believed he was approaching the target when in fact his nose was pointing towards the OP and Faley's laser. Zimmerman replied "Inbound" to Crusing, but never saying, "Target in sight, friendlies in sight" as procedure directed. The Hornet was in Air-to-

Ground "auto mode" and now targeting OP 10. Zimmerman gave one pulse on the trigger, one-second *before* the "CLEARED HOT ON SPARKLE" message from Crusing, causing the weapons release. When he heard the "CLEARED HOT" call, he pulsed the system again, a useless reaction, because the bombs were already away and sailing through the night, riding that laser beam straight toward OP 10. Crusing, instantly realizing that Zimmerman had targeted the OP, called "ABORT, ABORT, ABORT" but it was just too late. He screamed for everybody to clear out and took off running just as the three 500-pound bombs found their target.

At 7:01pm, just moments after the explosions, a badly injured Crusing put in a distress call for medical evacuation helicopters, while the less injured applied first aid and buddy care to the more gravely injured. Fifteen minutes later, two air ambulances from the 571st Medical company took off from nearby Camp Doha. The first one landed twenty minutes later, loaded the four injured men, including Crusing, and took off for the military hospital, arriving one hour and seven minutes after impact, and just as I was pulling into the parking lot. One man, EOD Staff Sergeant Richard Boudreau, died from his wounds in flight to the hospital. A short while later the second Medevac bird arrived with more dead: Staff Sergeant Faley, the other two EOD technicians, Specialists Philip M. Freligh and Jason D. Wildfong, Staff Sergeant Troy J. Westberg and the New Zealand officer, Major McNutt.

Two other soldiers, Sergeant First Class Donald Spencer, and Staff Sergeant Alton Adams, were treated and released. Crusing and Sergeant First Class William Sullivan, both badly injured, were later evacuated to Landstuhl Army hospital in Germany for further surgery.

Inside the hospital, the doctors and staff of the 126th Forward Surgery Team (FST), ably assisted by their KAF colleagues, conducted a swift triage, removing the injured to operating theaters and placing the dead in an unused surgical suite. I took an initial briefing from one of the less injured and began to put together a briefing for my boss, since he was the senior US officer in theater for Kuwait and would be responsible for briefing the KAF Chief of Staff and also the Commander of USCENTCOM in Tampa. This report was part of a joint and combined forces multinational incident and would include my initial identification of the injured and dead, so it became my job to ascertain that information which had to be correct the first time.

It's an odd sensation walking into a room with six dead bodies, none that appeared badly injured. Some showed just a bit of blood at their ears. Chris Kontogianis, an orthopedic surgeon and Bright Star deployment buddy from my time in Idaho, was there on a 90-day rotation. He shared his diagnosis that the men died from "blast lung injury" and had not felt a thing. He explained that high-order explosive detonations result in near instantaneous transformation of the explosive material into a highly pressurized gas, releasing energy at supersonic speeds. This results in the formation of a blast wave that travels out from the epicenter. Primary blast injuries are characterized by anatomical and physiological changes from the force generated by the blast wave impacting the body's surface, and affect primarily gas-containing anatomical structures (lungs, gastrointestinal tract, ears). This so-called "blast lung" is a clinical diagnosis and is characterized as respiratory difficulty and hypoxia without obvious external injury to the chest.

Meanwhile, I needed to locate the two stamped metal identification "dog" tags that contain the name, ID number, blood type, and religious affiliation. They're designed to survive any battlefield injury, but most special forces mask them with black electrical tape to eliminate any noise or reflection and that was the case here as well. Rather than removing a bunch of tape, after reading the name tag on the body, I pulled wallets from pockets and used the military identification card and driver's license information to create my list. To make sure the identifications remained correct until the remains could be airlifted to the mortuary affairs specialists in Germany, I wrote each name and service number in ink on their bare chests where only those technicians would see. I did this because I knew the anguish caused by a misidentification would be unforgivable.

In the process of going through the wallets and inventorying the contents before putting them in a plastic zip lock bag, I saw in their photos the happy faces of children, parents, wives, and girlfriends, in family portraits and candid moments, and thought about all the people who'd be getting a knock on the door in just a few hours. They'd be startled from their slumber and awakened to find two or more officers and NCOs in dress uniforms delivering the news nobody ever wanted to give or receive.

For his part in this tragedy, Zimmerman was relieved of his command, given a punitive letter of reprimand from a three-star Admiral at an Admiral's Mast hearing, and retired from the Navy. The crew of Latch 41 received career-killing letters of admonishment.

+++

# Running A Saloon In A Dry Country

For Americans living abroad, the US Embassy is that one solid contact with home and things American. Under international law, an embassy stands on soil of its homeland, and so it was in Kuwait. Once you passed through the gates, you were back in America, but that didn't quite assure that everything inside would be the same as in America.

The overarching cause for that was a State Department full of well-meaning people who understood diplomacy but didn't have the first clue about "quality of life" issues. This culture was unlike the Air Force which considered quality of life issues essential, because unhappy airmen might not get those multi-million dollar jets off the ground.

I discovered this lack of diplomatic enthusiasm during my first weekend in Kuwait when I was invited to the embassy to enjoy the American Employee's Welfare Association (AEWA) lounge. The lounge was located in an unused storage closet outside the Chancery building and near the swimming pool that no one could use because money for a life guard was not in the budget.

The "bar" was several sheets of ripped plywood stapled to a frame and looked like something a bunch of pre-teens might cobble together. Manned by the manager and the assistant manager, the sole employees, they slung just one type of beer and two types of wine, red or white, neither very good. These drink purveyors were paid seventeen dollars an hour in overtime pay, and they encouraged tips.

We arrived during the assignments season and many people were leaving Kuwait and heading off to new assignments, so there were vacancies on the AEWA board of directors. Every functional area, except the "Agency" guys, was expected to have a candidate stand for election to be their representative on the board of directors. The spooks got a break because they never admitted being there in the first place.

Having previously served on club boards of directors at RAF Upper Heyford and Howard Air Base in Panama, I didn't think this bar was very good and said so plainly and loudly. As a result, I ran unopposed for the OMC-K seat. At our first meeting, Brian, the administrative director, a dull and unimaginative fellow, announced that the AEWA was in danger of being shut down for reasons nobody could fathom. He said the lounge was hemorrhaging money and in two years had burned through most of a $130,000 cushion, losing around $45,000 a year. He announced that with the last fiscal year having just ended, all indications were that the losses would continue. Once the accounts balances were zero, the charter would have to be pulled and the pub closed. The entire board was stunned because this also meant the sole source of legal alcohol in a dry country would be gone and nothing to be done about it.

We sat silently as we processed the bad news. I felt an urge to relieve myself so I went off to the toilet. When I returned a few minutes later, I learned that in my absence I'd been voted in as Chairman of the Board. This was not a job I'd dreamed of, but the potential for the bar's closure jolted me into action. As the son of a wine salesman, and later as a teenager who came of age in Moran's bar in my hometown, and who also had enjoyed many good times in bars and nightclubs nationally and globally, let's just say I felt fully qualified to determine what was needed to create not just a bar, but a great bar. I'd also tended bar in the past and was not about to let all that practical experience and training go to waste. I certainly didn't want to be at the helm of a failed legal alcohol monopoly in a country that prohibited alcohol. I felt this was a moment of destiny calling.

I drew on all my life lessons: working in a catering hall, delicatessen, hamburger stand and bartending in college. I thought of all the different clubs in all the different locations on many different assignments. Sent from Saudi Arabia to investigate and adjudicate a governmental tort claim in Abu Dhabi in 1992, I'd had occasion to spend a week at a five-star hotel along the Gulf. This oasis offered three fabulous bars: a swim-up pool bar, a British pub, and a country western-themed saloon bar. It was in that saloon on a Wednesday night where I enjoyed "The

Mugabe Brothers," a Zimbabwean country-western band on tour. You haven't lived until you've seen three Zimbabweans in cowboy hats, pointy-toed cowboy boots, dashikis and sporting lion tooth necklaces, singing an African-accented cover of Johnny Cash's "I Walk the Line."

I knew if a bar that great could exist in a place as strange as Abu Dhabi, then it could also work in Kuwait. I applied the business lessons I'd learned at the University of South Florida, as well as everything I learned about people from being a cop and a lawyer.

The first thing I did was follow the money. I noticed the bar was a strictly cash affair; the money thrown into a cigar box that originally contained the dusty Tampa Nugget cigars for sale in the AEWA souvenir shop, cigars as dry and dusty as those, must have been sitting in the display case for years. During previous years, all the club's revenues were purportedly entered into a book somewhere and the whole thing reviewed and audited by the same big name, overcharging, American accounting firm, which reported all was well. That firm also said the AEWA owed them five thousand, for their auditing their own books; something they should never have done because they wrote them. This breach of "checks and balances" spurred a deeper look at those business records.

As the chairman, I requested all the books and records and sat with another board member, the Counselor Affairs officer, a non-practicing attorney, who had studied accounting as an undergrad. He soon discovered a receipt for five thousand dollars for a jukebox that had simply never shown up in the lounge. Soon he began finding other suspicious receipts and we realized the immediate steps to get on the road to fiscal wellness was to bring in a new management team, implement better cash accounting, and improve the beverages on offer. Happily, the annual summer PCS rotation took care of the management issue. The accounting issues were solved by buying a cash register and creating a system of rotating guest bartenders to work with our only full-time employee, Alfredo, a Filipino and long-term embassy employee.

I'd first seen the guest bartender concept when Mongo initiated it while we were assigned to Osan. He and any other qualified bartender would put on an apron and while wearing a Zorro mask, would sling drinks to the rail hangers at the bar. At Osan, it provided entertainment, in Kuwait, it provided a fiscal safeguard. I recalled that the East Germans would never let the same two soldiers work together because they might get some funny ideas about remaining on post, like defecting to the West. The guest bartender counted the receipts each night after closing, and a board member verified the tally. The bartenders were paid a flat rate of fifteen dollars an hour plus any tips which were considerable, sometimes over three hundred dollars in an evening, because people are surprisingly generous and thoughtful when you are the only source of booze.

I took an inspection tour, a terrain walk, to learn exactly what assets we had at our disposal and how to use those assets to boost business and save this failing enterprise. There were two unoccupied buildings just past the Marine barracks. One was empty, the other was divided into two spaces; the AEWA liquor store and a gift shop stocked with a small collection of souvenir key chains and shot glasses, all emblazoned with the Embassy logo and State department seal. These limited offerings were surrounded by bottles of wine with labels I'd last seen in the clearance aisle at the Great Falls Walmart. The other space had some counters and under counter sinks that to my trained eye bore an astonishing resemblance to a bar. I took my beliefs to the structures office and asked for a copy of the original plans for the building. Those plans labeled the area as an "ice cream parlor," but the design told me that was written to avoid offending any cultural sensibilities in a country which does not allow alcohol.

Like Moses pushing the promised land, I made a declaration at the next board meeting that I'd found our salvation and outlined my plan. The other board members were on board, but some warned I'd be fighting with the bureaucracy in the form of long-term groundskeeper and general curmudgeon, Norm, who believed that as groundskeeper he had a say in how any building on "his" facility was used. (This was a man who also insisted that children who lived on Embassy grounds could not run and play on the grass field in the center of the housing compound.)

There was some initial resistance from the community when I announced the plans for the new AEWA lounge, but the grumbling was made by those few people who don't like any change. Still, I was surprised they'd complain, given how crappy the current bar was. Over the next few weeks, the operation was examined, a plan for moving forward was formulated, and work began. I gave Alfredo a picture of the tall cocktail tables and solid wooden chairs I wanted and he was off to Shuwaikh, a district where different artisans plied their various trades. He visited an iron monger and showed him the picture. While the legs and stands were being fashioned, he found at the marble souk some green Italian marble left over from a palace update. He got the table tops made and mounted and came back proudly under budget.

The GS-12 property officer was happy to let us have exclusive use of both small buildings as long as we paid rent, the only organization on the entire compound to be so charged. We relocated all the remaining liquor supplies to our empty building and set up committees to identify the wines, beers, and liquors that would be most in demand. The Charge d'Affairs's French-born wife was in charge of selecting the red and white wines, while Tony, our USAF Postmaster and fellow board member, a veteran of multiple tours in Germany, headed the beer committee. We had two beer sub-committees: one solely for domestic US beers and the other for foreign brews. I headed the committee charged with selecting the distilled liquors and was especially proud of the seven single-malts representing the best of Scotland and two Irish whiskeys I'd put on order. As Eugene, an Irish guest, pointed out one evening, "This is the only time I'd ever seen Protestant Bushmills, and Catholic Jameson's whiskeys on the same shelf and next to each other." We'd used our remaining reserved monies to place the orders with the Dutch and Belgian suppliers. The occasional experience of going to work with my father when I was a kid helped while talking to the salesmen. Thanks to some of my fraternity brothers at Boise State, who worked promotions for beer distributors, I knew all about promotional items. I got the sales reps to throw in a bunch of Heineken bar accoutrements, including beer coasters, glassware, playing cards, ashtrays, bar towels, a clock, and even some patio umbrellas.

There would be an issue of how to position and store all the items we'd ordered once they arrived. I was able to call upon our newly assigned protocol officer, Bill, who when not arranging dinners for dignitaries, was a theoretical mathematician assigned to Wright-Patterson AFB in Ohio. He'd spent his entire career designing wing surfaces for stealth aircraft. He'd been selected for this assignment as a sabbatical, an opportunity to broaden his horizons and learn more about the rest of the USAF and other services, and even meet a few foreigners. Nobody bothered to share this news with Bill until his orders were in hand. What they didn't know was that Bill was a lifelong introvert. He'd also readily admit to having an anti-social personality and was really uncomfortable around other people generally, and certainly foreigners, who were all mysterious and, to him, unnerving, but nobody ever asked at all.

Thanks to these candid admissions shortly after his arrival, one of my new and additional duties was back-up protocol officer. I spent the next month assisting him with visits to each of the different offices in the Ministry of Defense (MoD) in order to orient him, help establish connections, and review plans for visits. This involved drinking a lot of coffee and tea while making small talk, another area where Bill did not excel. Despite these vocational limitations, I learned that having a theoretical mathematician as a friend had its advantages. I gave him a copy of the liquor orders we'd placed and, from those numbers, he was able to design an off-load and storage plan that would compensate for projected sales so that cases never had to be shuffled or moved to reach the desired supplies.

Liquor supplies came into Kuwait twice a year, in spring and autumn, under diplomatic seal and were not subject to inspection. Although we had the largest embassy in Kuwait and the most personnel assigned, our order could only fill thirty-five of the forty foot length of the shipping container. To fill the remaining few feet, we called on our friends at the Canadian embassy who happily put their order in with ours, but did not receive any of the promotional items since they had no bar to speak of and only few people assigned. We loved having them over because they did have a great rock band that played regularly at our club, and their frontman was their Charge d'Affairs. For other some embassies, providing liquor could be a great source of cash and influence. The Cubans, for example, routinely bought liquor for embassies of countries where alcohol use was restricted or prohibited and they made a killing in the Gulf.

Watching the operation taking place over his objection, at a Monday team meeting with the Ambassador, groundskeeper Norm first protested that because the plans labeled our bar as an ice cream parlor, it could only be used as one. I pointed out the "best use" doctrine for government facilities and his complaint was dismissed by the Ambassador without any discussion. Next Norm shifted to a complaint that storing liquor in our warehouse would constitute a fire hazard. At that point I offered that in my three-year experience as a firefighter for the US Army reserves while in law school, I was quite comfortable in opining that, "Beer cannot catch fire and neither can the wine, and since all of the liquor is under 100 proof, 50% alcohol, it can't burn either." He started to protest, but when I added that the hard liquor was also stored under the fire sprinklers, he finally gave up.

In relatively short order, our new bar was organized, equipped, staffed, and ready to be opened to the public.

+++

# Just Because They Look American Doesn't Mean They Are

It's hard to tell what an American looks like. After all, we are a nation of immigrants and our ethnic diversity means that, absent some sort of cultural dress or language, it's hard to tell who is or isn't an American just by looking. Often times, we assume people we meet have a background, education, experiences, and skills similar to ours, but realistically, they most often do not. There are myriad areas of commonality and universal experience inside our American culture that foreigners never see, learn, or experience.

Our bar's opening was just a few hours away and I had a job for one of the employees we'd hired for our cleaning staff. She was the wife of a state employee who worked in the vault, destroying classified materials. She was from Eritrea and had only recently married him, but under the rules of spousal preference we were able to employ her as a cleaner, which was great because she was also the only person to apply for the twelve-dollar-an-hour job. I'd completed a walk-through inspection and noticed the glass doors and full length glass windows were all very dirty, the result of a passing dust storm. I asked our cleaner to clean the windows. Her English wasn't very good and she told me she didn't understand. I wanted her to succeed so I fetched a bucket, rubber squeegee and sponge and brought them to her. For the next few moments, I pantomimed how to clean the window, first wiping down with the sponge and then wiping clean with the rubber blade, then looked at her and asked if she understood. Eager and happy for the work, she nodded up and down agreeably saying, "Yes sir, yes, sir." I took that as my cue to leave and went off to complete some other last minute tasks.

I returned about an hour later and saw her outside, in front of the last door as she was finishing. She reached up on tiptoes and wiped that sponge back and forth across the glass, then pulled out the rubber squeegee and wiped it down exactly as I'd instructed, which was fine; except I'd never told her to fill the bucket with water. I looked at the other glass and saw clearly that the sponge had rubbed the dirt and the squeegee left swirls when she whipped the rubber blade back and forth as I'd demonstrated, but all to no end.

At first I was aggrieved, thinking, "How could she not know how to clean a window?" but immediately realized she'd never been anyplace where the windows might get washed and simply didn't know water was a component of this operation. I brought her to the back sink and demonstrated how to fill the bucket, and even included how much white vinegar to add to the mix. She took the lesson and our windows never looked better, while I learned to never take for granted that another person understands what is required to complete a task and that nodding one's head up and down is no guarantee.

As a Navy guy in foreign military sales remarked, "You know how a Pakistani says, 'Fuck you?' He nods his head up and down, saying, 'Yes sir, Yes sir.'"

+++

# Satisfaction Guaranteed!

An embassy is really just a small community of a hundred or so people, staff, spouses and kids. One thing the State folks were very good at was putting out an internal phone book so that anybody on the country team could be reached on their government mobile phones or in their office.

It was late afternoon, toward the end of duty hours. I was sitting in my office reviewing a contract when my phone rang. It was a civilian assigned to our case who served as liaison for the Detroit company that made the M1A-2 main battle tanks owned by the KAF. If any related problems arose, like an engine burning up, he was also the guy who arranged to pack up and send that AGT-1500 gas turbine engine for a very expensive rebuild. He was also quite pleased, if the damage was severe enough, to order a brand new one from Honeywell, at just under one million dollars a copy.

The problem came down to tanks manned primarily by Bedoons, stateless Arabs who, while born in Kuwait, were not Kuwaiti citizens. Their nomad parents never got around to entering their family into the original and legally binding book that was created and opened for people to declare themselves citizens in 1962, when Kuwait became a country. These families were poor, but any Bedoon could work for the government and the military wages were good. Still, it's a hot and miserable job, so on Thursday nights, when they returned from training in the desert, some drivers would simply shut off the engine instead of idling it for the required thirty minutes to cool down. After that, like those two sailors who sunk that ship in Panama, they'd light out for the weekend.

After taking the lazy exit a few times, their engine would blow up. While this was good for Honeywell's bottom line, it was terrible for maintaining a combat readiness rate. This abuse became so rampant that I submitted a report to my Kuwaiti bosses that it'd be much cheaper to hire Indians as tank drivers. As a culture, the Indians are book and procedure oriented, and would only shut off those engines after properly allowing them time to cool, therefore fiscally prudent to "outsource" the driving to a foreigner.

The contractor opened our conversation by asking me if I was the Chairman of the Board for AEWA. I assured him that I most certainly was. He then let me know that he had a complaint. I was happy to inform him that our policy was "your satisfaction guaranteed or double your money back." He then went on to explain that he'd recently purchased five cases of Heineken beer, his total monthly allowance, and was concerned about the quality of the beer.

"I just finished drinking the second case and noticed I wasn't burping as much as I usually do, so I checked the date on the cans and these are a month past the last-sell date. What are you going to do about it?"

I had to take a moment while I considered my response. Here was a guy paying one dollar a can for imported Dutch beer in a dry country, and he wants to bitch about burping? Ignoring the chance for outright sarcasm, and recognizing he did deserve an answer and a solution, I offered, "OK, our motto at AEWA is 'You satisfaction guaranteed or double your money back, no questions asked!' Since you aren't satisfied and enjoying our offerings, tell you what, go buy two cases of beer at another store, bring in the receipt and we'll give you back twice what you paid for it."

He was quiet for a moment before saying, "But there aren't any other stores that sell beer in Kuwait."

"And there you have it," I consoled him, as I hung up the phone on another satisfied customer.

+++

# Everything Just Changed

It was ten minutes to four that Monday afternoon and the weekly classified country-team meeting for the Ambassador had just gotten underway. Representatives from the various intelligence agencies would attend and share their observations from on-going operations as they saw fit, never giving anything more than absolutely necessary to protect the integrity of their operations. These briefings served as coordination to avoid conflict on various intelligence collection programs any other agency might have running, and anything else the Ambassador needed to know about. This deconfliction is necessary. The Defense Intelligence Agency (DIA) is responsible for the collection of over eighty percent of all intelligence. Despite their press clippings, the CIA only gets twenty percent. The operations officer had just concluded his briefing on forces in the region when the door opened and the public affairs officer came rushing in.

An animated, but most disagreeable person, with terrible fashion sense, she had a fondness for brown polyester pantsuits and was dating the resident editor of *Pravda*, the Moscow news organization and long time KGB front. One spook remarked, "That guy ought to get the Order of Lenin for having sex with her." She whispered into the Ambassador's ear and both left. With the reason for the briefing gone, and no indication of when he'd be back, we began to talk among ourselves and after another minute, Bill, the anti-social protocol officer, came in, whispered in the Chief's ear and they were gone, with the chief calling over his shoulder, "Meetings over!"

With no further information, and realizing we needed some coffee, the Skipper and I zeroed in on the break room. A Navy reservist, Skipper and I became friends when he took a short-notice tour, replacing our Mr. Joe, that former civilian protocol officer who'd planned on dropping Fernanda off at the police station and hightail it to back to the States. Gregarious, self-starting, and a world-class schmoozer, Skipper was the exact opposite of his replacement, anti-social Bill.

After finishing that tour, Skipper returned to the States and picked up a job at CENTCOM headquarters at MacDill AFB, in Tampa, Florida. He hated the job because every day was a ten-hour day, thanks to a daily hour-long in-briefing to announce what happened since the last shift. In return, he had to prepare, and deliver, another hour-long out-briefing before he could drive the hour it took him to go north on Dale Mabry Highway and drive the thirty-four miles to his rented house in Odessa, up near the Pasco County line. He'd call when he got bored with staring at the big screen, while waiting for anything to happen. He always complained of his assignment as being at "MacDillabad in Tampistan." He often wondered aloud why he didn't get hazardous duty pay for living in Tampa. He'd note that CENTOM's area of responsibility was the entire Middle East, and Africa, but more Americans were killed each year in Tampa than the entire CENTCOM area of responsibility.

There never seemed to be a lot happening; but, even though CENTCOM was over eight thousand miles and seven time zones away, they still believed they were right there on the pointy end of the spear. This view was not shared by those of us actually out on the pointy end of the spear. This rigidity was born in part as guilty overcompensation for never sentencing any of their folks to a 179-day tour over in "the sandbox." The other part was nostalgia for, and missing, the spotlight. Those now decade-old halcyon few weeks of *Desert Storm,* were over a long, long time ago; and as the late Beatle, George Harrison might have noted, back "When they was fab."

A promotion board met and Skipper found out he'd been passed over for promotion to captain. Most passed-over officers chose to retire, but Skip got busy and forgot to do that. When the Navy guy serving as the Foreign Military Sales (FMS) director announced his retirement, Skip volunteered for a full tour at OMC. Given his popularity and demonstrated past-performance as the protocol guy, he was re-incarnated as the new FMS guy.

Shortly after he arrived back at the OMC, another Navy promotion board met. Too many passed-over commanders had bailed out, Skip got a second look, and ended up promoted after all, thus becoming the "Accidental Captain." He spent a lot of time enjoying the discomfort of one stiff-necked Army colonel who had been curt with Skip as the protocol guy. In a stunning reversal of fortune, Skip alone now controlled the case money and how it was spent, with no oversight. He also had the power to dispossess the now involuntarily obsequious and sycophantic senior officer from his 8,000-square-foot villa, and move him into a much smaller place, to cut costs.

A television was always on in the lobby and set to CNN because it was the best source of breaking news. I stopped right there when I saw the smoke coming from the building I recognized as one of the World Trade center towers. The camera was locked in position and it took a few moments to comprehend exactly what I was seeing because it shouldn't be happening. It was early morning in New York, and at first I thought it might have been a small plane accident. Skip and I mused about how skyscrapers are built to take a huge hit and recalled the only building strike we knew of was when a B-25 bomber got lost in fog and hit the Empire State building in 1945. Skip had a private pilot's license and was talking about how air traffic control shouldn't have let that happen. For three minutes we watched the North tower burn when what looked like a Boeing 737 (but was a 767) entered the frame and flew right into the southern wall of the South tower and exploded. I shook my head, as if that could shake out the image that I was beginning to understand. Skip said, "What the fuck was that?"

As it became clear we were not watching a loop of the original accident, it also became clear this was some kind of coordinated attack by a foreign entity.

Echoing what very many people said on that day and since, I looked at Skipper and said, "I think everything just changed."

My beliefs were confirmed when, thirty-four minutes later, word began popping up that a plane had just crashed into the western wall of the Pentagon E ring, killing 70 civilians and 55 military personnel. Lieutenant General Tim Maude was the highest ranking military officer killed that day. A combat veteran from Vietnam in 1967, he was the most senior US Army officer killed by foreign action since the 1945 combat death of Lieutenant General Simon Bolivar Buckner, Jr, at Okinawa.

Maude, the US Army's Deputy Chief of Staff for Personnel was in a meeting when American Airlines Flight 77 impacted. He'd only recently moved back into his office in this renovated section of the Pentagon. On that day, only 800 of 4,500 people who would have been in the area were there because of that on-going renovation work. Furthermore, the area hit, on the side of the Heliport facade, was the section best prepared for such an attack. These renovations contained security improvements resulting from the Oklahoma City bombing,[5] and were nearly completed.

While we were absorbing that horror, word came in about United Airlines flight 93. The doomed Boeing 757-222 departed Liberty Newark International with 33 passengers, seven crew and four terrorists, bound for San Francisco. After the terrorists took control of the plane, several passengers and flight attendants learned from phone calls that suicide attacks had already been made by hijacked airliners on the WTC in New York City and at the Pentagon.

Todd Beamer, a 32 year old businessman from Cranbury, New Jersey was on his way to a meeting with a Sony representative in San Francisco. When the passengers heard reports of the other attacks, they

---

[5] In the worst act of domestic terrorism, on April 19, 1995, Timothy McVeigh, a Desert Storm Army veteran, aided by Terry Nichols, bombed the Alfred P. Murrah Federal building in Oklahoma City killing 168 people, including 19 children in a day care, and injured more than 680 others. The blast destroyed one-third of the building and damaged 324 other buildings within a 16-block radius, shattered glass in 258 nearby buildings, and destroyed or burned 86 cars, causing an estimated $652 million worth of damage. McVeigh, a self described patriot, offered it was the book *"The Turner Diaries"* which depicts a violent revolution in America which leads to the overthrow of the federal government, nuclear war, and, ultimately, a race war, that guided his actions. The book also called for the extermination of Jews, gays and non-whites. McVeigh was convicted and executed in a Federal Prison in Indiana on June 11, 2001. Nichols is serving 161 consecutive life sentences without parole in the SuperMax facility in Florence, Colorado. He spends 23 hours a day in solitary confinement with one hour a day of solitary exercise while shackled.

realized the hijackers were suicidal and determined to go down swinging. Beamer, along with passengers Mark Bingham, Tom Burnett, and Jeremy Glick, formed a heroic plan to take the plane back from the hijackers.They were joined by fellow passengers Lou Nacke, Rich Guadagno, Alan Beaven, Honor Elizabeth Wainio, Linda Gronlun, William Cashman and flight attendants Sandra Bradshaw and Cee Cee Ross-Lyles. They decided they'd storm the cockpit and take back the plane. The pilots were dead, none of the passengers knew how to fly, and every one of them knew that this was going to be their final action on this planet. The group planned to "jump on" the hijackers and fly the plane into the ground before the hijackers' could strike their intended target, which they didn't know was the Capital in DC, the home of Congress and ultimate symbol of America. Beamer and the others recited the Lord's Prayer and the 23rd Psalm and when finished he said, "*Are you ready? Okay. Let's roll.*"

Those twelve American heroes triumphed over evil and United 93 went into a steep dive until auguring into a field by a reclaimed strip mine in Stoneycreek Township, near Shanksville, Pennsylvania, and about seven flight minutes from Washington DC.

It was late 2001, and now our operations tempo spiked rapidly. The duty days grew longer as our entire mission profile transformed from drinking coffee, making friends, and influencing people, to using our skills in preparation for the clouds of war that were appearing on the near horizon.

That Monday in September galvanized the nation. Our FP Con level had remained in Delta since the USS *Cole* was attacked eleven months earlier. In very short order, word began to flow that we were to prepare for what would become *Operation Enduring Freedom*, the beginning of the hunt in Afghanistan for Osama bin Laden, or OBL, the Saudi-born mastermind of 9-11.

Our mission had always been about getting to know people in "faces in places and spaces" and develop personal relationships and to that end an inordinate amount of time was spent drinking tea to build those relationships. All this social interaction led to a continuation of, and improvement on, the strong relationship between the US and Kuwait, a bond forged in the fires roaring in Desert Storm a decade earlier. The Kuwaitis never forgot the Americans who died for their freedom. Plaques and memorials honor the US efforts on their behalf, including a remembrance wall on the embassy grounds, of each and every American who gave their life during Desert Storm. After that war, ordinary citizens sponsored the families of the fallen to come to Kuwait and visit the place where their son or daughter, husband or wife, died in defense of freedom, which gave those families some closure and another way to deal with their loss and grief.

The day after the towers fell, I was driving into work, stopped at a traffic light. A car pulled up alongside and the Kuwaiti driver tapped his horn and lowered his window, so I lowered mine. With tears in his eyes, he told me he hated the people who destroyed the towers and killed so many people and "God Bless America."

I entered our compound, came into work and saw that the lobby and hallways of the Chancery were overflowing with literally thousands of floral arrangements and notes of sympathy. Thousands more were piled against the front wall of the Embassy, with notes of sympathy and solidarity and more than a few teddy bears.

Now, in our time of national need, the Kuwaitis opened their country to us.

On October 7, 2001, the fires in the ruins of the Twin Towers continued to burn and smolder 25 days after the sneak attack. While the NYFD continued to work the fire, the USAF was delivering the first bombs to Tora Bora and the pursuit of OBL began. +++

# If It Doesn't Fit, Cut The Rope

Not everybody enthusiastically supported the global efforts of countries that committed troops to hunting down OBL. Threats against Americans globally resulted in a decision that it was time to arm all the members of the OMC. For me, this meant making certain all our personnel, military and civilian employees, could be trained and qualified under the AF Instructions.

The new boss, Thom, was a Special Forces brigadier general. A warrior, scholar, and gentleman, he was a fully qualified expert in all the many areas of the military arts. A master of every weapon in the US and foreign inventories, he'd jumped out of airplanes from very high altitudes, hung suspended from helicopters, wandered through swamps, and engaged in global operations. An Eagle Scout from Pennsylvania who'd spent his entire Army career in special forces, he was the real deal.

I liked him. He had a wicked sense of humor, but was straight-forward, direct and no-nonsense. He gave everybody the maximum latitude and authority to do their job as they saw fit, but he also expected people to do that job better than anybody else. When he arrived on station he shared this philosophy with us. Fiercely competitive, he believed in not only working hard, but working smart. He emphasized the importance of playing hard, and to win. He also believed in assignments being completed on time and properly staffed. If a suspense date was going to be blown, he cautioned folks not to come whining and looking for some slack, offering only his personal credo:

*"If you want some slack, cut the rope."*

One day, while having coffee at the Ministry of Defense offices, one of my KAF buddies tossed me his cigarette lighter and told me to check out the purple flame, so I pressed the actuator. Thanks to thirty years of improvements to, and miniaturization of, super-capacitors since 1972, when that Mexican battery man shocked the crap out of me, I howled and dropped the lighter while yelling at my buddy, who thought it was a scream. He'd already tricked everybody he knew, including his mom, so gave me the toy to enjoy.

Pranks like these were also an integral part of the military lifestyle. They helped break up the monotony and boredom, like when the Accidental Captain declared the Agency guys in the spook shop "drones" who were way too uptight; and, more than a little too full of themselves. Skipper had been a legend in the Pentagon for his tormenting suspected military drones. The Pentagon was loaded with humorless, self-professed super-patriots who presented a mighty rich target environment.

Here in Kuwait, after some consideration, Skip identified his target, a fastidious dresser who bore a slight resemblance to JFK. To amplify that persona, the agent spoke with a polished New England accent and always wore *Dusty Khaki* colored J. Crew stretch chino pants. He was an East-coast yuppie prig who'd gone to the right New England prep school, and from there on to Yale and joined the right secret society. He was also certain to let a person know about his alma mater within the first fifteen minutes of meeting.

Early one morning, Skip followed him into the men's room and watched as the JFK lookalike stole a long look in the mirror to check his perfectly coifed hair, while Skip stepped up to the starboard side urinal and commenced operations. The dapper spook stepped up to the port urinal, alongside and at Skip's left. In conformity with the tenants of the Catholic church he was raised in, the spook nodded at the Skipper, all the while primly keeping his eyes firmly focused on a point somewhere straight ahead.

This was a pity, because he didn't see that Skip wasn't peeing. If only that preppie peeped, he might have seen the water pistol in Skip's left hand and put it together, but he didn't, which shouldn't have surprised anybody. Agency guys lived off an infallibility cachet generated by Hollywood. As Angus, a candid spook, remarked one night, "We hire guys who couldn't get night jobs at K-Mart."

That JFK clone didn't notice a thing until he felt the drops when they landed on his pants, right where the cuff broke over the tops of his expensive pair of Bass Weejun dark red Logan loafers. He dismissed it the first time as his imagination, but the second time, there wasn't any doubt and, horrified, he leapt back, before he'd completed his own offload. In his haste to avoid the suspected urine stream, a fair amount of his own efforts missed the rim, splashed on the floor and back-splattered his pants. Now, really upset and feeling his blood pressure rising, he was dumbstruck when a laughing Skipper held up the water pistol and went side-stepping back outside with a wave of the hand.

When I arrived back at the embassy with my new toy, I ran the gag on anybody I found. Osama Bill held that electrifying lighter the longest, a full two-seconds, deeply impressing me with his concentration and willpower, but concerning me about his apparent inability to register pain. I ran it on Thom but his reaction time was much quicker and he tossed it at me while I beat feet to the door.

Now, in the course of casual conversation, Thom discovered that I'd been a military and civilian policeman and was qualified as an expert marksman with pistols and rifles. When he also learned I'd attended the FBI firearms instructor course, I became the project officer charged with getting all sixty of our people out to the range and qualified. This meant that, in addition to running the attendant paperwork, I'd also be arranging and overseeing weapons qualifications. Once I'd run all those wickets, we'd be able to issue Beretta 9 mm pistols to everyone. It would be a lot of work.

Before any of that was accomplished, I had also been tasked with finding a holster suitable for carrying its weapon openly while the soldier was in uniform, but also concealed while in civilian clothing. Thom was also adamant about ordering lanyards for all personnel, that nylon cord with a clip that attaches to the pistol acts as a "runaway cord" so to eliminate its possible loss by accident. He emphasized this requirement, citing a number of instances where highly trained and experienced special operators left a sidearm in a bathroom.

After some considerable research, I found a small company that had designed a five-position leather holster. The ad showed it in a shoulder position, outer waistband, inner waistband, cross-draw style, or small-of-the-back position. I felt pretty comfortable that this utility would work to suit our needs and shared this with Thom. He liked the concept and told me to order two, one for each of us so we could field test them prior to ordering them for the entire unit.

It took a little over a week for the gear to arrive. I brought one into his office and left him to become familiar with it and adjust it to his frame. I returned to my office and worked the pistol into the holster. That took a bit of doing. The holster was expertly milled, made tight to retain the pistol while running. The Beretta would only fit one way, and that way was tight. I decided to wear it in the small of the back, a position I'd always favored and was most comfortable with. I'd strapped in the holster and practiced pulling the pistol out, and tucking it back in, until the action came smoothly. Drawing the pistol out was soon smooth enough; putting it back into the holster was a pain in the ass.

About the time I finished drawing and re-stuffing the Beretta for the fifth, and what I knew would be final time, my door opened and the Chief came walking in. He was fidgeting with his rig. He'd gone for the shoulder holster position and tried seating the pistol while the holster was half-twisted as he walked. I could see he was exerting some considerable effort but wasn't getting anywhere. He looked up at me, "Hey Judge! I think you got hustled. This holster isn't a good fit for the nine mil; I can't get the pistol to seat."

He then muttered something about "*air force guys*" while shaking his head. I knew he wasn't mad, and it wasn't a put down, he was just teasing me. Service members always razz members from other services; it comes as close to a statement of affection as stoic and unsentimental warriors allow.

Thom's broad shoulders and chest were blocking his view of the holster, so he was trying to do it by feel. As a firearms instructor, and knowing what a pain in the ass that holster was, I probably should have told him to just take the rig off to show him how to fit the pistol and then put the rig on, but this was just too good an opportunity to pass up. Besides, I was stuck with getting everybody assigned to OMC qualified and that was reason enough to let this moment play on. My challenges included several civilians we had assigned. One poor man, a contracting officer, confessed he was so afraid of guns he thought the only person he'd ever shoot would be himself, by accident.

In light of all this, and since it was Wednesday afternoon with happy hour imminent, I kept any smile off my face and feigned concern. I asked him to lift his arms, taking a look, while assuring him both holsters were the same size and I'd ordered them for the Beretta. He pulled his right hand away from the butt of the weapon and I saw the problem instantly.

I felt that little angel of my better nature calling softly to me, "He's a busy man, tell him to take it off and start again." That angel got his ass kicked when the little devil in a flight suit and holding a beer popped up and shouted in my ear, "Hey flyboy! You hear what he said about us? 'You want some slack? Cut the rope.'" With that admonishment fresh in my mind, I elected to "rip the bandage" and just be direct.

"Sir, you're putting that pistol in upside down."

He had been looking at me, but he turned his head towards his shoulder and began stretching his neck to look down and backward and said, "What?" Using just the tips of my fingers I pulled the few inches of pistol from the holster and flipping it over, started to slide it back in. He quickly took over, and worked to set it inside that tight compartment. I contemplated sharing my technique, of securing the pistol first and then putting on the rig, but his rejoinder about slack again came back to me unbidden.

I watched him set the thumb strap over the hammer and snap it in place. He moved his shoulders, checking for comfort, gave a small nod to himself and made his way to the door. He turned the handle down and stopped before pulling it open. He turned back and saw me grinning and said, "We're never gonna talk about this ever again…Right?"

+++

---

# Just Put It Right There

T he M1A2 SEP "Abrams" was built by General Dynamics at their Detroit Arsenal facility, a place in continuous operation since 1940, providing US, and other forces around the world, with outstanding hardware and unparalleled lethality. A model of modern engineering, the Abrams is designed to defeat any enemy tank in existence; it was something everybody wanted and the US government was happy to sell.

As happened that day, the Kuwaitis had been thinking about buying some more tanks. GD was happy to sell and, in true Detroit fashion, brought out the latest model, the "Special Enhanced Package," to the tank range. The assembled KAF senior leadership could then examine the upgraded weapon system and evaluate it themselves. As was the custom, GD thoughtfully brought enough ordinance so anybody who wanted to "put one downrange" could be accommodated.

The Kuwaitis were reticent to take a shot, given that all of the other senior leaders were there. To miss the target would reflect poorly upon them and they'd be teased about it at the various diwanyas until some new incident arose. Nobody wanted that, so it fell to the American advisors to rise to the challenge and show how easy it was.

My boss was the senior US officer in-country and all those KAF senior eyeballs lighted on him, and so he'd been silently selected to represent all of us.

"One shot, One kill, Judge." He casually repeated the Marine sniper's creed as he clapped me on the back and climbed up onto the machine and moved toward the hatch.

The tank range was just as you'd imagine it. A tank target was put in motion challenging the shooter to shift the aiming reticle until it targeted the enemy tank, then to press the side buttons that locked the targeting laser on the target, press the "fire button," and wait for impact.

Somehow, the Boss managed to wedge his six-foot tall body inside the confines of the very tight crew position and took up a position in the gunner seat. An instructor from the manufacturer gave him the necessary briefing, pointing out the different controls, how to work the sight, lock on the target, and fire. He touted the way that sight would account for the movement of the enemy vehicle and he confidently asserted that a kill could not be easier. I was leaning in the open commander's hatch, just another curious spectator with a back-stage pass.

With few objects in between, the target rapidly traversed across the range. It became clear that success demanded a quick assessment, or the laser would not lock on the target, and the round missed.

The briefing concluded, our champion gave a big thumbs up. I got off the tank, and we all waited. In very short order he fired and that depleted uranium dart was gone. He popped up in the hatch, came out of the tank, jumped down, walked over, and, always being a competitor, punched me in the shoulder and said, "Well, whattaya think of that, Judge?"

I was deeply impressed. I'd never been around tanks, unless you counted the video tank-battle game I wasted a lot of quarters on while I was in law school. We all saw his shot go, but couldn't see the hit. The range guys would report that in a few moments.

Turns out, it was really one of those "missed it by just this much" moments. Everybody understood because it was his first attempt with an unfamiliar weapon system. That might have been true, but recently coming in from the sangfroid world of nuclear missiles, I was steeped in the doctrine of: "Close only counts in horseshoes, hand grenades, and nuclear weapons." Given the look of disappointment that started forming on his brow as that announcement concluded, I felt it best to just study the dust on my boots for a while. The senior American officer in-country was a bit disappointed to say the least. I was watching a sand beetle making its way across the desert floor when he clipped me on the shoulder saying, "Think you could beat that? It's harder than it looks."

That wasn't a "yes or no" kind of question, but a dare. Coming on the heels of that shoulder holster moment, I certainly couldn't ask for any slack. There was nothing left to do but go with it, knowing full well I'd endure some considerable heat on the thirty mile ride back to the embassy if, being a marksman, I missed. I climbed up and squeezed on down while the instructor dropped his head in, saying, "You remember what I told the General?" I said I did; he verified I understood the fire control system, and then I was up.

I peered through the view screen, and was pleasantly surprised to see I was staring at a scene of what looked very much like an upgraded version of that tank game I played at a nearby video arcade during my law school days. The images presented looked just like the ones I destroyed while dumping a bunch of quarters and working my way on to the "highest score" chart. I clearly saw the target tank in the distance and muscle-memory took over. I began to track it, floating the reticule onto the body of the tank. Just as it drifted to the body's center, I snapped the lock on and put that Sabot round downrange.

I got out, clambered down, and my boss, competitor that he was, began telling me it was OK if I missed because I was *just* an Air Force lawyer. I'd never understood why people seemed to believe the USAF is just a bunch of civilians in blue clothing, wearing long hair and out-of-regulation mustaches, and all sitting around a flashing video screen while slurping lattes.

While this could possibly be in some part true, just because we opted for clean sheets, good coffee, and air conditioning, it doesn't mean we can't do all those manly soldier tasks, we simply prefer *not* to do them.

After a few moments, the range guys announced I'd been dead on and schwacked the target.

It was a long, quiet, but ultimately satisfying, ride back to the office.

+++

# You Like To Drink, Don't You?

**I**f that phrase had been uttered by a military officer superior to me I might have been concerned, but it was just Andy, the Political-Military affairs guy. He had a soft face, still boyish, despite rapidly graying hair and, like so many in the US Department of State, he projected the air of a slightly rumpled and mildly distracted adjunct professor at a private four year liberal arts college in New England. He often wore a bow tie to complete that persona. This day he'd come wandering casually into my office and leaned on the door frame. All he needed was a small briar pipe to fiddle with as he spoke to complete the professorial effect.

I was attached to the State Department and the OMC-K, as a Security Assistance agency, came under Andy's purview. Although I couldn't imagine why the question was asked, my reply was straight forward. "Of course I do. I'm the Chairman of the Board for the American Employees Welfare Association and you've been a direct beneficiary of my singularly heroic efforts on behalf of a most grateful and very thirsty community." Andy nodded slowly, taking it all in and said, "Well, good. It happens we need a guy who can drink to be the counter-intelligence handler for the Japanese Embassy and we've noticed you're very good with people."

I appreciated the effort to butter me up; it immediately signaled this would be a job none of his guys wanted. "OK, what do you want me to do?"

"We just want you to not tell them anything. We need you to be our liaison, to listen to any concerns, to find out whatever you can about them, but they're going to be aggressive and will ask a lot of questions that we'd prefer not to answer. You can't lie, you just can't say anything. The Ambassador (Ambo) thinks you are exactly the right guy for the job."

Fair enough, I was a lawyer and had often been accused of talking without saying anything. Who knew obfuscation would be an asset in the direct defense of the United States? I was happy to do this small service, but I told him I had one question, "Do I get a liquor allowance or do I have to buy the booze myself?"

This was an important question. My year in Korea taught me that most Asians cannot process brown liquor because they didn't grow up on it. Their 65,000 year genetic drinking experience, presumably since leaving Africa, was restricted to rice-based fermented drinks because that's what they had to work with. I learned this over many shared glasses of whiskey with Korean friends on the balcony of the Osan Officers club. I also knew they could drink heroic amounts of liquor before passing out and, even though our liquor was cheap, it wasn't that cheap.

This wasn't my first observation about cultural drinking capabilities. During the nuclear arms reduction period after the Cold War, the Russians sent inspectors to the missile base I was assigned to in Montana to "trust but verify" our compliance with SALT limitations, and we did the same. In the spirit of "glasnost" (openness) the inspectors were always invited to the club after work to toast the new spirit of friendship. For some reason, we always served vodka and our guests routinely drank us under the table. I submitted a report suggesting we stop playing to their strengths and make them play to ours. At the last session I attended, Jack Daniels and Jeremiah Weed defended the honor of the USAF and it was the Russians who quit the field first.

Andy told me I was cleared for unlimited Johnnie Walker Red from an account established with the AEWA; with that news I told him I was ready to go, fully committed, and asked only what time and where.

My first meeting was to be held at the Japanese Embassy, which is located in an area called "Jabriya," a part of the Hawalli district and named after the thirteenth Emir of Kuwait, Sheikh Jaber Al-Ahmed Al-Sabah. The Japanese uniformly love American hamburgers and fried chicken, so much so that the driving instructions from their embassy said, "Come to Jabriya, go through the roundabout near the Burger King and KFC and it will be on the next corner." The bedoon taxi driver didn't speak English and had no idea where or what the Japanese embassy was, but he homed right in on the brightly lit sign showing the Kentucky Colonel's smiling face.

I'd always believed it was important to learn enough of a host's language to be polite and demonstrate respect. Thanks to a quick internet search and audio files with a native speaker, I learned to give a passable greeting and could recite it in unaccented Japanese. I also reviewed the protocols on bowing. Armed with these social tidbits and a couple of 750 ml bottles of Red Label, I was off to the Embassy of Japan for my counter-intelligence debut.

I'd also studied up on Japanese drinking traditions and realized that I needed to get inside their OODA Loop, referring to the decision cycle of *observe, orient, decide, and act*, developed by military strategist and USAF Colonel John Boyd. Boyd applied the concept to the combat operations process, often at the strategic level in military operations. It is also applied to aid understanding of commercial operations and learning processes. The approach favors agility over raw power in dealing with human opponents in any endeavor, and my personal motto was "*Semper Gumby*" (always flexible).

In this case, I would attempt to leverage their societal customs to my fullest advantage and that knowledge came with the word "Kanpai" or "dry the glass." I also learned "Otsukare-sama deshita" means "I know you've worked hard today, so have a drink." That phrase also gave me some insight into he mind of the average Japanese man, horribly overworked and under-appreciated with not much to look forward to except more of the same. My plan was to fill their glasses and toast them into submission.

I also knew that Asian cultures particularly respected older people and, although only forty-seven, my hair was quite gray, so I was sure to be respected and my offer of drinks would not be refused. This level of deep respect was made clear one evening in Korea. Mira, a lovely young Korean woman, had become a part of our group on Friday evenings at the Osan Club. I'd only been introduced as Shyster and she didn't understand the nickname's derogatory meaning. Always polite, she insisted on calling me "Uncle Shyster," as befit my age and gray hair. One evening Mongo yelled, "Screw you, Shyster!" Mira responded with "No, Mongo! You must respect Uncle Shyster!" Of course this made Mongo and the others laugh; it infuriated Mira, who repeatedly called on them to "Respect Uncle Shyster" until she teared up, while others held their now aching sides.

I presented myself to the group, voiced my greetings, and was in turn greeted warmly and ushered into a large reception area. I was offered tea and we exchanged pleasantries for a few minutes before I opened my black helmet bag, pulling out the two bottles I'd figured would do the trick to make friends and influence people. This offering was well-received and to the apparent delight of the overworked servants of Japan who responded by clapping and suddenly producing glasses, ice buckets and club soda while I poured the American-sized drinks.

This initial meeting lasted five rounds, then one by one, my hosts and new-found friends were beginning to drop their heads down onto their forearms. By round seven, we were all done. I'd won, but I knew I'd hurt the next morning. I bid my new friends goodnight and hopped in a cab for the ride home. My latest additional duty as counter-intelligence "handler" was underway.

+++

# The Japanese Historian

The polished voice of the protocol officer was only lightly accented as he offered, "Good Morning, Michael-san, Embassy of Japan calling, we would be pleased to know if you would have any time to meet again with our historian, Dr. Inouye. He was very pleased to meet you the other night and would like an opportunity to talk again."

Dr. Inouye was about seventy years old, easily the oldest resident at the Embassy. He was introduced as a historian who was compiling the history of Japanese and Kuwaiti people. Given that relationship was only a few decades old, this left him plenty of time to make generalized inquiries regarding economic and military matters. All these areas were of extreme interest to the Japanese government and the doctor's actual job being the Chief of Station for the Japanese Intelligence services. It was early 2002 and tensions were on edge. The tragedy of September 11 had thrown the world into a tizzy and rumors of an invasion of Iraq were rife; but, Dr. Inouye was more concerned about the Iraqis invading Kuwait again, which was a fair concern and led to the next meeting.

"Dr. Inouye would like very much to visit you at the American Embassy and is hoping to enjoy lunch at your staff dining room. He understands it is very good and serves real American hamburgers."

I couldn't very well refuse the request, but I felt no compunction to tell him our hamburger chef was a some guy from suburban Goa, India, with no previous experience cooking an American hamburger or cheeseburger; and, the Australian ground beef came from the local Sultan Center Supermarket. I also didn't tell him he'd get a much better burger across the street from his embassy at the Burger King, but thought, "Who am I to ruin his fantasy about America?" The invitation was extended and the necessary clearances obtained from the regional security officer (RSO) for me to bring an intelligence agent of a foreign country on to embassy grounds. All that remained was to await the meeting.

The date arrived and at exactly the correct time my phone rang and the gate guards announced my guest. I left my office in the controlled-access area and made my way through the central atrium of the Embassy building to collect my guest at the front gate, which was actually guests, because the doctor brought his secretary, Miss Uchida. They deposited their cell phones and cameras at the gate, and I walked them down an outdoor path that led to the cafeteria which was in an ancillary "open access" area.

They eyed the menu but briefly, and each ordered the "*All American*" hamburger with cheese. We took our food and sojourned to the outdoor dining area where we could enjoy the nice weather and avoid sitting with the Defense Intelligence Agency (DIA) guys. They never read any of the memos concerning foreign agents visiting embassy grounds who might overhear something classified.

Prior to this luncheon and because I had watched a lot of old B&W movies, I carried the impression of the Japanese as a delicate people who savored their food after exquisitely preparing it. Of course, in the movies, it was always a tea ceremony and, if they ate, I only saw them eating with chop sticks. It was interesting to see that, once freed from holding their food between two skinny pieces of wood, they were able now to pack away as much of a half-pound hamburger and bun as the best of them. I was also amazed at the body weight to food-consumed ratio because those burgers were gone almost before I finished salting my fries. There couldn't have been a better result for our luncheon.

Thoroughly sated, Dr. Inouye thanked me profusely for the excellent food, then switched to the topic of his immediate concern: our defense agreement with the Government of Kuwait.

"So, Michael-san, we at the Embassy of Japan, are given to understand from our discussions with other diplomats that you have a SECRET arrangement with the government of Kuwait. Do you deny this?"

The Defense Cooperation Agreement (DCA) is a standard agreement that the US (or any other country) might enter into with another country. In the case of Kuwait, it was several pages long, and outlined each party's obligation to the other in the event of a war or other hostile act by a third country actor. It was nothing sexy, but for operational reasons, the exact levels of support could not be disclosed to any person(s) not a party to the agreement.

"I don't deny it."

Miss Uchida was furiously writing something on the notepad she had on her lap. I only noticed because the spirals of the notepad drew my attention to her shapely legs which were nicely displayed in the short, tight skirt she'd chosen to wear. Like the doctor, she was also an intelligence officer and wouldn't be averse to using her charms to see what could be gleaned from anybody enamored of her.

I had no objections to her memorializing the meeting because that would ensure accuracy when the notes were later transcribed, encoded, and sent off to their CIA, at Naicho center headquarters in Tokyo. As the station chief, Dr. Inouye would be responsible for providing an intelligence assessment attached to the transcript. He pressed his interrogation.

"So you don't deny this?"

"No, I do not deny this."

"Then please, will you tell me what the contents say?"

"Sorry, Doc, but it's a secret."

"So, you admit you have secret plans?"

"Yes."

"And will you also please tell us your secret intentions towards any invasion plans?"

"No can do, Doc, it's a secret."

"So you will not tell us your secret invasion plans?"

"No, sorry, I can't because they really wouldn't be much of a secret if I told you. Besides, you guys are way more into secret invasion plans than we are."

As Miss Uchida faithfully captured our every word, Dr. Inouye stiffened a bit with my words, catching the reference to Pearl Harbor. He gave a small bow, saying sincerely, "Ah, yes, that was regrettable." The air hung heavy for a moment before I leaned forward and patted him on the back. "That's OK, Doc, that whole August 6, 1945, Hiroshima thing was also regrettable, but hey! Whattaya gonna do?"

Lunch concluded pleasantly and I walked them out while looking forward to the next phone call from him.

++++

# The Ambo Wants To See You

In the early summer of 2002, in an abundance of caution, it was decided that the OMC would be responsible for developing an evacuation plan in the event of hostilities breaking out. The embargo had begun to crumble, which increased the possibility that Iraq could somehow manage to conjure up an army to invade Kuwait again. This had never been a concern before, but it was none other than Dr. Inouye who created that need for us.

On a Tuesday that spring, the good doctor called to wangle an invitation to the club for a happy hour. He asked if we could meet for drinks the next evening while flattering me by commenting that our bar was the talk of the diplomatic community. This was fair comment since we were in fact the *only* full service bar, every other embassy having nothing more than perhaps a small room, at best. Bringing in guests was never a problem since board members could bring up to five guests per evening, while other folks were limited to two. This rule was established by the RSO, convinced that mysterious and dangerous outside forces would arrange invitations to learn the inner workings of our compound. I dismissed his concerns, noting we'd had over two hundred guests for New Year's Eve parties. I shared with him that, in my experience, the greatest risk was Grace, the Indonesian-born Dutch wife of a British diplomat, who were both frequent guests. Grace drank quite heavily and would then affect a cockney accent and say the word "FUCK!" too loudly and far too often for our tastes.

I told the good doctor that the United States would be honored to have him pay our humble establishment a visit and that I'd look forward to seeing him and his guest Miss Uchida. I spent the remainder of the day sending emails to the appropriate personnel who would need to know so they could plan accordingly. The last part of the plan involved filling in our Filipino barman, Alfredo, on our hosting two guests from the Japanese Embassy. I told him I'd be ordering all their drinks, and to make all their drinks doubles and, my Cuba libré was to stop containing any rum after the first round. He saluted smartly and said, "Yes, Sir Mike, it will be my pleasure always!"

His enthusiasm was, in small part, due to the large raise he'd recently received for his outstanding work, but mainly he was so perfectly willing to long-shot our guests because he came from a large family with two uncles who had been some of the 18,000 prisoners who died on the infamous Bataan death march in April 1942. His uncles were part of almost four hundred Filipino officers and men whom Colonel Masanobu Tsuji, the Japanese commander, ordered summarily executed near the Pantingan River after they had surrendered. Like Polish barman Bobeslaw Jandy with the Nazis, and my Korean tailor, Mr. Kim, Alfredo was another guy whose family and life were directly impacted by WW II, and old animosities die hard.

The Japanese diplomats arrived promptly at half-past-four, right as the lounge was opening, and I escorted them into the bar. As the evening crowd began rolling in, I got them their drinks and also some hamburgers with French fries made by the Syrian cooks employed by one of the catering companies. Those two cooks had worked for some Southerners at the Saudi-Aramco oil refineries south of Kuwait City and they could prepare an astonishing variety of Tex-Mex food and cajun cuisine, in addition to the regular burgers and fries.

We took our table inside the air-conditioned lounge where Alfredo, now skilled in counter-intelligence bar operations, quickly began running up their blood alcohol levels. The doc was frank in his comments. "Michael-san, we have heard throughout the embassy community that Saddam might invade and we were wondering what your thoughts were on the matter."

I was curious why they'd ignore the shared intelligence estimates that Saddam's Army, once the fourth most powerful in the world, was now reduced to a threat-projection capability roughly equivalent to that of Jamaica. I was also wondering what the root cause of the concern was, but I knew I needed to put him at ease first. "Well, let me put it this way, Doc. If I ever thought Saddam might seriously launch an attack, you'd understand that, of course, I might not be able to call to give you a head's up." He nodded his understanding of my ethical dilemma, as I leaned in a bit closer to say softly, "But, if you ever call for me and somebody says, 'He went back to the States and we aren't sure when he'll be back' then it's probably a good bet that something bad is going to happen."

Satisfied with my answer and assurances, we spent the next thirty minutes discussing the evacuation of Japanese citizens from the country, should the need arise, because they'd been caught flat-footed, as had the rest of the world, when Iraq invaded on August 2, 1990. I shared some of our airlift experiences and a plan emerged. Since there were only about six hundred Japanese citizens in-country at any time, mostly engineers working on building a desalination plant, the solution was simple enough. Charter two Japan Airlines 747s to fly into KCIA, load everybody at the first hint of trouble, and fly them to Dubai, an hour and a half away, until the situation resolved itself. All was carefully noted by Miss Uchida. The visit was completed in short order, as Alfredo did a masterful job from the free-pour line. In under an hour both tipsy diplomats were ready to be assisted to their embassy car where a driver would run them back out to Jabriya. Upon my return, I gave no further thought to it as the club music got louder.

The summer came and school let out, so Laurie and Maggie returned to the US on a holiday to visit her folks in Idaho. I had no plans to take leave, preferring to use my vacation time to travel within the region. That changed when my wife called to let me know she'd had a serious medical issue pop up and I'd have to return home on emergency leave. I was out the door and on a plane the next morning with no real idea of when I'd be back. It turned out I only needed to be gone for two weeks and flew back to Kuwait, arriving on a Sunday night. On Monday I went to the club and ran into our security chief, Osama Bill, who greeted me by saying, "Oh hey! Welcome back, and by the way, the Ambo needs to see you — he's been getting phone calls from the Japanese Ambassador saying you've put out word that Saddam is going to invade Kuwait?"

+++

## Mysterious Crop Circles

From my discussions with the Ambassador, who laughed the incident off, it came to light that, while the USMC would be tasked to evacuate us if an invasion occurred, we currently had no alternative evacuation plan if the Marines were heavily engaged in any fighting. I brought those concerns back to my boss, telling him that no particular "plans officer" had been assigned to develop one. The General knew any plans for short-notice evacuation would require aviation assets, the only real question was "What type?" With that thought in mind and a wide grin on his face, he handed me the project suspense slip while congratulating me on my appointment. Still smiling, he assured me this project would count a great deal towards my being awarded the highly coveted USAF 5,000-hour Power Point operator's patch. As he turned and started whistling while walking away, I realized using the spent SABOT round casing from that day at the range as a door stop wasn't the smartest thing I'd ever done.

The embassy was now lightly manned, most families having left the country a few weeks earlier when school let out, and many of the unaccompanied State Department employees also left on holiday. One of those recently departed vacationers was the chief AEWA antagonist and obstructionist, Groundskeeper Norm.

I was coordinating the evacuation plan with fellow part-time VIP door stop, Osama Bill. We decided that Norm's grass field in the center of the housing compound could accommodate one Navy CH-53E Super Stallion helicopter capable of hauling out fifty-five passengers at a time, or two Army UH-60 Blackhawks hauling eleven persons each. The evacuees could be staged in the houses that faced the makeshift landing zone. All we needed to do was check the viability of our escape plan.

It happened that we'd invited our favorite Army reservist, a civil affairs major, "Jimmy the Mysterious," to come to happy hour that evening. Jimmy was purportedly a Buffalo, NY, fireman, but he hadn't seen a fire in years. NY law allowed emergency services workers unlimited time off for reserve and national guard duties, continuing their salary and allowing them to be promoted while away. He was currently a lieutenant fireman, but found working civil affairs more exciting because he operated on the frontier, often one of the first Americans to show up in an undeveloped country to start working on winning hearts and minds.

One day in early 2001, Jimmy showed up at a country team meeting and handed me a coin from Djibouti while telling me, "Watch this place, nobody's ever heard of it but it will be huge." I'd heard of

Djibouti, but after the meeting I pulled up the CIA World Fact book and learned the former French Territory of the Afars and the Issas became Djibouti in 1977, and an authoritarian, one-party state, was installed until civil war ended it in 2001. Since Djibouti occupies a strategic geographic location at the intersection of the Red Sea and Gulf of Aden, it serves as an important shipping portal for goods entering and leaving the African highlands. The location also provides a platform to monitor all shipments between Europe, the Middle East, and Asia. Our good friends, the French, maintain a significant military presence in the country.

It came as no surprise to me when, after negotiations in mid-2001, the Djiboutian government allowed Camp Lemonnier, a US operational base, to open within its borders. This camp provides support for de-mining, humanitarian, and counter-terrorism efforts. It serves as the location from which US and Coalition forces are operating in the Horn of Africa. That camp is also the centerpiece of a network of six US drone and surveillance bases stretching across the continent.

On this evening while we were discussing our project, Jimmy offered, "You want to test that theory? I can get some guys to fly in here and test it." We knew this offer was just too good to pass up and, if he could whistle up some helos, that was fine by us and we let him know that. We ordered another round of drinks to secure the deal.[6]

The next Monday, Jimmy attended the country team meeting and announced the helos were coming at noon to demonstrate the feasibility of using the lawn for evacuation. At the appointed hour, everyone from the OMC, along with the Ambassador, the Charge d'Affairs, and other important folks came to the AEWA lounge to watch the exercise.

---

[6] The last time I saw Jimmy the Mysterious was in Baghdad in March 2006, when I was working as a consultant helping reconstruct the Iraqi military justice system. I saw him in passing and he filled me in. In early 2004 he'd been appointed acting Iraqi Minister of Labor by the soon to be departed American caliphate, Paul Bremer. Bremer had seen him passing by in the hallway at the former Republican guard palace turned US Embassy and called him in. He asked Jimmy his name and then appointed him to his new office. As Labor Minister Jimmy created the National Fire Academy and appointed himself lifetime director.

Two Blackhawks orbited the compound and, while still in formation, set those machines down on the lawn using less than half the available area. The aircrew shut down, hopped out and were greeted by the Ambo and the rest of us. The crews were given a "grip and grin" photo op with all of us and a lunch served on the patio. As a thanks for supporting our efforts, the AEWA gave each crewman a souvenir sport shirt with embassy logo. What we didn't know then was that when they returned to Camp Doha and wore those shirts, they created some serious buzz and our sales started to rise as soldiers and airmen found any excuse to attend a meeting at the embassy with plans to visit the gift shop on the way out.

In response to that favorable reaction, we now carried a full line of men's and women's State Department logo'd clothing and gear such as Zippo lighters and key chains, plus the basic post cards and other sundries. In the first year of this change, the AEWA made a $27,000 profit, but it was later, when the war broke out, that our fortunes increased via the "can't keep 'em on the shelf" decks of Saddam Hussein "Most Wanted Cards" we'd had made up for pennies in Texas and sold for five bucks a pack. We eventually made $125,000 from selling those cards, plus all the other tchotchkes and tourist kitsch, effectively saving the club.

When it was time to go, I walked over to the lead pilot, a Chief Warrant Officer Three (CWO-3) sporting a dashing and completely beyond-regulation mustache. I liked that in an aviator and asked if he could do me a favor and maintain a low hover just a few feet off the deck, for a minute or so, before taking off back to Camp Doha. Stroking the end of his mustache, the aviator cocked his head and looked at me saying, "Sure, I'm happy to do that, but you need to understand the APU (Auxiliary Power Unit) is a little jet engine that spins the generator to make electricity and power up the airframe. The exhaust points down and if I hover it will leave some burn marks in the grass." He looked even more surprised when all I said was "Perfect."

Shortly thereafter, the crews said their goodbyes, hopped into their machines and fired them up. The blades were spinning, building up speed to lift off which set our Heineken umbrellas flying and our civilian guests scrambling to get away from the debris stirred up by the powerful wash of the rotor blades. In short order, both birds were sitting in a low hover about two feet off the ground. The pilot held it there for over a minute and I could see the brown circles forming. Thirty-seconds later, satisfied that the grass was good and truly dead enough to never come back, I gave the pilot a thumbs up and a wave. He applied more power, pulled up on the collective and, changing the pitch of the blades so they could take a bigger bite out of the air, began to lift off. Both machines cleared the roof top and the pilots pushed the cyclic forward and those big black machines nosed down and lit out. They circled once to allow us another photo op and were off into the ever-present brown haze.

Norm came back from his holiday a few weeks later and was confounded by the four mysterious and perfectly formed dead spots on his otherwise green and unused lawn.

+++

## Who are you and what are we to do with you?

A s the drumbeat for war grew louder after the horror of 9-11, the OMC became the current "Tip of the Spear," an overworked phrase. Every operation outside of the States and potentially in harm's way gets referred to as "The Tip of the Spear." This is meant to remind the troops that they have to maintain constant readiness and, like they said in Korea, "Be ready to fight *tonight*."

RAF Upper Heyford sat on the pointy-end in the cold war against communism. Howard air base in Panama was the stiletto tip in the bag of cocaine on the war on drugs. Korea was that blunt-tipped sword holding back the marauding hordes of the Evil Hermit Kingdom. Now, here I was in Kuwait, once again on the tip, as the bodies started flowing in country.

We could handle the tremendous influx of troops, thanks to our friendship and personal relationships with so many Kuwaitis in so many aspects of government service. We rapidly negotiated that coalition troops would be allowed in country without a passport or visa, using only their ID cards and unit orders. One Navy officer in the Foreign Military Sales (FMS) shop, thanks to his close and personal friendship with the Port director, managed to singlehandedly negotiate priority berthing rights at the Port of Shuwaikh, the country's most important commercial port. At that time, Shuwaikh was the only one that could serve ocean-going vessels at its deep-water berths and possessing ample modern container facilities to receive whatever goods and equipment the giant supply machine in the USA would churn out. These were the benefits of the secret Defense Cooperation Agreement Dr. Inouye was so interested in. They provided the necessary framework to begin operations, but it still took steady coordination to make those things run smoothly.

Working all these negotiations and agreements took a tremendous amount of time and involved many social commitments, while each day the number of requests grew for diplomatic clearance to visit troops, submitted by command elements left behind. This meant requiring more OMC advisors to serve as escorts to support the growing number of proposed visits. The visitor list included generals, admirals, colonels, governors, congressional delegations, USO shows, and anybody else who thought they could wangle a visit. We were the logical choice for escorts since our Embassy badges and KAF credentials gave us "all access and escort" to every military installation and KCIA.

These visitors believed their visits increased unit cohesion and morale by letting the troops know the command and all the good folks back home were thinking of them. Less commented upon was the habit of these proposed *morale visits* being scheduled to last for only two days, and the timing always having the visitors arriving at the end of the month, so that they could collect combat pay and earn a break on their income tax for the entire month just ending. Additionally, by being in-country for the first day of the next month, they caught the break again — two months of tax-free pay for a two-day visit.

This "gaming" of the generous release from income taxes while serving in a combat zone rubbed everybody the wrong way. It might have been legal, but the only morale being improved was the visitors, and troops resented them.

What those gadflies didn't understand was for seven months out of the year, Kuwait was like hell on earth. Daily temperatures routinely passed 100 degrees and in June, July and August, it was not unusual for temperatures to reach 120 degrees and all that nonsense about it being "a dry heat" is only said by people who live in air conditioned houses. These men and women in service in Kuwait at one of the many camps and airbases spent everyday living in tents, working in that heat and dust so, when some visitor popped in for a 48 hour photo op and then went back home, it just pissed people off.

Once we wised up to that practice, those end of month country-clearances were denied, citing volume, with mid-month dates offered instead, and interest in *troop welfare* began to drop off. This was well-received by those actual warriors on the tip of the spear and "no visits" was in fact good for unit cohesion. Morale actually improved anytime a unit was told a proposed visit was scrubbed, because all these visits amounted to yet another inspection by somebody who never has to do any cleaning or prep work. The reality for the troops was accommodating these important guests added many extra hours on to an already long duty day. Preparing to receive the guests meant developing slides to document readiness and planning every minute of the visit to ensure no visitor's time was ever wasted.

One sad outcome of this obsession with "leaving no chronological margin for error" resulted in the Commander of USCENTCOM having thirty minutes to kill between visits to two different Kuwaiti offices located within the vast Seif Palace downtown by the Sharq Mall. These offices were physically located next to each other, but protocol prohibited early arrivals and it wouldn't do for a four-star general to mill about in the hallway. It was midmorning so the general decided to get a coffee at Starbucks in the mall next door. That sent the security detail into a tizzy as if the Taliban in Afghanistan could use that time to cobble together and execute an assassination attempt. Despite the grave risk to his security, the general had a latte and survived.

Our unit had been ordered by USCENTCOM to commence twenty-four hour operations and that meant keeping the office open and staffed throughout the night. In a unit where any job is only one person deep that meant some primary staff would begin to suffer, like Bill the anti-social protocol guy. Because he couldn't attend to all the DVs (distinguished visitors) arriving in-country, he'd resorted to drafting field advisors to assist him, hence those KAF units were not being covered. The insertion of untrained protocol/escort officers into the mix led to a ball of confusion which often manifested about the time a DV was arriving.

+++

# Shanghai'd

A voice called out, "Hey Mike, you got a second?" It was Wednesday afternoon and I looked away from the screen where I was typing up the latest "beg" to the KAF. This time I was asking them to support a request to prohibit bird hunting that year. Many Kuwaitis love to hunt and enjoy an abundance of game birds in country. Hunting with shotguns was permitted, but some of the security forces expressed concern that those hunters could be mistaken for hostile forces and fired upon. Everybody obviously agreed that would be bad for relations, so the decision was made to cancel the hunting season. Remembering the USS Cole, the government also decided to close fishing within two miles of the shoreline. The fishermen received subsidy payments to ease the burden of lost income. One unanticipated outcome was that hunting and fishing the following year was the best in living memory.

I looked up and saw Hugh, an Army lieutenant colonel and the KAF artillery advisor standing in the doorway. Tall and slender, he was a very popular figure within both the OMC and KAF because of his easy-going nature and first rate abilities as a soldier and leader. I'd seen him come into the lobby thirty minutes earlier as he headed back towards the cubicles, but he hadn't popped in for a chat. He now stopped in and I noticed his coffee cup was full and steaming, so I figured he wanted to shoot the breeze for a bit and kill some time before heading off to

"All Hands," our final meeting of the week and, like the title says, one all personnel were required to attend. It was a mechanism to physically account for everybody assigned, and verifying before going into the weekend that everybody was alive and healthy when last seen officially. This also eliminated the possibility that we'd have to search for bodies in the desert over the weekend. After listening to all the official announcements and conducting any "hails and farewells," it was off to happy hour.

Hugh put his cup on my desk, stepped back and pressed the release on my door stop, taking his seat as the door closed. This was not uncommon in my office because people knew I kept confidences and, if nothing else, they could come in and vent about whatever nonsensical distraction might have come their way. Hugh picked up the cup and sat back. He looked at me and said, "So how the fuck do we do this?" He saw my surprise and added, "So you don't know about it either?" I shook my head and waited. He hunched forward as he told me, "Somebody thought it'd be a good idea if I escorted the Army Deputy Secretary for Personnel and some three-star general around the country." All I could think to say was, "Well, that really sucks!" He nodded and blew on the coffee. "Yes, it does! It sucks because they are coming in early tomorrow afternoon and I'd been planning on taking my wife and kids over to the science center to see the aquarium." Hugh lived in the former residence of Mr. Joe (of unwanted maid fame). Unlike Joe, he was very family oriented. His kids were always splashing about in the compound pool, and having come from an assignment in Hawaii where they threw a lot of BBQs and did other family oriented entertaining, giving up a weekend with the family during the pleasant winter weather was a bad break indeed.

I continued to nod sympathetically and alternately shake my head sideways in disgust, even muttering *those bastards*" periodically, a technique another basement-dwelling friend from law school taught me. My buddy Ron said, "Whenever there isn't anything to do assuage a person's complaint, just mutter 'those bastards' under your breath. Not only will it make them feel better but, if they are ever inclined towards work place violence they'll always remember you as one of the good guys and shoot somebody else," but even that magic phrase was unable to provide any genuine comfort or relief for Hugh. Satisfied that he'd gotten everything he needed to say off his chest, he sunk back into the chair and took a sip from his cup. He'd propped his elbows on chair's arms and was holding his cup with both hands while looking at me over the rim. "Glad you understand how rat-fucked this is because you're going to be my partner on this operation" and before I could think to respond he added, "The general already OK'd it." So that's what he was doing while he was wandering around; he was coordinating my kidnapping.

I wanted to say something but all that came out was "bastards."

+++

---

# Visitors

T he DV party stepped off the dedicated C-20 Gulfstream IV. The filed flight plan touted an earlier arrival, but in keeping with tradition, it landed a few hours late. It was Thursday evening, the first full day of our weekend, and we'd waited all those hours in our cars at the aircraft parking area on the tarmac.

On the ride to the hotel, Hugh got the news from one guest, a lieutenant general: "I want to do a terrain walk and see the Highway of Death." This was a command, not a request, a short-hand reference to the night of February 26-27, 1991, when coalition aircraft and ground forces attacked retreating Iraqi military personnel. Once attack jets disabled the lead and rear vehicles, the rest of the convoy stalled and the air attack was like shooting fish in a barrel. This resulted in the destruction of almost two thousand vehicles and the deaths of many of their occupants. The general giving Hugh this order had been a brigade commander during Desert Storm and, in that one hundred-hour war, he had seen a lot of action; the highlight of spending more than thirty-years in his beloved Army.

He wanted to see it all again and why shouldn't he? He'd done well in his career, and now owing to the sad events of September 11, when the previous occupant of his position had been killed, he was now chief of staff and on this visit with his civilian boss, the Deputy Secretary. A career bureaucrat, the Deputy was attending a series of classified briefings involving the entire CENTCOM area of operations, including all of the Arabian Gulf states, and most of Southwest Asia, on Saturday. This would let him get a complete picture of what the upcoming manpower requirements would be and to get a feel for just how big the theater of operations would become. Our guests would remain in Kuwait until Sunday morning when they would board a C-117 cargo plane bound for Bagram airfield in Afghanistan for further terrain walks, visits, and briefings.

Military protocol directs that the senior person present is always the distinguished visitor. For this group, the deputy secretary was the DV and the general, while certainly important, just wasn't *as* important. Hugh tried to explain to him that it'd been a few years since the war and the Kuwaitis had hauled away all the wreckage and ruin to a salvage yard way out in the desert. The General insisted he'd still like to see the highway and junkyard, so it fell to Hugh, as an Army officer and fellow Desert Storm vet, to take him where he needed to go.

I was given responsibility for the Deputy and planned to take him on a guided tour of Kuwait City to better orient him to the people while getting a feel for the culture. I couldn't read the signs in Arabic so I had memorized where everything was. I'd follow people to places to learn a route and I'd also drive around on weekends to become intimately familiar with the whereabouts of all the markets, especially the gold and rugs souks (shops). I knew all those places visitors want to see. I knew they wanted to buy carpets and gold necklaces, and also to see the mysterious side of Arabian Gulf region, the stuff they'd seen in movies like "Casablanca." We'd received loads of guests while living in the UK and I found making up day-trip itineraries to all the local tourist attractions was helpful, so I made one for Kuwait.

Where my old boss Bob in Panama made a list of restaurants he'd rated with number of guns, I made a similar list only instead of the number of guns, my restaurants were rated on the most authentic middle-eastern experience. Lebanese restaurants provided the fare most people know as middle eastern, but there was also Turkish, Persian, and Indian, as well as Italian or Chinese. I knew all those managers and our parties were always welcomed because a restaurant developed a certain cachet for the public if diplomats ate there. We'd order a never-ending supply of appetizers with several mixed grille platters ensuring no one left hungry, then finished the evening with nargilla water pipes, Turkish coffee, and sweets. We found all that effort allowed people to obtain a sense of having really visited an exotic place and come away more informed and with a better mental image about life there. I'd now become a tour guide for the current "*must visit*" place on the globe.

The next day was Friday and would serve as a recovery day for the party, since it was the equivalent of Sunday, with no business conducted. That made it a perfect time to show our visitors around in civilian clothes, which worked out well because somehow, in the fog of loading bags onto the flight, the general's bag containing all of his military uniforms had vanished. The general's aide d'camp approached us with the problem and, after ascertaining that every single bit of his military gear was gone, provided me with a list of required clothing, hat, and shoe sizes. I was left with the happy task of getting him dressed, and that meant an early morning drive out to Camp Doha, some twenty miles away.

Camp Doha was a sprawling concern. Routinely crowded with the normal National Guard rotations, it was one of the several facilities the Kuwaitis paid $262 million a year to keep open for our mutual benefit. For some of that money they got a full Brigade Combat Team, (BCT) and 4,413 soldiers on station at all times. A BCT consists of seven battalions: one cavalry, one support, one engineer, three infantry, and one field artillery. That rental fee worked out to around $45,000 per soldier, but they all came with full medical and dental, plus tanks, cannons, helicopters, and lots of ammo. Owing to the nearby port facilities, the camp was reaching its capacity and then some as the buildup got underway. It was shortly past dawn and I was in the traffic jam born of the twenty-five minute screening process to drive onto the base.

Because they came from a secured compound, embassy vehicles were supposed to be waved in without inspection, but the current commander, an Army colonel, was upset because his wife did not have the same color US Embassy access badge as all the other wives. The Regional Security Officer (RSO) rules directed that she needed an escort if she wanted to come into the chancery building, while the wives and kids with the correct color code could simply enter. She didn't understand that OMC didn't make the rules: the RSO, a credentialed federal agent just like the FBI, did. Her pride was hurt and she was pissed, so in her defense, her husband established a "tit for tat." Now all embassy vehicles were subjected to the morning search, just like the Bangladudes driving the garbage trucks. Once cleared of any suspicions of being a terrorist in a Hawaiian shirt, our vehicles could enter. After the *Cole* was attacked, we rarely wore our uniforms unless going out into the field or working other military operations. The threat assessment guys told us civilian apparel allegedly reduced our target profile, while our short hair, loud-spoken American accented English and Oakley issue wrap-around ballistic proof sunglasses evidently didn't.

I made my way to the supply building where a very accommodating buck sergeant, Rocky from Philadelphia, was delighted to provide me with every single item on my list. He guaranteed me that the general's name tag, rank, and required patches would be sewn onto three sets of desert camouflage uniforms, plus a pair of size 11 desert boots and service patrol cap, would be ready for pickup within an hour. This was very kind of him, especially since I'd told him that he and his two best friends would be invited as my guests one evening at our club. This amounted to a visit to America and included an overnight stay at one of our spare guest apartments for the sobering up.

My next stop: the BX, where I bought three sets of regulation underwear and picked up some bacon. While that might sound like a strange pairing, you might recall that pork is prohibited in Kuwait and other muslim countries, so the only place to buy that indispensable flavor-packed meat was at the BX. None of the Kuwaiti inspectors knew that "Virginia flat-nosed beef" on inventories and manifests was actually bacon. The only other place to procure bacon in Kuwait was the Korean shop in distant Fahaheel, and they bought it from the BX at

Camp Arifjan, applying the same methods as the ones used to get around the ox-tail ban at Osan.

After scoring the pork, I bought a latte at the coffee concession and then drifted back to the supply building to pick up the General's now perfectly prepared uniforms and boots. Rocky had found some buddies to bring along on his club night, and we made a date to visit on the next Wednesday. With all the official visitors flowing in who didn't need to be on a guest list, three more people wouldn't be a problem, but I was particularly pleased Wednesday evening when the smartest supply guy I'd ever met brought two of the most beautiful female soldiers I'd ever seen into the club with him.

He was certainly smarter than I am. In law school, a friend's father came down to Moscow for some business and invited me to lunch at the one nice restaurant in town. I brought my roommate Eric and as we sat down Pete said, "When I made the invitation, I thought you'd at least bring a good-looking FEMALE law student."

Current mission accomplished, I left the camp, drove back to Kuwait City, and dropped off the bacon with Laurie before heading on to the Radisson SAS hotel over on the Gulf Cooperative Road, just across the street from my friend Hassan's house. I brought the new duds inside and grabbed the Nepalese bellman. I told him the uniforms were clean but needed to be pressed, then the lot was to be delivered to the general's room as quickly as possible. I pressed a dinar ($3.35) into his hand and he was gone. I caught up with the aide d'camp who was working in the business center. He looked about beat to death so I didn't know if he'd been an early riser or just awake all night trying to keep up with the never ending modifications to the schedule, and I never asked.

I brought him up to speed and reviewed the current plan for the remains of the day. My "date," the deputy secretary, would be arriving for breakfast at the crack of nine and whenever he finished I would take him and his aide on a tour of Kuwait City. We'd return at four so the guest could have three hours of free time at the right time to call the states, or more likely, to take a nap before going to dinner. This plan was still being formulated, so it was marked TBD, for "to be determined." Meanwhile, Hugh would drive an hour north out of Kuwait City on Highway 80 to look for the carnage and soot marks that were no longer there.

A trip around Kuwait City, with a population of one million Kuwaitis and another million expat guest workers, always began with a visit to Mubarakiya, the oldest marketplace in the country, one with origins going back at least two hundred years. We strolled down the different lanes of the covered market and spent an hour examining the Persian and the tribal carpets offered at Ali & Hussein's carpet souk, a favorite among the state department employees.

Hussein was a figure rarely seen. He spent his days wandering about rural Afghanistan with a suitcase full of cash looking for new rugs. His trade route took him through some very remote hill country, starting in Herat in the Northwest corner of Afghanistan, then across the border of Turkmenistan into the small town of Mary. Turning south, he'd sneak across the Iranian border and on into Mashhad. He drove an old white Isuzu truck with metal side racks and went from village to village, buying carpets until the truck, loaded beyond capacity, could hold no more. From there he'd make his way to the port city of Bushehr, on the Arabian Gulf. After paying a few bribes, the carpets would be put aboard a dhow, a small sailing boat sporting a long thin hull used to carry heavy items, such as fruit, fresh water, or other heavy merchandise, along the Arabian Gulf coast for the 175 mile voyage to Kuwait City and ultimately, this basement souk.

Ali spoke very good English so he provided customers with the history of each and every carpet stacked wall to wall in the small showroom. A master story teller, Ali captivated prospective buyers as he shared the pedigree of each carpet. He'd look at some notes written on an index card attached with a pin to the rug. While we drank sweet tea, he explained what tribe and village the rug came from. He'd point out and provide the meaning of all the symbols on tribal rugs. His big finale was to bring out rare and exquisite handmade silk carpets that shifted color as you walked around them. This was not by accident. By bringing out the most expensive carpets, ones costing tens of thousands of dollars, a beautiful hand-made "bridal dowry" carpet only costing a few hundreds of dollars seemed like an amazing bargain.

Ali would break open a photo album of all the mud hut villages Hussein regularly visited. Girls in those villages learn to make the carpets and in their spare time they would design and create a carpet to demonstrate their proficiency. They could sell that carpet to Hussein and all that money became a dowry for a prospective husband. These artists worked whatever they saw in front of them into the design. After so many years of Russian occupation, a lot of the carpets had AK-47s, Russian Hind attack helicopters and RPGs (rocket propelled grenades). If a buyer was reticent Ali always asked, "This one of a kind piece of decorative art probably took that young girl five years and many thousands of hours to create. You are buying the efforts of years, how much would that be worth if it was your time?"

He'd set the hook and tell the buyers to take the carpet home so it could be seen in the lighting there and, if it wasn't the right carpet, to bring it back for a full refund, no questions asked. Ali knew that once people got it into their homes, it was never coming back.

After buying a carpet, we wandered about and passed antique stores full of brass oil lamps, handmade jewelry from some of the Bedouin tribes, and other exotic curios. We walked by tailor shops, perfume merchants, and money changers occupying small booths with glass display cases showcasing all the global currencies available for trade. They not only traded currencies for walk-up customers needing money for a trip; they also ran an informal, virtual bank. Families would station trusted members in different cities throughout southwest Asia that had a large expat population in Kuwait, like all the domestics from Goa, India. Expats needing to send money home could use Western Union and pay a large percentage as a facilitation commission, or they could go to the money changers who charged only a small transaction fee. One trader would call another in the designated city and he'd release the funds, in local currency, to the designated recipient, no fuss, no muss, and no paperwork.

We walked into the indoor covered market, examining bins of fruit, vegetables, dates, honey, spices, olives, and nuts, before touring one of the highlights for visitors, the gold and silver souks. I took care to avoid offending delicate American sensibilities so I didn't take them to view the bloody offerings in the butcher shops and fish market. Once our tour of the souks concluded, we stopped for lunch at one of the many small restaurants in an area looking very much like an American food court in any mall. My guests looked around and enjoyed experiencing the ebb and flow of people in exotic costumes, speaking a polyglot of languages, all of whom swirled around us in the course of living their lives.

After lunch, I drove the secretary and his assistant around the city, pointing out buildings of interest and we finally wound up taking an elevator to the observation deck located inside the larger ball on the iconic Kuwait Towers. Those two round balls sit impaled on pylons and were made famous by a photograph of Iraqi helicopters flying towards them during the initial invasion of Kuwait. The other smaller ball, is a water tower. We sipped coffee while taking in the view of Kuwait City as the cafe slowly turned 360 degrees. I'd just pointed out some of the buildings we'd seen from the ground when the deputy asked a question about women in Kuwait and what kind of freedoms they enjoyed and restrictions they endured.

That subject was too broad to be answered simply, but on the subject of women being veiled, I offered that it was largely the choice of the pertinent people in the particular family, but when at a family beach it was always required that any woman must wear an abaya, even when swimming. I heard the snort of derision and the deputy said quite plainly to me, "Oh, come on, I find that very hard to believe." It was about that time the platform turned enough so the view had moved away from Kuwait City and was facing out towards the gulf's shining blue waters. I looked around and saw a woman wearing an abaya that was flapping in the wind as she opened the throttle on her jet ski. She wore a regulation orange life vest over the abaya and her veil was held firmly in place by goggles and a bathing cap. I tugged at his elbow and pointed down saying, "Sir? Perhaps this will help?" He followed my pointing hand. First his jaw opened, but then he started laughing and, like Millie did all those years ago in Panama, the deputy learned about "*Kuwaiti rules.*"

We got back a little later than scheduled because the deputy saw a nut shop and decided he'd take advantage of the prices and also because he didn't think he'd see another one in Afghanistan. He'd loosened up quite a bit and seemed to be really enjoying his Kuwait City experience. I pulled into the SAS parking lot and dropped off my charges so they could relax in their hotel until dinner. As I drove away, I got a message from Protocol Bill that the dinner plans that had been set earlier had now changed, so I returned to the lot, parked, and walked into the hotel lobby.

The new plan was for the deputy to be the dinner guest of an important sheikh, the head of the Kuwaiti Engineering department. The dinner would be held in the five-star Chinese restaurant in the lobby of the SAS, this being easier for everyone. I saw Hugh who'd come in a half hour earlier. I asked if he'd gotten the latest change to the schedule. He hadn't so I brought him up to speed and as I was doing so the general walked up and listened in. When I finished, he braced me, obviously angry. He was upset that this change had occurred without anyone consulting him. He chastised me, insisting he should have been kept in the loop and informed immediately when a change was contemplated so that he could make a decision about it.

I wasn't the guy in charge of dinner and I hadn't imagined that eating Chinese food at a five-star hotel was a matter any general officer would consider important. But I apologized and offered that no disrespect was intended, while stressing that the sheikh was a very important person, in charge of all the engineers in Kuwait, therefore we'd always be needing his help for any building project we'd seek to undertake in the future.

The general wasn't having any of it. He was in a foul mood, no doubt in part due to the jet lag that comes with a seven-hour time zone switch and also in some part because he'd spent all day stuffed in a car driving around in the desert looking for the Highway of Death junkyard, and hadn't gotten lunch because he didn't want to eat at any local restaurants and nobody thought to bring any food.

He began to bawl me out in the lobby which, in addition to being unseemly, was uncalled for. I was inclined to remind him that the last human being to yell at me was my training instructor in basic, but instead tried to defuse the situation by offering that perhaps it'd be better if we moved into a less public space. He ignored that suggestion and kept up what was now becoming a tirade and which included the phrase "I'm going to call your boss and tell him just what a fucking incompetent you are and I'm not going to any goddamn dinner I didn't sign up to!"

While unexpected, this was something I had seen before in certain types of senior officers and I wasn't inclined to put up with it for much longer. I'd had previous occasion to remind a senior officer that his behavior was ungentlemanly, but never got the chance with this near hysterical man. As he amped up his volume and his tone became even more aggressive, I saw the deputy secretary had his ear cocked and was listening. He turned from the conversation he'd been engaged in and ambled up along side the irate senior officer and said quietly to us both, "I think its just terrific that we have a chance to make a great impression and, General, I want to be at that dinner, and if YOU think that's a problem I'm going to strongly suggest YOU order room service and I'll see YOU at the meetings tomorrow where we can talk further."

That mild admonishment was like a glass of cold water because he snapped out of his rage and now simply looked sullen and worn. He walked off to the elevator while the deputy said, "Now what time is dinner and can I see a menu beforehand?"

It was with great relief that Hugh and I stood on the tarmac just before dawn on Sunday morning and waited while the four  C-117 Globemaster III's four Pratt & Whitney F117-PW-100 turbofan engines spooled up and eventually vaulted our headaches away to some other poor bastards down range.

+++

# No Pony Rides

The Emperor's birthday is called 'Tennou Tanjyobi' and is celebrated globally on Dec 23. The Embassy of Japan was celebrating the day, but it was still a bit of a surprise in late November 2002, when I received the phone call from the now familiar voice of the protocol secretary for the Embassy of Japan extending an invitation. A nice enough fellow, he'd been unable to hold his liquor on the occasion of my visit and was unable to pronounce my surname, so I insisted he call me by my first name.

"Good Morning, Michael-san, Embassy of Japan calling. We are wondering if you would do us the very great honor of accepting our invitation to come to a reception in honor of Emperor's birthday, a party being held at our Embassy."

I took a look at my evening social schedule and although it conflicted with Monday night poker, I decided that representing the interests of the United States clearly outweighed eating chicken wings and losing thirty bucks, so I accepted his kind invitation. However, since I'd let the guy off the hook on my name, I decided I might as well have a bit of fun and learn about cultural reactions to unexpected information.

"Yes, that's very kind, please mark me down as excited to attend, but can I ask just a couple of questions?"

"Yes, please, Michael-san."

"OK, will they have face painting?"

There was a long pause while he mulled the question, so I added, "You know, like Kabuki dancers?" Although I was having a bit of fun, this was not an unreasonable question because, depending on the wealth of a nation, this most important national day can be simple, or quite extravagant, as countries show off their cultures both past and present.

In Kuwait, the USA traditionally offered a lightly attended outdoor BBQ which might have drawn a better crowd if not for the 4th of July being at the height (and heat) of summer when Kuwait was almost devoid of citizens. Making the celebration even less attractive was the bar's closure, the RSO citing vague security concerns. The AEWA donation for fireworks was significant but our best efforts could never compete with the fireworks that were routinely shot off at night by the people who did remain in country. At the other end of the party spectrum, the gulf states were known for hiring a massive ballroom at one of the five-star hotels to put on a party for a few thousand guests, bringing in bands, craftsmen, and others, to further showcase their countries to the world.

"Ahhhhh, no, I am sorry to say, that will not be available."

I made some scratching sounds on a legal pad I'd been doodling on. I waited a few moments, then asked, "Will you guys be serving any of those little hot dogs rolled up in dough? You know, pigs in a blanket?"

"Ahhhhhh, no, I am very sorry. I do not know the food being offered."

"OK, no worries. Last thing. Will they have a pony ride? Every time I see a photo of the Emperor, he's on a pony. Is that a part of it?"

"Ahhhhh, no, I regret there will be no animals at the reception."

Having expended all my curiosity questions, I told him, "OK, please mark me down as a single." As I rang off, I had an image of that poor man just shaking his head and wondering how we remained a superpower.

The birthday party was extravagant and truly an affair fit for an emperor. We were treated to an extensive buffet bar offering a variety of Japanese dishes, all prepared by the Kuwaiti-owned and Filipino-staffed sushi bar and restaurant at the Crowne Hotel. Chefs at various prep stations kept the offerings coming to the international crowd. I saw one food station that reminded me of once watching a flock of seagulls outside a Florida McDonald's fighting over french fries tossed by tourists. I soon realized it was in fact a chef making a *Benihana* style show, tossing bits of grilled shrimps to the assembled fans and causing the people respond much like the seagulls do.

I made a point to visit with the servers wandering about with their trays loaded with tasty morsels.Most people never acknowledged the servers or other hired help, but I did because I'd been one when I was a kid. This also resulted in me getting first dibs on any food trays brought out from the kitchen.

I recognized some of the staff from previous parties and when they'd ask what I'd like, I always responded, "Give me the good stuff that you eat, not that rubbish you serve the customers."

I traveled about the room nodding to people who nodded back politely. I'd no idea of how long I was supposed to remain, but the bar was open, the sake was warm, there was gin, and also champagne. I'd gotten a drink and was watching a server approach with a large silver tray offering giant gulf prawns that had been butterflied, coated in panko crumbs, and deep fried, when a man built like a Russian weightlifter came by and offered his hand.

"My name is Bronco. I am the Director of Tourism for Bulgaria. And who might you be, sir?"

"Hi! Mike Sciales, US Embassy Kuwait, an employee of absolutely no interest at all, but it is very nice to meet you," as I took his proffered hand and sadly watched as those prawns on that tray veered away, the server flagged down by a woman in a red dress. Bronco stood back, rising to his full five and a half feet, his eyes suggesting he was not necessarily buying my story, but all he said was, "And that is precisely what makes you the most interesting person in this room" as he cast his eyes among the myriad of national costumes swirling about. I liked this guy!

Bronco was an excellent tourism director; I could tell because he told me, "We were the place all the old Commie bosses stayed for their holidays, so you know it's nice. I can get you a dacha on the Black Sea for no more than ten dollars a day." After discussing the merits of visiting Sofia before the tourists ruined it, and exchanging business cards, he wandered off to either find another potential visitor or a drink, I wasn't sure. I lost him in the crowd of folks in dark suits.

Thinking about getting another drink myself, I was starting to shift when a voice, deep and brusque with a flinty edge, said, "Why is a good-looking man like you standing all alone?" and in a nanosecond I was transported back to 1960 and my first serious cartoon crush, Natasha Fatale, the hyper-sexualized evil partner to Boris Badenov, a staple of Saturday morning cartoons. I wasn't alone in this cartoon daydream, and she had a tremendous impact on a lot of guys, as I discovered one night in Korea.

We were in the Osan bar on a Friday night when a new intelligence officer, a twenty-three year old blonde lieutenant named Cheryl arrived on station. Her specialty was the Soviet Union but she could have been a model. She spoke excellent Russian and could drink as well as any of the pilots. Cheryl came from an Air Force family and wasn't intimidated by any aviator. She also had much snappier retorts than they did, so she was always welcome to stand at the rail with the other "non-affiliated" and lean on the bar. One night several of us begged her to teach us how to say, "Is big trouble for Moose and Squirrel" the pet phrase the spies always uttered. It took several drinks but we finally memorized the phrase, *"Eto bol'shaya problema dlya losya i belki."*

I'd had occasion to use the phrase one evening a few months later at Kimpo airport. While waiting for a flight back to the States, a tall and very attractive woman with pale skin, black hair, and a thick Russian accent, approached me and asked if I'd be kind enough to help her carry one of her bags through the inspection station. I was rendered stupid for a moment by her beauty, but snapped out of it when I saw a very large and unsmiling Korean policeman appear behind her. I was reaching for the proffered bag when I saw that his head was shaking slowly from side to side. I took his meaning and recalled my left hand as smoothly as Todd flicked that piece of meatball off that two-star's shoulder board at the Pentagon cocktail party, and stepped back. As the policeman and his partner moved in towards her, all I could think to say was, "Большая беда для лося и белки, извините!" The lovely, but arrested, Russian woman stared at me open-mouthed as the two policemen took her by the arms and led her away.

Finished with my flashback, I turned left to the voice and was delighted to see that a slightly smaller version of my childhood fantasy had sidled up next to me and was now looking at me evenly, waiting for a reply.

"You ask why I am alone? Well, probably because a good-looking woman like yourself hasn't come up to try to have her way with me yet, and frankly, I'm excited about the prospects."

This wasn't exactly the response she was anticipating. "So, you're an American" she said, as the flint got harder and her eyes narrowed just slightly. She let the sentence hang for a moment and said, "I am from Romania, do you think I am pretty?" She turned her head away, just slightly, so I could see and admire her firm jawline. Truth told, other than maybe spending a few dollars to reduce a downy upper lip, she was a very attractive woman and radiating a sexual heat usually only associated with Moroccan women who are taught to be sensual from an early age.

I very much admired her bold approach. Had I been a single man, or perhaps from California, like a particular defense attaché in Moscow, the evening might have taken a different tack. A married man, this army major made the acquaintance of a beautiful local woman he'd met in a bar. He began an affair with her and fell prey to a KGB sexual "honey-trap." The KGB later approached with their Kodachrome color photographs of him "in flagrante delicto." They offered to keep the matter quiet in return for a bit of cooperation from him. The officer snappily replied "I'm from California and have an open marriage. Any way I can get copies of those?"

While in another life, I might have been tempted, but, it was getting late and I was ready to go home, so I looked around and saw my friend Bronco working his way toward the dessert tables. I pointed at him and said, "Sorry, sweetie, I'm married, but that's my boss, he's single." I turned and started to walk away but, just before I left the room, I glanced back as she was sidling up to Bronco.

+++

## Make Sure The Strawberries Are Fresh!

L aurie was recruited before she arrived and took the job at a Kuwaiti girl's school as a history and English teacher. She enjoyed the job and the life but as the year went on, she seemed to be catching the pre-teens bugs more often than was reasonable. It was May 2002 and she was looking forward to returning to America for the first time since 9-11. She'd been feeling poorly, with low energy and suffering a general malaise which shouldn't have been the case since school was almost out for the summer. She finally went to the physician's assistant at the Embassy, but he could offer no relief or explanation. One of her teacher friends, a Nigerian woman named Riscat, was concerned for her health and pushed Laurie to see her husband, Shagoon, who was the doctor in charge of the serology department at the Kuwait royal hospital. He took blood samples, ran the tests several times and Laurie took those results back on the plane when she left. Her very dear friend since high-school, a doctor, took charge of her cancer treatment and found the doctor who knew how to cure her. Thanks to modern medicine and the military "single payer" socialized system, Laurie got the care she needed for complete remission and full recovery. She'd be back in Kuwait before Christmas.

What she didn't know was that while she was gone, I'd been reading all the message traffic for the region and knew we'd soon be getting into a shooting war.

The State department knew this too, and attention was given to evacuating the embassy if the need arose. A year earlier we had a full scale rehearsal during which US Marines picked us up on the beach by the Radisson SAS hotel and brought us by hovercraft to a Navy amphibious transport ship floating out in the Gulf. This was the option of last resort. Before that, they would encourage dependents to leave and take a "long holiday." If it came down to a mandatory evacuation, those remaining would get scant notice and only be able to pack two suitcases.

Since Laurie had been receiving medical care in the states, I decided to do an "early return of dependents package" citing her treatment. That request granted, she and our daughter, Maggie, would be leaving Kuwait on the last day in December, with their baggage to follow.

Before telling them about this, I decided to throw a really great *"Well-come"* back party. I knew this would most likely be the last party with any family members held at the OMC and I wanted to make it a grand affair for her, so to make this a reality, I got a hold of Hassan, and told him my idea. I also told him that I'd be using all my liquor points, as well as a one-time only additional liquor ration, to adequately stock the bar. Hassan assured me he'd take care of everything. Any time he catered an affair, he was always given all the beer, wine, and liquor that remained and people always made sure there was plenty left over. He would then host parties for a wide and eclectic group of expat friends and acquaintances.

We'd been friends since I'd arrived and during those times Hassan would regale me with tales of the antics of his multi-national staff, and after asking about what kind of cake we should have, he told me the latest misadventure by the cake chef and his staff.

It was an average day when the private secretary of the man who owned the hotel called to ask that a cake be made for the owner's birthday. She gave Hassan the particulars as to the type of cake and the inscription "Happy Birthday Ali" in English. As is the practice in the food service industry, Hassan wrote the instructions on a paper cake doily. Before letting him off the phone, the secretary admonished him to "make sure the strawberries are fresh!" and Hassan added this instruction in Arabic to be sure there was no confusion, as everybody in the bakery spoke and read Arabic.

The cake was sent off and received by the celebrants. The next day, the hotel owner called Hassan to thank him for the cake and birthday wishes, but before ringing off, laughed and said, "Why did you write, 'make sure the strawberries are fresh' in Arabic under my name?"

On the next evening after she arrived back in country, Maggie and I took Laurie to visit the Skipper and his wife, Steph, for dinner. When we got to their front door, Laurie walked into the three-thousand square foot living room, astonished to see her many friends and acquaintances. Off to one side was a cake in English and Arabic "Well-come back, Laurie We missed you!" Below it was written تأكد من الفراولة الطازجة and while a casual reader might think it repeated the message for our Kuwaiti friends present, instead it said: "Make sure the strawberries are fresh" which I'd requested as homage to that story. My daughter had been studying Arabic in school and I knew she'd read it when she asked the same question the owner did.

As Laurie was making her way to cut the cake, a sharp-eyed Bangladude waiter spotted the "gaffe" in the cake's message. Remembering the chewing out they'd all just gotten over the first cake-faux-pas, he raced up to this cake, grabbed a spoon, and started to smear the writing. What he'd failed to notice was Hassan, the man who was in on the joke, standing nearby waiting for Laurie to ask about it. Hassan was able to grab the young fellow by the arm and exclaim "What are you doing?" He sent the now trembling man away, terribly confused, to the kitchen.

The party was a great success, but the downside was that the hotel staff, after the cake fiasco, was now slow to exercise initiative to investigate matters or even bring any concerns to management for fear of making a mistake. That mindset certainly helped explain things a few weeks later, when the hotel's classically trained, and quite elderly Albanian piano player dropped dead over his keyboard one evening. With all the people coming and going through the lobby where he played, nobody noticed at first. The staff finally realized his cigarette break was running longer than expected, and thinking he was leaning over slightly and taking a nap, decided not to disturb him.

This staff apprehension and indecision did, however, disturb the lady who tapped the corpse to get a song request and watched it tumble to the floor.

+++

# Who Will Pay?

On Sunday, January 19, 2003, I heard a now familiar voice saying, "Well, hello, Mister Jag!" I looked up from the weekly report to the KAF Chief of Staff I was editing, and saw the smiling face of Chris, our new chief of staff and the deputy to the chief. He'd been a GIB, or "guy in back," as an F-4 navigator and later as an F-15E whizzo. When he aged out of the cockpit, he took staff positions until he'd reached his final grade, then had spent the previous three years as an ROTC training detachment commander at a large university as a way to stave off forced retirement.

Chris's OMC job came up as a "short-notice" because the previous deputy had agreed to cut short his assignment to provide a one year overlap of the chief and deputy for continuity. An added bonus was that this guy left early. Another GIB, he had the kind of people skills that hurt people. His organizational skills were still worse. As a fervent believer in the good word, he had racked up a fair number of complaints and received subsequent counseling over his on-duty proselytizing. I'd favored his early release since the day he came into my office, closed the door, and confided he believed one of the feral cats near his house was possessed by the devil, insisting he'd seen its eyes glowing red.

Chris was the guy notionally charged with overseeing day-to-day operations and, should the occasion arise, assuming command if the chief needed to return to DC or were to ever take leave. He was a colonel looking for a place to hang his hat for a few more years and stall retirement until the last possible day. Like so many other aviators before him, he'd made a number of bad calls in affairs of the heart and so the bulk of his retirement pay was already spoken for. What little remained would go to putting his kids through college.

He was leaning half into the office, casting an eye about as if checking to be sure my office didn't contain any new furniture or other items he might be authorized to have, or failing that, could purloin from my office. By USAF regulations, JAGs, regardless of rank, are authorized leather couches and chairs as well as real wood desks, an entitlement ordinarily reserved for colonels and generals. I had a leather swivel chair, but the wooden desk would have been bigger than my small office would allow, so I was fine with my IKEA work station. Chris did make note of my chair and later requested the same model.

With his pale skin, thinning light reddish blonde hair, and almost non-existent eyebrows, Chris usually looked like a guy who was trying to think of what he wanted to say and having trouble figuring it out. After completing his visual inventory of my office furniture, he turned to me and said, "I need you to cover something for me tomorrow; I've got a meeting with the awards and decorations committee I can't miss because I'm the chairman. The meeting I need you to cover starts at nine." He pushed off to leave when I had to stop him to ask "Can you help me out on this? I really need to know where to go and what kind of meeting it is I'm covering for you."

He crossed his arms and pursed his lips, pushing out the lower one while tapping it with his left forefinger. After a few beats he said, "It's out at the KPC (Kuwait Petroleum Company) and I'm not really certain what it's about, I think Todd set up it." He pointed his finger up to indicate the executive offices where our economics section had their shop. Those guys allegedly work with foreign governments, international organizations, non-governmental organizations (NGOs) and other USG agencies on technology, science, economic, trade, energy, and environmental issues both domestically and overseas. Well, at least that's what the job description said, because I sure didn't see much evidence of that since Todd, the bow-tie wearing EO, lived behind stout walls on the embassy compound and rarely left, striking me as a guy who preferred reading reports on economy and making power point slides to actually getting out and into the economy to do some hands-on research and field work.

I still wasn't satisfied with this mission brief, so I asked him directly, "Just exactly what is it I'm supposed to do at this meeting?" He turned back to look at me, cocking his head as if I'd missed something vital and said, "I really don't know. This is some kind of State meeting the Ambassador brokered, so just go there and keep an eye out for US interests under the Defense Cooperation Agreement."

Now understanding that he actually didn't have any idea what the meeting was going to be about because I knew he'd never read the DCA, I just nodded my head up and down, knowing I was getting shafted. The only good thing, as I saw it, was that any meeting with the KPC involved an outstanding luncheon buffet at the conclusion of business. As he walked towards the coffee room, Chris called back over his shoulder, "Oh yeah, and there's some fuels guy coming in from Atlanta you need to bring with you. He's staying at the Crowne."

Now thoroughly confused and more than a little annoyed, I shook my head slowly from side to side and told him, "I don't like going into an international meeting without any idea of its purpose." He nodded his head and walked back into his office and closed the door. I sat at my desk, picked up the phone, and dialed the EO. After a few rings, a smooth and confident voice came on the line. "Yes, this is Todd, how can I help?" I told him Chris had just notified me of this meeting, but I needed some further explanation.

There was a pause as Todd leaned back in his chair, the spring squeaking and I imagined that, like Andy the Political Officer, he'd also be fumbling for a pipe, using it to buy a bit of time, loading it before answering. At least that's what he would have been doing if employees were still allowed to smoke in a Federal building. I waited a moment before saying, "Todd?" He coughed and said, "Yes, well, about that meeting. I'm not really certain what it's about, but I might as well tell you, I won't be able to attend either, as I'm in the middle of preparing an important presentation." He excused himself and rang off.

I knew this was a bullshit story because he'd pulled that gag before. I'd been tasked last summer to help him get approval from the Kuwait Ministry of Defense for our pathetic National Day fireworks display. My job was to take him to the Minister's office and walk him and his paperwork about, and help if needed, because the Minister's senior military aid, a colonel named Bushari, was a friend from a diwanya we both attended.

A diwan is a traditional men's gathering. I was invited to one by Bill, our charge d'affaires, who told me "I have somebody I want you to meet." Arriving at the diwan, Bill introduced me to the host, Sheikh Hamad, who was a career diplomat and well-placed senior prince within the Kuwait royal family. He and I hit it off and I'd accepted his invitation to return often. After several visits, the Sheikh asked me and Skipper, the accidental captain, why we didn't wear dishdashas, the long flowing robes traditionally worn by gulf Arabs, since they were way more comfortable than a jacket and tie. We explained our guidance from State was that a westerner wearing a dishdasha would give great offense. The Sheikh looked mildly astonished and said, "It's only offensive if you buy a cheap dishdasha and wear it badly, like going to Texas and buying a cheap cowboy hat and wearing it sideways or something."

Hamad spoke excellent English; he had served as an interpreter with the US Army during Desert Storm, and attended basic training at Fort Dix in New Jersey. He'd traveled extensively and was very familiar with America and Americans. When we told him the "dishdasha cultural sensitivities warning," he sighed and said, "I prefer it when unemployment is higher in the States, you get smarter people in the State Department." As a result of that conversation, Skipper and I happily shopped for some nice dishdashas and the red and white checked head covering called a guthra and the egal, which looks like a fan belt and holds the guthra in place on ones head, but is also used to hobble a camel at night so it doesn't wander off. Hamad was then kind enough to spend time during the next few diwans teaching us the ins and outs of wearing our new garb properly.

Hamad's diwan was held on Tuesday evenings, which was perfect, it falling between Monday poker night and Wednesday happy hour. The event always offered a giant buffet including beef, chicken, fish, shrimp, lamb, and the occasional baby camel cooked in yoghurt sauce. During those evenings, I would meet any number of new people and develop friendships with others I'd met before. This networking helped me make friends throughout the various ministries since everyone came to Hamad's diwan. It was so popular that one evening some USAF officers from nearby Jaber Air Base came up to visit. As they made their way around the room, I recognized one guest as a former neighbor, Pete, the lieutenant colonel security police chief at my last assignment in Montana. I was wearing a dishdasha and after greeting him he complimented me on my English and was stunned when I said, "Well, thanks, Pete! I should hope so, it hasn't been that long since we were stationed together at Malmstrom."

Now, with Chris having dumped his KPC meeting on me, I was contemplating walking into a meeting I knew nothing about, and I thought about the last time that had happened with the fireworks. I'd also been a bit disappointed with this tasking because it was falling on the same day and time that the newly revitalized embassy cafe was having its grand reopening. The board, having tired of only Indian food being offered, solicited some American food favorites and recipes from our members. We prepared a new menu and presented it to the cook, who then received guidance from each recipe donor on how to prepare the dish. This was a project that had been a month in the undertaking and, as the chairman of the board, I was supposed to cut the ribbon to open it, but the mission always comes first. When the day came, I called upstairs and asked Todd if he was ready to go. He begged off, telling me he had an important presentation to finish and it had to be done before the close of business.

Realizing I was now stuck with the task, I took the request, drove over to the MoD office building and made my way to the executive suite. I saw my friend Bushari, told him what was going on, and he invited me to have a seat with him and visit a while. He gave the paper to the tea boy along with some instructions in Arabic. The boy returned a few minutes later with Turkish coffee, while we chatted amiably about mutual friends and acquaintances from the diwan as well as the Charlotte Hornets. Bushari's oldest son was a senior at UNC Charlotte studying Computer Engineering and Physics, and Bushari was an alumnus. They'd finished the season second in the Central Division with a 44–38 record, and qualified for their third straight playoff appearance where they got defeated 4-1 in the semi-finals by the NJ Nets.

The signed request was brought back in just fifteen minutes, right as we were finishing our coffee. Bushari glanced at the paper, which was adorned with a few stamps, some signatures, and an attached note. He read it and a bemused look crossed his face. He handed it to me and pointing at the Arabic handwriting said, "This is from the Minister, it says 'I'm not certain why the Americans want this, because in the entire history of our country nobody has ever asked permission to shoot anything, let alone fireworks.' "

I got back to the embassy at around half past twelve, just in time to see the opening ceremony ending and the crowds shuffling through the food line; leading the group was the formerly busy Todd. A guy I knew from the spook shop told me Todd had been talking up this luncheon all week because we were giving away free soft drinks with every meal.

With that experience turning in the back of my mind and realizing I didn't have the first clue as to what the purpose of the currently proposed meeting was, I decided to see if I couldn't guilt Todd into coming. I went upstairs and into his office. It was a small space and, like any working office, there were sheafs of paper everywhere, each containing information that might or might not have been of any importance. Along one wall was a map of the entire Kuwaiti royal family tree. This helped in identifying exactly which Sheikh Mohammed a person might be talking about at any given moment, as there were so many Mohammeds.

Todd was on the phone and leaning back in his squeaky government chair. I thought about going back to my office and bringing up a can of WD-40 for that squeak but thought better of it and just stared at him until he made his excuses and rang off. I cut right to the chase and told him, "Listen, I don't know what this meeting is about and I don't know who it is exactly I'm supposed to talk to, or what is expected of me, but this meeting was put together by the Ambassador, the President's personal representative in Kuwait, and I don't feel like embarrassing the diplomatic mission through my ignorance, so you want to tell me all about this vital presentation you're preparing for?"

Todd looked a bit sheepish as he glanced down at his desktop calendar, offering that it was some sort of academic exercise and discussion with members of the American business community that was coming up in two weeks time. At that point, he was busted and he knew it. I had been pretty upset about having the meeting fobbed off on me by Chris, but it was even more galling to have the very person most needed for the meeting also trying to fob it off. I might have to take the job from Chris because of his rank, but I absolutely didn't have to put up with this from a civilian state employee. I told him I'd be calling him at half past seven the next morning when I was picking up the fuels guy and leaving the hotel for the KPC offices in Farwaniya City, some twenty miles south and towards the Saudi border. I told him he needed to be there, and I left.

The next morning I drove over to the Crowne at just after six so I could have a leisurely breakfast with Hassan. I regularly took coffee with the general managers of all the nearby five-star hotels because they were a terrific source of information and gossip since everybody visiting our world stayed at one of those three choices. I met him in the lobby and, before we went in to breakfast, he pulled me aside and pointed to an older man with scraggly white fly-away hair sitting in the lobby. The gentleman was clad in a white ribbed sleeveless "wife beater" tee-shirt, the kind favored by tough guys from New Jersey and rural residents of mobile homes, and presenting a style not often seen in the lobby of a beautiful and upscale five-star hotel. Hassan looked at me and said in clipped English, "I know; he is a guest of the hotel, an American, working for your State department, but I'm hesitant to walk up and ask him if he forgot to get dressed before coming downstairs. Do you think you might make an inquiry?" I was always happy to be of some small service to this guy who managed to pull many a logistical "rabbit out of his hat" trick when sudden and unexpected arrivals popped up.

I wandered over to the area where the disheveled guy was seated and sat down next to him. "Good morning!" I offered as I took my ease. He barely looked at me, so after introducing myself, I continued. "Say, I just couldn't happen to notice you're missing a shirt and was wondering if your luggage got misplaced. Anything I can help you with?" He swiveled his head, and looking at me said, "I have some meetings later this morning and I've only got one clean shirt, so I'm waiting before I put it on." He held up a white shirt that had seen many meetings, a shirt, that while it might have been clean, was certainly wrinkled. I realized he was seriously jet-lagged so I called over a Sri Lankan bellman, handed him the shirt and a dinar, told him I needed it cleaned and pressed within thirty minutes. His smile grew wide and he told me, "No problem, Boss" and was off like a shot. The disheveled man thanked me and I came to find out he was an Ambassador "without portfolio," a long-time middle east hand who'd retired but had been brought back into service to begin discussions with some Iraqis who had emerged as the anti-Saddam element. These Iraqis were jockeying for position when the US invaded Iraq to kick Saddam's ass for the second and final time.

It was just then that I saw an Army lieutenant colonel come off the elevator with a look that told me he was looking for somebody to come get him and I knew that somebody was me. I excused myself from the rumpled diplomat and approached the colonel. I introduced myself, and realizing my breakfast with Hassan was not to be, took him into the lobby cafe for some Turkish coffee, where I was able to learn a bit about him. As I'd been previously informed, this officer was an engineer and fuels specialist assigned to the Army unit that dealt with everything involving petroleum, oils, and lubricants. It turned out that his particular specialty was the introduction of "fizzie," a static dissipater additive/corrosion inhibitor/lubricity improver, and fuel system icing inhibitor also containing antioxidant and metal deactivators. Adding fizzie to refined oil creates JP-8, a universal fuel that can burn in any DoD equipment.

Armed with this knowledge and seeing the bellman, carrying a freshly laundered and pressed shirt, running up to the rumpled ambassador without a country, I felt my work at the Crowne was done for the morning. Noticing it was just half past seven, I put in my call and found a clearly perturbed Todd assuring me that he was heading south on the King Abdul Aziz Expressway towards Farwaniya.

We met in the KPC parking lot where I introduced Todd to the fuels guy who still appeared mildly disoriented and confused, since he really wasn't sure why he'd been sent to Kuwait in the first place. Not understanding anything about the nature of the meeting we were about to enter, I followed Todd inside. We were greeted by a veiled secretary in a black hijab who led us to a rather large set of wooden doors that stood at least fifteen feet tall and were made of some dark and expensive looking wood. She knocked and a tea boy opened the door, bidding us welcome and directing us towards a group of forty men in business suits and dishdashas, all of whom stood up as we walked into the room.

It was my habit to always have with me some business cards, one side in English and the other Arabic, with me whenever I went to any meeting, it being so much easier to hand them out than to do the phone exchange thing while being introduced. I'd only put ten in my card holder and burned through them rapidly. I continued moving down the line greeting these oil executives and collecting their business cards. Introductions concluded, we three took our seats on the opposite side of the longest conference table I'd ever seen in my life.

It was made of a lighter, burnished wood that somehow screamed "Italian design, crazy price tag" and I made a note to be sure and use the coaster they provided for my cut crystal Waterford glass. I took a gander at the cards and came to realize that we were sitting across from the entire Kuwait Petrochemical industry. Clearly, this would be economic-type work, so I began to relax knowing that the onus for success was not on me.

I learned that the meeting had been brokered because, while the US and its coalition allies were preparing for an invasion and building up large forces locally, the need for fuel had become acute and 10,000 gallon deliveries by fuel trucks would not meet the energy needs of over 250,000 troops with tens of thousands of vehicles and hundreds of aircraft. To that end, the coalition had requested, and the Kuwaiti Engineering Department had just completed, construction of a series of six-inch pipelines running many miles from the refinery in Farwaniya to all the camps and airfields throughout Kuwait. This was no small feat as the Kuwait Engineering Department, under the leadership of that Sheikh from the Chinese dinner with the Deputy Secretary of the Army, oversaw the rapid design, contracted the builders, and executed creation of those pipelines within sixty days.

The general manager for KPC operations announced to the group that the pipelines had been completed. "Pigs," the metal slugs that perform hydrostatic testing and pipeline drying, internal cleaning, internal coating, liquid management, batching, and inspection had been pushed through the lines and all were ready to receive the petroleum. He concluded by offering all that remained was to give the order that would start the fuel flowing. One pressing matter was broached by the KPC-CEO who raised concerns about putting fizzie into the storage tanks and converting all the product contained into JP-8. The fuels guy took the question and showed his worth by assuring the audience that, in fact, the fizzie would be injected into the product only when it left the pipeline at the fuel-terminal end on the various installations.

Murmuring and head nodding ensued as the various board members discussed among themselves the answer in both Arabic and English. Satisfied that the entire petroleum reserves of Kuwait would not be adulterated, the mood became more relaxed. It was at this point that the Operations manager looked at the board and said hopefully, "So, you will now order the pipelines activated?" He held a portable radio in his hand to demonstrate his readiness to execute any orders instantly.

There was a bit of a gap in the conversation while the collected executives discussed any reasons to delay the start of pumping operations. It was our host, the KPC-CEO, who looked across the table at Todd and said, "The order to begin must come from the Minister of Oil. We will of course need a letter from your Ambassador requesting us to turn on the pipeline before we can proceed. Will you make the letter?" Todd pursed his lips and pondered the question. After a few moments, he looked at me and said, "This is a military thing, so I guess you'll write the letter?"

With no options and forty executives looking on, I told Todd and the assembled group that I would have the letter prepared that very day. Some noted their appreciation because they were not used to anything being completed on the same day, and the group dynamic now suggested the meeting was coming to an end as a few papers were shuffled and people began checking schedules on their Blackberry phones.

The Chairman nodded towards us to confirm my suspicions that the meeting was at a close, when one of his assistants, a spare man in a white dishdasha, leaned in and whispered in his ear. The exec nodded and extended his hands and arms, a signal for his colleagues to stay in their seats and pay attention, a final matter was at hand.

Cocking his head, the CEO looked at Todd and said simply, "Before we go, there is one last thing. Who will pay?"

This unanticipated question hung heavy in the air. In that silence, I could hear the ticking of a rather large and beautiful Swarovski crystal table clock just behind me. I glanced at Todd and noticed he was staring at the dust on his shoes. The fuels guy was looking up at an ornate mobile that hung suspended over the table.

This was a binding negotiation and only the Ambassador could obligate the United States to make any payments for fuel. The clock kept ticking and I could feel eyes beginning to concentrate on me, the only guy with his head still level. This was a big issue because military forces required fuel in the amounts of millions of gallons costing hundreds of millions of dollars.

I knew there wouldn't be any second meeting while a strategy was developed; this was the time and this was the place for the decision. The Kuwaitis reckoned since the Ambassador had requested this meeting, he must have given us guidance before dispatching us to represent him at an international negotiation. If we begged off now, the US would look foolish and incompetent, and any future negotiations would be made more difficult.

In an instant I flashed back to an administrative discharge board I'd participated in at RAF Greenham Commons in 1991. My client was an airman who'd spent the majority of his very short career screwing up in some form or fashion. Since the base was slotted for closure, thanks to the collapse of the Soviet Union, the Air Force decided his services would no longer be required and he was not being offered an honorable discharge. In fact, his record was so bad his service would be characterized as Under Other than Honorable Condition (UOTHC). This meant he'd lose any GI Bill or VA benefits except burial in a national cemetery. Because of the proposed characterization, he was entitled to have a lawyer represent him at his administrative discharge board.

I'd gone through his records and could not find one instance of him displaying any behavior that had been noted as positive in his file. Not a single letter of appreciation or commendation, no medals or ribbons for exemplary service to the nation or any other mitigating documents to help support any argument I might present for awarding a general discharge, under honorable conditions, characterization. The evening before the board, he had called to ask what would happen the next day. I told him it looked pretty bad and asked if he had any good things in his private records, like rescuing a little old lady from a canal or saving some kids in a burning building. He said he didn't, but this guy was so useless that I felt compelled to admonish him not to create any of those situations to try to get an award we could present to the board.

That next morning in the courtroom, I stared at my blank legal pad and tapped a pencil against it while the government lawyer brought in what seemed like a forklift full of bad acts and deeds to support his argument. The airman saw me looking at the blank pad and asked

"What's that for?" I turned to him and whispered, "This is all the good stuff I have to say about you." He looked stunned and hissed, "But it's blank!" Before I could say, "And there you have it" the senior officer hearing the case, my old boss, Dan Haas, caught my attention by saying, "Captain? Is there something you'd like to now share with the board?" It seemed the government had rested its case and I was up.

I had nothing except that wooden number two Ticonderoga pencil with well-worn eraser. I looked at it, looked at the board members in the jury box, and started. "You know why they put erasers on the end of a pencil? Because we all understand that people make mistakes…" I went on along that theme of redemption and mercy for seven long minutes before finally sitting down. The hearing was closed and the board members retired to their deliberation room. My client clapped me on the back, telling me what a great job I'd done. I told him he'd best wait until the board came back before he broke out the cigars. Knowing any deliberation took at least twenty minutes, I figured I had time to go and have a smoke and some coffee, so I started towards the exit. I was just pushing on the crash bar to open it when the door to the deliberation room opened and a board member signaled to Dan that they were done.

After a few moments to take their places, the board president announced to a stunned airman that he was also done and his service would be characterized as UOTHC, and the hearing was closed. My client sat in his chair looking down at the floor as he processed the news. One of the board members, an officer I knew from my previous visits to the base, paused before going back to the deliberation room to retrieve his jacket and hat. He caught my eye and said, "That was a great argument. We were thinking about giving him the General but then somebody reminded us about all the evidence."

So here I was, twelve years later, and again with nothing but a pencil. This time I stood up and looked at the board. I started by praising Allah in Arabic and switching to English while thanking them for the opportunity to speak before them. It was Martin Luther King Day and I'd recalled the passion of his oratory as I told the group, "Kuwait is a small country, and you think, what can **we** do against Saddam?"

Channeling Dr. King's speech cadence and energy, I went on, "I tell you, my brothers, that Allah above has given you a gift, a magnificent gift that flows from the ground and can provide the energy to fuel that mighty war machine being built to the north! By your generosity and support, and with Allah on our side on this righteous cause, together we will bring to life an engine of death and destruction that will avenge you and destroy the animal who invaded your country, raped your women, killed your children, and tried to destroy your national identity! Share but a fraction of your wealth, less than ten days output of this precious gift from Allah, and we will provide you with freedom from the fear and terror that is that bad bastard Saddam, and insha'Allah, (God willing) we will take our mighty sword and chop off his head!" For emphasis I spat on the ground at the mention of the hated dictator's name.

The CEO started clapping and was instantly joined by the others, some shouting "Insha'Allah" and "A ham dul'Allah" (God willing and with God's support) and the CEO said, "Yes! You are right! We will pay, we will pay! Now come and let us all have some lunch!" And with that pronouncement, the meeting was over, all relevant matters being settled.

I realized that I'd just concluded an international agreement and thought it best to let the Ambassador know immediately and receive any guidance he might have to offer. I rang into his office and his secretary put me right through. The Ambassador had graduated with a degree in Mathematics from Harvey Mudd College, thirty-five miles east of Los Angeles, one of America's top math, science, and engineering undergraduate colleges. He was pretty new at the job, but was fluent in Arabic and, thanks to that math background, he was also an excellent poker player and very well received by the entire leadership of Kuwait. He was also a semi-regular at our Monday night poker games, so when he came on the line, his greeting was a relaxed, "What's up, Judge?" I told him I'd negotiated an international agreement on behalf of the United States. His only question was "Is it in our favor?" He was happy with my reply and told me to bring him any correspondence whenever I had it ready and he'd sign off on it.

Satisfied with this result, I went into the buffet and enjoyed some of those massive gulf prawns.

Back at the office, I briefed my boss and drafted the requested letter to the Minister of Oil for the Ambassador's signature. I wasn't sure who the current Minister of Oil was so I called Bushari and asked for his guidance which was straightforward, "Start by sending me a copy of the letter," and he gave me the full name of the Minister. I printed a draft and faxed it over to him. He called me back in a few minutes and said the letter was fine and that I needed to take it to the Ministry of Information in downtown Kuwait City for the signature because the Minister was dual-hatted and acting as the Minister of Oil. I told him I owed him dinner because I'd have never found that out on my own. I ran a final version on the embossed and watermarked "good paper" and brought it upstairs where the Ambassador looked at it and signed off, telling me I'd done a good job. It was just half-past-two when I made a copy of the letter for the file, faxed a copy to Bushari for his file, and took off for downtown Kuwait City.

Governmental offices tended to empty out at two, so all the heavy traffic was heading out of the city and I made great time. I pulled into the circular drive of the Ministry and was directed by a policeman to park my car at the curb, directly behind the Minister's car that was awaiting his arrival; an arrival being delayed while he waited for me. A tea boy was holding open the doors to the private, non-stop express elevator that brought me to the thirteenth floor. The door opened and I was greeted by a secretary in a black pantsuit and wearing a hijab who said, "Mister Mike? His excellency will see you now" as she pointed me towards an open door. I thanked her and walked inside.

The Minister was watching a show on the cooking channel and he waved me in saying, "Mister Mike, please have a seat." I thanked him for his time and handed him the paper. He read it, then pulled out a Monte Blanc fountain pen and, with green ink, executed his signature on the bottom of the letter. He smiled and handed the letter across to me. It took him less time to sign than for the chef to finish chopping some onions for the rice he was making, and I realized the Minister had waited at his office until I arrived and he'd missed his lunch. Not wanting to delay him any longer, I stood up and thanked him in my best Arabic, as the smiling secretary escorted me back to the elevator.

The fuel began flowing at eight the next morning. In a small ceremony conducted in the operations suite at the KPC, engineers, fueled by Starbucks coffee and a wide assortment of Dunkin' Doughnuts, opened the pipelines to the cheers of all involved in this massive undertaking.

What we didn't know then, was that the total value of the fuel the Kuwaitis *donated* to the war effort was in excess of *half a billion dollars.*

Two months later, at a state department awards ceremony, I listened while Todd was awarded a five thousand dollar cash bonus for his work in getting the oil flowing. Newly enriched, he was getting ready to depart Kuwait for another assignment in some foreign locale, and came into the bar for a last drink. As it happened, I was guest bartending when he pulled up a stool and ordered. I made it and slid it in front of him. He looked at me and said, "I really feel kind of bad, I know I wasn't a lot of help that day." I smiled and put down the glass I was wiping and said, "Well, you're always free to salve your conscience by buying me a nice bottle of eighteen-year old Macallan single malt, only twenty-two bucks." I could see he thought about it for a nano-second before pushing back his stool and saying, "Nah, I don't think so" as he drifted off and into the crowd.

One month later I was awarded a one-inch rectangle of colored thread representing the Defense Meritorious Service Medal, along with the thanks of the nation for what the citation described as an "incontestably exceptional" noncombat meritorious achievement.

It was better than money.

# Jimmy The Cop & The Night Of The Living Dead

Jimmy the Cop was the NYPD captain in charge of the 14th Precinct, which is a part of Midtown south and occupying a good chunk of central Manhattan. It was early afternoon on January 23, 2003, and the last fires from the ruins of the World Trade Center had finally been extinguished just one month earlier. The precinct boundaries were small by the NYPD standards, but that small area was considered the heart and soul of the Big Apple. In those confines were commercial offices, hotels, Times Square, Grand Central Terminal, Penn Station, Madison Square Garden, Korea town and the Manhattan Mall Plaza. Every day the area was flooded with around 80,000 visitors in and among the 1.5 million natives, so it packed more people and generated a greater need for police services than any other precinct in the city.

Jimmy was in his upstairs office when the desk sergeant buzzed, asking him to come downstairs to see a mailman with a package he needed to sign for. Jimmy lived on a sailboat he kept moored at the World's Fair Marina on Northern Boulevard in Flushing, Queens. He rebelled at having his mail shuffled through by the snoopy pain in the ass dockmaster, so he sometimes used the precinct address. Walking downstairs, he was guessing that the package was something he'd ordered recently, so he was more than a little surprised when the mailman handed him a white envelope with "Department of the Army" embossed as the return address. Jimmy was a helicopter pilot for the NY National guard but was on inactive reserves status due to the demands of his current job. What Jimmy didn't know, because he was terribly busy running the busiest precinct in the largest police department in America, was that a decision recently had been made which would greatly affect him.

A few weeks earlier, after touring Kuwait and Afghanistan, the Army's Deputy Secretary for manpower had decided to activate over 20,000 reservists and to begin flowing those forces into the Middle East to prepare for threatened military operations against Iraq. Jimmy was one of those reservists. What absolutely stunned him was the line that ordered him to report to his home unit within twenty-four hours, and to be ready to deploy overseas at any time after that.

Jimmy hopped on the phone with his boss, the Chief of Patrol for Manhattan south, who immediately called the Chief of Patrol who called the Chief of Personnel who called the Deputy Commissioner for Legal Matters, who opined that Jimmy was screwed, and who then directed the Personnel Chief to instruct the Commanding Officer of the Personnel Orders Division to reach out to find a suitable replacement for Jimmy forthwith.

With best wishes for his safety and eventual return, the next afternoon his soon-to-be-former patrolman-driver loaded Jimmy's duffel bag and suitcase into the trunk of his soon-to-be former department car and dropped him off like an unwanted Indian maid at his aviation battalion headquarters in Ronkonkoma, out in Suffolk County.

Through sheer random luck, Jimmy, now "Major Jimmy," appeared on an in-bound personnel manifest assigning him to the OMC-K. He arrived at KCIA after a ten-hour overnight flight from JFK and was swiftly set up in a room at the Radisson SAS on the Gulf, where he started to develop an idea that perhaps this wasn't the worst thing that could happen.

Owing to his police experience and lacking any actual knowledge about Kuwait, Jimmy was appointed the night shift watch officer where his only job was answering the phones, if they ever rang. In theory, nothing out of the ordinary should ever happen, but to be prepared, he was armed with a phone roster and the ability to reach out to anybody who might be needed to restore normalcy. Jimmy was happy with his assignment; it reminded him of his younger days as a beat cop working the overnight tours.

Back then, a precinct always offered some quiet place where he could hide his marked NYPD patrol car and catch a few winks when things got slow at four in the morning. Ten years after leaving patrol and moving into management, he spent his first night sitting up in a chair watching CNN continuously repeating itself while he waited for the phone to ring.

The next day Jimmy brought in a fully reclining beach lounge chair he had borrowed from the pool area at the SAS. He also brought in his Army sleeping bag and a couple of hotel pillows, then settled in for the long haul. During the day, he spent his time by the pool at the Radisson SAS, working on his tan and not missing the New York City winter at all.

It was after two in the morning when Jimmy the Cop answered his phone. Then he promptly called me, his thick New York accent helped me shake the fog from my brain. Jimmy was pissed off and frustrated. "I got a call from some jabroni at the State Department duty desk telling me that some State people are over at the military side of KCIA who need to get to a hotel." I was confused because State department people were handled by State folks, not military, and told him so. "I know," he said, "That low-grade moron said it sounded military and he couldn't do anything for her, told me to deal with it, and hung up." Jim had been given a contact number for the woman who was the handler for the trip, so I told him to give her a call to get an idea of the scope of the problem, and that I'd be heading in to the office.

After my family left for Idaho, I'd moved into the top floor of a recently constructed building in the new neighborhood directly across the street from the Embassy. This building provided a direct line of sight into the embassy chancery building, which also meant the possibility of bad guys on our roof with an RPG, so the OMC took the opportunity of renting all the surrounding houses to keep everyone closer, while reducing the risk to the Embassy. I usually left my vehicle parked in the embassy-secured lot, so the walk only took a few minutes. I got into the office as Jimmy finished up the call.

It turned out that State had activated three long-retired politicians to a kind of "Ambassador at Large" position with the goal of working out some kind of arrangement with the many groups of Iraqis who had come forward identifying themselves as leaders in the various national unity movements that were sprouting up like mushrooms after a rain.

Jimmy informed me that the State department handler was beside herself after being blown off by the unhelpful night-duty officer. He said the group was waiting in the military departure lounge. Realizing that it wasn't in anybody's best interests to keep that group sitting in the lounge, I called the general manager at the SAS, another frequent guest at happy hour. From Australia, she'd once gone on a "walkabout," prior to beginning her career with the Raddison corporation as a maid. She came to Kuwait as the head of housekeeping and in two years was the general manager. I asked if she had four rooms for my unwanted Ambassadors and their escort. Always ready to accommodate any request she could, she told me to bring the group on down and she'd attend to them.

Jimmy and I got our vehicles and headed over to the military side of KCIA. We found the group waiting, and the twenty-six year old escort, on her first overseas trip, had tears in her eyes as we pulled up. She was standing a fair distance from her charges as she took my hand and kissed it, saying, "Thank you so much! I thought I'd be stuck with those mummies all evening. All they do is complain." She gave me the names of the three ambassadors who had neither portfolios nor rooms. I didn't recognize the first two names, but the last one, Lawrence Eagleburger, stood out as a name I should have known from history. What I didn't know was that he'd been a senior career state department official and had even served as an undersecretary of state in George H. W. Bush's tenure. An early opponent of any war or regime change in Iraq, Eagleburger was part of a last-ditch effort to avoid violence.

I didn't recall any of this and, for some reason, I thought of Thomas Eagleton, a former Senator from Missouri who was briefly in contention to be 1972 presidential candidate George McGovern's vice president, but withdrew after the media revealed he'd once been treated for depression. This confusion manifested while I was driving the handler and Eagleburger and Jimmy had dibs on the two unknown ambassadors. I got a call from the SAS asking for the names of my guests so they could prepare the paperwork and the key cards could be handed out upon arrival. This level of service was only available because I worked continuously at keeping our good relationship, and even so, this was a lot of people going out of their way to expedite getting three old guys into a bed.

I named the young woman, then said the name "Eagleton" whereupon I heard from the back of the car a tired and worn out voice saying, "Eagleburger, it's Eagleburger dammit!" and understood why that young woman kissed my hand when we'd first met.

+++

---

# Operation Iraqi Freedom

On March 23, 2003, a coalition of US-led forces and including troops from Afghanistan, Albania, Australia, Azerbaijan, Bulgaria, Colombia, the Czech Republic, Denmark, El Salvador, Eritrea, Estonia, Ethiopia, Georgia, Hungary, Italy, Japan, South Korea, Latvia, Lithuania, Macedonia, the Netherlands, Nicaragua, the Philippines, Poland, Romania, Slovakia, Spain, Turkey, United Kingdom, and Uzbekistan, entered Iraq and overwhelmed the token resistance.

Barely downshifting to a lower gear as those combined forces barreled into Iraq, the rapidity of the assault astonished Saddam, as well as all the folks in charge of military operations on either side of the battle. There was no surprise with the success of the plan, that was a given; rather it was the incredible number of Iraqis being picked up and detained by the MPs and intelligence officers, following the initial assault waves. The truth was most were happy to surrender. The troops were joined by thousands of ordinary Iraqis from Basra and the port at Umm Qassar who knew from the last war that the Americans always fed their detainees. These folks had been subjected to reprisals since a failed uprising against Saddam ten years earlier. The bulk of the detainees were tomato farmers, but there were a lot of other citizens as well.

A few days later and I was in a rental car, the guest of Vito, a Navy intelligence officer. I'd met him at an intelligence meeting at the Embassy where he had introduced me to his friend, a reserve Navy JAG. They would make any excuse to get out of their warehouse accommodations on Camp Arifjan in southern Kuwait to have the opportunity to change into civilian clothing, visit the embassy bar, and have dinner at one of the many fabulous restaurants in Kuwait City.

It was hot that day, just like it is every day in Kuwait after mid-March. We left the Embassy and drove north out of the city along the motorway. Being Navy guys, they wanted to see the Iraqi port at Umm Qassar. This meant we wouldn't travel on Highway 80, the infamous "Highway of Death." Instead we turned down highway 801, the Saad al Sabah Road, the lesser known "*Highway of some Death*," where several hundred more burning Iraqi vehicles had been left littering the roadside. No border station there, just a booth long abandoned by the Iraqi border guards who'd wanted to surrender before hostilities began.

In the hours before the invasion, one Iraqi NCO walked to the Kuwaiti border to ask if surrender was possible. After consultations, he was advised to return to his post, and to turn on the interior lights and the four-way vehicle hazard lights as soon as he heard aircraft approaching so the building wouldn't be fired upon. He was the first person captured because he couldn't be ignored. As soon as he heard the engines fire up, he turned on the booth's outside lights and began waving a white flag.

We crossed a trickle of water intersecting the road which put us inside Iraq. We drove into the town of Umm Qasr where we were immediately assailed by groups of small children, each begging for water. We had a few cases in our trunk to pass out but, when that supply was exhausted, there was nothing more we could do for them, so we pressed on. Everywhere we looked we saw destruction, not by military force, but decay brought about by sheer neglect.

This was Saddam's punishment for the Shia who had dared, of necessity, to rise up against Saddam's rule, and a sad legacy to a series of popular rebellions that began in northern and southern Iraq in March and April of 1991, shortly after the fighting stopped when Desert Storm ended. These fighters were fueled by the perception, after two failed wars (the other being the eight-year-long war with Iran), that their ruler was responsible for systemic social repression and had become vulnerable to regime change. Within two weeks, most of Iraq's cities and provinces fell to rebel forces, a diverse mix of ethnic, religious, and political affiliations, including military mutineers, Shia Islamists, Kurdish nationalists, and far-left groups. Following initial victories, the revolution was ultimately held back by internal divisions and the lack of anticipated American support.

Saddam's Sunni Arab-dominated Ba'ath Party maintained control over Baghdad and those thugs soon suppressed the rebels in a brutal campaign conducted by loyalist forces and spearheaded by the Iraqi Republican Guard. Tens of thousands died and nearly two million were displaced.

We trekked to the port facilities and saw Spanish Navy divers working to clear the wreckage of several small merchant ships. Saddam had ordered these scuttled to deny use of the port or access to the Tigris–Euphrates River system and Fertile Crescent delta, the rich farmlands that radiated from the rivers.

As we walked along the pier, I saw a large green canvas US Navy tent with a homemade sign reading "Morale and Welfare Store." I detoured inside to find a huge selection of comfort items that were usually not to be seen by the war fighters until the AAFES supply system caught up with them. Those sundry items included many drugstore staples such as aspirin, lip balm, suntan lotion, sunscreen, flying insect repellent, throat lozenges, mints, antacid tablets, superglue, plastic combs, magazines, antibiotic ointment, and bandaids, to name a few. A Navy petty officer manned the store. He looked up from the comic book he was reading when I asked, "What's the protocol here? Where do I pay?" The sailor just shook his head and said, "There isn't any charge, all you have to do is sign the book." His eyes led me towards a US government-issued green, fabric-bound, ruled-line notebook. I opened it up and saw the several pages of names and on the right side sentiments each amounting to a big "Thank you!" I asked him how this place came to be and all he knew was what he'd heard, "Some women in Kuwait sent all this stuff up and the book will be going back to let them know we got it."

+++

# The Kindness Of A Stranger

On a Tuesday afternoon, just after Thanksgiving, I was caught up and only attempting menial tasks in my office as I waited for the duty day to end because it was poker night and I was hosting. That meant a post-workday dash to one of the supermarkets to pick up comestibles for my guests. My reverie was interrupted when the senior enlisted advisor, Joe, strode into my office with a wide grin on his face as he closed the door. In his position he served as liaison and direct representative for all the enlisted personnel. In addition to his regular administrative duties, he was charged with keeping a finger on the pulse of the troops to keep a happy balance of discipline and esprit d'corps, always ensuring a motivated and well-functioning unit ready for combat. A master sergeant, he had recently come to us from the 504th Parachute Infantry Regiment, a part of the legendary 82nd Airborne Division, the "Battling Bastards of Bastogne" during WW II. He was a squared away, take charge kind of guy, with the confidence that came from knowing he was one of the best.

He sat down, leaned across my desk and in a conspiratorial whisper said, "You remember when the general told us to use our initiative and see what we could do to improve things?" I nodded. Our boss was special forces and knew the value of constantly improving one's position in the field, and he also valued subordinates using personal initiative to get things done. Joe continued, "Well, I was talking to some of the young Sheikhas a while back and they'd been watching the buildup. They told me that they wanted to do something for our boys going up to the front." He stopped and looked at me. "They said that, they said, 'our boys.'" He got a bit misty as the full import of those words hit him again. He pushed a folded check across to me, saying, "They told me they took up a collection. They said I could use it however I thought best." I opened the check. It was for $700,000.

We spent the next few days at the Sultan Center, the largest commercial supermarket in Kuwait, spending that money. He'd created a master list of items developed over a lifetime in the field complaining about items needed "right then." Joe worked the distribution through friends in the supply system, who arranged to pack all the comfort items into sturdy containers and to distribute them evenly so that every unit moving forward into Iraq would have these items.

I finished signing the green guest thank you book and asked the sailor, "So how is this working out?" He looked at me and said, "I don't know who those ladies are, but we sure do appreciate all this stuff, especially the sun screen." He looked at me and saw my embassy badge hanging from a chain around my neck. "Sir, you from Kuwait?" I told him that I was assigned to the Embassy there. He said, "Well, if you ever find out who sent this, would you please tell them how much we appreciate it?"

I did.

A week before Christmas, a sheikh, one who had spent a lot of time in the US, had hundreds of fresh Christmas trees flown in from Europe and distributed to all the military installations, including two airbases, plus five US and two British forward bases, so the troops would not feel so alone over the holidays. Then the sheikh remarked to one installation commander, "I remember having to spend the holidays in the States because of my course load. I know the feeling of missing home during the holidays."

A few days before Christmas, another sheikh ordered two thousand Christmas dinners with all the fixings from one of the five-star hotels. He was a former fighter pilot and wanted the dinners delivered to Ali al-Jaber airbase. The US security guys, forever believing everything represented a safety risk, denied entry to the hotel trucks when they arrived at the main gate to deliver the hundreds of tables and chairs that would be adorned with linen tablecloths, china and glassware to facilitate a massive sit down banquet. Upon hearing this, the sheikh simply called his cousin, the base commander, who ordered the parade field cleared and made available for the service, and large tents were set up. When airmen left the US side of the base and walked out the gate and into those tents, they were treated to a gala dinner served by waiters in tuxedos and, to the disappointment of the security guys, nobody was killed.

+++

# Camp Bucca, Iraq

Sometime in early April 2003, a decision was made to create a detention facility where detainees could be vetted and released if determined to be a non-combatant. If determined a combatant, the detainee was sent on for further examination: was he a draftee or a leader? I was in my office when the phone rang. It was Vito, asking if I wanted to serve on a tribunal, explaining that panels were being assembled to determine probable cause to release some of the many hundreds of Iraqi detainees who'd been swept up when the armed forces brushed aside token resistance while racing on to Baghdad. I'd be working with an intelligence officer and a Kurdish translator on one of the many panels. My boss OK'd me to go for one day, and one day only, because he didn't want to take a chance on me getting killed up north, not so much for sentimental reasons but because it would take some time to whistle up a short notice replacement. So, my name was added to the list of officers who would clear out the backlog.

We drove north again into Iraq, and to the newly established Camp Bucca, named for Ronald Bucca, an FDNY fire marshal who had died in the Towers. This primitive camp was a collection of large, locally sourced tents with huge machine-made carpets laid out on the floor, there being no chairs. Under the big top sat eighty or so detainees awaiting their turn in front of the tribunal. If the examination determined they were farmers or other non-combatants, they were given a chit for a fifty-pound bag of rice and a new pair of shoes, along with the sincerest apologies of the US government. This generous compensation for several days' detention resulted in more than a few former detainees arranging to be picked up again by giving false names, just to get more rice and one more pair of new shoes.

Inside a large pre-fab and air-conditioned room were tables for ten teams. There I was introduced to the intel guy and the Kurdish translator I'd be working with for the day. Everyone in the room except me was a recent arrival, including the Kurds who were mostly older guys whose parents had immigrated to the USA decades earlier. These first generation Americans were actively sought because of their mastery of both languages and good cultural understanding of "the old country." The intel guy showed me a checklist developed to examine detainees claiming to be farmers. The region typically produced nothing but tomatoes, which farmers sold to the markets in Basra, the nearest large city.

The checklist directed that, if the detainee claimed to be a tomato farmer, the next question was "What type of tomato?" I was given a list of correct answers any farmer would know: types of tomatoes, water requirements, nutrition requirements, harvesting period, harvesting method, and the like. We knew that in and among the crowd would be any number of our target bad guys, mainly Ba'ath party men, and so the processing began.

The Arab Socialist Ba'ath Party, meaning "resurrection" or "renaissance," is one of two parties (with identical names) which emerged from the 1966 split of the original Ba'ath Party. One half was led by the Damascus leadership of the Ba'ath Party of Syria, the other half with its leadership in Baghdad. The party governed Iraq between 1968 and 2003 under Saddam Hussein and was banned in 2003 by Ambassador Bremer of the Coalition Provisional Authority (CPA).

While interviewing the first detainee, I looked at the man and immediately ordered his release. Although only in his forties, I saw an old man who had the deep, perpetually dark and burnished tan of a man who has lived a hard life outdoors. His clothing was frayed, he was missing several teeth, and the few remaining were rotting. The creases in his hands and fingers were permanently marked by years of tilling the soil, dirt so deep those hands could never be cleaned even if he'd had clean water, soap, and a brush, luxuries he would not have possessed.

I looked at him and thought of my high school buddy Johnny's Uncle Bob, a small acreage vegetable farmer on Long Island. When we were fourteen, we hitch-hiked the five miles out to his farm near the Old Bethpage Restoration Village, a living history museum of thirty-six houses, barns, and buildings that provided visitors with a unique opportunity to step back in time and experience life as it was on Long Island during the 1770s. We spent the day experiencing that eighteenth century lifestyle by weeding, and then picking tomatoes and cucumbers for a few dollars. Uncle Bob had that same raw, worn look, though much better teeth. His hands were hard and calloused and there was dirt under his fingernails despite a rigorous cleaning.

I wouldn't need a bunch of questions to determine if a detainee was a farmer and so it went with the next fifteen or so men brought before me. During a later pause, I took the opportunity to brief the assembly on what a farmer should look like and remind them that they were expected to apply common sense and experience and if the guy clearly looked like a tomato farmer, then he was. This helped pick up the pace of operations considerably. A detainee would be brought in, I'd take one close look and kick him loose.

Thanks to an excessive amount of coffee and water, I had to take a break. I left our building and walked about looking for a port-a-potty and found none. What I did see was a sign saying, **"Piss Tube"** and an arrow pointing to a two-inch diameter white PVC pipe that was inserted at a downward angle into a berm of sand and extended to crotch height. Next to it was a bottle of hand sanitizer on a small wooden platform.

I was walking back to the hearing room and passing by the very large tent holding a bunch of detainees, each waiting his turn before the tribunal. I stopped and looked at the assembly, noting the worn clothing and the tired, but resigned faces. Then I saw him, a young man, around thirty. He had jet black hair, wore dark green pants, and he was staring at me. While it is not uncommon for people in the region to stare at strangers or things of interest, his was a hard stare, one that told me this was a tough guy and, thinking of my visit with Hassan a few weeks earlier, I knew this was the guy I was looking for.

The war had kicked off on March 20 and would end on May 1, 2003. As things were getting started, Saddam decided to begin a rocket campaign against Kuwait City, as he'd done against cities in Iran when he invaded that country on September 22, 1980. Saddam's Iraq war ended in August 1988 with no final outcome or change in borders and with over one million dead. It compared to World War I in terms of the tactics used, including large-scales trench warfare with barbed wire stretched across trenches, manned machine gun posts, bayonet charges, "human wave attacks," extensive use of chemical weapons by Iraq, and later deliberate attacks on civilians targets. The United States and Soviet Union, together with France and most Arab countries provided support for Iraq, while Iran, as a Persian and Islamic theocracy, was largely isolated.

On the night of that first missile attack, I was having drinks with the Skipper on the rooftop of our apartment building after all the families and other "non-essential personnel" had left for the States. He and his wife, Steph had the two lower floors and I had the top floor — a "mother-in-law suite" with a private elevator. Steph had refused all offers to evacuate in advance of any hostilities, always citing her position as the recently hired AEWA lounge manager, as an essential position, and the sales receipts proved it.

A former computer systems sales rep, Steph had watched a CNN broadcast about the Iraqi "Most Wanted" playing cards that USCENTCOM would be giving the troops to help them identify senior leadership targets for arrest and detention. She saw promise in offering the playing cards for sale, but found they were not made in any quantity; they had really just been part of the psychological operations campaign. Not deterred by that at all, she had a set made by a printer in Texas and got permission to use the State Department seal on the back of the cards. She ordered five thousand packs on spec and began selling them in the AEWA store for five bucks a pack. Those dependents might have been gone, but the number of visitors to the Embassy had skyrocketed as troops found any reason they could to get off their various primitive installations in the wilderness and into town. Visiting the AEWA shop, the troops went crazy for this now hugely popular item and commanders bought them as souvenirs and gifts to motivate the troops. Sales had already topped fifty-thousand dollars and she'd sell even more as soon as they arrived from the printers. Ultimately, she sold over $125,000 worth of those cards, ensuring the future growth and fiscal well-being of the AEWA.

Skipper and I were sitting on lounge chairs enjoying the cool night air, some Cuba libres, and telling war stories. Between active duty stints, Skip lived up to his pirate heritage as he and Steph sailed the Caribbean in his sailboat, the *Snow Goose,* looking for a place to drop anchor and enjoy the sunset with some island rum.

An explosion out over the gulf startled us as a Patriot missile intercepted an inbound Scud missile. A few moments later, the sirens announcing a rocket attack wailed. Knowing we were small targets on a large planet, we continued watching and freshened our drinks. We lit cigars and wandered over to the edge of the deck so we could get a wider field of view. We stood, smoking and joking, until one of the Kuwaiti national guardsmen who provided external security for all the embassies noticed us and alerted a patrol to a possible threat on the roof. A police vehicle came screaming up to the front of our building and an officer began ringing the doorbell, shouting for us to open the door. We both leaned across the roof and yelled that we were going inside. Once he heard our American-accented voices, he relaxed, waved and sped back off into the night. We'd set our cameras up to catch the excitement but didn't see anymore missiles that evening.

The one good thing that came of those missile attacks was the government's ban on using loudspeakers to call Adhan, summoning people to prayer. The Shia always start a few minutes after the Sunnis, so for about five minutes the generalized wailing encourages sleeping folks to get up, get dressed, and pray. In the old days, Adhan was called out by a muezzin five times a day and traditionally from the minaret, but, thanks to technology, they now used great big gray outdoor loudspeakers to summon the faithful for worship. A second call, known as iqama, (set up) summons Muslims to line up for the beginning of the prayers. Not all prayer callers are of equal capability or talent and many are paid by donations to the mosque. Some mosques are poor, so they get the less talented, but cheaper, and far more strident, Pakistani muezzin. Thanks to civil defense sirens, the call to prayer was becoming confused with the numerous false positive air raid warning sirens as they sounded remarkably similar. One poor sleep-deprived Kuwaiti man finally took a rifle and shot out the loudspeakers broadcasting one of those particularly offensive off-key callers; his heroic act made this an issue of public safety and the microphones were ordered turned off for the duration.

On March 28, Saddam fired a Chinese-made Silkworm missile at the Seif Palace, which is the Emir's work palace along the seawall in downtown Kuwait City. The missile's telemetry system wasn't quite where it needed to be and the low flying missile struck Souk Sharq, a nearby shopping mall, damaging the facade and scaring the hell out of a couple of yellow-suited Bangladudes who were sweeping the parking lot. Through the length of the war, this was the only missile to ever hit anything of value in Kuwait. The rest were destroyed by KAF Patriot missiles which validated the training and those well-deserved awards the KAF received at the international Patriot battery competition held at White Sands proving grounds in New Mexico.

Prior to this attack, Saddam had launched thirteen other rockets. During that bombing campaign, I got a call one evening from Hassan asking if I wanted to come over for drinks and to watch a funny movie with him and his buddy, Bassam. He told me I had to see it; he swore it was like somebody came to Damascus and filmed his family. Since he mentioned Bassam, I knew to bring a bottle of Jim Beam bourbon with me. Now an American citizen, Bassam had married a woman from Tennessee twenty years earlier where he made his living as a tennis coach. He lived a comfortable life in Knoxville, but got tired of teaching old ladies and kids how to serve and, hating driving in winter conditions, he opted to come to Kuwait, as an upscale Miami substitute. He'd still be teaching old ladies and kids, but would be getting paid much more money working at a very exclusive tennis club. He loved living in a place where it never snowed and, although he traded winter hazards for year-round bad drivers, he thought it a good deal. He and Hassan had grown up together and attended the same high school in Damascus and now Bassam lived just a few houses away.

I arrived with my "gift" for the evenings festivities, expecting to watch some Egyptian comedy but was surprised when Hassan slipped in the disc and "My Big Fat Greek Wedding," a story set in Chicago, came on the screen. Bassam and Hassan would laugh out loud at some of the characters, adding comments like "Remember Uncle Mahmoud? He was just like that!" We watched the movie, had drinks,, and snacked on some food sent over by the hotel. The movie ended and we put on the news, which was never very good.

A top news story out of Baghdad showed students protesting something to do with America. Bassam elbowed Hassan saying, "Remember when those Ba'ath assholes would make us march?" This led to stories about being sophomores in high school when members of the Ba'ath party, hard core loyalists to then President Hafez al-Assad, would come in and order the school closed. All the students were required to attend a mass protest against whatever it was the Ba'ath guys told them to protest. Bassam was wiping tears away of laughter as he said, "Do you remember the signs they gave us?" Hassan agreed, telling me, "We could barely read English. I didn't know I was holding my sign upside down until some asshole yelled at me. I hadn't the first clue about what it said."

I was curious about their experiences under the Ba'ath party and they freely shared. Bassam was the most candid, saying, "You could always tell who those arrogant assholes were by their green uniforms and wrap around sunglasses." He took a drink and added, "They would either wear a forest green jacket or forest green pants because they knew that color told everyone exactly who they were and to be afraid because they could kill anybody they wanted to and you couldn't say a thing about it." Hassan piled on, saying, "Those assholes were always in the barber shop, like every other day, getting their hair razor cut so it always looked sharp, and then they never paid or even tipped." He held his hands out, fingers extended. "I'd see them sitting in those chairs acting like they owned the place, just having their nails trimmed and clear polish applied, like they were ladies! Anything to demonstrate to everyone else that they were in charge and didn't have to work." Those aspersions would have resulted in a serious beating, or even death, if uttered in Syria back then, but now they both nodded their heads up and down and continued to heap the insults, which no doubt still felt good.

I asked if the Ba'ath party guys ever went undercover dressing like regular folks. Hassan put that notion to rest right away, telling me clothing was what gave them their power. He opined that all the Ba'ath party guys were just gangsters, no different from Al Capone and his expensive suit-wearing bunch. He thought the party was just another bunch of ill-educated and corrupt thugs who were hated by all the regular Syrians. Bassam added, "They ruined Iraq and they will also ruin Syria."

The reminiscences ended as the TV screen went blank, replaced by a solid blue screen with the image of an air raid siren spinning and wailing, with writing in Arabic and English warning to take shelter from an inbound missile attack. My pager and cell phone were also trying to alert me to that fact, and before any of us could even comment, or formulate a plan, we heard a terribly loud explosion from immediately behind the house. The lights flickered and the crystal glassware tinkled as their cabinet shook from the vibrations. The three of us, instantly sober, shouted in unison, "Jesus Christ!" Followed by "What the hell was that?" As thoughts of sarin gas beginning to waft outwards from the impact site of the warhead began to dawn on us, we stood stock still. Then we heard the sound from a military radio. Hassan looked out the back door and started laughing. Bassam and I joined him and were amazed to see that somehow, somebody in charge ordered a Patriot missile battery to position itself in a vacant field directly behind Hassan's house, and the explosion we heard was a missile launched at the incoming rocket. That KAF missile team's talent deserved our kudos, because none of the neighbors heard it arrive earlier in the day.

Now here I was in rural Iraq, walking back from relieving myself, and I looked at him closely, that guy with the serious stare. I noticed his hair was neatly trimmed, unlike the detainees sitting around him, and unlike the others, he wore forest green pants. What really convinced me he was a bad guy was comparing the other detainees body language to his. They were without exception leaning as far away from him as they could get without falling over. I called over an MP who was in the vicinity. As he reported to me, I instructed him to take that guy from the group, he was a Ba'ath party bad guy, and that Army intelligence and CIA folks would want to talk with him. The MP stood well over six feet tall with the build of a guy who spent a crazy amount of time in the gym. He saluted and proceeded to reach past the now scattering detainees and snatching up my suspected gangster, cuffing and swiftly marching him out of the area.

The remaining farmers noticeably relaxed as he left the area and one began to make a kissing sound with his fingers to his lips, then blowing the kisses towards me in a sign I recognized as "Thank you." I called over a Kurdish interpreter and proceeded to hand out cigarettes to the workers while the interpreter got their story. Some were weeping, and some were full of rage, as they collectively offered that this asshole had been swept up with them a day earlier and he'd warned them all to keep their mouths shut and not say a word or he would kill them and their families when he was released. I got their detention chits and ordered the release of every man in the tent because it was clear that they were farmers. The MPs led them from the tent and began the process of bringing in the next batch.

I realized I knew something that none of the others did, so I went back inside to brief the senior Intelligence and MP officers on what to look for to help speed up the bad-guy-detection rate, then waited while the MPs brought in my next contestant. Taking one good look, I paid close attention and could see he was a man who hadn't had much sleep or any opportunity to shave since being detained. He bore a passing resemblance to the actor Dennis Quaid, and wore a gray suit that, although dirty, was well cut and made from some very nice material. He sat down in the chair, crossed his legs, and ran his hand down the fading crease to straighten it as best he could.

I introduced myself and the Kurdish translator started to translate when the man said in unaccented English, "There is no need for a translator, I speak English." I was mildly surprised, so I looked at him and said, "I must commend you; your English is excellent. How did you come to learn it?" He told me he'd studied fluid hydraulics at the University of

Baghdad. He explained he'd taken his engineering degree with honors and had been employed at the Ministry of Industry and Minerals. While visiting his parents in Basra, he got swept up by the Army and detained.

Taking out my smokes, I shook one loose and offered it to him. He was happy to take it and I gave him an extra one to enjoy after his dinner later that evening. He smiled when he saw the packet. Although I'd quit smoking after Korea, I'd started carrying Marlboro lights when I traveled because I found them to be the most popular brand with foreigners. There is a discernible difference in the taste of cigarettes made in the USA with American tobacco. Cigarettes destined for overseas are not subjected to the same quality standards and as a Marlboro in the Gulf states is different from the one in England, neither is the same as an American cigarette. I also gave him a cup of sweet tea and we began to chat.

I asked him what he did at the ministry and he told me he was a minor functionary who worked on the third floor of the massive building. He volunteered that the ministry had a lot of weapons development responsibilities and shared the location of several of those facilities, including some he believed housed chemical weapon programs. I thought he knew quite a bit for being a no-name pencil pusher on the third floor of a large ministry, so I told him he was being far too modest and surely a man of his talents was not simply a low-level bureaucrat. He looked down and said, "Well, actually, I was the Minister." And there we had it. We chatted amiably for the next few minutes while the intel officer arranged for an MP to escort the Minster to his next appointment with the folks from one of the acronym agencies.

Before he left, I asked him how he came to be the Minister, since he was a very young man, only in his mid-thirties. He sighed and took a last drag on the cigarette, then said, "I was minding my business on the third floor when the phone rang and it was a deep voice saying, 'Do you know who this is?' It was Saddam, and of course I knew that voice, everybody in Iraq knew that voice. He asked me, 'Am I speaking with my new Minister?' This let me know the old minister had been retired." He pointed his index finger to his head and pulled the trigger. "So, what was I to do? Turning him down was not a good career choice, you see."

The MPs arrived and we both stood up. I shook out another cigarette for him and also shook his hand while wishing him the best of luck in the next round. I offered that his cooperation would work in his favor and while leaving he told me, "You know, I'm really glad this is finally over. At least now I can sleep at night."

With that he was gone.

+++

# Epilogue

And just like that, my time in the desert kingdom ended and I returned for a final time to the "base that time forgot" and put in my request for retirement. It was granted and I signed out of the big personnel book at half past eleven on a Monday morning in April 2004 to begin my one hundred-eleven day terminal leave.

I recalled the advice Jimmy the Mailman gave me right after I was discharged in 1975, "When you get out, it'll take about six months for you to forget all about it and get back to being a normal civilian." Heeding that advice, I started the process by taking a three-hundred mile hike from Boise to Moscow to see my older daughter, Kate, graduate from law school at my alma mater. I walked fifteen miles a day in solitude, camped in a tent alongside the highway and next to the Payette River that ran along side it. I grew a beard, and used my newly found free time to reflect on my sojourn. It had all started in November 1971, because six months after graduating high school, there I was, still flipping burgers at Wetson's, a local franchise, along Jericho Turnpike, in Syosset, New York and wondering what to do with my life.

It was raining; I went for a drive. I stopped into the recruiter on a whim and was gone and into the blue three weeks later.

Over the four decades since I'd arrived for basic training on Dec 7, 1971, I'd finally completed twenty years and a day of active service. I lived outside of the USA and was immersed in the local foreign cultures for twelve of those years. I'd seen the end of the Vietnam era and watched POWs coming back home. I was there for the re-heating of the Cold War and later for its demise. I was right up front for the War on Drugs, popped over for Desert Storm, watched in horror on 9-11, saw Operation Enduring Freedom in Afghanistan and Operation Iraqi Freedom crank up, and witnessed the beginnings of the Global War on Terror.

It was time to go.

Looking back now on everything I didn't know, and how it all turned out, nobody is more surprised than me.

Mike Sciales
Boise, Idaho

+++++

If you liked what you just read and wondered how I got this way, please spend less than the price of a cup of carmel-double-espresso-latte coffee and a blueberry muffin and purchase your copy of *Syosset Blues*. Find out what it was like to grow up on Long Island, New York, in the 1960s and joining the USAF during the height of the Vietnam war. A sample story is provided and I hope you'll like it.

Fair Warning: If you buy these books, I'll only write more.

**REMINDER**: One dollar from **each** sale goes to Veterans Squaring Away Veterans, a 501(c)(3) non-profit dedicated to helping those vets who fall through all the social safety nets to get stabilized and catch traction in the civilian world. Learn more at VSAV.org

Now, please enjoy "Getting There Is Half The Fun," my 1971 induction physical.

# Getting There Is Half The Fun

Few things are more dehumanizing than the bureaucratic medical machine processing thousands of men each day solely for the purpose of seeing if they are fit enough to fight and die. During the Vietnam war somewhere close to thirty percent of the guys fighting and seven percent of those dying were from the greater New York City area. The draft emptied ghettos in both the South Bronx and Harlem, as well all of the hundreds of hamlets, villages, and towns on Long Island and upstate. The machine vacuumed up all those unfortunate peasants not clever enough to get a university educational deferment that would spare them from selection or, if they were in school, fail to maintain a 2.0 GPA. This amounted to an academic eugenics program that created a huge bow wave of college graduates.

There were 58,220 combat deaths in Vietnam and 4,121 of them came from New York. Syosset High School had about 500 people in each graduating class and had already lost two people, Army private Mitchell Sandman, 20, at Quang Ngai Province, shot dead five months after arriving in country and Marine PFC Gregg Lavery, 18, a former track star who died in Quang Tri Province, just forty-eight days after stepping off the plane. Everybody in town knew about those young men.

Jimmy, a guy who worked at Gene's Esso gas station where we hung out, was one of those guys who got snatched up. To get into any school in the State University of New York (SUNY) system after 1969, you had to have at least a 3.5 GPA and score high on your SATs, the Scholastic Aptitude Test. A perfect score was 1600 and the average was 1000. I think I scored 500 combined, but learned not to take an important test while hung over.

In 1968, Jimmy got accepted into SUNY at Stony Brook but in his second year forgot why he came to college and his semester GPA slipped to a 1.8. The school sent copies of his semester grades to him, his parents and the draft board. He was gone within two weeks and sent off to Vietnam. Back in a little over a year, Jimmy was never quite right after that. Loud noises, like when Al the mechanic popped a tire off a rim, or July fireworks sent Jimmy diving under the cash register. He wasn't an exception, there were lots of other guys, older brothers of my friends, who also came back with physical and psychological wounds. They became some of the new crazy regulars down at Moran's.

I was one of the few volunteers that month and was told to report to Ft. Hamilton in the Bay Ridge area of Brooklyn. The original New York induction center was located at 39 Whitehall in Manhattan. It was an eight-story building with a portion designated as a barber shop used to shave the heads of individuals entering the military. After a bomb blast inside the building in October 1969, the "Whitehall Examining and Entrance Station" moved to the more secured Fort Hamilton Army Post and into a warehouse. Two years later and they hadn't spent a lot of money on the facility. I was instructed to show up at seven and told it would take two days to complete the physical. I drove myself in and, after getting a pass and parking the car, I walked up to the large MEPS building, the Military Entrance Processing Station, a huge machine that evaluates fitness for military service.

In 1971, the military would take in almost 700,000 people. Getting rejected was hard to accomplish. On the steps leading up to the entry doors, a hippie freak, wearing a tie-dyed shirt, Ho Chi Minh sandals made from old tires, and sporting a blown out white guy Afro, was saying, "Hey man" a lot and making a big production out of taking a tab of what he claimed was LSD. "Hey man, they can't take me if I'm high" he said to no one in particular. He walked inside while again making his pronouncement in front of concerned witnesses and was promptly escorted to a residential holding facility, where he could remain until the effects of the drug wore off. Uncle Sam absolutely needed bodies and could deal with him.

I walked in and a soldier directed me to the hatcheck booth. It was manned by a one-armed veteran of World War II. He smiled cheerily and said, "Give me all your clothes except your underwear and socks." I gave him my shoes, then took off my pants and handed them to him. With surprising dexterity, he put the hanger in his mouth, folded my pants along the crease, and added them to the hanger. He then took my shirt and jacket deftly putting them on the same hanger. He hung the clothes up, handed me a chit and directed me down the hallway.

I turned the corner and found myself in another hallway at the end of long line inching towards a sign that said, "Station 1." I soon found out there were about twenty stations where they checked your vitals, took fluid samples, checked hearing and vision, including color vision and generally evaluated your fitness. The line only moved as fast as the one technician conducting that particular part of the examination took. I spent the first morning getting through four stations. Everybody looked pretty much the same, a bunch of guys in white underpants, white T-shirts and white socks. We were separated only by skin tone and hair length, except for one guy. There is always one guy who stands out in any large event and at the Ft. Hamilton MEPS station on that cold November morning this guy was the stand out.

Homosexuality was an absolute bar to military service in 1971 because homosexuals were then considered to be mentally ill. This meant that an awful lot of formerly loud and proud heterosexual guys were willing to attempt switching their official sexual orientation to avoid getting their butts shot off like poor Ed. The challenge for the US Army was to determine if the inductee claiming to be a homosexual was in fact a homosexual and not just somebody trying to pass himself off as one. This required an examination by an Army psychiatrist, of which there was only one, the rest of his kind treating the massive numbers of drug addicted and psychologically wounded troops coming back from the meat grinder in South East Asia.

I was standing in line for the hearing test, and had been for about an hour; now it was 11:30, and time for lunch. Turned out it was lunch time for the medical technicians and, when they were ready to go, they'd simply tell the next specimen to wait until he got back, never saying when that would be. As the machine shut down, some of the fluorescent lights were turned off, and we were handed bag lunches to eat in the hallway, all of us reduced to leaning against the walls, chewing our bologna sandwiches on white bread. Some random Army person periodically came striding through, looking neither left nor right, but projecting an air of urgency and importance. I think it was mainly to see if anybody was trying to leave.

From somewhere behind me, I became aware of a high lilting voice, all breathy tones with rapidly changing pitch and a pronounced lisp, and I knew, thanks to Mario, exactly what to listen and look for. I confess that at the time, I had a rather considerable dislike of homosexuals. This guy was about twenty, had dyed blond hair with black roots, wore a tight fitting lavender sleeveless undershirt and sported a red and white polka dotted boxers. To complete the ensemble, he wore green, black and gray calf length argyle socks, and was cradling a trembling teacup poodle. He was slowly moving along the opposite wall excitedly saying, "I need to speak to the psychiatrist! I need to speak to the psychiatrist!" sounding about as stereotypically gay as I thought possible. Just as he was slowly drifting past me, having survived the blank stares and more than a few sniggers, a harried, burly, equally stereotypical United States Army Master Sergeant, a top non-commissioned officer and no-doubt genuine tough guy, turned the corner and came down our hallway, leaning forward from the waist as if he had a full head of steam and was eager to get somewhere.

The gay draftee stretched a slender right arm into the air and began a delicate wave while saying, "Yoo-hoo! Excuse me, Admiral!" which made that Master Sergeant stop dead in his tracks, most likely taking offense at being mistaken for a sailor. He eyeballed the candidate with unconcealed disgust. "Its MASTER SERGEANT, fruitcake, you got that?" The trembling fellow shrank back as much from terror as from the breath coming from a guy with a cigar stub set in his mouth. "Yes, Master Sergeant, I need to see the psychiatrist!" The NCO looked at him and said, "You can see him when he gets back." Not to be put off, the fellow spoke to the broad back of the now departing soldier and called after him, "Do you know when that will be?" The reply came back, "In two weeks, Cupcake, he's on leave!" and with that he was gone. The lights came back on full and the stations began to move. Another Army guy came along and ushered the now very distraught fellow away to some other location, while I shuffled along to get my hearing test.

Along the way, I heard varied and sundry experts share their foolproof plan for gaming the system, most of which centered on taking some kind of drug in front of the doctors. One fellow showed me two slivers of lye soap and said he was going to put them under his arms and that would raise his blood pressure and they wouldn't take him. I asked if it was painful and he said he didn't know, but heard it was okay, with maybe some slight burning. All of moaners and schemers were guys who'd been called up to report, and I could understand, because they knew where they were going, but that was their problem. I was going into the Air Force where I'd have great coffee, clean sheets every night and air conditioning.

Those final stations the next day became more degrading. The mass genitalia/hernia check was somewhat mortifying, but it was the final station, the hemorrhoid exam that remains the clearest. Twenty-five of us walked into a large room and were told to take a quarter turn to the left, drop our shorts, and spread our cheeks while keeping eyes straight ahead. I was somewhere towards the rear of the group. The examining physician started at the back of the line, accompanied by a technician with individual charts who would record the observation into the newly created medical record. He walked past me with no comment and continued down the line for another five or six butts when he stopped and said, "Hmmm?" which meant he was going in for a closer examination. Out of the corner of my right eye, I could see a medical technician and another doctor walk over and bend down by the inspecting physician who had snapped on an exam light and was waving it around. This hadn't taken but a few seconds and we were all waiting to see what was up. The doctor said, "Hmmmm" again and then asked, "Son, what's that in your ass?" The specimen, an absolute hippie freak with long blonde hair and a "Make Love Not War" tattoo on his forearm, reached behind with his right hand, stuck a finger between his butt checks (we were all looking now) pulled it out, stood up, stuck that brown-coated digit in his mouth and started sucking. This produced a quick display of revulsion as assembled viewers were taken aback. After a moment he withdrew that clean finger and proclaimed, "Peanut butter, sir!" The Doc just laughed and said, "Nice try, son, but you ain't crazy. Enjoy your time overseas."

I finished the process and was accepted for enlistment…

I'd taken my oath of enlistment on December 7, 1971, the 30th Anniversary of the sneak attack on Pearl Harbor, and just like that, I was gone.

+++

You've just finished one of the stories. If you liked what you read, these are the other stories.

# Table of Contents

- The Gap Year

**REMINDER**:  One dollar from each sale goes to Veterans Squaring Away Veterans, a 501(c)(3) non-profit dedicated to helping those vets who fall through all the social safety nets get stabilized and catch traction in the civilian world. Learn more at VSAV.org

**LEARN MORE AT VSAV.ORG**

# About the Author

Mike grew up in Syosset, New York. He originally wanted to run away and join the circus in 1971, but they'd left town, so, times being what they were, he joined the USAF. He was sent to three different assignments, each time entering a unique phase of cultural change as the USAF switched from a hot war, and draft-dodgers hiding in plain sight, to an all volunteer force of people looking for work in a post-war economy.

You'll learn all about this in the prequel, "*Syosset Blues*" available right now on Amazon. Subtitled "*Reflections On A Misspent Youth,*" this is his story of growing up in a small, newly created suburban neighborhood on Long Island during the height of the Vietnam War and all the turbulence and social unrest that was the Sixties, told through the people he met along the way, the villagers who helped prepare him for leaving Syosset.

After getting out in 1975, Mike kicked around Europe, traveling on a EurRail pass, returned to the States, went to college for a year but in 1977, due to being broke; and times again being what they were, took a job as a cop in a small logging town in Oregon. Over those three rain-soaked years he answered a number of interesting calls for police services -- told in a soon to be released book, "*Memoirs Of A Small Town Cop.*"

Tired of the never-ending rains, and heeding the admonishment of the Beatles, "*And so I quit the police department and got myself a steady job.*" Mike moved to Florida to complete his undergrad work, but tiring of the heat, humidity, and mosquitos with tail numbers assaulting him, he applied for, and was accepted at, the greatest law school in the state of Idaho, well, at the time, also the only law school. He spent three years amidst the wheat fields of the Palouse, studying law on occasion while also juggling the demands of being a house painter and combat engineer in an Army Reserve firefighting unit. All this led to meeting new people, having interesting roommates, and experiences, like TV's Judge Wapner, as commencement speaker, all told in another soon to be released book, "***For My Next Trick.***"

A serious photographer, after retiring from active duty, in 2004, Mike took up motorcycle riding and has spent the last fourteen years taking photos while putting some serious miles on his GoldWing. Along with his artist buddy, Paul Hill, (paulhillfineart.com) on his Harley, they've toured huge swaths of America and British Columbia, Canada.

He got stupid in 2006, during the height of the insurrection in Iraq, and took a "safe" job in the Green Zone with the Multi-National Security Transition Command, MNSTC-I, as an unarmed contractor working to restore, or try to re-establish, the Iraqi military justice system. He lived in the US Embassy trailer park on the grounds of the Former Republican Guard palace complex, in a 110-square foot room with a deaf guy named George, who always denied being deaf.

They shared a telephone-sized bathroom with two other guys, the MNSTC-I public affairs guy, and a guy from Missouri who was paid $80,000 a year to drive the shit-suck truck on the Embassy grounds and empty the porte-potties. After arriving and getting his room, "ghosted" and simply never went into work. Nobody missed him, they thought he hadn't arrived.

Despite being promised differently, he was living in the Green Zone, sometimes called "The Emerald City" because of the luxuries within the walls, but worked outside those massive walls, at the Ministry of Defense, and experienced the daily lives, and deaths, of ordinary Iraqis in the Red Zone.

After several near misses, he finally got blown up while investigating a report of corruption, during a briefing from a Romanian guy who looked like Count Chocula, namesake character of a chocolate breakfast cereal. This will be the final book in the series of memoirs and due out in December. *__The Thieves of Baghdad__*" and subtitled, "*Confessions Of A Sleazy Contractor In The Emerald City.*"

He'd begun writing short stories in the early autumn of 2015 and, after that admonishment, wrote a quarter-million word first draft during the "once every 500-year, Snowpocalypse," that was the winter of January 2016. He spent the next few years whittling, chopping and polishing, all for your entertainment, education and amusement. His works are best paired with anything containing alcohol, and in places where legal, some Maui-Wowie or other herbal remedies.

If you buy his books, he'll only write more of them.

Printed in Great Britain
by Amazon

71930103R00241